A·N·N·U·A·L E·D·I·T·I·O·N·S

Race and Ethnic Relations

02/03

Twelfth Edition

EDITOR

John A. Kromkowski

Catholic University of America

John A. Kromkowski is president of The National Center for Urban Ethnic Affairs in Washington, D.C., a nonprofit research and educational institute that has sponsored and published many books and articles on ethnic relations, urban affairs, and economic revitalization. He is Assistant Dean of the College of Arts and Sciences at the Catholic University of America, and he coordinates international seminars and internship programs in the United States, England, Ireland, and Belgium. He has served on national advisory boards for the Campaign for Human Development, the U.S. Department of Education Ethnic Heritage Studies Program, the White House Fellows Progam, the National Neighborhood Coalition, and the American Revolution Bicentennial Administration. Dr. Kromkowski has edited a series sponsored by the Council for Research in Values and Philosophy titled *Cultural Heritage and Contemporary Change*.

McGraw-Hill/Dushkin

530 Old Whitfield Street, Guilford, Connecticut 06437

Visit us on the Internet
http://www.dushkin.com

Credits

1. **Race and Ethnicity in the American Legal Tradition**
   Unit photo—Courtesy of Library of Congress.
2. **American Demography: Conquest, Colonies, Slavery, and Color**
   Unit photo—Courtesy of Library of Congress.
3. **Immigration and the American Experience**
   Unit photo—© 2002 by PhotoDisc, Inc.
4. **Indigenous Ethnic Groups**
   Unit photo—United Nations photo by Jerry Frank.
5. **Hispanic/Latino Americans**
   Unit photo—Courtesy of Digital Stock.
6. **African Americans**
   Unit photo—© 2002 by Cleo Freelance Photography.
7. **Asian Americans**
   Unit photo—© 2002 by Sweet By & By/Cindy Brown.
8. **The Ethnic Identity: The Experience and Persistence of Diversity**
   Unit photo—Courtesy of New York Convention and Visitors Bureau.
9. **The Ethno-Religious Factor: Challenges in an Era in Search of Order**
   Unit photo—United Nations photo by J. Isaac.
10. **Understanding Cultural Pluralism**
    Unit photo—Apple Computers photo.

Copyright

Cataloging in Publication Data
Main entry under title: Annual Editions: Race and Ethnic Relations. 2002/2003.
1. Race Relations—Periodicals. 2. United States—Race relations—Periodicals.
3. Culture conflict—United States—Periodicals. I. Kromkowski, John A., comp. II. Title: Race and ethnic relations.
ISBN 0–07–250711–X   305.8'073'05   ISSN 1075–5195

Twelfth Edition

Cover image © 2002 PhotoDisc, Inc.
Printed in the United States of America   1234567890BAHBAH5432   Printed on Recycled Paper

Editors/Advisory Board

Members of the Advisory Board are instrumental in the final selection of articles for each edition of ANNUAL EDITIONS. Their review of articles for content, level, currentness, and appropriateness provides critical direction to the editor and staff. We think that you will find their careful consideration well reflected in this volume.

EDITOR

John A. Kromkowski
Catholic University of America

ADVISORY BOARD

James Ajemian
San Diego State University

Henry Lee Allen
Wheaton College

Alan B. Anderson
University of Saskatchewan

Paul Barton-Kriese
Indiana University East

James M. Calderone
College Misericordia

Ellis Cashmore
Staffordshire University

Phillip T. Gay
San Diego State University

Tom Gerschick
Illinois State University

Cecil Hale
City College of San Francisco

Perry A. Hall
University of North Carolina - Chapel Hill

Vicki L. Hesli
University of Iowa

Mary R. Holley
Montclair State University

Joseph Hraba
Iowa State University

Margaret A. Laughlin
University of Wisconsin - Green Bay

Seymour Leventman
Boston College

Robert Lilienfeld
CUNY, City College

Mark Meister
North Dakota State University

Linda Moghadan
University of Maryland - College Park

Robin Perrin
Pepperdine University

Tyrone Powers
Anne Arundel Community College

Mitchell F. Rice
Texas A & M University

Dennis M. Rome
Indiana University

Parmatma Saran
CUNY - Baruch College

Thomas V. Tonnesen
Waukesha County Technical College

Staff

EDITORIAL STAFF

Ian A. Nielsen, Publisher
Roberta Monaco, Senior Developmental Editor
Dorothy Fink, Associate Developmental Editor
William Belcher, Associate Developmental Editor
Addie Raucci, Senior Administrative Editor
Robin Zarnetske, Permissions Editor
Marie Lazauskas, Permissions Assistant
Diane Barker, Proofreader
Lisa Holmes-Doebrick, Senior Program Coordinator

TECHNOLOGY STAFF

Richard Tietjen, Senior Publishing Technologist
Jonathan Stowe, Executive Director of eContent
Marcuss Oslander, Sponsoring Editor of eContent
Christopher Santos, Senior eContent Developer
Janice Ward, Software Support Analyst
Angela Mule, eContent Developer
Michael McConnell, eContent Developer
Ciro Parente, Editorial Assistant
Joe Offredi, Technology Developmental Editor

PRODUCTION STAFF

Brenda S. Filley, Director of Production
Charles Vitelli, Designer
Mike Campell, Production Coordinator
Laura Levine, Graphics
Tom Goddard, Graphics
Eldis Lima, Graphics
Nancy Norton, Graphics
Juliana Arbo, Typesetting Supervisor
Karen Roberts, Typesetter
Jocelyn Proto, Typesetter
Cynthia Vets, Typesetter
Cathy Kuziel, Typesetter
Larry Killian, Copier Coordinator

To the Reader

In publishing ANNUAL EDITIONS we recognize the enormous role played by the magazines, newspapers, and journals of the public press in providing current, first-rate educational information in a broad spectrum of interest areas. Many of these articles are appropriate for students, researchers, and professionals seeking accurate, current material to help bridge the gap between principles and theories and the real world. These articles, however, become more useful for study when those of lasting value are carefully collected, organized, indexed, and reproduced in a low-cost format, which provides easy and permanent access when the material is needed. That is the role played by ANNUAL EDITIONS.

The information explosion, which led to an increased awareness of ethnicity and race, has accelerated the search for explanations of diversity among and within societies. Prior to these shifts in perspective and social practice society was discussed in terms of universal determinants derived from the Enlightenment and its sense of common humanity. Differences between societies and the arrangements of economic production were noted, but they were usually explained in terms of theories of progressive development or of class conflict. The new horizons and aspirations that are reconstructing social reality are the products of creativity, imagination, and religion, which all appear to be influenced by contemporary articulations of racial and ethnic relations. Consciousness of the pluralism expressed in ethnic, racial, religious, and cultural diversity has emerged throughout the world, and various disciplines are recasting models and recalibrating variables to account for these powerful forces of cohesion and conflict. Modern ethnicities and races are simply primordial cultural forms; relationships among groups are significantly, if not essentially, shaped by social, economic, cultural, and, most importantly, political and communitarian processes.

This collection was designed to assist you in understanding ethnic and racial pluralism in the United States and in several other countries. Unit 1, for example, illustrates how the most basic legal principles of a society—and especially the U.S. Congress and Supreme Court's interpretation of them—are significant for the delineation of ethnic groups. The intersection of the aspirations for inclusion and the realities of economic, gender, and racial claims reveal a pattern of cultural pluralism and contemporary challenges to the promise of American liberties. Unit 2 addresses the specific historical, existential, demographic, and geographic characteristics of diversity and delineates three periods and significant features in American diversity related to conquest, colonization, slavery, and color consciousness. Another ongoing characteristic of demography and politics—large-scale immigration—is broached in Unit 3. The immigration of people into relatively young and mobile societies, governed by regimes that have across time reviewed policies toward receiving new populations, exposes the fragility of social continuity and a range of issues related to the ethnic composition of a country. It also illustrates the challenges of education for a democratic citizenship and reveals the unique role of immigrant scholars.

The contemporary experiences of indigenous groups throughout the world, including Native Americans, are described in Unit 4. Significantly large, marginated populations are treated in the selections found in Unit 5 on Hispanic/Latino Americans and Unit 6 on African Americans. Unit 7 explores various dimensions of the Asian American experience. Unit 8 extends the discussion of ethnic identity to the perceptions and experiences of Americans. It addresses a unique American ambivalence toward ethnicities, the issues of self-identification, and the social-politi-

cal salience of ethnicities associated with the Mediterranean and Eastern Europe. When such groups and their opinions are woven into the fabric of American diversity a fuller set of race and ethnic concerns can be discerned. Unit 9, "The Ethno-Religious Factor: Challenges in an Era in Search of Order," focuses on an acute dimension of regional ethnicity that profoundly influences American life. It invites the reader to explore and evaluate ethno-religious concerns and their impact on America and its foreign policy. Unit 10 focuses on understanding the origins of racialism, the religious and ethnic origins that shape the consciousness of group affinities, and especially, the emergence of scientific claims of racialism and religious exclusion in public affairs.

Americans, especially the children and grandchildren of immigrants, have become increasingly aware of the ways that group and personal identity are interwoven. This perspective on the American reality was fashioned from necessity and a moral imagination that broke through the dichotomous mentality of Anglo-conformists and their logic and practices of social division and divisiveness. The urban ethnic experience demanded a new evocation of cultural pluralism—beyond the insularity, isolation, and racialist mentalities derived from the rural foundations of Anglo-Scot-Irish American culture. A new overarching synthesis founded in the appreciation of American ethnic and religious pluralism must stand the test of social and political realism, with all the pressures of mono-culturalism, color consciousness, and anti-immigrant xenophobia. Divisive strategies of ethnic group relations exist. Today the global challenge is to fashion an even wider and more inclusive ethno-religious synthesis that supports the peaceful resolution of differences. Muslims in America and all others must address and explore the development of a pluralistic form of Islam. Such an exploration waits for creative leaders who can cast new forms of social imaginations that differentiate religious, ethnic, and cultural modes of conveying meaning to persons and toward their collective legacies as groups. And it requires the integrity and legitimacy of American political institutions and processes as a parallel form of social-economic order within which cultural, ethnic, religious, and economic relationships may flourish.

Readers may have input into the next edition of *Annual Editions: Race and Ethnic Relations* by completing and returning the prepaid *article rating form* in the back of the book. Thank you.

John A. Kromkowski

Editor

iv

Contents

UNIT 1
Race and Ethnicity in the American Legal Tradition

Six articles in this section present the foundational legal definitions of race and citizenship and the historical landmarks of equal protection and due process found in Supreme Court decisions that express the search for new directions in race and ethnic relations during the civil rights era.

The concepts in bold italics are developed in the article. For further expansion, please refer to the Topic Guide and the Index.

UNIT 2
American Demography: Conquest, Colonies, Slavery, and Color

Ten articles in this section explore the history of population diversity in America and establish certain demographic base-lines that are essential for the analysis of public policy, including migration, the various understandings of personal identity, and the legitimate participation of ethnic cultures that define race and ethnic relations in America.

The concepts in bold italics are developed in the article. For further expansion, please refer to the Topic Guide and the Index.

UNIT 3
Immigration and the American Experience

Five articles in this section review the historical record of immigration that reveals its ongoing process and refocuses current concerns regarding immigration and legal, social, cultural, community-specific, and personal identity aspects of the American experience.

The concepts in bold italics are developed in the article. For further expansion, please refer to the Topic Guide and the Index.

UNIT 4
Indigenous Ethnic Groups

Three articles in this section review the issues and problems of indigenous peoples, portray the new relationships indigenous people are forging with concurrent governments, and discuss group identity, new cultural and economic forms that are emerging, and processes that protect indigenous traditions within pluralistic societies.

UNIT 5
Hispanic/Latino Americans

Four articles in this section reveal the demographics of Hispanic/Latino Americans as well as economic and political cultural dynamics of these diverse ethnicities.

The concepts in bold italics are developed in the article. For further expansion, please refer to the Topic Guide and the Index.

UNIT 6
African Americans

Five articles in this section review historical experiences derived from slavery and segregation and then explore current contexts and persistent concerns of African Americans.

UNIT 7
Asian Americans

Three articles in this section explore dimensions of identity and loyalty among Asian American and issues related to the cultural, economic, and political dynamics of pluralism.

The concepts in bold italics are developed in the article. For further expansion, please refer to the Topic Guide and the Index.

UNIT 8
The Ethnic Identity: The Experience and Persistence of Diversity

Three articles in this section invite the reader to measure and examine ethnic identity, its origin in the migration experience, and its persistence in the intersection of ethnic consciousness and culture with American pluralism and current issues in America.

Unit Overview   157

UNIT 9
The Ethno-Religious Factor: Challenges in an Era in Search of Order

Seven articles in this section look at the intersection of religion and ethnicities and their impact on conflict and cooperation among peoples in an era that challenges conventional boundaries for the resolution of conflict and the idea of sovereignty.

Unit Overview   170

The concepts in bold italics are developed in the article. For further expansion, please refer to the Topic Guide and the Index.

UNIT 10
Understanding Cultural Pluralism

Five articles in this section examine issues related to human variety and address the various approaches to race and ethnic relations. They also discuss the range of challenges that must be addressed to forge a new understanding of cultural pluralism.

The concepts in bold italics are developed in the article. For further expansion, please refer to the Topic Guide and the Index.

The concepts in bold italics are developed in the article. For further expansion, please refer to the Topic Guide and the Index.

Topic Guide

This topic guide suggests how the selections in this book relate to the subjects covered in your course. You may want to use the topics listed on these pages to search the Web more easily.

On the following pages a number of Web sites have been gathered specifically for this book. They are arranged to reflect the units of this *Annual Edition*. You can link to these sites by going to the DUSHKIN ONLINE support site at *http://www.dushkin.com/online/*.

ALL THE ARTICLES THAT RELATE TO EACH TOPIC ARE LISTED BELOW THE BOLD-FACED TERM.

Affirmative action
5. *University of California Regents v. Bakke*
6. Freedom of Religious Expression: *Shaare Tefila Congregation v. Cobb* and *Saint Francis College v. Al-Khazraji*
16. All White, All Christian and Divided by Diversity
29. 10 Most Dramatic Events in African-American History
30. Academic Haven for Blacks Becomes Bias Battleground
31. Laying Down the Burden of Race

Civil rights
1. *Dred Scott v. Sandford*
2. Racial Restrictions in the Law of Citizenship
3. In a Judicial 'What If,' Indians Revisit a Case
4. *Brown et al. v. Board of Education of Topeka et al.*
5. *University of California Regents v. Bakke*
6. Freedom of Religious Expression: *Shaare Tefila Congregation v. Cobb* and *Saint Francis College v. Al-Khazraji*
8. American Indians in the 1990s
29. 10 Most Dramatic Events in African-American History
30. Academic Haven for Blacks Becomes Bias Battleground
31. Laying Down the Burden of Race
32. Reparations for American Slavery
33. Racism Isn't What It Used to Be
38. Who Are We?
45. Arab Americans: Protecting Rights at Home and Promoting a Just Peace Abroad

Court system
1. *Dred Scott v. Sandford*
2. Racial Restrictions in the Law of Citizenship
3. In a Judicial 'What If,' Indians Revisit a Case
4. *Brown et al. v. Board of Education of Topeka et al.*
5. *University of California Regents v. Bakke*
6. Freedom of Religious Expression: *Shaare Tefila Congregation v. Cobb* and *Saint Francis College v. Al-Khazraji*
30. Academic Haven for Blacks Becomes Bias Battleground
32. Reparations for American Slavery

Culture
2. Racial Restrictions in the Law of Citizenship
3. In a Judicial 'What If,' Indians Revisit a Case
5. *University of California Regents v. Bakke*
6. Freedom of Religious Expression: *Shaare Tefila Congregation v. Cobb* and *Saint Francis College v. Al-Khazraji*
7. New Answers to an Old Question: Who Got Here First?
8. American Indians in the 1990s
9. Migrations to the Thirteen British North American Colonies, 1770–1775: New Estimates
10. The Enduring Legacy of the South's Civil War Victory
11. Racial Viewing Habits Move Closer, but Big Gaps Remain
12. Black America
13. White Girl?
15. What's White, Anyway?
16. All White, All Christian and Divided by Diversity
17. Should Immigrants Assimilate?
20. Following the Chain: New Insights Into Migration
22. As Others Abandon Plains, Indians and Bison Come Back
23. Culture Corrosion in Canada's North
24. Inside the Arctic Circle, an Ancient People Emerge
26. Specific Hispanics
27. The Blond, Blue-Eyed Face of Spanish TV

29. 10 Most Dramatic Events in African-American History
35. Arranged Marriages, Minus the Parents
36. Wartime Hysteria
38. Who Are We?
39. Where We Stand on Issues
40. A City That Echoes Eternity
41. Tribal Warfare
42. Will Arafat Father a Country?
43. Belonging in the West
50. Arabs Have Nobody to Blame but Themselves
51. History Is Still Going Our Way

Demography
2. Racial Restrictions in the Law of Citizenship
6. Freedom of Religious Expression: *Shaare Tefila Congregation v. Cobb* and *Saint Francis College v. Al-Khazraji*
7. New Answers to an Old Question: Who Got Here First?
8. American Indians in the 1990s
9. Migrations to the Thirteen British North American Colonies, 1770–1775: New Estimates
11. Racial Viewing Habits Move Closer, but Big Gaps Remain
12. Black America
13. White Girl?
14. America 2000: A Map of the Mix
16. All White, All Christian and Divided by Diversity
19. Surveying the Backgrounds of Immigration Scholars: A Report
20. Following the Chain: New Insights Into Migration
21. Ellis Island Finds an Immigrant Wave Online
22. As Others Abandon Plains, Indians and Bison Come Back
26. Specific Hispanics
34. Misperceived Minorities: 'Good' and 'Bad' Stereotypes Saddle Hispanics and Asian Americans

Desegregation
4. *Brown et al. v. Board of Education of Topeka et al.*
10. The Enduring Legacy of the South's Civil War Victory
13. White Girl?
28. Latino, White Students Cling to Own Social Circles
32. Reparations for American Slavery
33. Racism Isn't What It Used to Be
34. Misperceived Minorities: 'Good' and 'Bad' Stereotypes Saddle Hispanics and Asian Americans
38. Who Are We?

Discrimination
1. *Dred Scott v. Sandford*
2. Racial Restrictions in the Law of Citizenship
3. In a Judicial 'What If,' Indians Revisit a Case
4. *Brown et al. v. Board of Education of Topeka et al.*
5. *University of California Regents v. Bakke*
6. Freedom of Religious Expression: *Shaare Tefila Congregation v. Cobb* and *Saint Francis College v. Al-Khazraji*
8. American Indians in the 1990s
10. The Enduring Legacy of the South's Civil War Victory
12. Black America
13. White Girl?
15. What's White, Anyway?
16. All White, All Christian and Divided by Diversity
25. Hispanic Diaspora
27. The Blond, Blue-Eyed Face of Spanish TV
29. 10 Most Dramatic Events in African-American History

World Wide Web Sites

The following World Wide Web sites have been carefully researched and selected to support the articles found in this reader. The easiest way to access these selected sites is to go to our DUSHKIN ONLINE support site at *http://www.dushkin.com/online/*.

AE: Race and Ethnic Relations 02/03

The following sites were available at the time of publication. Visit our Web site—we update DUSHKIN ONLINE regularly to reflect any changes.

General Sources

Library of Congress
http://www.loc.gov

Examine this extensive Web site to learn about resource tools, library services/resources, exhibitions, and databases in many different fields related to race and ethnicity.

Social Science Information Gateway
http://sosig.esrc.bris.ac.uk

Access an online catalog of thousands of Internet resources relevant to social science education and research at this site. Every resource is selected and described by a librarian or subject specialist.

Sociosite
http://www.pscw.uva.nl/sociosite/TOPICS/index.html

Open this enormous site of the University of Amsterdam's Sociology Department to gain insights into a number of social issues. A six-column alphabetical list provides links to activism, affirmative action, discrmination, poverty, race and ethnic relations, urbanization, women's issues, and much more.

University of Pennsylvania/Library
http://www.library.upenn.edu/resources/subject/social/sociology/sociology.html

This site provides a number of valuable indexes of culture and ethnic studies, population and demographics, and statistical sources.

UNIT 1: Race and Ethnicity in the American Legal Tradition

American Civil Liberties Union (ACLU)
http://www.aclu.org

This site contains links to the ACLU's archives of information about civil rights in the United States and around the world, now and historically. Consult the index to find discussions of such topics as racial equality and immigrants' rights.

Human Rights Web
http://www.hrweb.org

The history of the human-rights movement, text on seminal figures, landmark legal and political documents, and ideas on how individuals can get involved in helping to protect the rights of all peoples around the world can be found at this valuable site. Links to other related sites can also be accessed here.

Supreme Court/Legal Information Institute
http://supct.law.cornell.edu/supct/index.html

Open this site for current and historical information about the Supreme Court. The archive contains many opinions issued since May 1990 as well as a collection of nearly 600 of the most historical decisions of the Court.

UNIT 2: American Demography: Conquest, Colonies, Slavery, and Color

North American Demography
http://www.chrr.ohio-state.edu/~gryn/namerica.html

This page contains resources that deal with North American demographics, labor statistics, social statistics, and much more.

U.S. Census Bureau
http://www.census.gov

Here is a link to the U.S. Census bureau, which provides useful demographic research and statisitcs.

UNIT 3: Immigration and the American Experience

Child Welfare League of America (CWLA)
http://www.cwla.org

The CWLA is the United States' oldest and largest organization devoted entirely to the well-being of vulnerable children and their families. This site provides links to information about issues related to the process of becoming multicultural.

National Immigrant Forum
http://www.immigrationforum.org

This pro-immigrant organization offers this page to examine the effects of immigration on the U.S. economy and society.

The National Network for Immigrant and Refugee Rights (NNIRR)
http://www.nnirr.org

The NNIRR serves as a forum to share information, to educate communities, and to develop and coordinate plans of action on important immigrant and refugee issues.

U.S. Immigration and Naturalization Service (INS)
http://www.ins.usdoj.gov

Visit the home page of the INS to learn U.S. policy vis-à-vis immigrants, laws and regulations, and statistics.

UNIT 4: Indigenous Ethnic Groups

American Indian Science and Engineering Society (AISES)
http://spot.colorado.edu/~aises/aises.html

This AISES "Multicultural Educational Reform Programs" site provides a framework for learning about science, mathematics, and technology. There are useful links to programs for Native American education.

UNIT 5: Hispanic/Latino Americans

Latino On-Line News Network
http://www.latnn.com

The purpose of this site is to empower Latinos. The site and its links address housing, employment, ethnicity, income and political issues, and presents the latest world news daily.

www.dushkin.com/online/

National Council of La Raza (NCLR)
http://www.nclr.org

Explore NCLR's home page for links to health and education issues in the Hispanic community. Many other economic, political, and social concerns are also covered at this site.

UNIT 6: African Americans

National Association for the Advancement of Colored People (NAACP)
http://www.naacp.org

Open this home page to explore the NAACP's stances regarding many topics in race and ethnic relations. Many links to other organizations and resources are provided.

UNIT 7: Asian Americans

Asian American Resources
http://www.ai.mit.edu/people/irie/aar/

Search through the links presented here for information on the political, historical, legal, and other concerns and interests of a wide variety of Asian American groups.

UNIT 8: The Ethnic Identity: The Experience and Persistence of Diversity

American Ethnic Studies
http://www.library.yale.edu/rsc/ethnic/internet.html

This site, provided by Yale Unversity, contains a list of resources regarding ethnic identity research and links to organizations that deal with ethnic identity.

American Indian Ritual Object Repatriation Foundation
http://www.repatriationfoundation.org

Visit this home page of the American Indian Ritual Object Repatriation Foundation, which aims to assist in the appropriate return of sacred ceremonial material.

Center for Research in Ethnic Relations
http://www.warwick.ac.uk/fac/soc/CRER_RC/

This eclectic site provides links to a wealth of resources on the Internet related to race and ethnic relations.

The International Center for Migration, Ethnicity, and Citizenship
http://www.newschool.edu/icmec/

The Center is engaged in scholarly research and public policy analysis bearing on international migration, refugees, and the incorporation of newcomers in host countries.

UNIT 9: The Ethno-Religious Factor: Challenges in an Era in Search of Order

Africa News Online
http://www.africanews.org

Open this site for *Africa News* on the Web. This source provides extensive, up-to-date information on all of Africa, with reports from Africa's newspapers, and other sources.

Cultural Survival
http://www.cs.org

This nonprofit organization works to defend and protect the human rights and cultural autonomy of indigenous peoples and oppressed ethnic minorities around the world. Learn about policies intended to avoid genocide and ethnic conflict.

Human Rights and Humanitarian Assistance
http://www.pitt.edu/~ian/resource/human.htm

Through this site you can conduct research into a number of human rights concerns around the world. The site provides links to many topics of interest in the study of race and ethnicity.

The North-South Institute
http://www.nsi-ins.ca/ensi/index.html

Searching this site of the North-South Institute—which works to strengthen international development cooperation and enhance social equity—will help you find information on a variety of issues related to international race and ethnicity.

U.S. Agency for International Development
http://www.info.usaid.gov/

This Web site covers such issues as democracy, population and health, race and ethnicity, and economic growth.

UNIT 10: Understanding Cultural Pluralism

Anthropology Resources Page, University of South Dakota
http://www.usd.edu/anth/

Many cultural topics can be accessed from this site. Click on the links to find information about differences and similarities in values and lifestyles among the world's peoples.

National Center for Policy Analysis
http://www.ncpa.org

Through this site, you can read discussions on an array of topics that are of major interest in the study of American politics and government from a sociological perspective.

Patterns of Variability: The Concept of Race
http://www.as.ua.edu/ant/bindon/ant101/lectures/race/race1.htm

This site provides a handy, at-a-glance reference to the prevailing concepts of race and the causes of human variability since ancient times.

STANDARDS: An International Journal of Multicultural Studies
http://www.colorado.edu/journals/standards/

This site provides access to the STANDARDS archives and links to topics of interest in the study of cultural pluralism.

We highly recommend that you review our Web site for expanded information and our other product lines. We are continually updating and adding links to our Web site in order to offer you the most usable and useful information that will support and expand the value of your Annual Editions. You can reach us at: *http://www.dushkin.com/annualeditions/*.

UNIT 1

Race and Ethnicity in the American Legal Tradition

Unit Selections

1. **Dred Scott v. Sandford**, from *U.S. Reports*
2. **Racial Restrictions in the Law of Citizenship**, Ian F. Haney Lopez
3. **In a Judicial 'What If,' Indians Revisit a Case**, William Glaberson
4. **Brown et al. v. Board of Education of Topeka et al.**, from *U.S. Reports*
5. **University of California Regents v. Bakke**, from *U.S. Reports*
6. **Freedom of Religious Expression: Shaare Tefila Congregation v. Cobb and Saint Francis College v. Al-Khazraji**, from *U.S. Reports*

Key Points to Consider

- In the late 1960s, proposals that sought to depolarize race issues argued for a policy of benign neglect, meaning that although equal protection and opportunity were essential, economic and education policy should focus on the needs of persons, groups, and regions regardless of their race. What can be said in support of such criteria?

- Does competition for protection and specific remedies among minority groups exacerbate race and ethnic relations? Comment on the idea that the American political process has relied too extensively on the Supreme Court. What policy outcomes or initiatives in race relations do you support? Are all races, religions, and ethnic groups protected from discrimination? Does such general and universal protection assure equality and fairness in all circumstances?

- Does competition for protection and specific remedies among minority groups exacerbate race and ethnic relations? Comment on the idea that the American political process has relied too extensively on the Supreme Court. What policy outcomes or initiatives in race relations do you support? Are all races, religions, and ethnic groups protected from discrimination? Does such general and universal protection assure equality and fairness in all circumstances?

- Should affirmative action be based on race and ethnicity or economic standing and income? Defend your answer.

- Why was the constitutional penalty found in U.S. Constitution Amendment 14, Section 2, which reduces the number of members in the House of Representatives from states that denied voting rights, not applied?

- Do aspects of race relations in America vary from region to region and state to state? What dimensions of discrimination are most onerous? Which are declining and diminishing? How does the law influence group and personal behavior?

 **Links: www.dushkin.com/online/**
These sites are annotated in the World Wide Web pages.

American Civil Liberties Union (ACLU)
http://www.aclu.org

Human Rights Web
http://www.hrweb.org

Supreme Court/Legal Information Institute
http://supct.law.cornell.edu/supct/index.html

The legal framework established by the original U.S. Constitution illustrates the way that the American founders handled ethnic pluralism. In most respects, they ignored the cultural and linguistic variety within and between the 13 original states, adopting instead a legal system that guaranteed religious exercise free from government interference, due process of law, and freedom of speech and the press. The founders, however, conspicuously compromised their claims of unalienable rights and democratic republicanism with regard to the constitutional status of Africans in bondage and indigenous Native Americans. Even after the Civil War and the inclusion of constitutional amendments that ended slavery, provided for political inclusion of all persons, and specifically mandated the loss of representation in the House of Representatives for those states that denied equal protection of the laws to all, exclusionary practices continued. Decisions by the U.S. Supreme Court helped to establish a legal system in which inequality and ethnic discrimination—both political and private—were legally permissible.

The Supreme Court's attempt to redress the complex relationship between our constitutional system and the diverse society it governs is mediated by a political leadership that has not persistently sought "equal justice under the law" for all persons.

The legacies of African slavery, racial segregation, and ethnic discrimination established by the Constitution and by subsequent Court doctrines are traced in the following abbreviated U.S. Supreme Court opinions.

In *Dred Scott v. Sandford* (1856), the Supreme Court addressed the constitutional status of an African held in bondage who had been moved to a state that prohibited slavery. U.S. Supreme Court chief justice Roger B. Taney attempted to resolve the increasingly divisive issue of slavery by declaring that the "Negro African race"—whether free or slave—was "not intended to be included under the word 'citizens' in the Constitution, and can therefore claim none of the rights and privileges that instrument provides for and secures to citizens of the United States." Contrary to Taney's intentions, however, *Dred Scott* further fractured the nation, ensuring that only the Civil War would resolve the slavery issue.

In *Plessy v. Ferguson* (1896), the Supreme Court upheld the constitutionality of "Jim Crow" laws that segregated public facilities on the basis of an individual's racial ancestry. The Court reasoned that this "separate but equal" segregation did not violate any rights guaranteed by the U.S. Constitution, nor did it stamp "the colored race with a badge of inferiority." Instead, the Court argued that if "this be so, it is not by reason of anything found in the act but solely because the colored race chooses to put that construction upon it." In contrast, Justice John M. Harlan's vigorous dissent from the Court's *Plessy* opinion contends that "our Constitution is colorblind, and neither knows nor tolerates classes among citizens." The history of the Court's attention to citizenship provides a view of a culturally embedded character of color consciousness and the strict textual dependence of the justices who interpreted the Constitution. Another perspective, however, emerges from the congressional debate that occurred when a civil rights law ensuring equal protection and voting rights was passed shortly after the Civil War. That legislative history is cited extensively in *Shaare Tefila/Al-khazraji* (1987). The

expansive view of protection for all ethnic groups cited in these decisions and the origin of these views in congressional intention voiced by elected legislators were indications of the Court's new directions. The Court's dependence on statutes rather than on the exercise of constitutional authority as the judiciary, and thus as a policy maker and initiator, appeared to be waning. Moreover, the Court, under the influence of a color-blind doctrine, seemed ready to challenge policies that significantly rely on race and ethnicity, thus changing the landscape as well as the discussion of race and ethnicity, inviting all of us to reexamine both the intentions and outcomes of all legislation in this field.

In *Brown et al. v. Board of Education of Topeka et al.* (1954), the Supreme Court began the ambitious project of dismantling statesupported racial segregation. In *Brown,* a unanimous Court overturned *Plessy v. Ferguson,* arguing that "in the field of public education the doctrine of 'separate but equal' has no place," because "separate educational facilities are inherently unequal."

However, this era of civil rights consensus embodied in the landmark actions of the Supreme Court has been challenged by contemporary plaintiffs who have turned to the Court for clarification regarding specific cases related to the significance of race and ethnic criteria in public affairs. Moreover, the lack of popular support for the implementation of policies and the judicial leadership of those policies is a political and electoral constraint. Popular concern was played out in referenda suggesting that the country may well face tension and acrimony between the will of the people in particular states and the rule and supremacy of national law. The mediation between law and popular expression, the political nexus of state and federal legitimacy, will no doubt be challenged by these contentions and require national and community-based leadership prepared to clarify the purposes and goals of a multiethnic civil society.

Revisiting the legislative history of the civil rights era can shed new light on our national public understanding of the thrust of that period. By reviewing the congressional deliberation in support of the Civil Rights Act and its goal of equal protection and equality before the law and then juxtaposing the contemporary legal arguments and current politics of equal protection, the reader will discover a complex set of considerations. A careful analysis of the moral foundations of our legal system and its expectations and attention to the practical consequence of defining and achieving an epoch of equality and the limits of legal remedies will emerge from these reconsiderations and the attendant search for new remedies and assurance of fairness and nonexclusionary practices.

The implementation of desegregation remedies, affirmative action, and voting rights remedies have been challenged in judicial rulings as well as in the decision to avoid court action that might compromise hard-won gains for minority populations. The politics of affirmative action include advocates and opponents who have become more strident and have exacerbated competition for rewards and benefits; thus, the privileging of claims and all that is implied in such argumentation has massively shifted public discourse. Even the most popular accounts of race in the American legal tradition have been changed and revalued in the crucible of persistent racism and ongoing political and media manipulation of racial passion in pursuit of remedies and privilege.

DRED SCOTT v. SANDFORD

December Term 1856.

MR. CHIEF JUSTICE TANEY delivered the opinion of the court.

This case has been twice argued. After the argument at the last term, differences of opinion were found to exist among the members of the court; and as the questions in controversy are of the highest importance, and the court was at that time much pressed by the ordinary business of the term, it was deemed advisable to continue the case, and direct a re-argument on some of the points, in order that we might have an opportunity of giving to the whole subject a more deliberate consideration. It has accordingly been again argued by counsel, and considered by the court; and I now proceed to deliver its opinion.

There are two leading questions presented by the record:

1. Had the Circuit Court of the United States jurisdiction to hear and determine the case between these parties? And

2. If it had jurisdiction, is the judgment it has given erroneous or not?

The plaintiff in error, who was also the plaintiff in the court below, was, with his wife and children, held as slaves by the defendant, in the State of Missouri; and he brought this action in the Circuit Court of the United States for that district, to assert the title of himself and his family to freedom.

The declaration is in the form usually adopted in that State to try questions of this description, and contains the averment necessary to give the court jurisdiction; that he and the defendant are citizens of different States; that is, that he is a citizen of Missouri, and the defendant a citizen of New York.

The defendant pleaded in abatement to the jurisdiction of the court, that the plaintiff was not a citizen of the State of Missouri, as alleged in his declaration, being a negro of African descent, whose ancestors were of pure African blood, and who were brought into this country and sold as slaves.

To this plea the plaintiff demurred, and the defendant joined in demurrer. The court overruled the plea, and gave judgment that the defendant should answer over. And he thereupon put in sundry pleas in bar, upon which issues were joined; and at the trial the verdict and judgment were in his favor. Whereupon the plaintiff brought this writ of error.

Before we speak of the pleas in bar, it will be proper to dispose of the questions which have arisen on the plea in abatement.

That plea denies the right of the plaintiff to sue in a court of the United States, for the reasons therein stated.

If the question raised by it is legally before us, and the court should be of opinion that the facts stated in it disqualify the plaintiff from becoming a citizen, in the sense in which that word is used in the Constitution of the United States, then the judgment of the Circuit Court is erroneous, and must be reversed.

It is suggested, however, that this plea is not before us; and that as the judgment in the court below on this plea was in favor of the plaintiff, he does not seek to reverse it, or bring it before the court for revision by his writ of error; and also that the defendant waived this defence by pleading over, and thereby admitted the jurisdiction of the court.

But, in making this objection, we think the peculiar and limited jurisdiction of courts of the United States has not been adverted to. This peculiar and limited jurisdiction has made it necessary, in these courts, to adopt different rules and principles of pleading, so far as jurisdiction is concerned, from those which regulate courts of common law in England, and in the different States of the Union which have adopted the common-law rules.

In these last-mentioned courts, where their character and rank are analogous to that of a Circuit Court of the United States; in other words, where they are what the law terms courts of general jurisdiction; they are presumed to have jurisdiction, unless the contrary appears. No averment in the pleadings of the plaintiff is necessary, in order to give jurisdiction. If the defendant objects to it, he must plead it specially, and unless the fact on which he relies is found to be true by a jury or admitted to be true by the plaintiff, the jurisdiction cannot be disputed in an appellate court.

Now, it is not necessary to inquire whether in courts of that description a party who pleads over in bar, when a plea to the jurisdiction has been ruled against him, does or does not waive his plea; nor whether upon a judgment in his favor on the pleas in bar, and a writ of error brought by the plaintiff, the question upon the plea in abatement would be open for revision in the appellate court. Cases that may have been decided in such courts, or rules that may have been laid down by common-law pleaders, can have no influence in the decision in this court. Because, under the Constitution and laws of the United States, the rules which govern the pleadings in its courts, in questions of jurisdiction, stand on different principles and are regulated by different laws.

This difference arises, as we have said, from the peculiar character of the Government of the United States. For although it is sovereign and supreme in its appropriate sphere of action, yet it does not possess all the powers which usually belong to the sovereignty of a nation. Certain specified powers, enumerated in the Constitution, have been conferred upon it; and neither the legislative, executive, nor judicial departments of the Government can lawfully exercise any authority beyond the limits marked out by the Constitution. And in regulating the judicial department, the cases in which the courts of the United States shall have jurisdiction are particularly and specifically enumerated and defined; and they are not authorized to take cognizance of any case which does not come within the description therein specified. Hence, when a plaintiff sues in a court of the United States, it is necessary that he should show, in his pleading, that the suit he brings is within the jurisdiction of the court, and that he is entitled to sue there. And if he omits to do this, and should, by any oversight of the Circuit Court, obtain a judgment in his favor, the judgment would be reversed in the appellate court for want of jurisdiction in the court below. The jurisdiction would not be presumed, as in the case of a common-law English or State court, unless the contrary appeared. But the record, when it comes before the appellate court, must show, affirmatively that the inferior court had authority under the Constitution, to hear and determine the case. And if the plaintiff claims a right to sue in a Circuit Court of the United States, under that provision of the Constitution which gives jurisdiction in controversies between citizens of different States, he must distinctly aver in his pleading that they are citizens of different States; and he cannot maintain his suit without showing that fact in the pleadings.

This point was decided in the case of *Bingham v. Cabot*, (in 3 Dall., 382,) and ever since adhered to by the court. And in *Jackson v. Ashton*, (8 Pet., 148,) it was held that the objection to which it was open could not be waived by the opposite party because consent of parties could not give jurisdiction.

It is needless to accumulate cases on this subject. Those already referred to, and the cases of *Capron v. Van Noorden*, (in 2 Cr., 126) and *Montalet v. Murray*, (4 Cr., 46,) are sufficient to show the rule of which we have spoken. The case of *Capron v. Van Noorden* strikingly illustrates the difference between a common-law court and a court of the United States....

If, however, the fact of citizenship is averred in the declaration, and the defendant does not deny it, and put it in issue by plea in abatement, he cannot offer evidence at the trial to disprove it, and consequently cannot avail himself of the objection in the appellate court, unless the defect should be apparent in some other part of the record. For if there is no plea in abatement, and the want of jurisdiction does not appear in any other part of the transcript brought up by the writ of error, the undisputed averment of citizenship in the declaration must be taken in this court to be true. In this case, the citizenship is averred, but it is denied by the defendant in the manner required by the rules of pleading, and the fact upon which the denial is based is admitted by the demurrer. And, if the plea and demurrer, and judgment of the court below upon it, are before us upon this record, the question to be decided is, whether the facts stated in the plea are sufficient to show that the plaintiff is not entitled to sue as a citizen in a court of the United States....

We think they are before us. The plea in abatement and the judgment of the court upon it, are a part of the judicial proceedings in the Circuit Court, and are there recorded as such; and a writ of error always brings up to the superior court the whole record of the proceedings in the court below And in the case of the *United States v. Smith*, (11 Wheat., 172) this court said, that the case being brought up by writ of error, the whole record was under the consideration of this court. And this being the case in the present instance, the plea in abatement is necessarily under consideration; and it becomes, therefore, our duty to decide whether the facts stated in the plea are or are not sufficient to show that the plaintiff is not entitled to sue as a citizen in a court of the United States.

This is certainly a very serious question, and one that now for the first time has been brought for decision before this court. But it is brought here by those who have a right to bring it, and it is our duty to meet it and decide it.

The question is simply this: Can a negro, whose ancestors were imported into this country and sold as slaves, become a member of the political community formed and brought into existence by the Constitution of the United States, and as such become entitled to all the rights, and privileges, and immunities, guaranteed by that instrument to the citizen? One of which rights is the privilege of suing in a court of the United States in the cases specified in the Constitution.

It will be observed, that the plea applies to that class of persons only whose ancestors were negroes of the African race, and imported into this country and sold and held as slaves. The only matter in issue before the court, therefore, is, whether the descendants of such slaves, when they shall be emancipated, or who are born of parents who had become free before their birth, are citizens of a State, in the sense in which the word citizen is used in the Constitution of the United States. And this being the only matter in dispute on the pleadings, the court must be understood as speaking in this opinion of that class only, that is, of those persons who are the descendants of Africans who were imported into this country, and sold as slaves.

The situation of this population was altogether unlike that of the Indian race. The latter, it is true, formed no part of the colonial communities, and never amalgamated with them in social connections or in government. But although they were uncivilized, they were yet a free and independent people, associated together in nations or tribes, and governed by their own laws. Many of these political communities were situated in territories to which the white race claimed the ultimate right of dominion. But that claim was acknowledged to be subject to the right of the Indians to occupy it as long as they thought proper, and neither the English nor colonial Governments claimed or exercised any dominion over the tribe or nation by whom it was occupied, nor claimed the right to the possession of the territory until the tribe or nation consented to cede it. These Indian Governments were regarded and treated as foreign Governments, as must so as if an ocean had separated the red man from the white; and their freedom has constantly been acknowledged, from the time of the first emigration to the English colonies to the present day by the different Governments which succeeded each other. Treaties have been negotiated with them, and their alliance sought for in war; and the people who compose these Indian political communities have always been treated as foreigners not living under our Government. It is true that the course of events has brought the Indian tribes within the limits of the United States under subjection to the white race; and it has been found necessary, for their sake as well as our own, to regard them as in a state of pupilage, and to legislate to a certain extent over them and the territory they occupy. But they may, without doubt, like the subjects of any other foreign Government, be naturalized by the authority of Congress, and become citizens of a State, and of the United States; and if an individual should leave his nation or tribe, and take up his abode among the white population, he would be entitled to all the rights and privileges which would belong to an emigrant from any other foreign people.

We proceed to examine the case as presented by the pleadings.

The words "people of the United States" and "citizens" are synonymous terms, and mean the same thing. They both describe the political body who, according to our republican institutions, form the sovereignty and who hold the power and conduct the Government through their representatives. They are what we familiarly call the "sovereign people," and every citizen is one of this people, and a constituent member of this sovereignty. The question before us is, whether the class of persons described in the plea in abatement compose a portion of this people, and are constituent members of this sovereignty?

We think they are not, and that they are not included, and were not intended to be included, under the word "citizens" in the Constitution, and can therefore claim none of the rights and privileges which that instrument provides for and secures to citizens of the United States. On the contrary, they were at that time considered as a subordinate and inferior class of beings, who had been subjugated by the dominant race, and, whether emancipated or not, yet remained subject to their authority and had no rights or privileges but such as those who held the power and the Government might choose to grant them.

It is not the province of the court to decide upon the justice or injustice, the policy or impolicy of these laws. The decision of that question belonged to the political or law-making power; to those who formed the sovereignty and framed the Constitution. The duty of the court is, to interpret the instrument they have framed, with the best lights we can obtain on the subject, and to administer it as we find it, according to its true intent and meaning when it was adopted.

In discussing this question, we must not confound the rights of citizenship which a State may confer within its own limits, and the rights of citizenship as a member of the Union. It does not by any means follow, because he has all the rights and privileges of a citizen of a State, that he must be a citizen of the United States. He may have all of the rights and privileges of the citizen of a State, and yet not be entitled to the rights and privileges of a citizen in any other State. For, previous to the adoption of the Constitution of the United States, every State had the undoubted right to confer on whomsoever it pleased the character of citizen, and to endow him with all its rights. But this character of course was confined to the boundaries of the State, and gave him no rights or privileges in other States beyond those secured to him by the laws of nations and the comity of States. Nor have the several States surrendered the power of conferring these rights and privileges by adopting the Constitution of the United States. Each State may still confer them upon an alien, or any one it thinks proper, or upon any class or description of persons; yet he would not be a citizen in the sense in which that word is used in the Constitution of the United States, nor entitled to sue as such in one of its courts, nor to the privileges and immunities of a citizen in the other States. The rights which he would acquire would be restricted to the State which gave them. The Constitution has conferred on Congress the right to establish a uniform rule of naturalization, and this right is evidently exclusive, and has always been held by this court to be so. Consequently, no State, since the adoption of the Constitution, can by naturalizing an alien invest him with the rights and privileges secured to a citizen of a State under the Federal Government, although, so far as the State alone was concerned, he would undoubtedly be entitled to the rights of a citizen, and clothed with all the rights and immunities which the Constitution and laws of the State attached to that character.

It is very clear, therefore, that no State can, by any act or law of its own, passed since the adoption of the Constitution, introduce a new member into the political community created by the Constitution of the United States. It cannot make him a member of this community by making him a member of its own. And for the same reason it cannot introduce any person, or description of persons, who were not intended to be embraced in this new political family which the Constitution brought into existence, but were intended to be excluded from it.

The question then arises, whether the provisions of the Constitution, in relation to the personal rights and privileges to which the citizen of a State should be entitled, embraced the negro African race, at that time in this country or who might afterwards be imported, who had then or should afterwards be made free in any State; and to put it in the power of a single State to make him a citizen of the United States, and endue him with the full rights of citizenship in every other State without their consent? Does the Constitution of the United States act upon him whenever he shall be made free under the laws of a State, and raised there to the rank of a citizen, and immediately clothe him with all the privileges of a citizen in every other State, and in its own courts?

The courts think the affirmative of these propositions cannot be maintained. And if it cannot, the plaintiff in error could not be a citizen of the State of Missouri, within the meaning of the Constitution of the United States, and, consequently, was not entitled to sue in its courts.

It is true, every person, and every class and description of persons, who were at the time of the adoption of the Constitution recognised as citizens in the several States, became also citizens of this new political body; but none other; it was formed by them, and for them and their posterity but for no one else. And the personal rights and privileges guarantied to citizens of this new sovereignty were intended to embrace those only who were then members of the several State communities, or who should afterwards by birthright or otherwise become members, according to the provisions of the Constitution and the principles on which it was founded. It was the union of those who were at that time members of distinct and separate political communities into one political family, whose power, for certain specified purposes, was to extend over the whole territory of the United States. And it gave to each citizen rights and privileges outside of his State which he did not before possess, and placed him in every other State upon a perfect equality with its own citizens as to rights of person and rights of property; it made him a citizen of the United States.

It becomes necessary, therefore, to determine who were citizens of the several States when the Constitution was adopted. And in order to do this, we must recur to the Governments and institutions of the thirteen colonies, when they separated from Great Britain and formed new sovereignties, and took their places in the family of independent nations. We must inquire who, at that time, were recognised as the people or citizens of a State, whose rights and liberties had been outraged by the English Government; and who declared their independence, and assumed the powers of Government to defend their rights by force of arms.

In the opinion of the court, the legislation and histories of the times, and the language used in the Declaration of Independence, show, that neither the class of persons who had been imported as slaves, nor their descendants, whether they had become free or not, were then acknowledged as a part of the people, nor intended to be included in the general words used in that memorable instrument....

From *U.S. Reports,* 1856. Opinion of the Supreme Court, December Term, 1856.

Racial Restrictions in the Law of Citizenship

Ian F. Haney Lopez

The racial composition of the U.S. citizenry reflects in part the accident of world migration patterns. More than this, however, it reflects the conscious design of U.S. immigration and naturalization laws.

Federal law restricted immigration to this country on the basis of race for nearly one hundred years, roughly from the Chinese exclusion laws of the 1880s until the end of the national origin quotas in 1965.[1] The history of this discrimination can briefly be traced. Nativist sentiment against Irish and German Catholics on the East Coast and against Chinese and Mexicans on the West Coast, which had been doused by the Civil War, reignited during the economic slump of the 1870s. Though most of the nativist efforts failed to gain congressional sanction, Congress in 1882 passed the Chinese Exclusion Act, which suspended the immigration of Chinese laborers for ten years.[2] The Act was expanded to exclude all Chinese in 1884, and was eventually implemented indefinitely.[3] In 1917, Congress created "an Asiatic barred zone," excluding all persons from Asia.[4] During this same period, the Senate passed a bill to exclude "all members of the African or black race." This effort was defeated in the House only after intensive lobbying by the NAACP.[5] Efforts to exclude the supposedly racially undesirable southern and eastern Europeans were more successful. In 1921, Congress established a temporary quota system designed "to confine immigration as much as possible to western and northern European stock," making this bar permanent three years later in the National Origin Act of 1924.[6] With the onset of the Depression, attention shifted to Mexican immigrants. Although no law explicitly targeted this group, federal immigration officials began a series of round-ups and mass deportations of people of Mexican descent under the general rubric of a "repatriation campaign." Approximately 500,000 people were forcibly returned to Mexico during the Depression, more than half of them U.S. citizens.[7] This pattern was repeated in the 1950s, when Attorney General Herbert Brownell launched a program to expel Mexicans. This effort, dubbed "Operation Wetback," indiscriminately deported more than one million citizens and noncitizens in 1954 alone.[8]

Racial restrictions on immigration were not significantly dismantled until 1965, when Congress in a major overhaul of immigration law abolished both the national origin system and the Asiatic Barred Zone.[9] Even so, purposeful racial discrimination in immigration law by Congress remains constitutionally permissible, since the case that upheld the Chinese Exclusion Act to this day remains good law.[10] Moreover, arguably racial discrimination in immigration law continues. For example, Congress has enacted special provisions to encourage Irish immigration, while refusing to ameliorate the backlog of would-be immigrants from the Philippines, India, South Korea, China, and Hong Kong, backlogs created in part through a century of racial exclusion.[11] The history of racial discrimination in U.S. immigration law is a long and continuing one.

As discriminatory as the laws of immigration have been, the laws of citizenship betray an even more dismal record of racial exclusion. From this country's inception, the laws regulating who was or could become a citizen were tainted by racial prejudice. Birthright citizenship, the automatic acquisition of citizenship by virtue of birth, was tied to race until 1940. Naturalized citizenship, the acquisition of citizenship by any means other than through birth, was conditioned on race until 1952. Like immigration laws, the laws of birthright citizenship and naturalization shaped the racial character of the United States.

Birthright Citizenship

Most persons acquire citizenship by birth rather than through naturalization. During the 1990s, for example, naturalization will account for only 7.5 percent of the increase in the U.S. citizen population.[12] At the time of the prerequisite cases, the proportion of persons gaining citizenship through naturalization was probably somewhat higher, given the higher ratio of immigrants to total population, but still far smaller than the number of people gaining citizenship by birth. In order to situate the prerequisite laws, therefore, it is useful first to review the history of racial discrimination in the laws of birthright citizenship.

The U.S. Constitution as ratified did not define the citizenry, probably because it was assumed that the English common law rule of *jus soli* would continue.[13] Under *jus soli*, citizenship accrues to "all" born within a nation's jurisdiction. Despite the seeming breadth of this doctrine, the word "all" is qualified because for the first one hundred years and more of this country's history it did not fully encompass racial minorities. This is the import of the *Dred Scott* decision.[14] Scott, an enslaved man, sought to use the federal courts to sue for his freedom. However, access to the courts was predicated on citizenship. Dismissing his claim, the United States Supreme Court in the person of Chief Justice Roger Taney declared in 1857 that Scott and all other Blacks, free and enslaved, were not and could never be citizens because they were "a subordinate and inferior class of beings." The decision protected the slave-holding South and infuriated much of the North, further dividing a country already fractured around the issues of slavery and the power of the national government. *Dred Scott* was invalidated after the Civil War by the Civil Rights Act of 1866, which declared that "All persons born… in the United States and not subject to any foreign power, excluding Indians not taxed, are declared to be citizens of the United States."[15] *Jus soli* subsequently became part of the organic law of the land in the form of the Fourteenth Amendment: "All persons born or naturalized in the United States, and subject to the jurisdiction thereof, are citizens of the United States and of the state wherein they reside."[16]

Despite the broad language of the Fourteenth Amendment—though in keeping with the words of the 1866 act—some racial minorities remained outside the bounds of *jus soli* even after its constitutional enactment. In particular, questions persisted about the citizenship status of children born in the United States to noncitizen parents, and about the status of Native Americans. The Supreme Court did not decide the status of the former until 1898, when it ruled in *U.S. v. Wong Kim Ark* that native-born children of aliens, even those permanently barred by race from acquiring citizenship, were birthright citizens of the United States.[17] On the citizenship of the latter, the Supreme Court answered negatively in 1884, holding in *Elk v. Wilkins* that Native Americans owed allegiance to their tribe and so did not acquire citizenship upon birth.[18] Congress responded by granting Native Americans citizenship in piecemeal fashion, often tribe by tribe. Not until 1924 did Congress pass an act conferring citizenship on all Native Americans in the United States.[19] Even then,

however, questions arose regarding the citizenship of those born in the United States after the effective date of the 1924 act. These questions were finally resolved, and *jus soli* fully applied, under the Nationality Act of 1940, which specifically bestowed citizenship on all those born in the United States "to a member of an Indian, Eskimo, Aleutian, or other aboriginal tribe."[20] Thus, the basic law of citizenship, that a person born here is a citizen here, did not include all racial minorities until 1940.

Unfortunately, the impulse to restrict birthright citizenship by race is far from dead in this country. Apparently, California Governor Pete Wilson and many others seek a return to the times when citizenship depended on racial proxies such as immigrant status. Wilson has called for a federal constitutional amendment that would prevent the American-born children of undocumented persons from receiving birthright citizenship.[21] His call has not been ignored: thirteen members of Congress recently sponsored a constitutional amendment that would repeal the existing Citizenship Clause of the Fourteenth Amendment and replace it with a provision that "All persons born in the United States… of mothers who are citizens or legal residents of the United States… are citizens of the United States."[22] Apparently, such a change is supported by 49 percent of Americans.[23] In addition to explicitly discriminating against fathers by eliminating their right to confer citizenship through parentage, this proposal implicitly discriminates along racial lines. The effort to deny citizenship to children born here to undocumented immigrants seems to be motivated not by an abstract concern over the political status of the parents, but by racial animosity against Asians and Latinos, those commonly seen as comprising the vast bulk of undocumented migrants. Bill Ong Hing writes, "The discussion of who is and who is not American, who can and cannot become American, goes beyond the technicalities of citizenship and residency requirements; it strikes at the very heart of our nation's long and troubled legacy of race relations.[24] As this troubled legacy reveals, the triumph over racial discrimination in the laws of citizenship and alienage came slowly and only recently. In the campaign for the "control of our borders," we are once again debating the citizenship of the native-born and the merits of *Dred Scott*.[25]

Naturalization

Although the Constitution did not originally define the citizenry, it explicitly gave Congress the authority to establish the criteria for granting citizenship after birth. Article I grants Congress the power "To establish a uniform Rule of Naturalization."[26] From the start, Congress exercised this power in a manner that burdened naturalization laws with racial restrictions that tracked those in the law of birthright citizenship. In 1790, only a few months after ratification of the Constitution, Congress limited naturalization to "any alien, being a free white person who shall have resided within the limits and under the jurisdiction of the United States for a term of two years."[27] This clause mirrored not only the de facto laws of birthright citizenship, but also the racially restrictive naturalization laws of several states. At least three states had previously limited citizenship to "white persons": Virginia in 1779, South Carolina in 1784, and Georgia in 1785.[28] Though there would be many subsequent changes in the requirements for federal naturalization, racial identity endured as a bedrock requirement for the next 162 years. In every naturalization act from 1790 until 1952, Congress included the "white person" prerequisite.[29]

The history of racial prerequisites to naturalization can be divided into two periods of approximately eighty years each. The first period extended from 1790 to 1870, when only Whites were able to naturalize. In the wake of the Civil War, the "white person" restriction on naturalization came under serious attack as part of the effort to expunge *Dred Scott*. Some congressmen, Charles Sumner chief among them, argued that racial barriers to naturalization should be struck altogether. However, racial prejudice against Native Americans and Asians forestalled the complete elimination of the racial prerequisites. During congressional debates, one senator argued against conferring "the rank, privileges, and immunities of citizenship upon the cruel savages who destroyed [Minnesota's] peaceful settlements and massacred the people with circumstances of atrocity too horrible to relate."[30] Another senator wondered "whether this door [of citizenship] shall now be thrown open to the Asiatic population," warning that to do so would spell for the Pacific coast "an end to republican government there, because it is very well ascertained that those people have no appreciation of that form of government; it seems to be obnoxious to their very nature; they seem to be incapable either of understanding or carrying it out."[31] Sentiments such as these ensured that even after the Civil War, bars against Native American and Asian naturalization would continue.[32] Congress opted to maintain the "white person" prerequisite, but to extend the right to naturalize to "persons of African nativity, or African descent."[33] After 1870, Blacks as well as Whites could naturalize, but not others.

During the second period, from 1870 until the last of the prerequisite laws were abolished in 1952, the White-Black dichotomy in American race relations dominated naturalization law. During this period, Whites and Blacks were eligible for citizenship, but others, particularly those from Asia, were not. Indeed, increasing antipathy toward Asians on the West Coast resulted in an explicit disqualification of Chinese persons from naturalization in 1882.[34] The prohibition of Chinese naturalization, the only U.S. law ever to exclude by name a particular nationality from citizenship, was coupled with the ban on Chinese immigration discussed previously. The Supreme Court readily upheld the bar, writing that "Chinese persons not born in this country have never been recognized as citizens of the United States, nor authorized to become such under the naturalization laws."[35] While Blacks were permitted to naturalize beginning in 1870, the Chinese and most "other non-Whites" would have to wait until the 1940s for the right to naturalize.[36]

World War II forced a domestic reconsideration of the racism integral to U.S. naturalization law. In 1935, Hitler's Germany limited citizenship to members of the Aryan race, making Germany the only country other than the United States with a racial restriction on naturalization.[37] The fact of this bad company was not lost on those administering our naturalization laws. "When Earl G. Harrison in 1944 resigned as United States Commissioner of Immigration and Naturalization, he said that the only country in the world, outside the United States, that observes racial discrimination in matters relating to naturalization was Nazi Germany, 'and we all agree that this is not very desirable company.'"[38] Furthermore, the United States was open to charges of hypocrisy for banning from naturalization the nationals of many of its Asian allies. During the war, the United States seemed through some of its laws and social practices to embrace the same racism it was fighting. Both fronts of the war exposed profound inconsistencies between U.S. naturalization law and broader social ideals. These considerations, among others, led Congress to begin a process of piecemeal reform in the laws governing citizenship.

In 1940, Congress opened naturalization to "descendants of races indigenous to the Western Hemisphere."[39] Apparently, this "additional limitation was designed 'to more fully cement' the ties of Pan-Americanism" at a time of impending crisis.[40] In 1943, Congress replaced the prohibition on the naturalization of Chinese persons with a provision explicitly granting them this boon.[41] In 1946, it opened up naturalization to persons from the Philippines and India as well.[42] Thus, at the end of the war, our naturalization law looked like this:

The right to become a naturalized citizen under the provisions of this Act shall extend only to—

> (1) white persons, persons of African nativity or descent, and persons of races indigenous to the continents of North or South America or adjacent islands and Filipino persons or persons of Filipino descent;
>
> (2) persons who possess, either singly or in combination, a preponderance of blood of one or more of the classes specified in clause (1);
>
> (3) Chinese persons or persons of Chinese descent; and persons of races indigenous to India; and
>
> (4) persons who possess, either singly or in combination, a preponderance of blood of one or more of the classes specified in clause (3) or, either singly or in combination, as much as one-half blood of those classes and some additional blood of one of the classes specified in clause (1).[43]

This incremental retreat from a "Whites only" conception of citizenship made the arbitrariness of U.S. naturalization law increasingly obvious. For example, under the above statute, the right to acquire citizenship depended for some on blood-quantum distinctions based on descent from peoples indigenous to islands adjacent to the Americas. In 1952, Congress moved towards wholesale reform, overhauling the naturalization statute to read simply that "[t]he right of a person to become a naturalized citizen of the United States shall not be denied or abridged because of race or sex or because such person is married."[44] Thus, in 1952, racial bars on naturalization came to an official end.[45]

Notice the mention of gender in the statutory language ending racial restrictions in naturalization. The issue of women and citizenship can only be touched on here, but deserves significant study in its own right.[46] As the language of the 1952 Act implies, eligibility for naturalization once depended on a woman's marital status. Congress in 1855 declared that a foreign woman automatically acquired citizenship upon marriage to a U.S. citizen, or upon the naturalization of her alien husband.[47] This provision built upon the supposition that a woman's social and political status flowed from her husband. As an 1895 treatise on naturalization put it, "A woman partakes of her husband's nationality; her nationality is merged in that of her husband; her political status follows that of her husband."[48] A wife's acquisition of citizenship, however, remained subject to her individual qualification for naturalization—that is, on whether she was a "white person."[49] Thus, the Supreme Court held in 1868 that only "white women" could gain citizenship by marrying a citizen.[50] Racial restrictions further complicated matters for noncitizen women in that naturalization was denied to those married to a man racially ineligible for citizenship, irrespective of the woman's own qualifications, racial or otherwise.[51] The automatic naturalization of a woman upon her marriage to a citizen or upon the naturalization of her husband ended in 1922.[52]

The citizenship of American-born women was also affected by the interplay of gender and racial restrictions. Even though under English common law a woman's nationality was unaffected by marriage, many courts in this country stripped women who married noncitizens of their U.S. citizenship.[53] Congress recognized and mandated this practice in 1907, legislating that an American woman's marriage to an alien terminated her citizenship.[54] Under considerable pressure, Congress partially repealed this act in 1922.[55] However, the 1922 act continued to require the expatriation of any woman who married a foreigner racially barred from citizenship, flatly declaring that "any woman citizen who marries an alien ineligible to citizenship shall cease to be a citizen."[56] Until Congress repealed this provision in 1931,[57] marriage to a non-White alien by an American woman was akin to treason against this country: either of these acts justified the stripping of citizenship from someone American by birth.

Indeed, a woman's marriage to a non-White foreigner was perhaps a worse crime, for while a traitor lost his citizenship only after trial, the woman lost hers automatically.[58] The laws governing the racial composition of this country's citizenry came inseverably bound up with and exacerbated by sexism. It is in this context of combined racial and gender prejudice that we should understand the absence of any women among the petitioners named in the prerequisite cases: it is not that women were unaffected by the racial bars, but that they were doubly bound by them, restricted both as individuals, and as less than individuals (that is, as wives).

Notes

1. U.S. COMMISSION ON CIVIL RIGHTS, THE TARNISHED GOLDEN DOOR: CIVIL RIGHTS ISSUES IN IMMIGRATION 1–12 (1990).

2. Chinese Exclusion Act, ch. 126, 22 Stat. 58 (1882). *See generally* Harold Hongju Koh, *Bitter Fruit of the Asian Immigration Cases*, 6 CONSTITUTION 69 (1994). For a sobering account of the many lynchings of Chinese in the western United States during this period, *see* John R. Wunder, *Anti-Chinese Violence in the American West, 1850–1910*, LAW FOR THE ELEPHANT, LAW FOR THE BEAVER: ESSAYS IN THE LEGAL HISTORY OF THE NORTH AMERICAN WEST 212 (John McLaren, Hamar Foster, and Chet Orloff eds., 1992). Charles McClain, Jr., discusses the historical origins of anti-Chinese prejudice and the legal responses undertaken by that community on the West Coast. Charles McClain, Jr., *The Chinese Struggle for Civil Rights in Nineteenth Century America: The First Phase, 1850–1870*, 72 CAL. L. REV. 529 (1984). For a discussion of contemporary racial violence against Asian Americans, *see* Note, *Racial Violence against Asian Americans*, 106 HARV. L. REV. 1926 (1993); Robert Chang, *Toward an Asian American Legal Scholarship: Critical Race Theory, Post-Structuralism, and Narrative Space*, 81 CAL. L. REV. 1241, 1251–58 (1993).

3. Act of July 9, 1884, ch. 220, 23 Stat. 115; Act of May 5, 1892, ch. 60, 27 Stat. 25; Act of April 29, 1902, ch. 641, 32 Stat. 176; Act of April 27, 1904, ch. 1630, 33 Stat. 428.

4. Act of Feb. 5, 1917, ch. 29, 39 Stat. 874.

5. U.S. COMMISSION ON CIVIL RIGHTS, *supra*, at 9.

6. *Id. See* Act of May 19, 1921, ch. 8, 42 Stat. 5; Act of May 26, 1924, ch. 190, 43 Stat. 153.

7. U.S. COMMISSION ON CIVIL RIGHTS, *supra*, at 10.

8. *Id.* at 11. *See generally* JUAN RAMON GARCIA, OPERATION WETBACK: THE MASS DEPORTATION OF MEXICAN UNDOCUMENTED WORKERS IN 1954 (1980).

9. Act of Oct. 2, 1965, 79 Stat. 911.

10. Chae Chan Ping v. United States, 130 U.S. 581 (1889). The Court reasoned in part that if "the government of the United States, through its legislative department, considers the presence of foreigners of a different race in this country, who will not assimilate with us, to be dangerous to its peace and security, their exclusion is not to be stayed." For a critique of this deplorable result, *see* Louis Henkin, *The Constitution and United States Sovereignty: A Century of Chinese Exclusion and Its Progeny*, 100 HARV. L. REV. 853 (1987).

11. For efforts to encourage Irish immigration, *see, e.g., Immigration Act of 1990*, § 131, 104 Stat. 4978 (codified as amended

at 8 U.S.C. § 1153 (c) [1994]). Bill Ong Hing argues that Congress continues to discriminate against Asians. "Through an examination of past exclusion laws, previous legislation, and the specific provisions of the Immigration Act of 1990, the conclusion can be drawn that Congress never intended to make up for nearly 80 years of Asian exclusion, and that a conscious hostility towards persons of Asian descent continues to pervade Congressional circles." Bill Ong Hing, Asian Americans and Present U.S. Immigration Policies: A Legacy of Asian Exclusion, *ASIAN AMERICANS AND THE SUPREME COURT: A DOCUMENTARY HISTORY 1106, 1107 (Hyung-Chan Kim ed., 1992).*

12. Louis DeSipio and Harry Pachon, Making Americans: Administrative Discretion and Americanization, *12 CHICANO-LATINO L. REV. 52, 53 (1992).*

13. CHARLES GORDON AND STANLEY MAILMAN, IMMIGRATION LAW AND PROCEDURE § 92.03[1][b] (rev. ed. 1992).

14. Dred Scott v. Sandford, 60 U.S. (19 How.) 393 (1857). For an insightful discussion of the role of *Dred Scott* in the development of American citizenship, see *JAMES KETTNER, THE DEVELOPMENT OF AMERICAN CITIZENSHIP, 1608–1870, at 300–333 (1978); see also KENNETH L. KARST, BELONGING TO AMERICA: EQUAL CITIZENSHIP AND THE CONSTITUTION 43–61 (1989).*

15. Civil Rights Act of 1866, ch. 31, 14 Stat. 27.

16. U.S. Const. amend. XIV.

17. 169 U.S. 649 (1898).

18. 112 U.S. 94 (1884).

19. Act of June 2, 1924, ch. 233, 43 Stat. 253.

20. Nationality Act of 1940, § 201(b), 54 Stat. 1138. See generally *GORDON AND MAILMAN*, supra, *at § 92.03[3][e].*

21. Pete Wilson, Crack Down on Illegals, *USA TODAY, Aug. 20, 1993, at 12A.*

22. H. R. J. Res. 129, 103d Cong., 1st Sess. (1993). An earlier, scholarly call to revamp the Fourteenth Amendment can be found in PETER SCHUCK and ROGER SMITH, CITIZENSHIP WITHOUT CONSENT: ILLEGAL ALIENS IN THE AMERICAN POLITY (1985).

23. Koh, supra, *at 69–70.*

24. Bill Ong Hing, Beyond the Rhetoric of Assimilation and Cultural Pluralism: Addressing the Tension of Separatism and Conflict in an Immigration-Driven Multiracial Society, *81 CAL. L. REV. 863, 866 (1993).*

25. Gerald Neuman warns against amending the Citizenship Clause. Gerald Neuman, Back to *Dred Scott? 24 SAN DIEGO L. REV. 485, 500 (1987). See also Note*, The Birthright Citizenship Amendment: A Threat to Equality, *107 HARV. L. REV. 1026 (1994).*

26. U.S. Const. art. I, sec. 8, cl. 4.

27. Act of March 26, 1790, ch. 3, 1 Stat. 103.

28. KETTNER, supra, *at 215–16.*

29. One exception exists. In revisions undertaken in 1870, the "white person" limitation was omitted. However, this omission is regarded as accidental, and the prerequisite was reinserted in 1875 by "an act to correct errors and to supply omissions in the Revised Statutes of the United States." Act of Feb. 18, 1875, ch. 80, 18 Stat. 318. See *In re Ah Yup, 1 F.Cas. 223 (C.C.D.Cal. 1878) ("Upon revision of the statutes, the revisors, probably inadvertently, as Congress did not contemplate a change of the laws in force, omitted the words 'white persons.'").*

30. Statement of Senator Hendricks, 59 CONG. GLOBE, 42nd Cong., 1st Sess. 2939 (1866). See also *John Guendelsberger*, Access to Citizenship for Children Born Within the State to Foreign Parents, *40 AM. J. COMP. L. 379, 407–9 (1992).*

31. Statement of Senator Cowan, 57 CONG. GLOBE, 42nd Cong., 1st Sess. 499 (1866). For a discussion of the role of anti-Asian prejudice in the laws governing naturalization, see generally *Elizabeth Hull*, Naturalization and Denaturalization, *ASIAN AMERICANS AND THE SUPREME COURT: A DOCUMENTARY HISTORY 403 (Hyung-Chan Kim ed., 1992).*

32. The Senate rejected an amendment that would have allowed Chinese persons to naturalize. The proposed amendment read: "That the naturalization laws are hereby extended to aliens of African nativity, and to persons of African descent, and to persons born in the Chinese empire." BILL ONG HING, MAKING AND REMAKING ASIAN AMERICA THROUGH IMMIGRATION POLICY, 1850–1990, at 239 n.34 (1993).

33. Act of July 14, 1870, ch. 255, § 7, 16 Stat. 254.

34. Chinese Exclusion Act, ch. 126, § 14, 22 Stat. 58 (1882).

35. Fong Yue Ting v. United States, 149 U.S. 698, 716 (1893).

36. Neil Gotanda contends that separate racial ideologies function with respect to "other non-Whites," meaning non-Black racial minorities such as Asians, Native Americans, and Latinos. Neil Gotanda, "Other Non-Whites" in American Legal History: A Review of *Justice at War, 85 COLUM. L. REV. 1186 (1985). Gotanda explicitly identifies the operation of this separate ideology in the Supreme Court's jurisprudence regarding Asians and citizenship. Neil Gotanda*, Asian American Rights and the "Miss Saigon Syndrome," *ASIAN AMERICANS AND THE SUPREME COURT: A DOCUMENTARY HISTORY 1087, 1096–97 (Hyung-Chan Kim ed., 1992).*

37. Charles Gordon, The Racial Barrier to American Citizenship, *93 U. PA. L. REV. 237, 252 (1945).*

38. MILTON KONVITZ, THE ALIEN AND THE ASIATIC IN AMERICAN LAW 80–81 (1946) (citation omitted).

39. Act of Oct. 14, 1940, ch. 876, § 303, 54 Stat. 1140.

40. Note, The Nationality Act of 1940, *54 HARV. L. REV. 860, 865 n.40 (1941).*

41. Act of Dec. 17, 1943, ch. 344, 3, 57 Stat. 600.

42. Act of July 2, 1946, ch. 534, 60 Stat. 416.

43. Id.

44. Immigration and Nationality Act of 1952, ch. 2, § 311, 66 Stat. 239 (codified as amended at 8 U.S.C. 1422 [1988]).

45. Arguably, the continued substantial exclusion of Asians from immigration not remedied until 1965, rendered their eligibility for naturalization relatively meaningless. "[T]he national quota system for admitting immigrants which was built into the 1952 Act gave the grant of eligibility a hollow ring." Chin Kim and Bok Lim Kim, Asian Immigrants in American Law: A Look at the Past and the Challenge Which Remains, *26 AM. U. L. REV. 373, 390 (1977).*

46. See generally *Ursula Vogel*, Is Citizenship Gender-Specific? *THE FRONTIERS OF CITIZENSHIP 58 (Ursula Vogel and Michael Moran eds., 1991).*

47. Act of Feb. 10, 1855, ch. 71, § 2, 10 Stat. 604. Because gender-based laws in the area of citizenship were motivated by the idea that a woman's citizenship should follow that of her husband, no naturalization law has explicitly targeted unmarried women. GORDON AND MAILMAN,

supra, *at § 95.03[6]* ("*An unmarried woman has never been statutorily* barred from naturalization.").

48. PRENTISS WEBSTER, LAW OF NATURALIZATION IN THE UNITED STATES OF AMERICA AND OTHER COUNTRIES 80 (1895).

49. Act of Feb. 10, 1855, ch. 71, § 2, 10 Stat. 604.

50. Kelly v. Owen, 74 U.S. 496, 498 (1868).

51. GORDON AND MAILMAN, *supra* at § 95.03[6].

52. Act of Sept. 22, 1922, ch. 411, § 2, 42 Stat. 1021.

53. GORDON AND MAILMAN, *supra* at § 100.03[4][m].

54. Act of March 2, 1907, ch. 2534, § 3, 34 Stat. 1228. This act was upheld in MacKenzie v. Hare, 239 U.S. 299 (1915) (expatriating a U.S.-born woman upon her marriage to a British citizen).

55. Act of Sept. 22, 1922, ch. 411, § 3, 42 Stat. 1021.

56. *Id.* The Act also stated that "[n]o woman whose husband is not eligible to citizenship shall be naturalized during the continuance of the marriage."

57. Act of March 3, 1931, ch. 442, § 4(a), 46 Stat. 1511.

58. The loss of birthright citizenship was particularly harsh for those women whose race made them unable to regain citizenship through naturalization, especially after 1924, when the immigration laws of this country barred entry to any alien ineligible to citizenship. Immigration Act of 1924, ch. 190, § 13(c), 43 Stat. 162. *See, e.g.*, Ex parte (Ng) Fung Sing, 6 F.2d 670 (W. D. Wash. 1925). In that case, a U.S. birthright citizen of Chinese descent was expatriated because of her marriage to a Chinese citizen, and was subsequently refused admittance to the United States as an alien ineligible to citizenship.

From *White by Law: The Legal Construction of Race*, 1996, Chapter 2, pp. 37-47, 235-240. © 1996 by New York University Press. Reprinted by permission.

Legal Journal

In a Judicial 'What If,' Indians Revisit a Case

By WILLIAM GLABERSON

LAWRENCE, Kan., Oct. 21—It was all white men on the Supreme Court who handed down the milestone rulings that helped decide the fate of American Indians more than a century ago.

Now, here at the University of Kansas School of Law, Indian lawyers are acting out a legal "what if" experiment: What if Indians had been on the Supreme Court of the 1800's?

Eight American Indian lawyers gathered here on Oct. 10 and played the roles of Justices in an elaborate moot court. The panel heard a full "reargument" of one of the most important of the early Supreme Court cases, Cherokee Nation v. Georgia. In the 1831 decision, Chief Justice John Marshall ruled that tribes were not foreign nations entitled to be dealt with equally but more "domestic dependent nations." The ruling in Georgia's favor laid the legal foundation for much that was to come in America's relations with the Indians.

Although fictitious, the reconsideration of the case is not a carefree task. Years ago in law school at the University of Wisconsin, said Laura Soap, one of the moot-court Justices, she felt no emotion as she studied the famous Supreme Court rulings dealing with Indians. But as the arguments have been replayed in the moot court, she said, "I find myself getting a little angry, the more I think about it. I find myself thinking: How am I going to explain this to my kids?" Ms. Soap is a Kickapoo Indian; her husband is a Cherokee.

A milestone ruling that set course for American relations with the Indians.

The moot-court judges surprised no one by announcing after the arguments that, this time, the Cherokee Nation had won. But, just like real Justices, the eight Indian lawyers are deliberating over a written opinion to justify their decision. It is to be published in a law review.

At the invitation of a reporter, Ms. Soap and another of the moot-court Justices, Russell A. Brien, a member of the Iowa tribe, met at the law school to hash out their views in the drafting of an opinion the way real judges might. On a bright Kansas afternoon, they struggled with the history of the legal system's treatment of their people.

Justice Marshall concluded 167 years ago that, no matter how real their grievances might be, tribes could not appeal to the Supreme Court. The ruling left the tribes with no redress for acts like the breaking of treaties and the forced removal of native people from their homelands.

Ms. Soap, 38, is an associate justice of the real Supreme Court of the Sac and Fox Nation of Kansas and Missouri. If she had the chance to hear the Cherokee case, she said, she would try to be practical in contending with Justice Marshall's view that the Supreme Court lacked jurisdiction to hear the Cherokees' case.

Perhaps she could concede, she said, that the Indians could not enforce their treaties. But closing the door of the country's highest court to Indians, she said, diminished the ideals of America. "I would talk to Marshall," she said, "and I would say: 'Maybe the treaties are no good. But we need to do it the way the Americans do it: We need to have the issues heard in court.'"

In real life, Mr. Brien, 32, is a lawyer in a Kansas City firm who works on repackaging mortgage loans as securities. He tried a legalistic approach to the Cherokees' case.

"Clearly the Indians were here first," Mr. Brien said. "The Indians' title to the land has not been extinguished."

He said that one way to deal with Justice Marshall's view was to convince him that if the court did not treat the Indians' claims as legitimate in 1831, the Indians' anger could fester for a long time. "You might as well address it now, rather than wait till later," Mr. Brien said.

Before the meeting of the two justices, the professor who convened the moot court, Robert B. Porter, had explained the goal of the exercise.

Mr. Porter, a Harvard-education lawyer and a member of the Seneca Nation, is the director of the Tribal Law and Government Center at the law school here.

As Indian nations across the country struggle to reassert their sovereign powers over their own people, he said, Indian lawyers must study the way America used the law to establish what he called colonial domination. The moot court and similar exercises, he said, are intended "to lay the intellectual foundation for our decolonization."

It is not an easy task. Mr. Brien and Ms. Soap said that as lawyers trained in the American system, it was nearly impossible for them to view the Cherokees' case of 1831 with anything like the eyes of their ancestors.

Mr. Brien said that his family left the reservation years ago and he had become involved in tribal matters only in recent years. As he learned his tribe's modern legal system, he said, he discovered that over the generations it had come to mirror the American system. Older ways, he said, had been forgotten.

"I don't have my tribe's dispute resolution system," he said. "That's lost to me. And I am still in the process of trying to learn my tribe's traditions."

How would an Indian Justice of the Supreme Court view the Cherokees' case? Mr. Brien said it was hard for him to know.

BROWN et al.

v.

BOARD OF EDUCATION OF TOPEKA et al.

347 U.S. 483 (1954)

MR. CHIEF JUSTICE WARREN delivered the opinion of the Court.

These cases come to us from the States of Kansas, South Carolina, Virginia, and Delaware. They are premised on different facts and different local conditions, but a common legal question justifies their consideration together in this consolidated opinion.[1]

In each of the cases, minors of the Negro race, through their legal representatives, seek the aid of the courts in obtaining admission to the public schools of their community on a nonsegregated basis. In each instance, they had been denied admission to schools attended by white children under laws requiring or permitting segregation according to race. This segregation was alleged to deprive the plaintiffs of the equal protection of the laws under the Fourteenth Amendment. In each of the cases other than the Delaware case, a three-judge federal district court denied relief to the plaintiffs on the so-called "separate but equal" doctrine announced by this Court in *Plessy v. Ferguson*, 163 U.S. 537. Under that doctrine, equality of treatment is accorded when the races are provided substantially equal facilities, even though these facilities be separate. In the Delaware case, the Supreme Court of Delaware adhered to that doctrine, but ordered that the plaintiffs be admitted to the white schools because of their superiority to the Negro schools.

The plaintiffs contend that segregated public schools are not "equal" and cannot be made "equal," and that hence they are deprived of the equal protection of the laws. Because of the obvious importance of the question presented, the Court took jurisdiction.[2] Argument was heard in the 1952 Term, and reargument was heard this Term on certain questions propounded by the Court.[3]

Reargument was largely devoted to the circumstances surrounding the adoption of the Fourteenth Amendment in 1868. It covered exhaustively consideration of the Amendment in Congress, ratification by the states, then existing practices in racial segregation, and the views of proponents and opponents of the Amendment. This discussion and our own investigation convince us that, although these sources cast some light, it is not enough to resolve the problem with which we are faced. At best, they are inconclusive. The most avid proponents of the post–War Amendments undoubtedly intended them to remove all legal distinctions among "all persons born or naturalized in the United States." Their opponents, just as certainly, were antagonistic to both the letter and the spirit of the Amendments and wished them to have the most limited effect. What others in Congress and the state legislatures had in mind cannot be determined with any degree of certainty.

An additional reason for the inconclusive nature of the Amendment's history, with respect to segregated schools, is the status of public education at that time.[4] In the South, the movement toward free common schools, supported by general taxation, had not yet taken hold. Education of white children was largely in the hands of private groups. Education of Negroes was almost nonexistent, and practically all of the race were illiterate. In fact, any education of Negroes was forbidden by law in some states. Today in contrast, many Negroes have achieved outstanding success in the arts and sciences as well as in the business and professional world. It is true that public school education at the time of the Amendment had advanced further in the North, but the effect of the Amendment on northern States was generally ignored in the congressional debates. Even in the North, the conditions of public education did not approximate those existing today. The curriculum was usually rudimentary; ungraded schools were common in rural areas; the school term was but three months a year in many states; and compulsory school attendance was virtually unknown. As a consequence, it is not surprising that there should be so little in the history of the Fourteenth Amendment relating to its intended effect on public education.

In the first cases in this Court construing the Fourteenth Amendment, decided shortly after its adoption, the Court interpreted it as proscribing all state-imposed discriminations against the Negro race.[5] The doctrine of "separate but equal" did not make its appearance in this Court until 1896 in the case of *Plessy v. Ferguson, supra*, involving not education but transportation.[6] American courts have since labored with the doctrine for over half a century. In this Court, there have been six cases involving the "separate but equal" doctrine in the field of public education.[7] In *Cumming v. County Board of Education*, 175 U.S. 528, and *Gong Lum v. Rice*, 275 U.S. 78, the validity of the doctrine itself was not challenged.[8] In more recent cases, all on the graduate school level, inequality was found in that specific benefits enjoyed by white students were denied to Negro students of the same educational qualifications. *Missouri ex rel. Gaines v. Canada*, 305 U.S. 337; *Sipuel v. Oklahoma*, 332 U.S. 631; *Sweatt v. Painter*, 339 U.S. 629; *McLaurin v. Oklahoma State Regents*, 339 U.S. 637. In none of these cases was it necessary to reexamine the doctrine to grant relief to the Negro plaintiff. And in *Sweatt v. Painter, supra*, the Court expressly reserved decision on the question whether *Plessy v. Ferguson* should be held inapplicable to public education.

In the instant cases, that question is directly presented. Here, unlike *Sweatt v. Painter*, there are findings below that the Negro and white schools involved have been equalized, or are being equalized, with respect to buildings, curricula, qualifications and salaries of teachers, and other "tangible" factors.[9] Our decision, therefore, cannot turn on merely a comparison of these tangible factors in the Negro and white schools involved in each of the cases. We must look instead to the effect of segregation itself on public education.

In approaching this problem, we cannot turn the clock back to 1868 when the Amendment was adopted, or even to 1896 when *Plessy v. Ferguson* was written. We must consider public education in the light of its full development and its present place in American life throughout the Nation. Only in this way can it be determined if segregation in public schools deprives these plaintiffs of the equal protection of the laws.

Today education is perhaps the most important function of state and local governments. Compulsory school attendance laws and the great expenditures for education both demonstrate our recognition of the importance of education to our democratic society. It is required in the performance of our most basic public responsibilities, even service in the armed forces. It is the very foundation of good citizenship. Today it is a principal instrument in awakening the child to cultural values, in preparing

him for later professional training, and in helping him to adjust normally to his environment. In these days, it is doubtful that any child may reasonably be expected to succeed in life if he is denied the opportunity of an education. Such an opportunity, where the state has undertaken to provide it, is a right which must be made available to all on equal terms.

We come then to the question presented: Does segregation of children in public schools solely on the basis of race, even though the physical facilities and other "tangible" factors may be equal, deprive the children of the minority group of equal educational opportunities? We believe that it does.

In *Sweatt v. Painter, supra*, in finding that a segregated law school for Negroes could not provide them equal educational opportunities, this Court relied in large part on "those qualities which are incapable of objective measurement but which make for greatness in a law school." In *McLaurin v. Oklahoma State Regents, supra*, the Court, in requiring that a Negro admitted to a white graduate school be treated like all other students, again resorted to intangible considerations: "… his ability to study, to engage in discussions and exchange views with other students, and, in general, to learn his profession." Such considerations apply with added force to children in grade and high schools. To separate them from others of similar age and qualifications solely because of their race generates a feeling of inferiority as to their status in the community that may affect their hearts and minds in a way unlikely ever to be undone. The effect of this separation on their educational opportunities was well stated by a finding in the Kansas case by a court which nevertheless felt compelled to rule against the Negro plaintiffs:

> "Segregation of white and colored children in public schools has a detrimental effect upon the colored children. The impact is greater when it has the sanction of the law; for the policy of separating the races is usually interpreted as denoting the inferiority of the negro group. A sense of inferiority affects the motivation of a child to learn. Segregation with the sanction of law, therefore, has a tendency to [retard] the educational and mental development of negro children and to deprive them of some of the benefits they would receive in a racial[ly] integrated school system."[10]

Whatever may have been the extent of psychological knowledge at the time of *Plessy v. Ferguson*, this finding is amply supported by modern authority.[11] Any language in *Plessy v. Ferguson* contrary to this finding is rejected.

We conclude that in the field of public education the doctrine of "separate but equal" has no place. Separate educational facilities are inherently unequal. Therefore, we hold that the plaintiffs and others similarly situated for whom the actions have been brought are, by reason of the segregation complained of, deprived of the equal protection of the laws guaranteed by the Fourteenth Amendment. This disposition makes unnecessary any discussion whether such segregation also violates the Due Process Clause of the Fourteenth Amendment.[12]

Because these are class actions, because of the wide applicability of this decision, and because of the great variety of local conditions, the formulation of decrees in these cases presents problems of considerable complexity. On reargument, the consideration of appropriate relief was necessarily subordinated to the primary question—the constitutionality of segregation in public education. We have now announced that such segregation is a denial of the equal protection of the laws. In order that we may have the full assistance of the parties in formulating decrees, the cases will be restored to the docket, and the parties are requested to present further argument on Questions 4 and 5 previously propounded by the Court for the reargument this Term.[13] The Attorney General of the United States is again invited to participate. The Attorneys General of the states requiring or permitting segregation in public education will also be permitted to appear as *amici curiae* upon request to do so by September 15, 1954, and submission of briefs by October 1, 1954.[14]

It is so ordered.

NOTES

1. In the Kansas case, *Brown v. Board of Education*, the plaintiffs are Negro children of elementary school age residing in Topeka. They brought this action in the United States District Court for the District of Kansas to enjoin enforcement of a Kansas statute which permits, but does not require, cities of more than 15,000 population to maintain separate school facilities for Negro and white students. Kan. Gen. Stat. § 72–1724 (1949). Pursuant to that authority, the Topeka Board of Education elected to establish segregated elementary schools. Other public schools in the community, however, are operated on a nonsegregated basis....

In the South Carolina case, *Briggs v. Elliott*, the plaintiffs are Negro children of both elementary and high school age residing in Clarendon County. They brought this action in the United States District Court for the Eastern District of South Carolina to enjoin enforcement of provisions in the state constitution and statutory code which require the segregation of Negroes and whites in public schools....

In the Virginia case, *Davis v. County School Board*, the plaintiffs are Negro children of high school age residing in Prince Edward County. They brought this action in the United States District Court for the Eastern District of Virginia to enjoin enforcement of provisions in the state constitution and statutory code which require the segregation of Negroes and whites in public schools....

In the Delaware case, *Gebhart v. Belton*, the plaintiffs are Negro children of both elementary and high school age residing in New Castle county. They brought this action in the Delaware Court of Chancery to enjoin enforcement of provisions in the state constitution and statutory code which require the segregation of Negroes and whites in public schools....

2. technical footnote deleted.
3. technical footnote deleted.
4. technical footnote deleted.
5. technical footnote deleted.
6. technical footnote deleted.
7. technical footnote deleted.
8. technical footnote deleted.
9. technical footnote deleted.
10. technical footnote deleted.
11. K. B. Clark, Effect of Prejudice and Discrimination on Personality Development (Midcentury White House Conference on Children and Youth, 1950); Witmer and Kotinsky, Personality in the Making (1952), c. VI; Deutscher and Chein, The Psychological Effects of Enforced Segregation: A Survey of Social Science Opinion, 26 J. Psychol. 259 (1948); Chein, What Are the Psychological Effects of Segregation Under Conditions of Equal Facilities?, 3 Int. J. Opinion and Attitude Res. 229 (1949); Brameld, Educational Costs, in Discrimination and National Welfare (MacIver, ed., 1949), 44–48; Frazier, The Negro in the United States (1949), 674–681. And see generally Myrdal, An American Dilemma (1944).
12. technical footnote deleted.
13. technical footnote deleted.
14. technical footnote deleted.

From *U.S. Reports*, 1954. Opinion of the Supreme Court, 1954.

UNIVERSITY OF CALIFORNIA REGENTS v. BAKKE

428 U.S. 269 (1977)

MR. JUSTICE POWELL announced the judgment of the Court.

This case presents a challenge to the special admissions program of the petitioner, the Medical School of the University of California at Davis, which is designed to assure the admission of a specified number of students from certain minority groups. The Superior Court of California sustained respondent's challenge, holding that petitioner's program violated the California Constitution, Title VI of the Civil Rights Act of 1964, 42 U.S.C. § 2000d *et seq.,* and the Equal Protection Clause of the Fourteenth Amendment. The court enjoined petitioner from considering respondent's race or the race of any other applicant in making admissions decisions. It refused, however, to order respondent's admission to the Medical School, holding that he had not carried his burden of proving that he would have been admitted but for the constitutional and statutory violations. The Supreme Court of California affirmed those portions of the trial court's judgment declaring the special admissions program unlawful and enjoining petitioner from considering the race of any applicant.† It modified that portion of the judgment denying respondent's requested injunction and directed the trial court to order his admission.

For the reasons stated in the following opinion, I believe that so much of the judgment of the California court as holds petitioner's special admissions program unlawful and directs that respondent be admitted to the Medical School must be affirmed. For the reasons expressed in a separate opinion, my Brothers THE CHIEF JUSTICE, MR. JUSTICE STEWART, MR. JUSTICE REHNQUIST, and MR. JUSTICE STEVENS concur in this judgment.

I also conclude for the reasons stated in the following opinion that the portion of the court's judgment enjoining petitioner from according any consideration to race in its admissions process must be reversed. For reasons expressed in separate opinions, my Brothers MR. JUSTICE BRENNAN, MR. JUSTICE WHITE, MR. JUSTICE MARSHALL, and MR. JUSTICE BLACKMUN concur in this judgment.

Affirmed in part and reversed in part.

Opinion of Powell, J.

I‡

The Medical School of the University of California at Davis opened in 1968 with an entering class of 50 students. In 1971, the size of the entering class was increased to 100 students, a level at which it remains. No admissions program for disadvantaged or minority students existed when the school opened, and the first class contained three Asians but no blacks, no Mexican-Americans, and no American Indians. Over the next two years, the faculty devised a special admissions program to increase the representation of "disadvantaged" students in each Medical School class.[1] The special program consisted of a separate admissions system operating in coordination with the regular admissions process.

Under the regular admissions procedure, a candidate could submit his application to the Medical School beginning in July of the year preceding the academic year for which admission was sought. Record 149. Because of the large number of applications,[2] the admissions committee screened each one to select candidates for further consideration. Candidates whose overall undergraduate grade point averages fell below 2.5 on a scale of 4.0 were summarily rejected. *Id.,* at 63. About one out of six applicants was invited for a personal interview. *Ibid.* Following the interviews, each candidate was rated on a scale of 1 to 100 by his interviewers and four other members of the admissions committee. The rating embraced the interviewers' summaries, the candidate's overall grade point average, grade point average in science courses, scores on the Medical College Admissions Test (MCAT), letters of recommendation, extracurricular activities, and other biographical data. *Id.,* at 62. The ratings were added together to arrive at each candidate's "benchmark" score. Since five committee members rated each candidate in 1973, a perfect score was 500; in 1974, six members rated each candidate, so that a perfect score was 600. The full committee then reviewed the file and scores of each applicant and made offers of admission on a "rolling" basis.[3] The chairman was responsible for placing names on the waiting list. They were not placed in strict numerical order; instead, the chairman had discretion to include persons with "special skills." *Id.,* at 63–64.

The special admissions program operated with a separate committee, a majority of whom were members of minority groups. *Id.,* at 163. On the 1973 application form, candidates were asked to indicate whether they wished to be considered as "economically and/or educationally disadvantaged" applicants; on the 1974 form the question was whether they wished to be considered as members of a "minority group," which the Medical School apparently viewed as "Blacks," "Chicanos," "Asians," and "American Indians." *Id.,* at 65–66, 146, 197, 203–205, 216–218. If these questions were answered affirmatively, the application was forwarded to the special admissions committee. No formal definition of "disadvantaged" was ever produced, *id.,* at 163–164, but the chairman of the special committee screened each application to see whether it reflected economic or educational deprivation.[4] Having passed this initial hurdle, the applications then were rated by the special committee in a fashion similar to that used by the general admissions committee, except that special candidates did not have to meet the 2.5 grade point average cutoff applied to regular applicants. About one-fifth of the total number of special applicants were invited for interviews in 1973 and 1974.[5] Following each interview, the special committee assigned each special applicant a benchmark score. The special committee then presented its top choices to the general admissions committee. The latter did not rate or compare the special candidates against the general applicants, *id.,* at 388, but could reject recommended special candidates for failure to meet course requirements or other specific deficiencies. *Id.,* at 171–172. The special committee continued to recommend special applicants until a number prescribed by faculty vote were admitted. While the overall class size was still 50, the prescribed number was 8; in 1973 and 1974, when the class size had doubled to 100, the prescribed number of special admissions also doubled, to 16. *Id.,* at 164, 166.

From the year of the increase in class size—1971—through 1974, the special program resulted in the admission of 21 black students, 30 Mexican-Americans, and 12 Asians, for a total of 63 minority students. Over the same period, the regular admissions program produced 1 black, 6 Mexican-Americans, and 37 Asians, for a total of 44 minority students.[6] Although disadvantaged whites applied to the special program in large numbers, see no. 5, *supra,* none received an offer of admission through that process. Indeed, in 1974, at least, the special committee explicitly considered only "disadvantaged" special applicants who were members of one of the designated minority groups. Record 171.

Allan Bakke is a white male who applied to the Davis Medical School in both 1973 and 1974. In both years Bakke's application was considered under the general admissions program, and he received an interview. His 1973 interview was with Dr. Theodore C. West, who considered Bakke "a very desirable applicant to [the] medical school." *Id.,* at 225. Despite a strong benchmark score of 468 out of 500, Bakke was rejected. His application had come late in the year, and no applicants in the general admissions process with scores below 470 were accepted after Bakke's application was completed. *Id.,* at 69. There were four special admissions slots unfilled at that time, however, for which Bakke was not considered. *Id.,* at 70. After his 1973 rejection, Bakke wrote to Dr. George H. Lowrey, Associate Dean and Chairman of the Admissions Committee, protesting that the special admissions program operated as a racial and ethnic quota. *Id.,* at 259.

Bakke's 1974 application was completed early in the year. *Id.,* at 70. His student interviewer gave him an overall rating of 94, finding him "friendly, well tempered, conscientious and delightful to speak with." *Id.,* at 229. His faculty interviewer was, by coincidence, the same Dr. Lowrey to whom he had written in protest of the special admissions program. Dr. Lowrey found Bakke "rather limited in his approach" to the problems of the medical profession and found disturbing Bakke's "very definite opinions which were based more on his personal viewpoints than upon a study of the total problem." *Id.,* at 226. Dr. Lowrey gave Bakke the lowest of his six ratings, an 86; his total was 549 out of 600. *Id.,* at 230. Again, Bakke's application was rejected. In neither year did the chairman of the admissions committee, Dr. Lowrey, exercise his discretion to place Bakke on the waiting list. *Id.,* at 64. In both years, applicants were admitted under the special program with grade point averages, MCAT scores, and benchmark scores significantly lower than Bakke's.[7]

After the second rejection, Bakke filed the instant suit in the Superior Court of California.[8] He sought mandatory, injunctive, and declaratory relief compelling his admission to the Medical School. He alleged that the Medical School's special admissions program operated to exclude him from the school on the basis of his race, in violation of his rights under the Equal Protection Clause of the Fourteenth Amendment,[9] Art. I, § 21, of the California Constitution,[10] and § 601 of Title VI of the Civil Rights Act of 1964, 78 Stat. 252, 42 U.S.C. § 2000d.[11] The University cross-complained for a declaration that its special admissions program was lawful. The trial court found that the special program operated as a racial quota, because minority applicants in the special program were rated only against one another, Record 388, and 16 places in the class of 100 were reserved for them. *Id.,* at 295–296. Declaring that the University could not take race into account in making admissions decisions, the trial court held the challenged program violative of the Federal Constitution, the State Constitution, and Title VI. The court refused to order Bakke's admission, however, holding that he had failed to carry his burden of proving that he would have been admitted but for the existence of the special program.

Bakke appealed from the portion of the trial court judgment denying him admission, and the University appealed from the decision that its special admissions program was unlawful and the order enjoining it from considering race in the processing of applications. The Supreme Court of California transferred the case directly from the trial court, "because of the importance of the issues involved." 18 Cal. 3d 34, 39, 553, P. 2d 1152, 1156 (1976). The California court accepted the findings of the trial court with respect to the University's program.[12] Because the special admissions program involved a racial classification, the Supreme Court held itself bound to apply strict scrutiny. *Id.,* at 49, 553 P. 2d, at 1162–1163. It then turned to the goals the University presented as justifying the special program. Although the court agreed that the goals of integrating the medical profession and increasing the number of physicians willing to serve members of minority groups were compelling state interests, *id.,* at 53, 553 P. 2d, at 1165, it concluded that the special admissions program was not the least intrusive means of achieving those goals. Without passing on the state constitutional or the federal statutory grounds cited in the trial court's judgment, the California court held that the Equal Protection Clause of the Fourteenth Amendment required that "no applicant may be rejected because of his race, in favor of another who is less qualified, as measured by standards applied without regard to race." *Id.,* at 55, 553 P. 2d, at 1166.

Turning to Bakke's appeal, the court ruled that since Bakke had established that the University had discriminated against him on the basis of his race, the burden of proof shifted to the University to demonstrate that he would not have been admitted even in the absence of the special admissions program.[13] *Id.,* at 63–64, 553 P.2d, at 1172. The court analogized Bakke's situation to that of a plaintiff under Title VII of the Civil Rights Act of 1964, 42 U.S.C. § § 2000e-17 (1970 ed., Supp. V) see, *e.g., Franks v. Bowman Transportation Co.,* 424 U.S. 747, 772 (1976). 18 Cal. 3d, at 63–64, 553 P. 2d, at 1172. On this basis, the court initially ordered a remand for the purpose of determining whether, under the newly allocated burden of proof, Bakke would have been admitted to either the 1973 or the 1974 entering class in the absence of the special admissions program. App. A. to Application for Stay 48. In its petition for rehearsing below, however, the University conceded its inability to carry that burden. App. B. to Application for Stay A19–A20.[14] The California court thereupon amended its opinion to direct that the trial court enter judgment ordering Bakke's admission to the Medical School. 18 Cal. 3d, at 64, 553 P.2d, at 1172. That order was stayed pending review in this court. 429 U.S. 953 (1976). We granted certiorari to consider the important constitutional issue. 429 U.S. 1090 (1997)....

V

A

It may be assumed that the reservation of a specified number of seats in each class for individuals from the preferred ethnic groups would contribute to the attainment of considerable ethnic diversity in the student body. But petitioner's argument that this is the only effective means of serving the interest of diversity is seriously flawed. In a most fundamental sense the argument misconceives the nature of the state interest that would justify consideration of race or ethnic background. It is not an interest in simple ethnic diversity, in which a specified percentage of the student body is in effect guaranteed to be members of selected ethnic groups, with the remaining percentage an undifferentiated aggregation of students. The diversity that furthers a compelling state interest encompasses a far broader array of qualifications and characteristics of which racial or ethnic origin is but a single though important element. Petitioner's special admissions program, focused *solely* on ethnic diversity, would hinder rather than further attainment of genuine diversity.[50]

Nor would the state interest in genuine diversity be served by expanding petitioner's two-track system into a multitrack program with a prescribed number of seats set aside for each identifiable category of applicants. Indeed, it is inconceivable that a university would thus pursue the logic of petitioner's two-track program to the illogical end of insulating each category of applicants with certain desired qualifications from competition with all other applicants.

The experience of other university admissions programs, which take race into account in achieving the educational diversity valued by the First Amendment, demonstrates that the assignment of a fixed number of places to a minority group is not a necessary means toward the end. An illuminating example is found in the Harvard College program:

> "In recent years Harvard College has expanded the concept of diversity to include students from disadvantaged economic, racial and ethnic groups. Harvard College now recruits not only Californians or Louisianans but also blacks and Chicanos and other minority students....
>
> "In practice, this new definition of diversity has meant that race has been a factor in some admission decisions. When the Committee on Admissions reviews the large middle group of applicants who are 'admissible' and deemed capable of doing good work in their courses, the race of an applicant may tip the balance in his favor just as geographic origin or a life spent on a farm may tip the balance in other candidates' cases. A farm boy from Idaho can bring something to Harvard College that a Bostonian cannot offer. Similarly, a black student can usually bring something that a white person cannot offer...."

In such an admissions program,[51] race or ethnic background may be deemed a "plus" in a particular applicant's file, yet it does not insulate the individual from comparison with all other candidates for the available seats. The file of a particular black applicant may be examined for his potential contribution to diversity without the factor of race being decisive when compared, for example, with that of an applicant identified as an Italian-American if the latter is thought to exhibit qualities more likely to promote beneficial educational pluralism. Such qualities could include exceptional personal talents, unique work or service experience, leadership potential, maturity, demonstrated compassion, a history of overcoming disadvantage, ability to communicate with the poor, or other qualifications deemed important. In short, an admissions program operated in this way is flexible enough to consider all pertinent elements of diversity in light of the particular qualifications of each applicant, and to place them on the same footing for consideration, although not necessarily according them the same weight. Indeed, the weight attributed to a particular quality may vary from year to year depending upon the "mix" both of the student body and the applicants for the incoming class.

This kind of program treats each applicant as an individual in the admissions process. The applicant who loses out on the last available seat to another candidate receiving a "plus" on the basis of ethnic background will not have been foreclosed from all consideration for that seat simply because he was not the right color or had the wrong surname. It would mean only that his combined qualifications, which may have included similar nonobjective factors, did not outweigh those of the other applicant. His qualifications would have been weighed fairly and competitively, and he would have no basis to complain of unequal treatment under the Fourteenth Amendment.[52]...

B

In summary, it is evident that the Davis special admissions program involves the use of an explicit racial classification never before countenanced by this Court. It tells applicants who are not Negro, Asian, or Chicano that they are totally excluded from a specific percentage of the seats in an entering class. No matter how strong their qualifications, quantitative and extracurricular, including their own potential for contribution to educational diversity, they are never afforded the chance to compete with applicants from the preferred groups for the special admissions seats. At the same time, the preferred applicants have the opportunity to compete for every seat in the class.

The fatal flaw in petitioner's preferential program is its disregard of individual rights as guaranteed by the Fourteenth Amendment. *Shelley v. Kraemer,* 334 U.S., at 22. Such rights are not absolute. But when a State's distribution of benefits or imposition of burdens hinges on ancestry or the color of a person's skin, that individual is entitled to a demonstration that the challenged classification is necessary to promote a substantial state interest. Petitioner has failed to carry this burden. For this reason, that portion of the California court's judgment holding petitioner's special admissions program invalid under the Fourteenth Amendment must be affirmed.

C

In enjoining petitioner from ever considering the race of any applicant, however, the courts below failed to recognize that the State has a substantial interest that legitimately may be served by a properly devised admissions program involving the competitive consideration of race and ethnic origin. For this reason, so much of the California court's judgment as enjoins petitioner from any consideration of the race of any applicant must be reversed....

NOTES

† technical footnote deleted.
‡ technical footnote deleted.
1. technical footnote deleted.
2. technical footnote deleted.
3. technical footnote deleted.
4. technical footnote deleted.
5. technical footnote deleted.
6. technical footnote deleted.
7. technical footnote deleted.
8. technical footnote deleted.
9. technical footnote deleted.
10. technical footnote deleted.
11. technical footnote deleted.
12. technical footnote deleted.
13. technical footnote deleted.
14. technical footnote deleted.
50. technical footnote deleted.
51. technical footnote deleted.
52. technical footnote deleted.

Opinion of Marshall, J.

MR. JUSTICE MARSHALL.

I agree with the judgment of the Court only insofar as it permits a university to consider the race of an applicant in making admissions decisions. I do not agree that petitioner's admissions program violates the Constitution. For it must be remembered that, during most of the past 200 years, the Constitution as interpreted by this Court did not prohibit the most ingenious and pervasive forms of discrimination against the Negro. Now when a State acts to remedy the effects of that legacy of discrimination, I cannot believe that this same Constitution stands as a barrier.

I

A

Three hundred and fifty years ago, the Negro was dragged to this country in chains to be sold into slavery. Uprooted from his homeland and thrust into bondage for forced labor, the slave was deprived of all legal rights. It was unlawful to teach him to read; he could be sold away from his family and friends at the whim of his master; and killing or maiming him was not a crime. The system of slavery brutalized and dehumanized both master and slave.[1]...

II

The position of the Negro today in America is the tragic but inevitable consequence of centuries of unequal treatment. Measured by any benchmark of comfort or achievement, meaningful equality remains a distant dream for the Negro.

A Negro child today has a life expectancy which is shorter by more than five years than that of a white child.[2] The Negro child's mother is over three times more likely to die of complications in childbirth,[3] and the infant mortality rate for Negroes is nearly twice that for whites.[4] The median income of the Negro family is only 60% that of the median of a white family,[5] and the percentage of Negroes who live in families with incomes below the poverty line is nearly four times greater than that of whites.[6]

When the Negro child reaches working age, he finds that America offers him significantly less than it offers his white counterpart. For Negro adults, the unemployment rate is twice that of whites,[7] and the unemployment rate for Negro teenagers is nearly three times that of white teenagers.[8] A Negro male who completes four years of college can expect a median annual income of merely $110 more than a white male who has only a high school diploma.[9] Although Negroes represent 11.5% of the population,[10] they are only 1.2% of the lawyers and judges, 2% of the physicians, 2.3% of the dentists, 1.1% of the engineers and 2.6% of the college and university professors.[11]

The relationship between those figures and the history of unequal treatment afforded to the Negro cannot be denied. At every point from birth to death the impact of the past is reflected in the still disfavored position of the Negro.

In light of the sorry history of discrimination and its devastating impact on the lives of Negroes, bringing the Negro into the mainstream of American life should be a state interest of the highest order. To fail to do so is to ensure that America will forever remain a divided society.

III

I do not believe that the Fourteenth Amendment requires us to accept that fate. Neither its history nor our past cases lend any support to the conclusion that a university may not remedy the cumulative effects of society's discrimination by giving consideration to race in an effort to increase the number and percentage of Negro doctors....

IV

While I applaud the judgment of the Court that a university may consider race in its admissions process, it is more than a little ironic that, after several hundred years of class-based discrimination against Negroes, the Court is unwilling to hold that a class-based remedy for that discrimination is permissible. In declining to so hold, today's judgment ignores the fact that for several hundred years Negroes have been discriminated against, not as individuals, but rather solely because of the color of their skins. It is unnecessary in 20th-century America to have individual Negroes demonstrate that they have been victims of racial discrimination; the racism of our society has been so pervasive that none, regardless of wealth or position, has managed to escape its impact. The experience of Negroes in America has been different in kind, not just in degree, from that of other ethnic groups. It is not merely the history of slavery alone but also that a whole people were marked as inferior by the law. And that mark has endured. The dream of America as the great melting pot has not been realized for the Negro; because of his skin color he never even made it into the pot....

It is because of a legacy of unequal treatment that we now must permit the institutions of this society to give consideration to race in making decisions about who will hold the positions of influence, affluence, and prestige in America. For far too long, the doors to those positions have been shut to Negroes. If we are ever to become a fully integrated society, one in which the color of a person's skin will not determine the opportunities available to him or her, we must be willing to take steps to open those doors. I do not believe that anyone can truly look into America's past and still find that a remedy for the effects of that past is impermissible.

It has been said that this case involves only the individual, Bakke, and this University. I doubt, however, that there is a computer capable of determining the number of persons and institutions that may be affected by the decision in this case. For example, we are told by the Attorney General of the United States that at least 27 federal agencies have adopted regulations requiring recipients of federal funds to take "'*affirmative action* to overcome the effects of conditions which result in limiting participation... by persons of a particular race, color, or national origin.'" Supplemental Brief for United States as *Amicus Curiae* 16 (emphasis added). I cannot even guess the number of state and local governments that have set up affirmative-action programs, which may be affected by today's decision.

I fear that we have come full circle. After the Civil War our Government started "affirmative action" programs. This Court in the *Civil Rights Cases* and *Plessy v. Ferguson* destroyed the movement toward complete equality. For almost a century no action was taken, and this nonaction was with the tacit approval of the courts. Then we had *Brown v. Board of Education* and the Civil Rights Acts of Congress, followed by numerous affirmative-action programs. *Now,* we have this Court again stepping in, this time to stop affirmative-action programs of the type used by the University of California.

NOTES

1. technical footnote deleted.
2. technical footnote deleted.
3. technical footnote deleted.
4. technical footnote deleted.
5. technical footnote deleted.
6. technical footnote deleted.
7. technical footnote deleted.
8. technical footnote deleted.
9. technical footnote deleted.
10. technical footnote deleted.
11. technical footnote deleted.

From *U.S. Reports,* 1977. Opinion of the Supreme Court, 1977.

FREEDOM OF RELIGIOUS EXPRESSION

SHAARE TEFILA CONGREGATION v. COBB

Cite as 107 S.Ct. 2019 (1987)

JUSTICE WHITE delivered the opinion of the Court.

On November 2, 1982, the outside walls of the synagogue of the Shaare Tefila Congregation in Silver Spring, Maryland, were sprayed with red and black paint and with large anti-Semitic slogans, phrases and symbols. A few months later, the Congregation and Federal District Court, alleging that defendants' desecration of the synagogue had violated 42 U.S.C. § § 1981, 1982, 1985(3) and the Maryland common law of trespass, nuisance, and intentional infliction of emotional distress. On defendants' motion under Fed.Rule Civ.Proc. 12(b)(1) and (6), the District Court dismissed all the claims. The Court of Appeals affirmed in all respects. 785 F.2d 523 (CA4 1986). Petitioners petitioned for writ of certiorari. We granted the petition, 479 U.S. ____, 107 S.Ct. 62, 93 L.Ed.2d 21 (1986), and we now reverse the judgment of the Court of Appeals.

[1] Section 1982 guarantees all citizens of the United States, "the same right… as is enjoyed by white citizens… to inherit, purchase, lease, sell, hold, and convey real and personal property." The section forbids both official and private racially discriminatory interference with property rights, *Jones v. Alfred H. Mayer Co.,* 392 U.S. 409, 88 S.Ct. 2186, 20 L.Ed.2d 1189 (1968). Petitioners' allegation was that they were deprived of the right to hold property in violation of § 1982 because the defendants were motivated by racial prejudice. They unsuccessfully argued in the District Court and Court of Appeals that Jews are not a racially distinct group, but that defendants' conduct is actionable because they viewed Jews as racially distinct and were motivated by racial prejudice. The Court of Appeals held that § 1982 was not "intended to apply to situations in which a plaintiff is not a member of a racially distinct group but is merely *perceived* to be so by defendants." 785 F2d, at 526 (emphasis in original). The Court of Appeals believed that "[b]ecause discrimination against Jews is not racial discrimination," *id.,* at 527, the District Court was correct in dismissing the § 1982 claim.

[2] We agree with the Court of Appeals that a charge of racial discrimination within the meaning of § 1982 cannot be made out by alleging only that the defendants were motivated by racial animus; it is necessary as well to allege that defendants' animus was directed towards the kind of group that Congress intended to protect when it passed the statute. To hold otherwise would unacceptably extend the reach of the statute.

[3–5] We agree with petitioners, however, that the Court of Appeals erred in holding that Jews cannot state a § 1982 claim against other white defendants. That view rested on the notion that because Jews today are not thought to be members of a separate race, they cannot make out a claim of racial discrimination within the meaning of § 1982. That construction of the section we have today rejected in *Saint Francis College v. Al-Khazraji,* ____ U.S., at ____, 107 S.Ct., at ____. Our opinion in that case observed that definitions of race when § 1982 was passed were not the same as they are today and concluded that the section was "intended to protect from discrimination identifiable classes of persons who are subjected to intentional discrimination solely because of their ancestry or ethnic characteristics." At ____, 107 S.Ct., at 2028. As *St. Francis* makes clear, the question before us is not whether Jews are considered to be a separate race by today's standards, but whether, at the time § 1982 was adopted, Jews constituted a group of people that Congress intended to protect. It is evident from the legislative history of the section reviewed in *Saint Francis College,* a review that we need not repeat here, that Jews and Arabs were among the peoples then considered to be distinct races and hence within the protection of the statute. Jews are not foreclosed from stating a cause of action against other members of what today is considered to be part of the Caucasian race.

The judgment of the Court of Appeals is therefore reversed and the case is remanded for further proceedings consistent with this opinion.

SAINT FRANCIS COLLEGE v. AL-KHAZRAJI

Cite as 107 S.Ct. 2022 (1987)

JUSTICE WHITE delivered the opinion of the Court.

Respondent, a citizen of the United States born in Iraq, was an associate professor at St. Francis College, one of the petitioners here. In January 1978, he applied for tenure; the Board of Trustees denied his request on February 23, 1978. He accepted a 1-year, nonrenewable contract and sought administrative reconsideration of the tenure decision, which was denied on February 6, 1979. He worked his last day at the college on May 26, 1979. In June 1979, he filed complaints with the Pennsylvania Human Relations Commission and the Equal Employment Opportunities Commission. The State agency dismissed his claim and the EEOC issued a right to sue letter on August 6, 1980.

On October 30, 1980, respondent filed a *pro se* complaint in the District Court alleging a violation of Title VII of the Civil Rights Act of 1964 and claiming discrimination based on national origin, religion, and/or race. Amended complaints were filed, adding claims under 42 U.S.C. § § 1981, 1983, 1985(3), 1986, and state law. The District Court dismissed the 1986, 1985(3) and Title VII claims as untimely but held that the § § 1981 and 1983 claims were not barred by the Pennsylvania 6-year statute of limitations. The court at that time also ruled that because the complaint alleged denial of tenure because respondent was of the Arabian race, an action under § 1981 could be maintained. Defendants' motion for summary judgment came up before a different judge, who construed the pleadings as asserting only discrimination on the basis of national origin and religion, which § 1981 did not cover. Even if racial discrimination was deemed to have been alleged, the District Court ruled that § 1981 does not reach claims of discrimination based on Arabian ancestry.[1]

The Court of Appeals rejected petitioners' claim that the § 1981 claim had not been timely filed. Under the Court of Appeals' holding in *Goodman v. Lukens Steel Co.*, 777 F.2d 113 (CA 2 1985), that the Pennsylvania 2-year statute of limitations governed § 1981 cases, respondent's suit would have been barred. The Court of Appeals, however, relying on *Chevron Oil Co. v. Huson*, 404 U.S. 97, 92 S.Ct. 349, 30 L.Ed.2d 296 (1971), held that *Goodman* should not be retroactively applied and that this suit was timely under its pre-*Goodman* cases which had borrowed the State's 6-year statute.

Reaching the merits, the Court of Appeals held that respondent had alleged discrimination based on race and that although under current racial classifications Arabs are Caucasians, respondent could maintain his § 1981 claim.[2] Congress, when it passed what is now § 1981, had not limited its protections to those who today would be

considered members of a race different from the race of the defendant. Rather, the legislative history of the section indicated that Congress intended to forbid "at the least, membership in a group that is ethnically and physiognomically distinctive." 784 F.2d 505, 517 (CA 3 1986). Section 1981, "at a minimum," reaches "discrimination directed against an individual because he or she is genetically part of an ethnically and physiognomically distinctive sub-grouping of *homo sapiens*." *Ibid.* Because respondent had not had full discovery and the record was not sufficient to determine whether he had been subjected to the sort of prejudice § 1981 would redress, respondent was to be given the opportunity to prove his case.[3]

We granted certiorari. 479 U.S. ____, 107 S.Ct. 62, 93 L.Ed.2d 21 (1986), limited to the statute of limitations issue and the question whether a person of Arabian ancestry was protected from racial discrimination under 1981, and now affirm the judgment of the Court of Appeals.

I

[1] We agree with the Court of Appeals that respondent's claim was not time barred. *Wilson v. Garcia*, 471 U.S. 261, 105 S.Ct. 1938, 85 L.Ed.2d 254 (1985), required that in selecting the applicable state statute of limitations in § 1983 cases, the lower federal courts should choose the state statute applicable to other personal injury torts. Thereafter, the Third Circuit in *Goodman* held that *Wilson* applies to § 1981 cases as well and that the Pennsylvania 2-year statute should apply. The Court of Appeals in this case, however, held that when respondent filed his suit, which was prior to *Wilson v. Garcia*, it was clearly established in the Third Circuit that a § 1981 plaintiff had six years to bring an action and that *Goodman* should not be applied retroactively to bar respondent's suit.

Insofar as what the prevailing law was in the Third Circuit, we have no reason to disagree with the Court of Appeals. Under controlling precedent in that Circuit, respondent had six years to file his suit, and it was filed well within that time. See 784 F.2d, at 512–513. We also assume but do not decide that *Wilson v. Garcia* controls the selection of the applicable state statute of limitations in § 1981 cases. The Court of Appeals, however, correctly held that its decision in *Goodman* should not be retroactively applied to bar respondent's action in this case. The usual rule is that federal cases should be decided in accordance with the law existing at the time of decision. *Gulf Offshore Co. v. Mobil Oil Corp.*, 453 U.S. 473, 486, n. 16, 101 S.Ct. 2870, 2879, n. 16, 69 L.Ed.2d 784 (1981); *Thorpe v. Durham Housing Authority*, 393 U.S. 268, 281, 89 S.Ct. 518, 526, 21 L.Ed.2d 474 (1969); *United States v. Schooner Peggy*, 1

Cranch 103, *110, 2 L.Ed. 49 (1801). But *Chevron Oil Co. v. Huson, supra,* counsels against retroactive application of statute of limitations decision in certain circumstances. There, the Court held that its decision specifying the applicable state statute of limitations should be applied only prospectively because it overruled clearly established circuit precedent on which the complaining party was entitled to rely, because retroactive application would be inconsistent with the purpose of the underlying substantive statute, and because such application would be manifestly inequitable. The Court of Appeals found these same factors were present in this case and foreclosed retroactive applications of its decision in *Goodman.* We perceive no good reason for not applying *Chevron* where *Wilson* has required a Court of Appeals to overrule its prior cases. Nor has petitioner persuaded us that there was any error in the application of *Chevron* in the circumstances existing in this case.

II

Section 1981 provides:

> "All persons within the jurisdiction of the United States shall have the same right in every State and Territory to make and enforce contracts, to sue, be parties, give evidence, and to the full and equal benefit of all laws and proceedings for the security of persons and property as is enjoyed by white citizens, and shall be subject to like punishment, pains, penalties, taxes, licenses, and exactions of every kind, and to no other."

[2] Although § 1981 does not itself use the word "race," the Court has construed the section to forbid all "racial" discrimination in the making of private as well as public contracts. *Runyon v. McCrary,* 427, U.S. 160, 168, 174–175, 96 S.Ct. 2586, 2593, 2596–2597, 49 L.Ed.2d 415 (1976). The petitioner college, although a private institution, was therefore subject to this statutory command. There is no disagreement among the parties on these propositions. The issue is whether respondent has alleged *racial* discrimination within the meaning of § 1981.

[3] Petitioners contend that respondent is a Caucasian and cannot allege the kind of discrimination § 1981 forbids. Concededly, *McDonald v. Sante Fe Trail Transportation Co.,* 427 U.S. 273, 96 S.Ct. 2574, 49 L.Ed.2d 493 (1976), held that white persons could maintain a § 1981 suit; but that suit involved alleged discrimination against a white person in favor of a black, and petitioner submits that the section does not encompass claims of discrimination by one Caucasian against another. We are quite sure that the Court of Appeals properly rejected this position.

Petitioner's submission rests on the assumption that all those who might be deemed Caucasians today were thought to be of the same race when § 1981 became law in the 19th century; and it may be that a variety of ethnic groups, including Arabs, are now considered to be within the Caucasian race.[4] The understanding of "race" in the 19th century, however, was different. Plainly, all those who might be deemed Caucasian today were not thought to be of the same race at the time § 1981 became law.

In the middle years of the 19th century, dictionaries commonly referred to race as a "continued series of descendants from a parent who is called the *stock,*" N. Webster, An American Dictionary of the English Language 666 (New York 1830) (emphasis in original), "[t]he lineage of a family," N. Webster, 2 A Dictionary of the English Language 411 (New Haven 1841), or "descendants of a common ancestor," J. Donald, Chambers's Etymological Dictionary of the English Language 415 (London 1871). The 1887 edition of Webster's expanded the definition somewhat: "The descendants of a common ancestor; a family, tribe, people or nation, believed or presumed to belong to the same stock." N. Webster, Dictionary of the English Language (W. Wheeler ed. 1887). It was not until the 20th century that dictionaries began referring to the Caucasian, Mongolian and Negro races, 8 The Century Dictionary and Cyclopedia 4926 (1911), or to race as involving divisions of mankind based upon different physical characteristics. Webster's Collegiate Dictionary 794 (1916). Even so, modern dictionaries still include among the definitions of race as being "a family, tribe, people, or nation belonging to the same stock." Webster's Third New International Dictionary Mass.1870 (1971); Webster's Ninth New Collegiate Dictionary 969 (Springfield, Mass. 1986).

Encyclopedias of the 19th century also described race in terms of ethnic groups, which is a narrower concept of race than petitioners urge. Encyclopedia Americana in 1858, for example, referred in 1854 to various races such as Finns, vol. 5, p. 123, gypsies, 6 *id.,* at 123, Basques, 1 *id.,* at 602, and Hebrews, 6 *id.,* at 209. The 1863 version of the New American Cyclopaedia divided the Arabs into a number of subsidiary races, vol. 1, p. 739; represented the Hebrews as of the Semitic race, 9 *id.,* at 27, and identified numerous other groups as constituting races, including Swedes, 15 *id.,* at 216, Norwegians, 12 *id.,* at 410, Germans, 8 *id.,* at 200, Greeks, *id.,* at 438, Finns, 7 *id.,* at 513, Italians, 9 *id.,* at 644–645 (referring to mixture of different races), Spanish, 14 *id.,* at 804, Mongolians, 11 *id.,* at 651, Russians, 14 *id.,* at 226, and the like. The ninth edition of the Encyclopedia Britannica also referred to Arabs, vol. 2, p. 245 (1878), Jews, 13 *id.,* at 685 (1881), and other ethnic groups such as Germans, 10 *id.,* at 473 (1879), Hungarians, 12 *id.,* at 365 (1880), and Greeks, 11 *id.,* at 83 (1880), as separate races.

These dictionary and encyclopedic sources are somewhat diverse, but it is clear that they do not support the claim that for the purposes of § 1981, Arabs, Englishmen, Germans and certain other ethnic groups are to be considered a single race. We would expect the legislative history of § 1981, which the Court held in *Runyon v. McCrary* had its source in the Civil Rights Act of 1866, 14 Stat. 27, as well as the Voting Rights Act of 1870, 16 Stat. 140, 144, to reflect this common understanding, which it surely does. The debates are replete with references to the Scandinavian races, Cong.Globe, 39th Cong., 1st Sess., 499 (1866) (remarks of Sen. Cowan), as well as the Chinese, *id.*, at 523 (remarks of Sen. Davis), Latin, *id.*, at 238 (remarks of Rep. Kasson during debate of home rule for the District of Columbia), Spanish, *id.*, at 251 (remarks of Sen. Davis during debate of District of Columbia suffrage) and Anglo-Saxon races, *id.*, at 542 (remarks of Rep. Dawson). Jews, *ibid.*, Mexicans, see *ibid.*, (remarks of Rep. Dawson), blacks, *passim*, and Mongolians, *id.*, at 498 (remarks of Sen. Cowan), were similarly categorized. Gypsies were referred to as a race. *Ibid.*, (remarks of Sen. Cowan). Likewise, the Germans:

> "Who will say that Ohio can pass a law enacting that no man of the German race... shall ever own any property in Ohio, or shall ever make a contract in Ohio, or ever inherit property in Ohio, or ever come into Ohio to live, or even to work? If Ohio may pass such a law, and exclude a German citizen... because he is of the German nationality or race, then may every other State do so." *Id.*, at 1294 (Remarks of Sen. Shellabarger).

There was a reference to the Caucasian race, but it appears to have been referring to people of European ancestry. *Id.*, at 523 (remarks of Sen. Davis).

The history of the 1870 Act reflects similar understanding of what groups Congress intended to protect from intentional discrimination. It is clear, for example, that the civil rights sections of the 1870 Act provided protection for immigrant groups such as the Chinese. This view was expressed in the Senate. Cong.Globe, 41st Cong., 2d Sess., 1536, 3658, 3808 (1870). In the House, Representative Bingham described § 16 of the Act, part of the authority for § 1981, as declaring "that the States shall not hereafter discriminate against the immigrant from China and in favor of the immigrant from Prussia, nor against the immigrant from France and in favor of the immigrant from Ireland." *Id.*, at 3871.

[4–6] Based on the history of § 1981, we have little trouble in concluding that Congress intended to protect from discrimination identifiable classes of persons who are subjected to intentional discrimination solely because of their ancestry or ethnic characteristics. Such discrimination is racial discrimination that Congress intended § 1981 to forbid, whether or not it would be classified as racial in terms of modern scientific theory.[5] The Court of Appeals was thus quite right in holding that § 1981, "at a minimum," reaches discrimination against an individual "because he or she is genetically part of an ethnically and physiognomically distinctive sub-grouping of *homo sapiens*." It is clear from our holding, however, that a distinctive physiognomy is not essential to qualify for § 1981 protection. If respondent on remand can prove that he was subjected to intentional discrimination based on the fact that he was born an Arab, rather than solely on the place or nation of his origin, or his religion, he will have made out a case under § 1981.

The Judgment of the court of Appeals is accordingly affirmed.

NOTES

1. technical footnote deleted.
2. technical footnote deleted.
3. technical footnote deleted.
4. There is a common popular understanding that there are three major human races—Caucasoid, Mongoloid, and Negroid. Many modern biologists and anthropologists, however, criticize racial classifications as arbitrary and of little use in understanding the variability of human beings. It is said that genetically homogeneous populations do not exist and traits are not discontinuous between populations; therefore, a population can only be described in terms of relative frequencies of various traits. Clear-cut categories do not exist. The particular traits which have generally been chosen to characterize races have been criticized as having little biological significance. It has been found that differences between individuals of the same race are often greater than the differences between the "average" individuals of different races. These observations and others have led some, but not all, scientists to conclude that racial classifications are for the most part sociopolitical, rather than biological, in nature.
5. technical footnote deleted.

From *U.S. Reports,* 1987. Opinion of the Supreme Court, 1987.

UNIT 2

American Demography: Conquest, Colonies, Slavery, and Color

Unit Selections

Key Points to Consider

- In what respect does location define race and ethnic relations?

- In your opinion, are the issues of the South associated with those of the rest of the country? Explain.

- Does the 1998 racially motivated murder of African American James Byrd Jr. in Jasper, Texas, revive images of lynchings?

- What impact does the grouping of people into divisions such as black or white have for self-identification? for government policy? for the law? for understanding pluralism in America?

- What stereotypes of American regions have you encountered? Discuss the tension between regional and universal values.

- Does diversity in entertainment and segmented marketing fractionate the common elements of American culture?

- Explore the racial and ethnic diversity of neighborhoods, towns, and counties that are within your experience and compare them to state and national data. Use the U.S. Census ancestry data. What levels of dissimilarity do you notice?

- Does historical archaeology have social significance?

- Should the U.S. Census collect religious data?

 **Links: www.dushkin.com/online/**
These sites are annotated in the World Wide Web pages.

North American Demography
http://www.chrr.ohio-state.edu/~gryn/namerica.html

U.S. Census Bureau
http://www.census.gov

American demography is a neglected dimension of race and ethnic relations. The aspects of demography are broached in the articles selected for this unit. The following three complex features of American reality become more apparent when attention to American demography is a mode of analysis:

- The variety and specificity of indigenous, migrant, and imported populations,

- The particular scale and regional uniqueness of demographic configurations and patterns of settlement, and

- The historically embedded characteristics of dominant cultures and the history of their interaction with minority groups.

The concept of original populations is addressed in the first article of this section, which reveals a historical account based in anthropological archaeology. Attention to the demography during the founding of America is provided in material on the colonial populations, which extended the variety of European groups into The New World, and a contemporary geographic and economic profile of Native Americans. The relationship between indigenous populations and modern states will be taken up in Unit 4 of this reader.

The demography of the American South and its ongoing influence on the continuum of cultural experiences from slavery, segregation, and racialism are certainly aspects of its isolation. Its persistent small towns, its ethos of agriculture, its rurality, and its isolation and independence from currents of northern intellectualism and literary expression have differentiated the South's culture, arts, architecture, folkways, and learning. The South, unlike New England and much of the northern industrial states, has deeper ambiguities about the uprooting force of bourgeois and market-driven universalism. The absence of large-scale immigration and urbanization has limited its historical experience with diversity and pluralism. Southern regional culture is not homogeneous but does have embedded in it a particularity that is well worth exploring in more detail for its impact on ethnic and racial group formation. Interaction in the context of the southern experience and the process of separation and integration is unique. The contextual character of group relations is well established in the social sciences as a powerful explanatory variable. In fact, ethnicity as a local identity may be utterly and entirely contextual. The ongoing emergence of southern cultural and social histories produced by Lewis P. Simpson and Joel Williamson and the ongoing impact of the works of William Faulkner, Toni Morrison, Sarah Orne Jewett, Alice Walker, Flannery O'Connor, Maya Angelou, Robert Penn Warren, John Crowe Ransom, Eudora Welty, and Cleanth Brooks fashioned profound interpretative ground upon which fuller understanding of this regional clustering of group relations rests. The particular demography of a region clearly shapes its self-articulation. The articles grouped in the second section of this unit express the ongoing presence of the past and reveal its impact on the present state of race relations.

Interestingly, the South has by far the largest population of African Americans. The South and West are the only regions of the United States that have a measurable white population. The South has by far the largest percentage and absolute number of persons claiming the United States as their ancestry. In addition, unlike other regions with large immigrant populations and descendants of nineteenth-century immigrants, over 15 percent of the population of the South didn't answer the question regarding ancestry on the 1990 Census.

The third section of this unit probes concerns raised in a very provocative book by Michael Novak, *The Rise of the Unmeltable Ethnics,* written at the beginning of the 1970s, the author makes the following observation: "Two forms of prejudice stamped the immigrants. Both had a peculiar 'northern' quality: one was racial and the other 'progressive.' According to one view, it was his race and religion that made the southern European inferior. According to the other, it was his social and political backwardness." Although acknowledgment of ethnicity and cultural pluralism emerged as an intellectual and cultural force in the mid1960s, its origins were formed even before the period of mass immigration to America.

The American experience from 1870 to 1924 addressed the influence of these groups and in so doing shifted American consciousness of itself. Even 100 years later, America's public mind continues to identify and divide its history as an immigrantreceiving country into two periods: The Old Immigration, meaning Northern Europeans, and the New Immigration, meaning Others—the Mediterranean and eastern European as well as Asian and Hispanic populations. One marker of this division can be found in the *Report of the Dillingham Commission* (1910), a congressional and presidential blue ribbon panel that warned America that the eastern European and Mediterranean character was less capable of Americanization than the Nordics and Teutonics who had peopled America.

Because of the considerable fluidity of the immigrant experiences, the complex processes of cultural identity, and the political use of cultural symbols such as race and ethnicity, the search for more analytical rigor in the field of race and ethnic relations is far from complete. A guide to discernible and measurable features of ethnic phenomena and characteristics that are attributes of ethnicity was developed in a fine collection of materials on this topic, *The Harvard Encyclopedia of American Ethnic Groups,* which lists the following markers of ethnic groups: common geographic origin; migratory status; language/dialect; religious faith(s); ties that transcend kinship, neighborhood, community boundaries; shared traditions, values, symbols; literature; folklore; music; food preferences; settlement and employment patterns; special interests in regard to politics in the homeland and in the United States; institutions that specifically serve and maintain the group; and internal sense of distinctiveness and an external perception of distinctiveness. The contributions and concerns of various ethnic immigrant groups over many generations provided a deeply woven pattern of material and a complex social history of America.

New Answers to an Old Question: Who Got Here First?

By JOHN NOBLE WILFORD

SANTA FE, N.M.—For most of the 20th century, the solution to the mystery of the original Americans—where did they come from, when and how?—seemed as clear as the geography of the Bering Strait, the climate of the last ice age and the ubiquity of finely wrought stone hunting weapons known as Clovis points.

According to the ruling theory, bands of big-game hunters trekked out of Siberia sometime before 11,500 years ago. They crossed into Alaska when the floor of the Bering Strait, drained dry by the accumulation of water in a frozen world's massive glaciers, was a land bridge between continents, and found themselves in a trackless continent, the New World when it was truly new.

People may have arrived tens of thousands of years sooner than believed.

The hunters, so the story went, moved south through a corridor between glaciers and soon flourished on the Great Plains and in the Southwest of what is now the United States, their presence widely marked by distinctive stone projectile points first discovered near the town of Clovis, N.M. In less than 1,000 years, these Clovis people and their distinctive stone points made it all the way to the tip of South America. They were presumably the founding population of today's American Indians.

Europe and Australia as possible cradles for the Americas.

Now a growing body of intriguing evidence is telling a much different story. From Alaska to Brazil and southern Chile, artifacts and skeletons are forcing archaeologists to abandon Clovis orthodoxy and come to terms with a more complex picture of earliest American settlement. People may have arrived thousands to tens of thousands of years sooner, in many waves of migration and by a number of routes. Their ancestry may not have been only Asian. Some of the migrations may have originated in Australia or Europe.

The Clovis-first paradigm "has become increasingly improbable," said Dr. Robson Bonnichsen, an archaeologist at Oregon State University in Corvallis, opening a recent conference here titled "Clovis and Beyond" at which archaeologists looked beyond the shards of old theory in search of new explanations. "Clovis was not the only culture in America 11,000 years ago," Dr. Bonnichsen said.

Two discoveries—the remains of a pre-Clovis camp at Monte Verde in Chile and the skull and bones of the Kennewick Man, possibly as old as 9,300 years and bearing little physical resemblance to later American Indians—are primarily responsible for the profound shift in thinking. Freed from the restrictive Clovis model, archaeologists and other scholars have aired a wide assortment of alternative explanations for the initial occupation of America.

"Monte Verde puts the peopling of America in a new light," said Dr. David J. Meltzer of Southern Methodist University in Dallas. Two years ago, Dr. Meltzer was a member of a blue-ribbon panel of archaeologists, including some resolute skeptics, who inspected the Monte Verde site, which had been excavated by Dr. Tom D. Dillehay of the University of Kentucky. The visitors took a close look at the stone, wood and bone artifacts, remnants of hide-covered huts and a child's footprint. These were judged to be clear evidence that humans had reached southern Chile 12,500 years ago, more than a millennium before the first signs of Clovis hunters in North America.

After years of stout resistance from many establishment archaeologists, the Clovis barrier had finally been breached. Monte Verde was not only the first confirmed pre-Clovis site, but it was nowhere near the Bering Strait and bore little resemblance to the Clovis culture. It seemed time to examine more seriously other migration hypotheses.

Because the ice-free corridor on the eastern flank of the Rockies did not open before 13,000 years ago, and does not appear to have had many plants or animals to feed travelers, many scholars have revived speculation of coastal migration routes.

Some of the early people may have come from northeast Asia in hide-covered boats, hugging the southern shore of the Bering land bridge, putting in from time to time for food and water. They could have continued down the west coast of North America long before the glacial corridor was available to them. They could have traveled great distances in relatively short periods, conceivably reaching South America much faster and more easily than by any land routes. Prehistoric people at least as early as the Australian colonists some 50,000 years ago had boats capable of open-sea navigation.

Coastal migration is an attractive idea, archaeologists at the conference said, because it could explain the existence of Monte Verde and other possibly pre-Clovis sites in several places in South America and why their cultures, by Clovis times, bore few similarities to North American settlers. Perhaps, Dr. Meltzer said, "there were more, rather than fewer, migratory pulses to the Americas."

Establishing a coastal migration was once thought to be hopeless. At the end of the ice age, melting glaciers raised sea levels and inundated what had been ancient shorelines. But recent artifact discoveries off British Columbia, in the Channel Islands off California and along the coast of Peru have bolstered arguments favoring coastal routes as one of many migration theories.

"Clovis first and Clovis everywhere was a regional North American phenomenon, and a late one at that," said Dr. Ruth Gruhn of the University of Alberta in Edmonton, reflecting a view long held by a few archaeologists working at South American sites. "North Americans have been discounting South American evidence because it did not fit their models."

Monte Verde also inspired researchers in North America to dig deeper. They have found possibly pre-Clovis remains in South Carolina and Virginia and are beginning to reinterpret findings at the Meadowcroft rock shelter, a site near Pittsburgh.

This was how Dr. Albert Goodyear, a University of South Carolina archaeologist, discovered likely pre-Clovis traces at the Topper site near the Savannah River. "I had stopped a little below the Clovis stratum," Dr. Goodyear explained. "You don't look for what you don't believe in. But in light of Monte Verde, I thought, maybe this might be a place to look for pre-Clovis."

Increasing evidence of early Clovis, and possibly pre-Clovis, remains in the Eastern United States has raised eyebrows. Perhaps the hunters who came through the ice-free corridor went east first, then moved west. An even bolder idea is attracting debate: perhaps ancestors of the Clovis hunters arrived not by the Bering land bridge, but from Europe by boats skirting the ice of the North Atlantic.

Dr. Dennis Stanford of the Smithsonian Institution, a leading proponent of the possible European connection, cited as evidence the stylistic similarities between the stone tools of Clovis and those of the Solutrean culture from Spain and southwestern France, dated from 20,000 to 16,000 years ago. The idea has drawn little support from most archaeologists.

But if Monte Verde encouraged thinking about multiple migrations, the discovery of the Kennewick Man, a skeleton found in 1997 in Washington State and dated between 8,000 and 9,300 years old, raised unsettling questions about the origins of the first Americans. Were they all from Asia? Are American Indians actually direct descendants from the first migrants?

Early descriptions of the Kennewick skull led to reports that the man was Caucasoid and possibly European. After a more careful analysis, the skull appeared to be longer and narrower than those of modern American Indians. Dr. Joseph Powell of the University of New Mexico reported last month that its physical affinities appeared to be closer to those of South Asians or Polynesians than either Europeans or American Indians.

At the conference, Dr. Douglas Owsley of the Smithsonian Institution and Dr. Richard Jantz of the University of Tennessee at Knoxville reported that close examination of the craniums of several other skeletons and mummies found in the Americas produced similar results. The evidence, they said, suggested that either more than one group of people migrated into the New World or the settlers underwent significant physical changes in the time after their arrival. It is even possible that the first migrants became extinct, replaced by subsequent groups.

The issue is central to a legal case pitting American Indians, who claim Kennewick Man as an ancestor and want his remains turned over to them for reburial, and anthropologists, who are seeking access to the skeleton for more detailed studies, including DNA tests of the man's genetic background.

Another skeleton, of a woman being called Luzia, which was found in Brazil, has prompted speculation of another origins scenario. The skeleton, estimated to be possibly 11,500 years old and thus older than any previous human bones in the Western Hemisphere, appeared to be more Negroid in its cranial features than Mongoloid.

Dr. Walter Neves of the University of Sao Paulo said this suggested that some of the first people in South America might have originated in Australia, or at least South Asia. Last month, he said Luzia might have belonged to a nomadic people who began arriving in the New World as early as 15,000 years ago. They may have come across the Pacific, but more probably, he said, they were a branch of Southeast Asians, some of whom settled in Australia as the Aborigines while others navigated northward along the Asian coast and then across the Bering Strait.

It may be a long time before the shattered Clovis-first hypothesis is replaced by a single new paradigm. In the meantime, some Clovis partisans are not giving up without a fight.

In the current issue of the magazine Scientific American Discovering Archaeology, Dr. Stuart J. Fiedel of John Milner Associates in Alexandria, Va., which conducts archaeological excavations under contract, said that Dr. Dillehay's Monte Verde report was riddled with errors and omissions that "raised doubts about the provenience of virtually every" artifact excavated there. Monte Verde, he concluded, "should not be construed as conclusive proof of a pre-Clovis human occupation in South America."

Dr. C. Vance Haynes Jr. of the University of Arizona, one of the staunchest defenders of the Clovis orthodoxy, said that, though he had been a member of the panel of experts that authenticated Monte

Verde's pre-Clovis credentials, he now had serious second thoughts. After further study of the evidence, he said, "To my surprise, I found these data to be inadequate and therefore unconvincing."

The attack on Monte Verde, published just before the conference here, raised cries of foul. Many archaeologists complained that Dr. Fiedel's review was biased and ignored material that did not support his critical thesis. They deplored his tactic of airing his critique in a popular magazine rather than a peer-reviewed journal.

In a defense of Monte Verde, also published in the magazine, Dr. Dillehay acknowledged that some errors had crept into the 1,300-page report and would be corrected, but none of them undercut an interpretation of the place where pre-Clovis hunter-gatherers camped 12,500 years ago. At the conference, he called Dr. Fiedel's review "ungrounded accusations" and one more example of North American archaeologists' dismissal of South American sites because they lacked the familiar Clovis stone-tool technology.

"The half-century-long emphasis on Clovis projectile points and related durable lithic artifacts," argued Dr. James M. Adovasio of Mercyhurst College in Erie, Pa., who excavated the long-disputed Meadowcroft site and thus sees himself as another victim of Clovis chauvinism, "has actually served to mask rather than elucidate the nature of

late ice age adaptations in the New World."

Warming to the attack, Dr. Adovasio charged that evidence of "soft technologies" such as cordage, netting and basketry was seldom given its due at many early American sites. The result, he said, was a failure to appreciate fully the way of life of the first American colonizers.

"Nets suggest a subsistence strategy carried out by both sexes and all age groups in stark contrast to the traditional model based on highly mobile groups of spear-wielding, mammoth-killing macho men," Dr. Adovasio said to another round of hearty applause.

The loss of a paradigm has thus plunged American archaeology into a new period of tumult and uncertainty over its oldest mystery, one critical to understanding how modern humans spread out through the world. For their entry into America was the last time in history when people occupied an entirely new land, alone and with little more than their own ingenuity and an eye on far horizons.

"We're going to have to open our minds," Dr. Michael B. Collins of the University of Texas said at the conference. "We're going to have to explore some ideas that may not get us very far. We're going to have to be tolerant of each other as we explore these ideas. My God, this is an exciting time to be involved in research in the peopling of America and the earliest cultures of the Americas."

American Indians in the 1990s

The true number of American Indians may be unknowable, but a rapidly growing number of Americans are identifying with Indian culture. The Anglo appetite for Indian products is creating jobs on poverty-plagued reservations. Gambling and tourism are the most lucrative reservation businesses. Meanwhile, the middle-class Indian's urge to "go home" is growing.

Dan Fost

When Nathan Tsosie was growing up in the Laguna Pueblo in New Mexico, he was not taught the Laguna language. The tribe's goal was to assimilate him into white society.

Today, Tsosie's 9-year-old son Darren learns his ancestral language and culture in the Laguna schools. He speaks Laguna better than either of his parents. "They're trying to bring it back," says Darren's mother, Josephine. "I'm glad he's learning. I just feel bad that we can't reinforce it and really teach it."

The strong bonds American Indians still feel to their native culture are driving a renaissance in Indian communities. This cultural resurrection has not yet erased the poverty, alcoholism, and other ills that affect many Indians. But it has brought educational and economic gains to many Indians living on and off reservations. A college-educated Indian middle class has emerged, American Indian business ownership has increased, and some tribes are creating good jobs for their members.

The census counted 1,878,000 American Indians in 1990, up from fewer than 1.4 million in 1980. This 38 percent leap exceeds the growth rate for blacks (6 percent) and non-Hispanic whites (13 percent), but not the growth of Hispanics (53 percent) or Asians (108 percent).

The increase is not due to an Indian baby boom or to immigration from other countries. Rather, Americans with Indian

heritage are increasingly likely to identify their race as Indian on census forms. Also, the Census Bureau is doing a better job of counting American Indians.

Almost 2 million people say that their race is American Indian. But more than 7 million people claim some Indian ancestry, says Jeff Passel at the Urban Institute. That's about 1 American in 35.

"A lot of people have one or more ancestors who are American Indian," says Passel. "There's a clear trend over the last three censuses for increasing numbers of those people to answer the race question as American Indian. But it doesn't tell you how 'Indian' they are in a cultural sense.

"The strength of this identification in places that are not Indian strongholds is transitory. If it becomes unfashionable to be American Indian, it could go down."

People who try to count American Indians employ many different means that often confound demographers. Tribes keep tabs on enrollment, but the rules vary on how much Indian blood makes one a member. Some tribes are not recognized by the federal government. Local health services may keep one set of records, while federal agencies like the Bureau of Indian Affairs will keep another. Some Indians are nomadic; Navajos, for example, may maintain three residences. Rural Indians can be hard to find, and minorities are always more prone to census undercounts. A

growing number of mixed marriages blurs the racial boundaries even further.

"I don't know what an Indian is," says Malcolm Margolin, publisher of the monthly *News from Native California*. "Some people are clearly Indian, and some are clearly not. But the U.S. government figures are clearly inadequate for judging how many people are Indian."

Even those who can't agree on the numbers do agree that Indians are returning to their roots. "In the early 1960s, there was a stigma attached to being American Indian," Passel says. These days, even Anglos are proud of Indian heritage.

IDENTIFYING WITH INDIANS

When white patrons at Romo's restaurant in Holbrook, Arizona, learn that their host is half Navajo and half Hopi, they frequently exclaim, "I'm part Cherokee!" The host smiles and secretly rolls his eyes. More *bahanas* (whites) are jumping on the Indian bandwagon.

"In the last three years, interest in Indian beliefs has really taken off," says Marzenda McComb, the former co-owner of a New Age store in Portland, Oregon. To celebrate the sale of her store, a woman performed an Indian smudging ritual with burnt cedar and an eagle feather. Most of McComb's customers were non-Indian.

INDIAN STATES

During the 1980s, Oklahoma replaced California as the state with the largest American Indian population. South Dakota dropped off the top ten list as New York moved into ninth place.

(population of the ten states with the largest American Indian populations, in thousands)

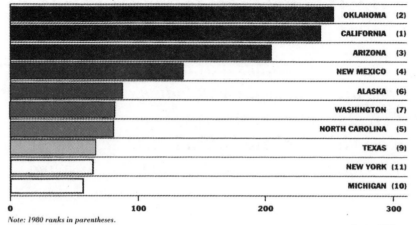

	OKLAHOMA (2)
	CALIFORNIA (1)
	ARIZONA (3)
	NEW MEXICO (4)
	ALASKA (6)
	WASHINGTON (7)
	NORTH CAROLINA (5)
	TEXAS (9)
	NEW YORK (11)
	MICHIGAN (10)

0   100   200   300

Note: 1980 ranks in parentheses.

Source: 1990 census

INDIAN INDUSTRIES

American Indian specialty contractors had receipts of $97 million in 1987. But automotive and food-store owners may earn higher profits.

(ten largest industry groups in receipts for firms owned by American Indians and Alaska Natives)

rank	industry group	firms	receipts (in thousands)	receipts per firm (in thousands)
1	Special trade contractors	2,268	$97,400	$43
2	Miscellaneous retail	1,799	85,400	47
3	Agriculture services, forestry, and fishing	3,128	84,000	27
4	Automotive dealers and service stations	222	65,300	294
5	Food stores	301	54,300	180
6	Business services	2,532	48,600	19
7	Eating and drinking places	464	35,300	76
8	Construction	461	34,200	74
9	Trucking and warehousing	590	32,200	55
10	Personal services	1,719	26,500	15

Source: 1987 Economic Censuses, Survey of Minority-Owned Business Enterprises

Controversy often accompanies such practices. Some Indians bristle at the sharing of their culture and spiritual practices with whites. But others welcome people of any race into their culture. And many tribal leaders recognize that Indian art and tourism are hot markets.

Anglos are not the only ones paying more attention to Indian ways. Indian children are showing a renewed interest in their culture. Jennifer Bates, who owns the Bear and Coyote Gallery in California, says her 9-year-old son has taken an independent interest in Northern Miwok dance. "It's nice, knowing that we're not pushing it on him," she says. "He wanted to dance and make his cape. It's up to us to keep things going, and if we don't, it's gone."

The oldest generation of California Indians "grew up among people who recalled California before the arrival of whites," says Malcolm Margolin. These people have "something in their tone, their mood,

THE BEST STATES FOR Indians in Business

This table shows how the states rank on the basis of business ownership among American Indians. States in the South may offer the most opportunity for American Indians, white midwestern states may offer the least.

The number of Indian-owned businesses in a state is not closely related to the business ownership rate. Business ownership rates are calculated by dividing the number of Indian-owned businesses by the number of Indians and multiplying by 1,000. The top-ranked state, Alaska, is one of only five states with more than 1,000 Indian-owned firms. But the state that ranks last, Arizona, has the seventh-highest number of Indian-owned businesses.

Statistical analysis also indicates that the pattern of business ownership among American Indians is not driven by the rate of growth in a state's Indian population during the 1980s, or by a state's overall level of business ownership.

There appear to be strong regional biases in patterns of Indian business ownership. The business ownership rate was 12.2 Indian-owned firms per 1,000 Indians in the South, 10.3 in the West, 9.6 in the Northeast, and only 7.4 in the Midwest.

One clue to a state's business ownership rate among Indians could be the share of its Indian population living on reservations. The lowest-ranking state, Arizona, contains seven of the ten most populated reservations in the U.S., including a large share of the huge Navajo reservation (1990 Indian population of 143,400 in Arizona, New Mexico, and Utah). South Dakota, ranking 47th, contains the large and economically troubled Pine Ridge, Rosebud, and Standing Rock reservations. Indians living on a reservation have limited entrepreneurial opportunities. Another factor that may be related to the Indian business rate is the state's general economic health: several states near the bottom of the ranking, Kentucky, Nebraska, and Michigan, have experienced weak economic growth during the 1980s.

But the most powerful predictor is probably the business skill of a state's Indian tribes. Third-ranking North Carolina is home to one branch of the Cherokee tribe, which has large investments in lumber and tourism. And Alaska may rank first because its native American, Eskimo, and Aleut population received billions of dollars in a federal land claim settlement. These data do not contain businesses owned by Eskimos or Aleuts. But many of Alaska's Indians live in isolated towns where small businesses have a captive, all-native audience.

—**William O'Hare**

William O'Hare is Director of Population and Policy Research Program, University of Louisville.

INDIAN OPPORTUNITY

(states with more than 100 American Indian-owned businesses in 1987, ranked by business ownership rate)

rank	state name	number of firms 1987	American Indian population 1987	business ownership rate*
1	Alaska	1,039	28,700	36.2
2	North Carolina	1,757	75,600	23.2
3	Texas	872	57,500	15.2
4	Virginia	188	13,300	14.1
5	Colorado	343	24,600	13.9
6	California	3,087	225,600	13.7
7	Louisiana	221	16,600	13.3
8	Massachusetts	132	10,700	12.4
9	Kansas	225	20,000	11.3
10	Florida	348	30,900	11.3
11	Maryland	123	11,300	10.9
12	Pennsylvania	139	12,800	10.8
13	Georgia	122	11,400	10.7
14	New Jersey	131	12,800	10.3
15	New Mexico	1,247	126,400	9.9
16	Illinois	182	19,600	9.3
17	Montana	405	44,700	9.1
18	Oklahoma	2,044	229,300	8.9
19	Oregon	306	34,500	8.9
20	North Dakota	208	24,300	8.6
21	Wisconsin	306	36,300	8.4
22	Ohio	149	17,700	8.4
23	Washington	602	72,300	8.3
24	Nevada	146	17,700	8.3
25	New York	425	54,800	7.8
26	Missouri	133	17,500	7.6
27	Minnesota	333	45,400	7.3
28	Michigan	304	50,900	6.0
29	South Dakota	267	49,000	5.5
30	Utah	109	22,700	4.8
31	Arizona	843	189,100	4.5

* Number of American Indian-owned firms per 1,000 Indians.

Source: Bureau of the Census, 1987 economic census, and author's estimates of 1987 Indian population

their manners—a very Indian quality." Younger generations are more comfortable in the white world, he says, but they sense "something very ominous about the passing of the older generation. It's the sense of the younger generation that it's up to them."

The Zuni tribe is trying to revive ancient crafts by opening two tribal-owned craft stores—one in their pueblo in New Mexico, and one on San Francisco's trendy Union Street. The most popular items are fetishes—small stone carvings of animals that serve as good-luck charms. "After *Dances with Wolves* came out, we weren't able to keep the wolf fetishes in stock," says Milford Nahohai, manager of the New Mexico store.

JOBS ON RESERVATIONS

Many Indians on and off the reservation face a well-established litany of problems, from poverty and alcoholism to unemployment. Many tribal leaders say that only jobs can solve the problem. Promoting Indian-owned businesses is their solution.

The number of Indian-owned businesses increased 64 percent between 1982 and 1987, compared with a 14 percent rise for all U.S. firms, according to the Census Bureau. "A whole new system of role models is being established," says Steven Stallings, president of the National Center for American Indian Enterprise Development in Mesa, Arizona. "Indians see self-employment as a viable opportunity."

In boosting reservation-based businesses, Stallings aims to create sustainable, self-reliant economies. In some areas, 92 cents of every dollar earned on a reservation is spent outside the reservation, he says. Non-Indian communities typically retain as much as 85 cents.

Stallings's center hopes to start by attracting employers to Indian country. The next step is to add retail and service businesses that will "create a revolving economy on the reservation."

This strategy is at work in Laguna, New Mexico. The Laguna Indians were hit hard in 1982, when the price of uranium plummeted and the Anaconda Mineral Company closed a mine located on their reservation. But the Lagunas have bounced back with several enterprises, including Laguna Industries, a tribal-owned manufacturing firm that employs 350 people.

Laguna Industries' clients include the Department of Defense, Raytheon, and Martin Marietta. Its flagship product is a communications shelter that U.S. forces used in the Gulf War. "It's pretty nice to see your own people getting involved in high-tech stuff," says welding supervisor Philip Sarracino, 44.

Laguna Indians are given first priority for jobs at the plant, but several middle managers are white. Conrad Lucero, a plant group leader and former tribal governor, says that non-Indian supervisors are often retirees who lend their expertise until Indians can run things on their own.

"I have an 8-year-old daughter," says Sabin Chavez, 26, who works in the quality control division. "I'm hoping to keep this company going, so our kids can live on the reservation. It's a long shot, but we have to believe in long shots."

High morale at Laguna Industries is tempered by the risks of relying on the government. The Lagunas realize that their dependence on military contracts makes them vulnerable to cuts in the defense budget. And in August 1994, the tribe's right to bid on minority set-aside contracts will expire—partly because the business has been so successful.

"We have to be able to meet and beat our competitors on the open market," Lucero says. The Lagunas may succeed: Martin Marietta Corporation has already awarded Laguna Industries a contract based on price and not minority status, says Martin Marietta customer representative Michael King.

Laguna Industries has not solved all the tribe's problems, however. Tribal planner Nathan Tsosie estimates that unemployment runs as high as 35 percent on the reservation. Much of the housing is substandard, water shortages could impede future development, and alcoholism still tears Indian families apart. But Tsosie has an answer: "We just need to develop more. People leave the reservation to get jobs. If there were jobs here, they'd stay."

GAMBLING AND TOURISM

Indians bring some real advantages to the business world. The Lagunas show that a cohesive community can be organized into an efficient production facility. Other reservations have rich natural resources. But the biggest benefit may be "sovereignty," or the suspension of many local, state, and federal laws on Indian territory. Reservations have no sales or property tax, so cigarettes, gasoline, and other items can be sold for low prices. They can also offer activities not permitted off-reservation.

Like gambling.

"Bingo is a way for tribes to amass funds so they can get into other economic development projects," says Frank Collins, a Mescalero Apache from San Jose who specializes in development.

Bingo can be big business. One parlor on the Morongo reservation, just north of Palm Springs, California, draws 5,000 people a week and employs more than 140 people. The Morongo tribe's main objective is to develop as a major resort destination, says bingo general manager Michael Lombardi.

Lombardi won't say how much money bingo generates for the Morongos. He will say that 113 reservations allow some form of gaming, and he attributes bingo's popularity to the effects of Reagan-era cutbacks in the Bureau of Indian Affairs budget. Lombardi says then-Secretary of the Interior James Watt told Indians, "Instead of depending on the Great White Father, why don't you start your own damn business?"

Indian culture also can create unique business opportunities. On the Hopi reservation in northern Arizona, Joe and Janice Day own a small shop on Janice's ancestral property. They swap elk hooves and cottonwood sticks, useful in Indian rituals, for jewelry, and baskets to sell to tourists.

The Days would like to credit their success to their shrewd sense of customer service. But they confess that the difference between profit and loss may be their wildly popular T-shirts, which read "Don't worry, be Hopi."

Not long ago, Hopis had to leave the reservation to go to school or find work. Today, the tribe has its own junior and senior high school and an entrepreneurial spirit. But small schools and small businesses won't keep people on the reservation. The Days still make a two-hour drive to Flagstaff each week to do their banking, laundry, and shopping. "The first Hopi you can get to build a laundromat is going to be a rich man," says Joe Day.

The Days lived in Flagstaff until their children finished high school. At that point, they decided to come "home." Janice's daughter is now an accountant in San Francisco, and she loves the amenities of the big city. "But who knows?" Janice says. "She may also want to come home someday. No matter where you are, you're still going to end up coming home."

THE URGE TO GO HOME

"Going home" may also mean renewing a bond with one's Indian heritage. While the population in 19 "Indian states" grew at predictable levels during the 1980s, the Urban Institute's Jeff Passel says it soared in the non-Indian states.

"Instead of depending on the Great White Father, why don't you start your own damn business?"

For example, Passel estimated the 1990 Indian population in Arizona at 202,000 (the 1980 population of 152,700, plus the intervening 58,600 births and minus the intervening 10,300 deaths)—a figure close to the 1990 census number (203,500). But in Alabama, a non-Indian state, Passel found a huge percentage increase that he could not have predicted. Alabama's Indian population grew from 7,600 in 1980 to 16,500 in 1990, a 117 percent increase. Higher birthrates, lower death rates, and migration from other states do not explain the increase.

Passel explains the gap this way: "The people who are Indians always identify themselves as Indians. They tell the census they are Indians, and they register their newborns as Indians." These people are usually found in the Indian states. "People who are part Indian may not identify them-

INDIAN MARKETS

The 1990 census showed rapid increases among American Indians who live in large metropolitan areas. Some of the increases reflect an increasing willingness to declare one's Indian heritage.

(top ten metropolitan areas, ranked by American Indian, Eskimo, and Aleut population in 1990; and percent change in that population, 1980–90)

rank	metropolitan area	1990 population	percent change 1980–90
1	Los Angeles-Anaheim-Riverside, CA	87,500	5%
2	Tulsa, OK	48,200	41
3	New York-Northern New Jersey-Long Island, NY-NJ-CT	46,200	101
4	Oklahoma City, OK	45,700	82
5	San Francisco-Oakland-San Jose, CA	40,800	19
6	Phoenix, AZ	38,000	66
7	Seattle-Tacoma, WA	32,100	42
8	Minneapolis-St. Paul, MN-WI	24,000	49
9	Tucson, AZ	20,300	36
10	San Diego, CA	20,100	37

Source: 1990 census

selves as American Indians. But they don't do that consistently over time."

Today, for reasons of ethnic pride, part-Indians may tell the Census Bureau they are Indian. At the hospital, they may identify themselves as white to avoid discrimination. This is most common in non-Indian states, which Passel generally defines as having fewer than 3,000 Indians in 1950.

California ranks second only to Oklahoma in its Indian population, but its mixture of tribes is unique in the nation. Some Indian residents trace their roots to native California tribes, says Malcolm Margolin. Others came west as part of a federal relocation program in the 1950s. In California cities, Cherokees, Chippewas, and other out-of-state Indians congregate in clubs.

"What has happened is the formation of an inter-tribal ethic, a pan-Indian ethic," Margolin says. "People feel that America has a lot of problems. That cultural doubt causes them to look for their ethnic roots, for something they can draw strength from. And for Indians, it's right there. It's ready-made."

Dan Fost is a contributing editor of American Demographics *in Tiburon, California.*

Reprinted with permission from *American Demographics*, December 1991, pp. 28–34. © 1991 by American Demographics, Inc. For subscription information, please call (800) 828–1133.

Migrations to the Thirteen British North American Colonies, 1700–1775: New Estimates

Aaron Fogleman

Mainstream historians have finally begun to study the long-neglected, yet extremely important topic of eighteenth-century immigration. Bailyn and DeWolfe's study, *Voyagers to the West,* and other monographs and articles on this subject appeared with increasing frequency during the 1980s.[1] Accurate statistics for immigration during the eighteenth century as a whole are lacking, however, and this gap has forced historians to rely on approximations which are sometimes sketchy and do not reveal much about the varied and complex nature of immigration during that century.

Although it is difficult to compile immigration statistics for the eighteenth century, it is still possible to update the work of previous historians, and for many reasons it is important to do so. With better information on immigration available, historians can compare the relative effects of immigration and natural increase in causing the phenomenal population growth of the colonies in the eighteenth century and of the United States during the early national period. Also, if one simply wants to know approximately how many people of each ethnic or racial group arrived and helped to shape early American society, a single reference with this information would be valuable. In this article, I review some recent estimates of eighteenth-century immigration, showing their accomplishments and problems, and then present an alternative method which corroborates some earlier estimates and provides more information for reference purposes than was heretofore available.

It is impossible to establish definitively the volume of eighteenth-century immigration to America. The only records kept over a long period of time for any ethnic group are the ship lists maintained in Philadelphia for German-speaking passengers arriving from 1727 to 1808.[2] Still, there is enough demographic and other data available for eighteenth-century America to allow historians cautiously to estimate the levels of immigration (and other demographic measures)—not crude, "ballpark" guesses, but cautious estimates which can illuminate a great deal about life in early America. Historians will con-

tinually correct and hopefully improve these estimates as they rework old data, discover new data, and develop new methods. But what we have now is suggestive.

Whereas in the past historians relied on rough guesses of the levels of eighteenth-century immigration, they have recently begun to use sophisticated residual methods which may be more accurate. Twenty-five years ago, Potter estimated that 350,000 whites immigrated from 1700 to 1790—an estimate which was, in his own words, "little more than a shot in the dark." About ten years later, Henretta concluded that "nearly 400,000" whites arrived between 1700 and 1775. Higham suggested that about 450,000 came in the eighteenth century, over half of whom were Irish. More recently, Fogel and several of his colleagues used a simulation model of generational progression and an estimated set of mortality, net reproduction, and gross reproduction rates to measure net migration as a residual, concluding that 822,000 more whites arrived in the colony-states from 1607 to 1790 than migrated out of this region. For the period 1700 to 1790 their figure was 663,000 whites. Yet in 1981 Galenson, using a different residual method, in which he took into account the high mortality of immigrants shortly after their arrival, as they adjusted to the new disease environment, concluded that a net migration of 435,694 whites and 220,839 blacks took place between 1650 and 1780, and that 346,099 whites and 196,411 blacks arrived from 1700 to 1780, a figure close to Potter's.[3]

Still more recently, Gemery has provided the best summation of all these estimates, as well as many older ones, and pointed out some problems with their sources and methodologies. Given the scarcity of appropriate statistics for the eighteenth century, it is not surprising that the range for net migration calculated by the previously mentioned historians is fairly substantial—from 350,000 to 663,000 for 1700 to 1790. Realizing that estimates of early mortality and fertility rates were tenuous at best, Gemery opted to present a set of plausible immigration estimates from 1700 to 1820, rather than making a single estimate. Using a scale of annual rates of natural increase based on various estimates by historians measuring fertility and mortality, along with his own estimates for mortality during the overseas passage and the period of adjustment by migrants thereafter, Gemery concludes that the "New England pattern" was the most favorable for demographic growth and all other regions were moving in that direction during the eighteenth century. He calculates net migration as a residual, with the results being a plausible range of 765,000 to 1,300,000 white immigrants for the period 1700 to 1820 and a more precise one of 278,400 to 485,300 for the period 1700 to 1780. Allowing for the fact that this estimate does not cover the decade 1780 to 1790, his range runs only somewhat below that established by previous estimates. Gemery understands the difficulties in measuring and generalizing from mortality and fertility rates in early America. He concludes his article with a call for more research—more precise demographic data—so that the range of migration estimates can be narrowed.[4]

This note suggests an alternative method for measuring eighteenth-century migration—one that avoids the impasse created by relying too heavily on fertility and mortality rates, which are difficult to establish for the colonial period. My method is also somewhat simpler, yet corroborates the results of residual methods, especially Gemery's, while yielding more detailed information. The method relies on three sources of information for estimating the volume and timing of eighteenth-century immigration, all of which yield strong estimates for some ethnic groups and time periods, and somewhat weaker estimates for others. The first source is the work of ethnic-group historians who have produced plausible estimates of immigration for their respective groups. The second source (most important for the British and Irish immigration) is the more qualitative aspects of the ethnic-group historians' work on the timing, flow, and general conditions of the various migrations. The last source is an improved surname analysis of the first federal census in 1790, which, when used in conjunction with the above two sources, allows one to infer what the levels of migration may have been in previous decades, producing what Gemery calls "quasi-numbers."

The first source produces the strongest estimates. Ethnic-group historians have used information on ship departures and arrivals, as well as samples of how many immigrants could be carried by different kinds of ships, to arrive at reasonable estimates of total immigration of Germans, northern and southern Irish, Scots, African slaves, and others. Grouping the best of these estimates by decade and ethnic group into an estimate of overall immigration in the eighteenth century conveys a clear sense of how immigration varied over time and between ethnic groups, something other estimates have not done.

In the past, relying heavily on the estimates of ethnic-group historians would have been a risky enterprise. However, the recent trend among historians has been to lower the estimates of their perhaps more filiopietistic

predecessors. Since Dunaway's calculation of at least 250,000 Scots-Irish immigrants in the eighteenth century, Leyburn estimated 200,000 from 1717 to 1775. Still later, Dickson found approximately 109,000 to 129,000 for the years 1718 to 1775. And very recently, Wokeck has found even Dickson's estimates to be too high. For Germans, older estimates of 200,000 to North America before 1800 by both Mönckmeier, along with 225,000 to 250,000 before 1770 by Clarence Ver Steeg, have been revised downward by Fenske (125,000 for the entire century) and Wokeck (about 100,000 in the years 1683 to 1776). Butler has drastically revised the immigration estimates for French Huguenots by Higonnet from 14,000 to about 1,500 (or at most 2,000)—all before 1700. On the other hand, Bailyn and DeWolfe conclude that 100,000 to 150,000 Scots-Irish came before 1760 and over 55,000 Protestant Irish arrived from 1760 to 1775. Furthermore, they raise Graham's estimate for Scots from less than 25,000 for 1763–1775 to approximately 40,000 for 1760–1775. And Doyle has recently emphasized that there was a large southern Irish immigration into the colonies, which Dickson may have overlooked. Extreme accuracy will never be possible, given the nature of eighteenth-century statistics, but given such recent work, we can make significantly better estimates of the volume of immigration of some ethnic groups than was previously possible.[5]

The second source of information for this method, the discussions by the ethnic-group historians of the more qualitative aspects of migration, helps give one a sense of when peaks and valleys in immigration occurred, even when no actual data on volume are available. Population pressure, famine, unemployment, rack-renting (the doubling or tripling of rents after the expiration of long-term leases in order to accelerate the removal of tenants from the land), and active recruitment by colonials were major causes of the British and Irish emigration to the colonies. Extended discussions of these developments throughout the eighteenth century give a rough indication of how the total estimated immigration for each group should be distributed over the decades.

The third source of information, Purvis' recent surname analysis of the 1790 federal census, serves as a check and a supplement to estimates of immigration of each ethnic group by indicating to some extent the plausible proportions of the total immigration one could expect from various groups. Purvis calculated the percentage distribution of each white ethnic group (immigrants and their descendants) in the total population of 1790. His work contains some problems, but represents a marked improvement over Hansen and Barker, and the McDonalds, who did not include non-British ethnic groups.[6]

The method allows one to make use of the expertise of those who best understand the history of immigration. Using conservative estimates for each group tends to correct any bias toward inflation of numbers for filiopietistic or other reasons. This method essentially represents a trade-off: instead of the residual methods using decennial

Table 1

Estimated Decennial Immigration by Ethnic Group into the Thirteen Colonies, 1700–1775

DECADE	AFRICANS	GERMANS	NORTHERN IRISH	SOUTHERN IRISH	SCOTS	ENGLISH	WELSH	OTHER	TOTAL
1700–09	9,000	(100)	(600)	(800)	(200)	<400>	<300>	<100>	(11,500)
1710–19	10,800	(3,700)	(1,200)	(1,700)	(500)	<1,300>	<900>	<200>	(20,300)
1720–29	9,900	(2,300)	(2,100)	(3,000)	(800)	<2,200>	<1,500>	<200>	(22,000)
1730–39	40,500	13,000	4,400	7,400	(2,000)	<4,900>	<3,200>	<800>	(76,200)
1740–49	58,500	16,600	9,200	9,100	(3,100)	<7,500>	<4,900>	<1,100>	(110,000)
1750–59	49,600	29,100	14,200	8,100	(3,700)	<8,800>	<5,800>	<1,200>	(120,500)
1760–69	82,300	14,500	21,200	8,500	10,000	<11,900>	<7,800>	<1,600>	157,800
1770–75	17,800	5,200	13,200	3,900	15,000	7,100	<4,600>	<700>	67,500
Total	278,400	84,500	66,100	42,500	35,300	<44,100>	<29,000>	<5,900>	(585,800)

NOTE Figures were rounded to the nearest 100 immigrants. Estimates are divided into three categories: most accurate–no demarcation, less accurate–( ), and least accurate–< >.
SOURCES See Appendix.

Table 2

Estimated Proportional Distribution of Ethnic-Group Immigrants in the Thirteen Colonies by Decade 1700–1775

DECADE	AFRICANS	GERMANS	NORTHERN IRISH	SOUTHERN IRISH	SCOTS	ENGLISH	WELSH	OTHER	TOTAL
1700–09	.03	(.00)	(.01)	(.02)	(.01)	<.01>	<.01>	<.02>	(.02)
1710–19	.04	(.04)	(.02)	(.04)	(.01)	<.03>	<.03>	<.03>	(.03)
1720–29	.04	(.03)	(.03)	(.07)	(.02)	<.05>	<.05>	<.03>	(.04)
1730–39	.14	.15	.07	.17	(.06)	<.11>	<.11>	<.14>	(.13)
1740–49	.21	.20	.14	.22	(.09)	<.17>	<.17>	<.19>	(.19)
1750–59	.18	.35	.21	.19	(.11)	<.20>	<.20>	<.20>	(.20)
1760–69	.30	.17	.32	.20	.28	(.27)	<.27>	<.27>	.27
1770–75	.06	.06	.20	.09	.42	.16	<.16>	<.12>	.12
Total	1.00	1.00	1.00	1.00	1.00	1.00	1.00	1.00	1.00

NOTE The estimates are divided into three categories: most accurate–no demarcation, less accurate–( ), and least accurate–< >. Slight adjustments were made to account for rounding errors.
SOURCE From Table 1.

population figures from *Historical Statistics* and the sketchy fertility and mortality data compiled by other historians, my method relies on an improved surname analysis of the 1790 census as a check for the increasing expertise of ethnic-group historians who, in turn, rely on actual data regarding immigrants—ship and passenger lists. The results are presented in Tables 1, 2, and 3.

The quality of the estimates varies by time and ethnic group, but the tables as a whole are useful. The "most accurate" estimates are based on solid information produced by the ethnic-group historians. The "less accurate" estimates should be used with care, but the sum totals for these ethnic groups, especially Africans, Germans, north-

ern and southern Irish, and to some extent the Scots, and Welsh, are plausible and the distribution by decade probably reflects a small margin of error in most cases. It is only the "least accurate" estimates that are dubious, and for this reason they should be used with the greatest care, if at all.

In spite of the problem with filling in the gaps which ethnic-group historians have not yet thoroughly covered, this method as a whole produces enlightening results for most ethnic groups during most of the period in question. The sum total of 585,800 immigrants—278,400 blacks and 307,400 whites—is consistent with Gemery's findings (from 278,400 to 485,300 whites). Indeed, the two meth-

Table 3

Estimated Proportional Distribution of Immigration per Decade in the Thirteen Colonies by Ethnic Group, 1700–1775

	1700–09	1710–19	1720–29	1730–39	1740–49	1750–59	1760–69	1770–75	TOTAL 1700–75
Africans	.78	.53	.45	.53	.53	.41	.52	.26	.48
Germans	(.01)	(.18)	(.10)	.17	.15	.24	.09	.08	.14
Northern Irish	(.05)	(.06)	(.09)	.06	.08	.12	.14	.20	.11
Southern Irish	(.07)	(.08)	(.14)	.10	.08	.07	.05	.06	.07
Scots	(.02)	(.03)	(.04)	(.03)	(.03)	(.03)	.06	.22	(.06)
English	<.03>	<.06>	<.10>	<.06>	<.07>	<.07>	(.08)	.10	<.08>
Welsh	<.03>	<.05>	<.07>	<.04>	<.05>	<.05>	<.05>	<.07>	<.05>
Other	<.01>	<.01>	<.01>	<.01>	<.01>	<.01>	<.01>	<.01>	<.01>
Total	1.00	1.00	1.00	1.00	1.00	1.00	1.00	1.00	1.00

The estimates are divided into three categories: most accurate–no demarcation, less accurate–( ), and least accurate–< >. Slight adjustments were made to account for rounding errors.
SOURCE From Table 1.

ods, one using fertility and mortality data calculating immigration as a residual, and the other relying on actual estimates of immigration by the ethnic-group historians, tend to provide a check for each other. Yet the second method provides much more reference information, listing immigration by decade and ethnic group instead of merely the sum total.

Further study of individual ethnic groups will surely require that adjustments be made to these tables, but they do reflect in a simpler and more usable way the approximate magnitude of colonial immigration in the eighteenth century. I do not mean to evoke the old, filiopietistic practice of inflating numbers (I have used conservative estimates for each ethnic group), but it is ironic that the work of ethnic-group historians, once looked upon with disdain by many, may have provided the beginning of a methodology which yields important and usable results that corroborate the work of more sophisticated techniques.

APPENDIX

AFRICANS   If immigrants are people who voluntarily leave their homeland to find a better life elsewhere, then African slaves are not immigrants. But in strictly demographic terms immigrants are people who came from somewhere else, as opposed to being a product of the natural increase in the indigenous population. In this sense everyone who came from elsewhere was an immigrant, including slaves, transported convicts, and so forth. I have included Africans in these tables of immigration by "ethnic" group because they contributed to early American demographic growth in the same ways as the other groups in the tables. The Africans actually came from a

variety of different ethnic backgrounds, but taken together, their numbers more than triple those of the largest European group, the Germans. (On the importance of ethnicity among African slaves in the American colonies see, for example, Ira Berlin, "Time, Space, and the Evolution of Afro-American Society," *American Historical Review*, LXXXV [1980], 44–78.)

Since the appearance of Philip D. Curtin, *The Atlantic Slave Trade, A Census* (Madison, 1969), a bitter debate has arisen on the volume of the Atlantic slave trade and Curtin's figures are no longer acceptable without qualification. (For a good summary of the debate see David Henige, "Measuring the Immeasurable: The Atlantic Slave Trade, West African Population and the Pyrrhonian Critic," *Journal of African History*, XXVII [1986], 295–313.) I have used Curtin's figures for North America (137) as modified by Paul E. Lovejoy in "The Volume of the Atlantic Slave Trade: A Synthesis," *Journal of African History*, XXIII (1982), 487.

GERMANS   I have used my own method to calculate the volume and distribution of colonial German immigration. The large majority of Germans came through the port of Philadelphia, for which there are good records (passenger lists), especially for the period after 1726. The greatest difficulty occurs when one tries to measure the volume and distribution for other ports. To do this I divided the ethnic-German population of 1790 into two geographical groups—one settled overwhelmingly by immigrants through the port of Philadelphia, the other settled by immigrants through all other ports. Next, a ratio of immigrants to 1790 population was calculated for the first, or Philadelphia, group which was then extended to the second group to estimate the number of immi-

Exhibit A

GROUP I

State	1790 white population	% German	Total Germans
Tennessee	31,913	6.6	2,106
Kentucky	61,913	4.9	2,996
New Jersey	169,954	6.5	11,047
Pennsylvania	424,049	38.0	161,139
Delaware	46,310	2.6	1,204
2/3 Maryland	139,099	12.7	17,666
2/3 Virginia	294,745	4.5	13,264
7/8 North Carolina	252,179	5.1	12,861
TOTAL	1,420,162	15.7	222,283

GROUP 2

State	1790 white population	% German	Total Germans
Maine	96,002	1.2	1,152
New Hampshire	141,097	0.1	141
Vermont	85,268	0.2	171
Massachusetts	373,324	0.3	1,120
Rhode Island	64,470	0.1	64
Connecticut	232,374	0.4	929
New York	314,142	9.1	28,587
1/3 Maryland	69,550	12.7	8,833
1/3 Virginia	147,372	4.5	6,632
South Carolina	140,178	5.5	7,710
1/8 North Carolina	36,025	5.1	1,837
Georgia	52,886	3.5	1,851
TOTAL	1,752,688	3.4	59,027

grants necessary to produce the known 1790 population for that group.

Using Purvis' surname analysis of the ethnic-German population in 1790 ("European Ancestry," 98), the two geographical groups [see Exhibit A] were created. The German population of some states had to be divided because its roots were in the immigration through Philadelphia and other ports.

To measure the immigration through Philadelphia I used a variety of sources. For the early period (1700–1726) these included the text from Strassburger and Hinke, *Pennsylvania German Pioneers*; Julius F. Sachse, *The German Pietists of Provincial Pennsylvania* (Philadelphia, 1895), 1–10; Martin G. Brumbaugh, *A History of the German Baptist Brethren in Europe and America* (Morris, Ill., 1899), 54–70. Also, I estimated that approximately 500 Germans, who

were part of the large migration to New York beginning in 1709, eventually moved to Pennsylvania and contributed to the growth of the population in Group 1—see Walter A. Knittle, *Early Eighteenth Century Palatine Emigration* (Philadelphia, 1937); Henry Z. Jones, *The Palatine Families of New York* (Universal City, Calif., 1985).

For the period 1727–1775 I used the passenger lists in Strassburger and Hinke, which are not entirely comprehensive, but do represent the best collection of immigrant lists for any ethnic group in the eighteenth century. They include all male passengers sixteen years and older well enough to disembark at Philadelphia and sign an oath of allegiance to the king. Further, many of the more than 300 ship lists for this period also contain lists of women and children, or list a total number of passengers and/or "freights" (children were counted as half freights or not at all). This allows one to calculate the ratio of total passengers to adult males, a figure that changed over the decades. After controlling for these changes, the difference between "passengers" and "freights," and adding the Moravian immigrants, who settled in Pennsylvania but immigrated primarily through New York (see John W. Jordan, "Moravian Immigration to Pennsylvania, 1734–1765," *Pennsylvania Magazine of History and Biography*, III [1909], 228–248; *idem*, "Moravian Immigration to America, 1734–1800," unpub. ms. [Historical Society of Pennsylvania, Philadelphia, n.d.]), a fairly complete picture of German immigration through Philadelphia for the years 1700–1775 can be compiled.

Records for other ports are incomplete, although historians and genealogists constantly make new discoveries. I have reproduced data from several sources here to give an idea of the distribution through other ports which produced the ethnic-German population for Group 2 in 1790. These sources include Knittle, *Early Eighteenth Century Palatine Emigration*; Jones, *Palatine Families in New York*; Daniel I. Rupp, *Thirty Thousand Names of German, Swiss, Dutch, French, and Other Immigrants in Pennsylvania from 1727 to 1776* (Philadelphia, 1875); newspaper and other accounts located in the research files of the Museum of Early Southern Decorative Arts in Winston-Salem, N.C.; Jane Revill, (ed.), *A Compilation of the Original Lists of Protestant Immigrants to South Carolina, 1763–1773* (Columbia, 1939).

The following is the estimated distribution by decade for all known immigrants by port of entry (Group 1—Philadelphia, Group 2—other ports). Group 1 is fairly complete, but Group 2 is incomplete:

	GROUP I		GROUP 2	
	N	%	N	%
1700–09	0	0	50	0
1710–19	1,000	2	2,548	41
1720–29	2,161	3	0	0
1730–39	12,477	19	138	2
1740–49	14,201	21	594	9
1750–59	24,971	37	1,033	16
1760–69	7,712	12	1,690	27
1770–75	4,211	6	242	4
TOTAL:	66,733	100%	6,295	100%

Because the data in Group 2 is so incomplete, I have extended the ratio of immigrants-to-1790 population for Group 1 to Group 2, for whom the 1790 population is known. The following results were achieved:

	GROUP I		GROUP 2	
1700–75 immigration:	66,700	=	x	x ≈ 17,700
1790 population:	222,300		59,000	

Total immigration through 1770–75: 66,700 + 17,700 = 84,400.
(All figures were rounded to the nearest 100 persons.)

About 17,700 Germans (21 percent of the total) immigrated through ports other than Philadelphia, and 84,400 immigrated through all ports of the thirteen colonies during the period 1700–1775. (The final estimate in Table 1 was adjusted to account for rounding errors.)

The validity of this calculation rests on two assumptions (in addition to the assumption that Purvis' surname analysis is reasonably accurate). The first is that the fertility/mortality experience, or rate of natural increase, was the same for both groups. The second is that the time pattern of arrival was the same for both groups, or that the differences were such that the net effect was the same.

To deal with the first assumption, the work of Gemery must be addressed ("European Immigration to North America"). He found that the widest discrepancies in the rate of natural increase during the colonial period occurred between northern and southern colonies in the seventeenth century. By the eighteenth century the fertility/mortality experience for whites in all regions was becoming similar. This, along with the fact that both Group 1 and Group 2 contain inhabitants from northern and southern colonies, tends to make this assumption reasonable, although there is some error introduced in the final estimates because of it.

The second assumption is more difficult to make, since the above table clearly shows a discrepancy in the distribution of known immigrants in the two groups. There are many factors which could have contributed to the same number of immigrants from 1700 to 1775 producing differing numbers of inhabitants in 1790. These include when they arrived, their age, and to what degree they came as families (early or late in the reproductive period), or single individuals. Group 2 contains more earlier immigrants, which means they had time to produce more descendants by 1790 than their counterparts in Group 1. On the other hand, there were also more immigrants in Group 2 in the 1760s and 1770s (relative to the middle decades of the century) than were in Group 1, which means that more of Group 2 had relatively less time to reproduce by 1790 than was true for Group 1. These two characteristics tend to cancel one another out, at least to a degree. There is no doubt some error was introduced by assuming equal growth rates and timing of immigration for both groups, but the reasons outlined above and the fact that a large majority clearly emigrated to Philadelphia tends to indicate that the margin of error in the final estimates of Tables 1–3 is small.

Lastly, German immigration from 1775 to 1790 did have some effect on the population of 1790, but it was very slight. During the war years, 1775–1783, German immigration ceased almost completely, except for some 3,000 "Hessian" deserters (see Rodney Atwood, *The Hessians: Mercenaries from Hessen-Kassel in the American Revolution* [Cambridge, 1980], 254). Immigration into Philadelphia resumed in 1785, and by 1790 only 1,467 persons had arrived (calculated from Strassburger and Hinke, III. 3–44).

The final estimate in Table 1—84,500—is lower than Wokeck's generally accepted figure of 100,000 German-speaking persons immigrating through all ports before 1776 (see "German Immigration to Colonial America," 12). I distributed the final total, including the "unknown" immigrant figure arrived at by the above calculation, according to that of the known immigrants listed above. Some adjustments were made for the early decades, however, because there are fairly complete records for the large emigration from 1709 to 1714 to New York and North Carolina (represented in Group 2). Therefore few "unknown" immigrants in Group 2 were added to the period before 1720.

NORTHERN AND SOUTHERN IRISH Estimates of the volume of northern Irish, which includes primarily people of Scottish descent ("Scots-Irish"), but also native Irish from the northern counties, have fluctuated wildly through the years. Dunaway estimated 250,000 Scots-Irish arrived in the eighteenth century (The Scotch-Irish of Colonial Pennsylvania, 41) and Maldwyn A. Jones calculated the same number for the entire colonial period ("Scotch-Irish," in Thernstrom, Harvard Encyclopedia of American Ethnic Groups, 896). Further, Leyburn concluded that 200,000 Scots-Irish immigrants arrived from 1717 to 1775 (The Scotch-Irish, 180–181). Until recently, Dickson was the only historian to present some quantitative evidence justifying his calculations, and to show how the flow of immigration varied over time. He concluded that 109,000 to 129,000 Ulster Irish immigrated into the colonies from 1718 to 1775.

On the other hand, the immigration of Catholic, "southern," or non-Ulster Irish was largely ignored until the work of Audrey Lockhart, *Some Aspects of Emigration from Ireland to the North American Colonies between 1660 and 1775* (New York, 1976) and David N. Doyle, *Ireland, Irishmen and Revolutionary America, 1760–1820* (Dublin, 1981) appeared. Although Lockhart does not attempt to estimate the numbers of immigrants arriving, she does present important evidence on the volume of immigrant-carrying ships, which, when used with other evidence, allows one to make an estimate of the total number of immigrants arriving and to show how this migration varied over time. Doyle's work has helped alert historians to this large immigration. He also showed with qualitative evidence how southern Irish

emigration varied over the decades, paralleling to a large degree Ulster Irish emigration.

But Doyle has overestimated the numbers of this emigrant group. He states that about 90,000 southern Catholic Irish came before 1776 (almost all in the eighteenth century), up to 30,000 native (that is, Catholic) Ulster Irish, and 10,000 southern Anglo-Irish (Protestant), even though there were only 156,000 to 166,000 inhabitants in the United States in 1790 who descended from all these groups. He attributes their slow natural growth rate to the large number of single men emigrating, who had to marry non-Irish women in America (51–76, especially 61 and 70–71). They did marry and have children, however, and even if all "Irish" found by surname analysis in the 1790 census were not really "100 percent" Irish (due to marriage migration), the number of immigrants from which they descended must have been much lower than Doyle indicates.

My estimates of 66,100 northern and 42,500 southern Irish in Table 1 are based upon Lockhart, Dickson, and the very recent work of Wokeck, who has found passenger lists for the Delaware ports which allowed her to calculate approximate passenger-per-ship ratios for both northern and southern Irish and extend them to the number of ships arriving from 1729 to 1774. See "Irish Immigration to the Delaware Valley." Wokeck calculated 17,296 southern Irish and 35,399 northern Irish arriving in the Delaware ports from 1729 to 1774. I have grouped them by decade as follows:

DECADE	SOUTHERN	NORTHERN	TOTAL
1729	723	296	1,019
1730–39	3,328	2,510	5,838
1740–49	4,106	5,225	9,331
1750–59	3,639	8,099	11,738
1760–69	3,811	12,067	15,878
1770–74	1,689	7,202	8,891
TOTAL	17,296	35,399	52,695

According to Lockhart's tables, 45 percent of all the immigrant-carrying ships went to the Delaware ports during this same time period (calculated from Appendix C, 175–208). From Dickson's tables (Appendix E, 282–287) one can calculate that 57 percent of immigrant-carrying ships from northern Ireland went to Delaware Valley ports, although this data only reflects the situation in the years 1750 to 1775. If one extends Dickson's figure to the entire period 1729–1774, the following calculations can be made for total Irish immigration into all ports of the thirteen colonies in the years 1729 to 1774:

SOUTHERN IRISH				TOTAL
1729	723 ÷	.45	=	1,607
1730–39	3,328 ÷	.45	=	7,396
1740–49	4,106 ÷	.45	=	9,124
1750–59	3,639 ÷	.45	=	8,087
1760–69	3,811 ÷	.45	=	8,469
1770–74	1,689 ÷	.45	=	3,753
TOTAL	17,296 [3]	.45	=	38,436

NORTHERN IRISH				TOTAL
1729	296 ÷	.57	=	519
1730–39	2,510 ÷	.57	=	4,404
1740–49	5,225 ÷	.57	=	9,167
1750–59	8,099 ÷	.57	=	14,209
1760–69	12,067 ÷	.57	=	21,170
1770–74	7,202- ÷	.57	=	12,635
TOTAL	35,399 ÷	.57	=	62,104

To estimate immigration for the remaining years, 1700–1728 and 1775, the following steps were taken. According to Lockhart's tables, 13 percent of all immigrant-carrying ships from southern Ireland from 1700 to 1775 arrived in the first three decades of the eighteenth century—2 percent from 1700 to 1709, 4 percent from 1710 to 1719, and 7 percent from 1720 to 1729. Thus 87 percent arrived in the years 1730 to 1775. Subtracting the 1,903 that Wokeck found for 1729, and extending her passenger-per-ship ratio for 1770–1774 to the nine ships Lockhart found arriving in the colonies in 1775, one can calculate total southern Irish immigration from 1700 to 1775 as follows:

$$38,436 \ -1,903 + 180 = .87x$$
$$x = 42,199 \text{ immigrants}$$

This total number is distributed as follows for 1700–1729:

$$1700–09 \quad .02 \times 42,199 = 844$$
$$1710–19 \quad .04 \times 42,199 = 1,688$$
$$1720–29 \quad .07 \times 42,199 = 2,954$$

In Table 1, I inflated the figure for the 1720s to 3,500 because of the higher passenger-per-ship ratio prevalent for

that decade in the few instances in Lockhart's tables where this information was given.

Since Dickson's tables do not include the number of ships arriving before 1750, and since Wokeck has shown that Dickson's method consistently overestimated the number of immigrants per ship, the only option remaining for calculating northern Irish immigration from 1700 to 1728 is to make use of the proportion of southern Irish to total Irish for the period closest to 1700–1728. From 1729 to 1739 southern Irish immigration equaled 58 percent of the total. Thus one can calculate:

	SOUTHERN		TOTAL	NORTHERN		
1700–09	844 ÷ .58	=	1,455	1,455 –	844 =	611
1710–19	1,688 ÷ .58	=	2,910	2,910 –	1,688 =	1,222
1720–29	2,954 ÷ .58	=	5,093	5,093 –	2,954 =	2,139

All these calculations can be summarized as follows:

Total Irish Immigration Through All Ports, 1700-1775

DECADE	SOUTHERN	NORTHERN	TOTAL
1700–09	844	611	1,455
1710–19	1,688	1,222	2,910
1720–29	2,954	2,139	5,093
1730–39	7,396	4,404	11,800
1740–49	9,124	9,167	18,291
1750–59	8,087	14,209	22,296
1760–69	8,469	21,170	29,639
1770–75	3,933	13,185	17,118
TOTAL	42,495	66,107	108,602

In Table 1 all figures were rounded to the nearest 100 immigrants. Purvis found 16.3 percent (c. 520,000 persons) of the white population in 1790 to be of Scots-Irish and Irish descent, or northern and southern Irish (see "European Ancestry," 98). The ratio of immigrants 1700–1775 to the total population in 1790 was thus .21 (108,600 ÷ 520,000), a factor which will be used to help calculate immigration for other ethnic groups with less quantitative evidence available than the Irish.

SCOTS   It is difficult to get a sense of the overall number of Scottish immigrants in eighteenth-century America. Graham estimates that emigration to America was "sporadic" from 1707 to 1763. From 1763 to 1775 less than 25,000 departed. Emigration was truly massive only in the years 1768 to 1775, when 20,245 left Scotland for America, see *Colonists from Scotland*, 185–189. Graham's figures, however, are probably too low. Using the same ratio of immigrants to 1790 population as existed for the northern and southern Irish (.21), combined with Purvis' finding that 5.3 percent (or c. 168,000) of the white population in 1790 was of Scottish descent ("European Ancestry," 98) allows an estimate of 35,300 Scottish immigrants from 1700 to 1775.

The lack of good data for pre-1760 immigration prohibits the labeling of these estimates as "most accurate." Nevertheless, because of the similarities between the Scottish and Irish emigration experience to America— both began in the early eighteenth century, and were caused by population pressure, rack-renting, and agricultural dislocations which occurred in both places at about the same time—I have opted to distribute the total immigration for the period 1700–60 in the same manner as the Irish (both northern and southern combined). It is only in the late 1760s and 1770s that Scottish emigration to the North American colonies noticeably differs from the Irish. The Irish emigration was larger in real numbers, but the Scottish emigration became relatively more intense (compared to the earlier Scottish migrations) as Graham has shown. For these reasons I have labeled the pre-1760 estimates as "less accurate" and the post-1760 estimates, based on Graham's work, as "most accurate."

ENGLISH   Estimates of English immigrants are even scarcer than those for Scottish. Furthermore, the English are the only ethnic group for which significant immigration occurred in both the seventeenth and eighteenth centuries, which makes it impossible to use Purvis' surname analysis of the 1790 census to assist in calculating eighteenth-century immigration. E. Anthony Wrigley and Roger S. Schofield, *Population History of England, 1541– 1871: A Reconstruction* (Cambridge, Mass., 1981) found net migration in England from 1701 to 1775 to be 423,162 (calculated from Table 7.11, 219), but the only period for which there are statistics available for arrivals in the thirteen colonies is the 1770s. Here Bailyn and DeWolfe found about 4,500 English emigrants bound for America during the years 1773–1776 in the Register maintained in London, as opposed to 3,600 Scottish emigrants (*Voyagers to the West*, 92). In the absence of any other data I have made the assumption that the ratio of English to Scottish emigrants in the 1770s extended back to 1700, which would mean about 44,100 English immigrants arrived in the colonies during the period in question. This is not to say that the emigration history of Scotland and England are exactly parallel and there is little reason to accept this figure as being very accurate, but it does compare well with Richard S. Dunn's estimate of 25,000 English servants arriving in the colonies during these years, see "Servants and Slaves: The Recruitment and Employment of Labor," in Jack P. Greene and J.R. Pole (eds.), *Colonial British America: Essays in the New History of the Early Modern Era* (Baltimore, 1984), 159. Similar to the Scottish and Irish emigrants, the English, too, were plagued by population pressure and agricultural dislocations that coincided with these developments elsewhere in the realm. Thus I have distributed the total figure throughout the decades in the same manner as the southern and northern Irish. My figures for English immigrants are no doubt the weakest in Table 1 and for this reason I have labeled them "least accurate."

WELSH   There is little literature on Welsh immigration in eighteenth-century America and quantitative estimates are virtually nonexistent. Rowland Berthoff found the first "sizable" Welsh immigration to have taken place in the years 1680 to 1720, when a few hundred arrived in Pennsylvania. But he does not discuss any other Welsh immigration before the nineteenth century. See "Welsh," in Thernstrom, *Harvard Encyclopedia*, 1011–1012. Yet Arthur H. Dodd did find Welsh settlements in Maryland (1703), North Carolina (1733), South Carolina (1737 and 1780), and Virginia (1740 and 1762), although he made no estimate of their numbers. See *The Character of Early Welsh Emigration to the United States* (Cardiff, 1953), 2. In contrast to the English, most Welsh emigration to the colonies appears to have taken place in the eighteenth century, making it possible to use Purvis' work in this calculation. My estimate of 29,000 Welsh immigrants is based upon his estimate of 4.3 percent of the white population being of Welsh descent in 1790 (Purvis, 98), or about 138,000 people, and the same ratio of immigrants to 1790 population used for the Irish (.21). The 29,000 figure is distributed over the decades in the same manner as the Irish. The advantage of being able to use Purvis' work is offset, however, by the lack of discussion in the literature of the causes, conditions, and timing of the Welsh emigration in the eighteenth century, which has led me to label all these estimates "least accurate."

OTHERS   Purvis ("European Ancestry," 98) gives the following percentages for white ethnic distribution in 1790: Dutch 3.1, French 2.1, and Swedish 0.3. Most of these groups arrived before 1700, but there were occasional immigrations of these and other groups during the eighteenth century. For example, over 200 French-speaking passengers arrived in Charleston from 1763 to 1773 (calculated from Revill, *Protestant Immigrants to South Carolina*, [Columbia, 1939], 18, 112, 127). I have placed "other" immigration at a minimal 1 percent of the total per decade to cover this and other such scattered examples during this period and labeled them "least accurate."

Notes

1. See Bernard Bailyn, with the assistance of Barbara De-Wolfe, *Voyagers to the West: A Passage in the Peopling of America on the Eve of the Revolution* (New York, 1986). This book, along with Bailyn's companion volume, *The Peopling of British North America: An Introduction* (New York, 1986), provide important bibliographic material on the subject.

2. The most comprehensive and best-edited publication of these lists is Ralph B. Strassburger and William J. Hinke (eds.), *Pennsylvania German Pioneers. A Publication of the Original Lists of Arrivals in the Port of Philadelphia from 1727–1808*, (Norristown, Pa., 1934), 3 v. They list all males sixteen years and older (and some women and children) well enough to disembark upon arrival and sign oaths of loyalty to the British king. Because the large majority of Germans landed in Philadelphia after 1726, these lists are the starting point for any estimation of German immigration into all ports during the colonial period.

3. See James Potter, "The Growth of Population in America, 1700–1860," in David V. Glass and D.E.C. Eversley (eds.), *Population in History: Essays in Historical Demography* (London, 1965), 645; James A. Henretta, *The Evolution of American Society, 1700–1815: An Interdisciplinary Analysis* (Lexington, Mass., 1973), 11; John Higham, *Send These to Me. Immigrants in Urban America* (Baltimore, 1984; rev. ed.), 18; Robert W. Fogel et al., "The Economics of Mortality in North America, 1650–1910: A Description of a Research Project," *Historical Methods*, XI (1978), 100; David W. Galenson, *White Servitude in Colonial America: An Economic Analysis* (Cambridge, 1981), 212–218.

4. Henry A. Gemery, "European Immigration to North America, 1700–1820: Numbers and Quasi-Numbers," *Perspectives in American History*, I (1984), 318, 320.

5. Wayland F. Dunaway, *The Scotch-Irish of Colonial Pennsylvania* (Chapel Hill, 1944), 41; James G. Leyburn, *The Scotch-Irish: A Social History* (Chapel Hill, 1962), 180–181; R. J. Dickson, *Ulster Emigration to Colonial America, 1718–1775* (London, 1966), 20–64; Marianne Wokeck, "Irish Immigration to the Delaware Valley before the American Revolution," forthcoming in David B. Quinn (ed.), *Ireland and America, 1500–1800*; Wilhelm Mönckmeier, *Die deutsche überseeische Auswanderung. Ein Beitrag zur deutschen Wanderungsgeschichte* (Jena, 1912), 13; Clarence Ver Steeg, *The Formative Years, 1607–1763* (New York, 1964), 167; Hans Fenske, "International Migration: Germany in the Eighteenth Century," *Central European History*, (1980), 344; Marianne Wokeck, "German Immigration to Colonial America: Prototype of a Transatlantic Mass Migration," in Frank Trommler and Joseph McVeigh (eds.), *America and the Germans: An Assessment of a Three-Hundred-Year History* (Philadelphia, 1985), I, 12; Jon Butler, *The Huguenots in America: A Refugee People in New World Society* (Cambridge, Mass., 1983), 49; Patrice L. R. Higonnet, "French," in Stephan Thernstrom, Ann Orlov, and Oscar Handlin (eds.), *Harvard Encyclopedia of American Ethnic Groups* (Cambridge, Mass., 1980), 381; Bailyn and DeWolfe, *Voyagers to the West*, 25–26; Ian C.C. Graham, *Colonists from Scotland: Emigration to North America, 1707–1783* (Ithaca, 1956), 185–189; David N. Doyle, *Ireland, Irishmen and Revolutionary America, 1760–1820* (Dublin, 1981), 51–76.

6. The oft-quoted figures from U.S. Bureau of the Census, *Historical Statistics of the United States, Colonial Times to 1970, Bicentennial Edition, Part 2* (Washington, D.C., 1975), Series Z 20–23, 1168 originate from a study conducted primarily by Howard F. Barker and Marcus L. Hansen, "Report of the Committee on Linguistic and National Stocks in the Population of the United States," American Historical Association, *Annual Report for the Year 1931* (Washington, D.C., 1932), I, 107–441. Forrest McDonald and Ellen Shapiro McDonald recently revised these estimates, "The Ethnic Origins of the American People, 1790," *William and Mary Quarterly*, XXXVII (1980), 179–199. See Thomas L. Purvis, "The European Ancestry of the United States Population, 1790," *William and Mary Quarterly*, XLI (1984), 98. A symposium in that volume contains an enlightening discussion between Purvis, Donald H. Akensen, and the McDonalds on the problems and merits of the various estimates available for the 1790 population.   Purvis improves upon previous work by more carefully analyzing distinctive surnames known to be borne by a certain percentage of a European group and then calculating an arithmetical coefficient sufficiently accurate to allow computation of the proportion of people belonging to that nationality within the United States in 1790. The number of individuals with the same surnames, multiplied by the appropriate numerical constant, equals the approximate size of the group in the United States. The problem with this method is that the surnames from the base population with which Purvis initially worked was not always representative of the actual immigrant population. For immigrants from the European continent he found sufficient passenger lists and other information which adequately reflect the actual population of immigrants. For British and Irish immigrants, however, the dearth of seventeenth- and eighteenth-century passenger lists and censuses forced Purvis to rely on nineteenth-century surname lists from Britain and Ireland, rather than surname lists from the actual immigrant population. Another problem with Purvis' method is that he was unable to distinguish between Scots-Irish and Scottish surnames, which forced him to assume that the number of Scots-Irish was twice the number of Scots in 1790.

In spite of these problems, Purvis' work is the best available, and significantly better than the much older research on which historians have often relied. He completed it diligently and without any apparent bias.

Aaron Fogleman is Assistant Professor of History at the University of South Alabama.

The author thanks John Shy, Kenneth Lockridge, and Rosalind Remer for their helpful comments on this article.

From *Journal of Interdisciplinary History*, Spring 1992, pp. 691–709. © 1992 by the Massachusetts Institute of Technology and the editors of *The Journal of Interdisciplinary History*. Reprinted by permission.

Free at Last

The Enduring Legacy of the South's Civil War Victory

This debate isn't just about reparations. It is about putting slavery in its place.

By DAVID BRION DAVIS

THE United States is only now beginning to recover from the Confederacy's ideological victory following the Civil War. Though the South lost the battles, for more than a century it attained its goal: that the role of slavery in America's history be thoroughly diminished, even somehow removed as a cause of the war. The reconciliation of North and South required a national repudiation of Reconstruction as "a disastrous mistake"; a wide-ranging white acceptance of "Negro inferiority" and of white supremacy in the South; and a distorted view of slavery as an unfortunate but benign institution that was damaging for whites morally but helped civilize and Christianize "African savages."

The current national debate about slavery and its role in American history is finally forcing not only a discussion of reparations, but, more important, a re-examination of the long-accepted message conveyed by respected white scholars whose textbooks on slavery, the Civil War and Reconstruction were still being assigned to college students in the 1950's and even later. It was the message reinforced at countless Memorial Day celebrations, where white Union and Confederate veterans shook hands and recalled their collective heroism, while survivors of the 200,000 black Union soldiers and sailors crucial in helping win the war were not welcome. It was the message bestowed on the white veterans by Woodrow Wilson, the first Southerner elected president after the Civil War, during the huge 50th reunion at Gettysburg in 1913.

Consider that Wilson's most beloved film was the popular "The Birth of a Nation," of 1915, which glorified the Ku Klux Klan and depicted freed male slaves as beasts lusting after white women; and that the later big commercial success about the South was the 1936 novel and 1939 film "Gone With the Wind," which romanticized the region as a victim of an unjust war. (Of course, the relatively few black historians had a different view.)

Partly as a result of this denial of slavery's centrality in American history, few Americans today know that black bondage had long been legal in all 13 colonies when the American Revolution began. Indeed, black slavery also flourished in 16th-century Mexico, Peru and Brazil. In the 17th century, it made possible factory-like plantations in the British, French, Danish and Dutch Caribbean—the center of wealth in the Western Hemisphere, as slave-grown sugar and tobacco became the first luxury goods for an international mass market. In fact, in 1688, Governor Denonville of French Canada wrote to King Louis XIV, begging him to end the manpower shortage by authorizing shipments of African slaves. Though France granted permission, Canada could not afford the high prices of prized African slaves paid in the South. In 1716, a high Canadian official attributed the success of New York and New England to black slave labor, and insisted Canada could vie for the profitable West Indies markets if given credit to buy more slaves.

While no New World colony began with a blueprint for becoming a slave society, the entire Western Hemisphere had become implicated by the paradox of trying to reconcile racial slavery with aspirations to escape the sins of the Old World. If some Africans abetted this by enslaving and making available millions of cheap laborers, it was Western European and then American entrepreneurs who exploited it. From the 1440's, when the Portuguese began transporting black slaves to Iberia, to the 1860's, when the illegal slave trade to Cuba finally came to an end, Africa exported an estimated 11 million slaves.

AFTER decades of research, historians are only now beginning to grasp the complex interdependencies of a society enmeshed in slavery. There were shifting interactions among West African enslavers, sellers and European buyers; European investors in the slave trade, who ranged from small-town merchants to well-known figures like the philosophers John Locke and Voltaire; wealthy Virginian and Brazilian middlemen who purchased large numbers of Africans off the slave ships to sell to planters; New Englanders who shipped foodstuffs, timber, shoes and clothing as supplies for slaves in the South and the West Indies; and, finally, the European and American consumers of slave-produced sugar, rum, rice, cotton, tobacco, indigo (for dyes), hemp (for rope-making) and other goods.

Missouri Historical Society

A slave nurse and her master, photographed around 1850.

Today, it is difficult to understand why slavery was accepted from prebiblical times in virtually every culture and not seriously challenged until the late 1700's. But the institution was so basic that genuine antislavery attitudes required a profound shift in moral perception. This meant fundamental religious and philosophic changes in views of human abilities, responsibilities and rights. By the time of the American Revolution, the isolated critiques of slavery by early Quakers and philosophers like Montesquieu had begun to win public support in Britain, France and even some bastions of slavery, like Virginia. Yet, though the American Revolution catalyzed the first antislavery movements around the world, slavery in America was a far stronger institution in 1800 than in 1770—largely because of the invention of the cotton gin.

Even most history books fail to convey the extent that the American government was dominated by slaveholders and proslavery interests between the inaugurations of Presidents Washington and Lincoln. Partly because of the clause in the Constitution that gave the South added political representation for three-fifths of its slave population, Southern slaveholding presidents governed the nation for roughly 50 of those 72 years. And four of the six Northern presidents in that span catered to Southern proslavery policies. For example, Martin Van Buren, who came from a New York slaveholding family, sought to undermine the nation's judicial process and send the captives from the slave ship Amistad back to Cuba—and certain death. Millard Fillmore, also from New York, signed the Fugitive Slave Law of 1850, which enforced return of escaped slaves even from free states.

From the start, America's foreign policy favored slaveholding interests, and administrations refused to cooperate with efforts by Britain to suppress the international slave trade, even though the United States had defined the African slave trade in 1820 as piracy, a capital crime. The one exception to this proslavery stand was the support John Adams's administration gave to Toussaint Louverture during the Haitian Revolution— both to help the slaves gain freedom and to expel the French.

There were strong economic reasons for the broad national reach of American slavery. Though Northerners gradually eliminated slavery in their states, Southern slave-grown cotton was the nation's leading export. It powered textile-manufacturing revolutions in both New England and Europe, and paid for American imports of everything from steel to capital. In addition, the demand for slave labor in southwestern states like Mississippi, Louisiana and Texas drove up slave prices and land values throughout the South. In the 19th century, slave values more than tripled. By 1860, a young "prime field hand" in New Orleans would sell for the equivalent of an expensive car, say a Mercedes-Benz, today. American slaves represented more capital than any other asset in the nation, with the exception of land. In 1860, the value of Southern slaves was about three times the amount invested in manufacturing or railroads nationwide.

Not surprisingly, the richest Americans were concentrated in the South, which, in turn, attracted many Northern college graduates and ministers, who often married into prosperous Southern families. Rich Southern planters also summered in cooler locales like Boston, Newport, R.I., and Saratoga, N.Y., where marriages and other relationships between wealthy Southerners and Northerners reinforced business alliances based on cotton.

The fortunes of New England manufacturers and New York merchants increasingly depended on a northward flow of cotton, a fact that carried the deepest implications for politics as well as banking, insurance and shipping. The Southern "lords of the lash" forged ever closer ties with Northern "lords of the loom." For example, as the owners of major textile mills in Lowell and Lawrence, Mass., established cordial relations with Southern planters, it became increasingly necessary to reassure slaveholders that abolitionists like William Lloyd Garrison represented a lunatic fringe, and that Northerners generally agreed that the Constitution prevented any interference with slavery.

Such reassurances became more difficult, however, after the 1850 Fugitive Slave Law, which was extremely unpopular in the North. Under its terms, any citizen could be drafted into a posse and any free black person seized without a jury trial. Then the Kansas-Nebraska Act of 1854 seemed to open all the Western territories to slavery.

Before the Mexican War and the resulting acquisition of a vast Western territory raised the possibility of an expanding slave empire, the abolitionist movement appealed to a small minority of Northern whites, who along with free black abolitionists faced violent mobs from Ohio to Rhode Island. In the 1830's, it took real courage to speak out against slavery in the North. Abolitionist speakers were shunned by "respectable society," even disowned by family members.

THOUGH these reformers faced rejection at home, they had a disproportionate influence on the South. Nat Turner's insurrection in Virginia in 1831 was blamed on abolitionist propaganda. Southerners grew convinced that slaves only became dangerous if incited by abolitionists. It was the South's extreme reaction to this fear, evident in escalating demands to nationalize slavery, that led to the creation of the North's Republican Party in the 1850's and to President-elect Lincoln's stand against any expansion of "the peculiar institution."

The Confederacy's ideological victory, which the nation is still struggling with, would not have been possible without the North's deeply embedded racism and complicity in repudiating Reconstruction as an embarrassing failure. This was cited regularly, despite Reconstruction's many achievements in promoting black suffrage, education and civil rights. Because most of the Northern white public was unprepared to face the consequences of slave emancipation in 1865, it was easy to popularize a new history of America, in which slavery occupied a far less central role. Beginning in the 1870's, as the price of recon-

ciliation, the North accepted the demands of Southern whites that they manage "Negroes" as they pleased—an acquiescence to an era of lynching and Jim Crow.

Nonetheless, considering that slavery had been globally accepted for millennia, it is encouraging that people were able to make such a major shift in their moral view, especially when a cause like abolition conflicted with strong national economic interests. As the nation tries in this cynical age to avoid "generational chauvinism"—the assumption that the current generation is morally superior to all past generations—we can still learn from history the invaluable lesson that an enormously powerful and profitable evil can be overcome.

Future historians will need to explain the remarkable recent upsurge of public interest in slavery and the Civil War. Professors who confront the hundreds of new scholarly and popular books each year, to say nothing of the re-enactments of Civil War battles and slave sales, can only speculate. Certainly the growing black middle class sees little shame in the old stigma of slave origins and instead uses it as an opportunity to clarify its own identity.

In this era of relativism, an interest in the debates over slavery and America's most destructive war can reflect a discontent with the present, on the part of both blacks and whites, and a longing for an era when moral issues seemed clear cut. Like World War II, the Civil War was deemed a "good war," when people fought for what they believed in. While the slavery era may serve as a screen on which current conflicts are acted out, the nation is now freeing itself from the old Confederate-dominated paradigm, and can finally see the period from 1790 to 1865 as a deeply stained but defining era in the history of this strange nation.

David Brion Davis is the director of the Gilder Lehrman Center for the Study of Slavery, Resistance and Abolition at Yale University.

Racial viewing habits move closer, but big gaps remain

By Gary Levin USA TODAY

ABC's *My Wife and Kids* is the new most popular show among black viewers.

A new report from ad-buying firm TN Media, based on analysis of Nielsen Media Research data, shows 20% of black homes watched the Damon Wayans comedy in the survey period, from October through March, compared with just 7.5% of white homes. (The sitcom premiered in mid-March, so only the first few episodes were measured.)

But eight of the other most popular shows in black homes also rank in the top 20 among whites, up from seven with such crossover appeal in last year's survey.

All six broadcast networks are represented in the top-20 ranking, but CBS leads among black homes, with five series in the top 20, and the most homes in general among all networks this season. Lower-rated WB ranks last, despite placing two of its shows among that list.

"Blacks watch more than whites, and old people watch more than young people, so they score on both areas," says analyst Stacey Lynn Koerner, the study's author. The canceled *City of Angels* was its most popular among black homes, but CBS has several shows with leading black characters.

Although total TV viewership among both blacks and whites has remained flat, blacks are watching less prime-time network TV this season, while whites are watching roughly the same amount.

The average rating in black homes across all six broadcast networks is 7.4% this season, down from 7.7% last season, while the white average was 6.8%, down slightly from 7%.

"Usage hasn't declined, but (blacks) could be finding more things on cable," Koerner says.

Apart from *My Wife and Kids*, UPN's entire Monday sitcom block, featuring largely black casts, showed up near the top of the black chart but ranked among the least popular shows among whites.

ER, The Practice, Survivor, Law & Order, 60 Minutes and *Who Wants to Be a Millionaire* were popular across all homes, though more so with whites than blacks. *CSI* was about equally popular among both groups. And *Temptation Island*—the only Fox show to perform strongly among blacks—was more popular with that group than among whites.

Little middle ground between black, white viewers

Top 20 shows among blacks	Rank among white viewers	Top 20 shows among whites
1 *My Wife and Kids* (ABC)	56	*Survivor* (CBS)
2 *Monday Night Football* (ABC)	13	*ER* (NBC)
3 *The Parkers* (UPN)	141	*Who Wants to Be a Millionaire*-Wed. (ABC)
4 *The Hughleys* (UPN)	137	*Millionaire*-Tue. (ABC)
5 *Moesha* (UPN)	137	*Everybody Loves Raymond* (CBS)
6 *Girlfriends* (UPN)	141	*Friends* (NBC)
7 *City of Angels* (CBS)	104	*Millionaire*-Sun. (ABC)
8 *The Steve Harvey Show* (WB)	140	*Millionaire*-Thu. (ABC)
9 *Temptation Island* (Fox)	22	*Law & Order* (NBC)
10 *ER* (NBC)	2	*Will & Grace* (NBC)
10 *The Practice* (ABC)	11	*The Practice* (ABC)
10 *WWF Smackdown!* (UPN)	108	*The West Wing* (NBC)
13 *The District* (CBS)	42	*NFL Monday Night Football* (ABC)
14 *Who Wants to Be a Millionaire*-Wed. (ABC)	3	*Becker* (CBS)
14 *Millionaire*-Tue. (ABC)	4	*60 Minutes* (CBS)
14 *CSI* (CBS)	19	*Frasier* (NBC)
17 *Survivor* (CBS)	1	*Millionaire*-Fri. (ABC)
18 *For Your Love* (WB)	136	*Just Shoot Me* (NBC)
19 *Touched by an Angel* (CBS)	23	*CSI* (CBS)
20 *Law & Order* (NBC)	9	*The Weber Show* (NBC)

Source: Nielsen Media Research

Black America

The heart of Chicago—Cook County, Illinois—is home to 1.3 million blacks, more than any other county in the country. Chicago's new African-American Marketing and Media Association has only 18 members, but president Ken Smikle is targeting another 300 black-owned or -operated advertising agencies, public relations firms, market research companies, television stations, magazines, and film production companies across the country.

"Chicago businesses are increasingly aware of the importance of black consumers," says Smikle. "People have to learn to speak to this population, and the best way is to use the marketing expertise of local black professionals." In Chicago, these resources include six black-oriented newspapers and four radio stations.

The black population grew by 13.2 percent during the 1980s, faster than the national average of 9.8 percent but not as fast as the growth rate for Hispanics or Asians. Blacks now comprise 12.1 percent of all Americans. They live where whites live: the four most populous states (California, New York, Texas, and Florida) are also the top-ranking states for blacks.

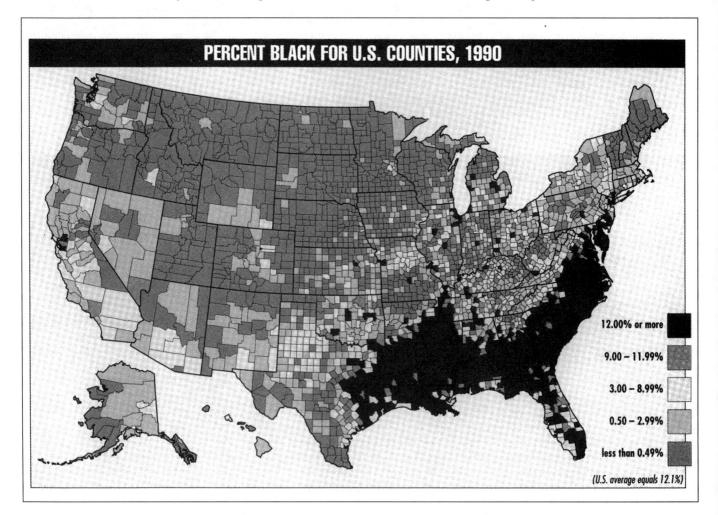

PERCENT BLACK FOR U.S. COUNTIES, 1990

12.00% or more

9.00 – 11.99%

3.00 – 8.99%

0.50 – 2.99%

less than 0.49%

(U.S. average equals 12.1%)

FASTEST-GROWING COUNTIES FOR BLACKS

(counties with black populations of 5,000 or more in 1990, ranked by percent change in black population, 1980-90)

rank/county		state	1990 black population	1980 black population	percent change 1980-90
1	Jefferson County	New York	6,501	274	2,272.6%
2	Gwinnett County	Georgia	18,175	4,094	343.9
3	Clayton County	Georgia	43,403	10,494	313.6
4	Cobb County	Georgia	44,154	13,055	238.2
5	Arapahoe County	Colorado	23,279	8,446	175.6
6	Cleveland County	Oklahoma	5,271	2,132	147.2
7	San Bernardino County	California	114,934	47,813	140.4
8	Essex County	Massachusetts	15,809	6,675	136.8
9	Kings County	California	8,243	3,583	130.1
10	Fort Bend County	Texas	46,593	20,420	128.2
11	Denton County	Texas	13,569	6,173	119.8
12	Johnson County	Kansas	6,917	3,161	118.8
13	Prince William County	Virginia	25,078	11,597	116.2
14	San Luis Obispo County	California	5,727	2,726	110.1
15	Virginia Beach (city)	Virginia	54,671	26,291	107.9
16	Stanislaus County	California	6,450	3,124	106.5
17	Riverside County	California	63,591	30,857	106.1
18	Plymouth County	Massachusetts	16,520	8,144	102.8
19	Norfolk County	Massachusetts	12,089	6,014	101.0
20	Douglas County	Georgia	5,597	2,818	98.6
21	DuPage County	Illinois	15,462	7,809	98.0
22	Osceola County	Florida	5,902	3,012	95.9
23	Chesterfield County	Virginia	27,196	13,910	95.5
24	Kitsap County	Washington	5,107	2,704	88.9
25	Dane County	Wisconsin	10,511	5,688	84.8
26	Fairbanks North Star	Alaska	5,553	3,006	84.7%
27	Kenosha County	Wisconsin	5,295	2,886	83.5
28	Hennepin County	Minnesota	60,114	32,986	82.2
29	Montgomery County	Maryland	92,267	50,756	81.8
30	Fairfax County	Virginia	63,325	34,985	81.0
31	Oneida County	New York	13,661	7,721	76.9
32	DeKalb County	Georgia	230,425	130,980	75.9
33	Collin County	Texas	10,925	6,260	74.5
34	Worcester County	Massachusetts	15,096	8,724	73.0
35	Broward County	Florida	193,447	113,608	70.3
36	Orange County	California	42,861	25,287	68.8
37	Bristol County	Massachusetts	8,054	4,795	68.0
38	Williamson County	Texas	6,861	4,111	66.9
39	Solano County	California	45,839	27,785	65.0
40	Sacramento County	California	97,129	58,51	64.8
41	Lehigh County	Pennsylvania	6,776	4,134	63.9
42	Henrico County	Virginia	43,827	27,096	61.7
43	Oakland County	Michigan	77,488	47,962	61.6
44	Sonoma County	California	5,547	3,466	60.0
45	Washoe County	Nevada	5,680	3,552	59.9
46	Clay County	Florida	5,513	3,470	58.9
47	Middlesex County	Massachusetts	40,236	25,358	58.7
48	Howard County	Maryland	22,019	13,899	58.4
49	Baltimore County	Maryland	85,451	53,955	58.4
50	Cochise County	Arizona	5,078	3,224	57.5

Source: 1990 census

BIGGEST BLACK METROS

(metropolitan statistical areas ranked by size of black population in 1990)

rank/metro area		1990 black population
1	New York, NY PMSA	2,250,026
2	Chicago, IL PMSA	1,332,919
3	Washington, DC-MD-VA MSA	1,041,934
4	Los Angeles-Long Beach, CA PMSA	992,974
5	Detroit, MI PMSA	943,479
6	Philadelphia, PA-NJ PMSA	929,907
7	Atlanta, GA MSA	736,153
8	Baltimore, MD MSA	616,065
9	Houston, TX PMSA	611,243
10	New Orleans, LA MSA	430,470
11	St. Louis, MO-IL MSA	423,185
12	Newark, NJ PMSA	422,802
13	Dallas, TX PMSA	410,766
14	Memphis, TN-AR-MS MSA	399,011
15	Norfolk-Virginia Beach-Newport News, VA MSA	398,093
16	Miami-Hialeah, FL PMSA	397,993
17	Cleveland, OH PMSA	355,619
18	Oakland, CA PMSA	303,826
19	Richmond-Petersburg, VA MSA	252,340
20	Birmingham, AL MSA	245,726
21	Boston-Lawrence-Salem-Lowell-Brockton, MA NECMA*	233,819
22	Charlotte-Gastonia-Rock Hill, NC-SC MSA	231,654
23	Kansas City, MO-KS MSA	200,508
24	Milwaukee, WI PMSA	197,183
25	Nassau-Suffolk, NY PMSA	193,967

*New England County Metropolitan Area (NECMA)

Census data for blacks are not as accurate as data for non-blacks. The bureau counted between 97.5 percent and 98 percent of all Americans, according to estimates from its post-enumeration survey. But it counted only 94.2 percent to 96.3 percent of black women and 93.0 percent to 95.3 percent of black men. Census data are still the most accurate available, but they miss about 1 in 20 black Americans.

Most of the hot spots for black population growth are outer-ring suburbs of central cities, also the national focus of population growth. The black population of Gwinnett county, Georgia, north of Atlanta, increased 344 percent, for example, while its total population doubled during the 1980s, says planner Patrick Quinn. Gwinnett's affordable housing and job growth attract working families of all races; still, only 9 percent of its residents are nonwhite, compared with a national average of 20 percent.

Some metropolitan areas are disproportionately black, and some black hot spots are not suburbs. Baltimore is the 17th-largest metropolitan area in the U.S., for example, but it has the 8th-largest black population. New Orleans ranks 41st overall, but 10th in number of blacks. Among counties with 1990 black populations of 5,000 or more, the fastest-growing black county is in northern New York. The reason is Fort Drum, a military base that swelled from 3,600 soldiers in the mid-1980s to 11,000 soldiers last year.

The counties with the highest proportion of blacks remain in a southern region sociologists call the "Black Belt." Among the 50 counties with the highest proportion of blacks in 1990, Mississippi has 14, Georgia has 10, Alabama has 8, and South Carolina has 7. These counties are the former home of many blacks who now live in Cook County. Blacks who remain in the Black Belt have incomes that are among the lowest in the nation. In Jefferson County, Mississippi, 86 percent of residents are black, 23 percent of residents are unemployed, and the median household income ranks in the bottom 2 percent.

The share of blacks living in the South fell steadily for most of the 20th century, from 90 percent in 1900 to 53 percent in 1980. But in the wake of the civil rights movement of the 1960s, blacks began leaving the South in fewer numbers. And as southern cities such as Atlanta became economic powerhouses, the migration stream stabilized. Today, the South is still home to 53 percent of America's blacks, and the share who live in the Midwest is decreasing.

Kathy Bodovitz

Reprinted with permission from *American Demographics*, Desk Reference Series, No. 1, 1991. © 1991 by American Demographics, Inc. For subscription information, please call (800) 828-1133.

WHITE GIRL?

Cousin Kim is passing. But Cousin Lonnae doesn't want to let her go.

BY LONNAE O'NEAL PARKER
Washington Post Staff Writer

I have a 20-year-old white girl living in my basement. She happens to be my first cousin. I happen to be black.

Genetics is a funny thing. So are the politics of racial declaration.

My 5-year-old daughter, Sydney, calls her Cousin Kim. Kim's daddy calls my mother his baby sister. Kim's father is black. Her mother is white. And Kim calls herself white. At least that's what she checks off on all those forms with neat little boxes for such things.

She grew up in southern Illinois. Sandoval, population about 1,500. There were 33 people in her high school graduating class. Counting Cousin Kim, there was half a black. I used to think Kim lived in a trailer park. But one day she corrected me. We live in a trailer home, she said—"my mother owns the land."

The black side of Kim's family is professional. Lawyers, doctors, Fortune 500 company execs. We have an uncle who got a PhD in math at 21. The white side of Kim's family is blue collar. Less formally educated. Some recipients of government entitlement programs. Not to

draw too fine a distinction, but color is not the only thing that separates us.

I brought Kim to Maryland to live with me after my second child, Savannah, was born. She is something of an au pair, if au pairs can hail from Sandoval.

Back home, Kim had run into some trouble. Bad grades, good beer. She came to D.C. to sort it all out. To find a way to get her life back on track. And she came to get in touch with the black side of her family—and possibly herself.

She may have gotten more than she bargained for.

This is a story about how a close family can split right down a color line without ever saying a word about it. The details belong to Cousin Kim and me, but the outline is familiar to anyone for whom race is a secret or a passion or an issue or a decision. The story is scary in places. Because to tell it, both Kim and I have to go there. Race Place, U.S.A. It is a primal stretch of land. It shares a psychic border with the place where we compete for the last video, parking space at the mall or kindergarten slot in that elite

magnet school. Where we fight over soccer calls, and elbow each other to secure Tickle Me Elmos for our kids. It is the place where we grew up hearing black people smell like copper and white people smell like wet chickens. Where everybody knows that whites are pedophiles and gun nuts. And blacks smoke crack. Where interracial couples still bother us.

You've gotta pass through Race Place in order to make it to Can We All Get Along, but most everybody is looking for a shortcut.

For Kim and me, there are no shortcuts. We meet in the middle, from opposite sides of a racial divide. It is the DMZ and our shields are down. We may lose friends, black and white, for telling this truth so plainly. Still, alone together, we begin.

The First Time

Do you remember the first time somebody called you "nigger"?

I do. I was on vacation in Centralia, Ill., where both of my parents were born and raised. Five minutes from where Cousin Kim grew up. It was the early 1970s, and I was maybe 5 years old.

Two white girls walked up to me in a park. They were big. Impossibly big. Eleven at least. They smiled at me.

"Are you a nigger?" one of the girls asked.

On the segregated South Side of Chicago where I lived, it was possible for a black child to go a very long time and never hear the word "nigger" directed at her. But I wasn't on the South Side, and after five years, my time was up.

I stood very still. And my stomach grew icy. My spider senses were tingling. Where had I heard that word before? "I, I don't know," I told her, shrugging my shoulders high to my ears.

The first girl sighed, exasperated. Then the other repeated, more forcefully this time, "Are you a nigger? You know, a black person?" she asked.

I wanted to answer her. To say something. But fear made me confused. I had no words. I just stood there. And tried not to wet my panties.

Then I ran. I turned quickly to look over my shoulder just in time to hear a rock whiz past my ear and plop into a nearby creek.

"You better git, you little Ne-gro!" somebody else, a white boy, yelled at me from a few feet away. I kept running, and this time, I didn't look back.

For the rest of the day, I harbored a secret. I harbored the shame for longer. I knew I was black. I had found out the year before. I remember because I had confronted my father, demanding to know when my blond hair and blue eyes would kick in. Like the Miss Breck shampoo girl on television. Like the superheroes on "Superfriends."

"I hate the N-word.... I hate that the first thing they associate with that word is me."

Only white people have blond hair and blue eyes, my dad said. "And we're black."

The wicked witch, the headless horseman, the evil stepmother and all the bad guys on "The New Adventures of Scooby Doo" wore black. Black eye,

black heart, Black Death. Black ass. Mine was a negative, visceral reaction to the word.

Five years old was old enough to know I was black. It was old enough for somebody to call me a nigger.

And it was certainly old enough to feel like one.

That would be the first time.

One Black Drop

It is early June, and Cousin Kim and I are about to watch "Roots," the landmark 1970s television miniseries about a slave family. Kim says she's heard of the movie but has never seen it. So I go to queue the video in the cassette player, but first I make a cup of tea. And straighten the pillows on my couch. Then I check my voice mail.

I am puttering. Procrastinating. Loath to begin. Because I don't know if our blood ties are strong enough to withstand slavery. And I am scared to watch "Roots" with a white girl. Scared of my anger. Scared of my pain. Scared that she won't get it. Scared of how much I want her to. Scared of the way race can make strangers out of family.

It has been nearly a year since Kim first came to live with me. She was a cousin I barely knew. She had visited my husband and me in the summer of 1994, when our daughter Sydney was a baby. The first time she had ever seen so many black people in her life, she would later say.

Before that, there were brief visits with my mom and quick kisses at my college graduation. Over the years, I heard much more than I ever saw of Cousin Kim. Kim's father had a black family. His kids were adults when Kim was born. Later, his wife died. And though they are now a public couple, my uncle and Kim's mom never married.

My girls adore Kim. And when she goes to get Sydney from school, the little black prekindergartners rush her at the door, greeting her with wide smiles and hugs and shouts of "Hi, Cousin Kim!"

This past year, we've laughed over sitcoms and shared private jokes. We've talked about old boyfriends, gone shopping and giggled over family gossip. Still, up to now, we've never been down that black-and-white brick road.

I was shocked to hear that Cousin Kim considered herself white. I found out only because she had to fill out some forms to

get into community college. Because I asked her if they had a box for race. Then I asked her what she checked. I was ready to tease her pointedly for checking off "other." In between. Not quite either.

I was prepared to lobby—to drop science about the "one-drop rule." In slave days, that meant that if you had a drop of black blood, you were singing spirituals and working for somebody for free. Trying not to get beaten, and trying to keep your babies from being sold—even if the massa was their daddy. Color gradations were a legacy of the plantation system. And although light was favored, one drop gave us a common destiny. Shackled all of us darkies together.

Later, one drop meant that blacks were able to form a common cultural identity. To agitate for the common good. Because light mulattoes lynched as easily as dark Africans. But one drop also meant there have always been those who could pass. Who required writ, or testimony, or a declaration of intent to make them black. For whom race has always been a choice.

I have The Sight. Like my mother before me. Like most black people I know. It is a gift. …we can spot some Negro on you three generations away.

Cousin Kim would be one of these. Her eyes are bright blue-gray and her skin has only a suggestion of color. Generations of careful breeding have worked out all her kinks. To white folks, she looks white. And mostly, that is how they treat her. Like one of their own.

Still, I was ready to cast her lot with the sisters. You know half-black is black, I was ready to say. I was ready for "other." I wasn't ready for "white." Or that familiar sting of rejection.

Passing Away

I have The Sight. Like my mother before me. Like most black people I know. It is a gift. A special kind of extrasensory perception. We may not be clairvoyant enough to determine the location of the rebel base. Or have the telekinesis it takes to shatter a glass ceiling.

But we can spot some Negro on you from three generations away.

It reveals itself in a flash of expression. A momentary disposition of features in repose. The curl of a top lip that seems to say "Nobody knows the trouble I've seen."

We have The Sight because we are used to looking at black people. Used to loving them. We know the range of colors black comes in. Because there's always somebody at our family reunions who could go either way. And because we are a worldly people, and we know how these things go.

The Sight is a nod to solidarity. It is a reaction against dilution and division. It is the recognition that when people face overwhelming odds, you need to know who can be compelled to ante up and kick in.

We use it to put a black face on public triumphs that look lily white. And to "out" folks who might act against our interests without sharing in the consequences.

No matter how many times she thanked "the black community" for embracing her music, we knew Mariah Carey was part black. And long before he opened his mouth, we saw something in Rock Newman's eyes, even though they are blue.

When people wanted to call actresses Jennifer Beals or Troy Beyer beautiful, we were eager to point out their black roots. Eager to claim New York Yankee Derek Jeter and Channel 4 newscaster Barbara Harrison. Old folks swear Yul Brynner was black and that was why he kept his head shaved. And speculation persists, despite the fact that Georgia representative Bob Barr has affirmed his whiteness.

Understand. It's not that we don't respect Tiger Woods's right to call himself a Cablinasian. We just don't think it will help him get a cab in D.C.

My cousin calls herself white and I see a side of me just passing away. Swallowed up by the larger, more powerful fish in the mainstream. And I wonder if that will be the future for my family, some who look like Kim—others who look like me but have married white, or no doubt will. And I wonder, ultimately, if that will be the future for black people. Passing themselves right out of existence. Swearing it was an accident. Each gen-

eration trading up a shade and a grade until there is nothing left but old folks in fold-up lawn chairs on backyard decks who gather family members close around to tell nostalgic tales that begin "Once upon a time when we were colored…"

And I think to myself, I wish there were some things that we just wouldn't do for straight hair. And I think of the struggle and the history and the creativity lost. And I trust that the universe will register my lament.

When my cousin calls herself white, I see red. And I hear echoes. "Well, I don't really consider myself black…"

Or maybe it is laughter.

The Real World

Cousin Kim is having a hard time with "Roots." Not her own, the movie. I'm not having an easy time myself.

She isn't ready for the stuff they left out of her history books. I am unable to restrain my commentary. Or my imagination. Sometimes my tears.

Ever heard of Calvert County, I ask Kim bitterly when a teenage African girl is sold at an Annapolis auction as a bed wench to Robert Calvert. Kim didn't know that Maryland had ever been a slave state.

There is a scene where kidnapped African Kunte Kinte won't settle down in his chains. "Want me to give him a stripe or two, boss?" the old slave, Fiddler, asks his Master Reynolds.

"Do as I say, Fiddler," Reynolds answers. "That's all I expect from any of my niggers."

"Oh, I love you, Massa Reynolds," Fiddler tells him. And instantly, my mind draws political parallels. *Ward Connerly*, I think to myself. *Armstrong Williams. Shelby Steele.* Hyperbole, some might say. I say dead-on.

"Clarence Thomas," I say to Cousin Kim. And she just stares at me. She may be a little tender yet for racial metaphors. I see them everywhere.

Kim is 20 in the way of small-town 20-year-olds all over the country. Her best-best friends are Jenny and Nikki and Theresa. They send letters, e-mail one another and run up my phone bill. She takes classes, takes care of my children and passes time painting her nails and watching "The Real World," on MTV. I tease her about being Wal-Mart-obsessed.

Cousin Kim walked out of the movie "Glory" when she was in 11th grade. When Denzel Washington got lashed with a whip and cried silently. Couldn't handle it, she said. "I just didn't want to see it. I couldn't stand the idea of seeing someone literally beat." Avoidance and denial are twins in my family. In others as well.

When Kim was growing up in Sandoval, they didn't celebrate Black History Month, she says. "Not even Black History Week. We just had Martin Luther King Day."

The town was not integrated. Her father was the only black person she saw regularly. "And I don't consider him black," Kim says. My uncle is not one to disabuse her of that notion.

Kim's dad ran his own sanitation business. He was a hard-working, astute, sometimes charming businessman. A moneymaker. And my mother says people used to say if he had been white, he would have been mayor of Centralia. Of course, Kim has never heard this. In fact, "we've never had a conversation about race in my house," Kim says casually. And for a moment, I am staggered. But I am not surprised.

Making the Grade

My mama's people have always been color-struck. Daddy's, too, for that matter. Black folks know the term. It is part of an informal caste system that has always existed in the black community.

It is a form of mental colonialism. A shackle for the mind. A value system that assigns worth and power to those traits that most closely resemble the massa.

If you're light, you're all right. If you're brown, stick around. If you're black, get back, people used to say.

I am light; my husband is dark. When my daughter Sydney was born, everybody wanted to know who she looked like. They weren't asking about her eyes. They wanted to know what black folks always want to know when a baby who can go either way on the light-dark thing is born. Whose color is she? What kind of hair does she have?

The hair can be a tricky thing. Nothing for that but to wait a few months until the "grade" comes in good. But for color, we've got it down. We're a race of mad scientists, fervently checking the nail beds and ear tips of newborns to precisely determine where they'll fall over the rainbow.

My paternal grandmother was a very light woman with straight hair and black features. She had an inspection ritual she performed on all new babies in the family. A careful once-over to check for color and clarity before she pronounced judgment. I didn't know this until I introduced her to Sydney when she was about 6 months old.

She sat my baby on her lap. After a few minutes, she announced her findings. "Well, her color is good. And her hair ain't half bad considering how black that nigger is you married."

Hmmmm.

You know these days we try to stay away from divisive pronouncements on color, I wanted to tell her. We don't want to handicap our daughter with crippling hair issues.

But please. My grandmother might have hit me if I had tried to spout some nonsense like that. More to the point, particularly among the elders, there is a certain unassailable quality to the color caste logic. A tie-in with life chances. And my grandmother was nearly 80. So I took the only option available under the circumstances. I smiled sweetly and said thank you. Because, after all, this was high praise.

"Watch out for your children!" had been a favorite admonition passed down from my maternal grandmother. The one I shared with Cousin Kim. She wasn't talking about bad influences or oncoming traffic. She was talking about a kind of Breeders' Cup standard for black love. At least the kind that ended in marriage. Light skin, good-hair (a compound word), light eyes. That was the Triple Crown.

Early on, I learned there is a premium placed on my particular brand of mongrel.

I am Red, as in Red Bone. Or Yellow, for High Yellow. Or light, bright and damn near white.

I used to be able to break into a full genealogy incantation in an instant, with attention paid to the whites and Native Americans in my family tree. Because that white girl was still running around my head asking me if I was black. Because black and ugly always came in the same breath.

But I credit white folks with my slow evolution toward racial consciousness.

We moved to a suburb of Chicago when I was 9. And we arrived squarely in a middle-class dream.

I had always been shy. A good student. With long hair. Teachers loved me. And always, a few black girls hated me. "White dog," they called me—no, wait, that's what they called my sister. I was a "half-white bitch." Theirs was a reaction. A rage. A demonstration of the only power they had, the only power perhaps they thought they would ever have. The power to bully. But back then, I didn't know that. I had "A Foot in Each World" but couldn't get my head into either.

I don't remember my moment of political and aesthetic epiphany. It was more of a slow dawn, I think. An incremental understanding of the forces that were working around me. Certainly, watching white folks pack up and leave the neighborhood in herds made an imprint. And when a white boy spat on me at a park, I took that very personally. But it was the trickle of small slights that accumulated over the years that combined to make one point very clear.

High Yellow was just a lighter shade of black.

To be in Chicago in 1983 when Harold Washington, a big, dark, deep-black intellectual, was elected mayor was to see the face of racism. To watch the way that hate contorts the features and purples the skin. White folks were rabid. Foaming at the mouth. A few white newscasters could barely read their copy. A flier circulated through my high school featuring a big-lipped black caricature chowing down on watermelon. The city would have to be renamed Chicongo, it said. And I understood.

Ultimately, race is political. And I am a partisan.

Sometimes I still hear that white girl ask me if I am black. And now I have an answer.

Pitch.

Cold.

Blacker than three midnights.

As black as the ace of spades.

I'm so black that when I get into my car, the oil light comes on.

I've decided that it is unhealthy for us to surrender to white sensibilities, including the ones that mock us from inside our own heads.

We have all been guilty of dumbing down our expectations of white humanity—like white folks can't process nappy hair—and it's time to help them raise the bar.

Playing the Race Card

Kim has a friend whose daddy was in the Ku Klux Klan. A poster-sized picture of a finger-pointing Klansman adorned her living room wall. "I felt like Clarice Starling in 'The Silence of the Lambs' whenever I went over there," Kim says. "Like the first time she went to the jail and saw Hannibal Lecter."

The father didn't ask if Kim was part black. Kim didn't tell. She just sat on the edge of the couch with her hands and legs folded. "I kept praying, oh God, he's going to see something on me and know that I am mixed." So she stared straight ahead. And she sucked her lips in a reverse pucker the whole time she was there. Trying not to make herself too obvious, she says. Trying not to look black.

When she was in fifth grade, Kim's dad took her to a basketball game. And the bleachers went silent. Then they got whispery. Some folks already knew her dad was black. After that, everybody did.

"They used to tease me," Kim says with a shrug. She is reluctant to talk. So I press her. "Let's see, it went something like this, "Nigger-lips, nigger-lips, nigger-lips." Kim won't look at me.

The grandparents of one of Kim's friends didn't like black people. They didn't know about Kim's daddy. When the girls visited these folks, they weren't allowed to watch "The Cosby Show" because the grandfather didn't want a black man in his living room.

"I hate the N-word," Kim says. It is late. We've finished another installment of "Roots," and Kim is unsettled. Ready to talk. Tripping over her pent-up thoughts. "Whenever somebody said 'nigger' in class, everyone would turn around and look at me. I *hate* that word. I *hate* that the first thing they associate with that word is me."

When she was a freshman at Sandoval High, Kim wore a T-shirt with Martin Luther King Jr. on the front and Malcolm X on the back. "They all looked at me as if to say 'Oh, my God, she really isn't white.'" She grins when she says this.

Around 1993, Kim says she started getting into the "movement." Started watching "Yo! MTV Raps" and "The Cosby Show." Started being hungry for black culture.

She gave a civil rights speech to her sophomore English class. Her teacher thought it was a little angry. That summer, when my daughter Sydney was a baby, Kim came to D.C. We toured the

White House and saw the first lady. But it was the Father's Day tribute at a friend's house where a group of us read proclamations and praised all the things we loved best about black men that got her. That let her know there was a different world than where she came from.

Her mother said she seemed different when she returned. Kim says she's always been different. In a town where everybody knows everybody and the social hierarchy is simple and uncolored, Kim is an anomaly.

"I've never technically fit in Sandoval," Kim says. "I've never had the small-town mentality. Then, after I moved out here, I thought maybe I do. Maybe I'm just a little bit country."

"I'm really trying to figure out who I am."

Some of that goes with 20-year-old territory. It's a no woman's land. Biologically grown, legally not quite, emotionally uneven. But Cousin Kim's 20 is more complex than most. She's never tried to deny the fact that her dad was black. But she has never had the resources or the tools to embrace that side of herself. She is provincial. Unexposed. Underdressed as a black girl. Searching.

On the phone or when she goes home to visit, Kim is still white. But in my house, she is a real root sister. Neither are affectations. It's just the way her cards fall. Kim is, I suppose, the ultimate insider. Privy to our private jokes. The ways we laugh at white people. And at each other. A black spy in her world. A white fly on the wall in mine. A study in duality.

We have also had some growing pains in my house. And I am quick to assign blame. Quick to play the race card.

Cousin Kim smokes. I am hard pressed to name anybody else who smokes. Especially anybody young and black. I want her to stop, and I make the questionable leap. "You need to leave that nasty white girl [expletive] alone," I tell her. Initially when I said it, Kim just looked at me meekly. Now, she gives me the finger.

Ours is a jocularity. Aided by silent code. Reinforced by a power imbalance.

Reverse racism, I suppose some would call it. I don't think so. I believe white folks would know if blacks were ever to really reverse racism. We call them countermeasures. Cousin Kim, I ask her, if you hate me because I am black and I hate you because you killed my babies, is that the same?

It is a rhetorical question. Because in my house, we do not hate. We merely understand that there are those who do. So we strive for balance. We try not to resort to negative campaigning. Sometimes we succeed. Occasionally we fail. But we always make the effort. Because fear leads to anger, anger leads to hate and hate leads to suffering. We do not need Yoda to tell us this. It is something people on the dark side have always known.

Killing Me Softly

A couple of months ago, Katie Couric made me mad. I had to vent with Cousin Kim. For a week, the "Today" show devoted a segment to tracing family histories. And Couric's roots go back to Alabama. When cotton was king and the Courics were part of the ruling family.

You could buy fertile land cheap, the segment said. And the Courics did. The family prospered and included a Civil War governor and a member of Congress.

Couric toured the family cemetery and recounted the stories behind the headstones. Then she said, "Slaves lie in unmarked but well-tended graves nearby."

That was it. No acknowledgment that these "slaves" were people her family bought and sold. That some of them might be her kin. That no matter how smart or talented or hard-working she is, her privilege was codified, her head start generations long. That it came at the expense of somebody else's freedom. No mention of any attempt to trace those other lives to see how they fared. Maybe that would have been too much to hope for. But how about an expression of regret. A mea culpa. An "I'm sorry—wish you were here."

Genealogy is about "our simple stories, not forgotten," Couric said. Interesting choice of words. Black families have stories, too. Ones we don't forget. That get passed down to our kids.

My great-grandmother shot a white man who tried to rape her in Mississippi, and the family had to scatter. My grandmother's family, who hadn't been able to get in on that fertile-land-for-cheap deal, was dirt poor and although she was the only one of her people to finish high school, there was no money for college. At 17, my mother sat outside a Birmingham train station crying because they told her she was too colored for the white side and too white for the colored side.

On a family vacation, we were turned away from an empty motel lot because the manager said there were no vacancies. In college, when I told a white journalism professor I wanted to work at The Washington Post, he said, "Doing what? Sweeping floors?"

Cousin Kim, I say. Which is better? The kindly massa or the sadistic overseer? And Kim doesn't answer. Neither, I tell her. They are the same. Two parts of a whole. Today, folks won't just walk up to you and call you "nigger lips." Well, they might, but mostly it is the benign racists who are killing me softly. They don't recognize themselves in the mirror. They didn't mean anything by it. They harbor no ill will. They just don't care enough to step outside their comfort zone.

I understand that proclivity. Often I share it. Most of us are too self-involved to dig up the psychic pain of others. But when your family has owned slaves, indifference is a self-indulgence you forfeit.

More than 300 years of chattel slavery. 129 years of terrorism and de jure Jim Crow. Thirty-four years—one generation—of full legal enfranchisement. I don't know, seems a little corrupt for white folks to cry colorblind now. We go to the Race Place because these days, I find privileged indifference as culpable as malice aforethought. When you step on my toes, I may not retaliate in kind, but you must know that I will say ouch. Loudly. Such that it disturbs your peace. Then you say, "I'm sorry." Then help me heal. After that, we can all get along nicely.

Cousin Kim nods her head yes. I believe she really gets it this time. But perhaps that's just wishful thinking.

Black for Me

Cousin Kim and I have watched all six parts of Alex Haley's "Roots." And three parts of "Queen." Then we did an hour of WHMM's "Black Women on the Light Dark Thing." We have talked and we have shared. And still she is white. And I am as black as ever.

"We're lucky," the biracial woman Alice said in "Queen." "We can choose. Who'd choose to be black? Black is hard. White is so much easier."

Still.

I want my cousin to be black for me. For the little girl who ran from a rock thrown at her head. For all the niggers I have been. I want her to be black because I'm still afraid of casual monsters in white-girl clothes. Not because they might hurt me, but they might hurt my children. Not because they hate. But because they teach 5-year-old black girls to hate themselves. And black people of all ages to suck in their lips.

Cousin Kim still chooses white not only because she looks white, she says, but "because I was raised white," and because most white folks don't know the difference. Probably it is easier. Maybe to some people she is selling out—but I also know that is an option a lot of black folks would like to have.

If I'm honest with myself, maybe I'm one of them. At least sometimes, if I think about my husband or brother getting stopped by the police for speeding. Or maybe at Tysons Corner, when tears burn my eyes as I watch a sales clerk wait on everybody but me. My anger is hot and righteous. But I'd give it up for a simple "May I help you?" any day.

Every day the world lets me know I'm black. And I wonder what it would feel like not to carry that, just for a while. Probably guilty. Probably relieved. Probably a lot like Cousin Kim.

There are no easy choices, but I think I understand my cousin's. Maybe I did all along. I just had to tell our story to realize it. But understanding and acceptance are not the same. Cousin Kim is white but conflicted, and I still sting with rejection. So alone together, we linger.

The Magic Kingdom

Race. The final frontier.

The Race Place isn't crossed in a day. You can't pass through it in the time it takes to watch a miniseries. We traverse the Race Place in fits and starts, inch by inch, over the course of a lifetime. Or maybe two. Sometimes our progress is steady. And sometimes we are dragged for miles back to the beginning, chained behind a pickup truck, and have to start all over.

The overarching reality is that realities overarch. And jockey for head space.

The extremes are easy to condemn, but the vast middle is where most of us live. Where we raise our families. And where we hope that life's lessons land a little softer on the behinds of our children than they did on our own.

A few days ago, Cousin Kim said she got into an argument with her ex-boyfriend over "The Wonderful World of Disney." The characters in the old cartoons are racists, Kim said. Look at the crows in "Dumbo." "I won the argument," she says. "He told me 'Kim, you think too much.' "

Cousin Kim smiled. And I smiled. Because this is what I want for her. To think. To challenge. To recognize. To get it. If she does that, then maybe she doesn't have to be black.

Still, I can't help giving her a silent "right on, little sister." You just take your time. We're family. And I'll be here to hip-you-up if you ever change your mind.

From the *Washington Post*, August 8, 1999, pp. F1, F4–F5. © 1999 by The Washington Post Writers Group. Reprinted by permission.

America 2000: A Map of the Mix

As the country becomes more and more diverse, three states and the capital city have seen nonwhites gain majority status

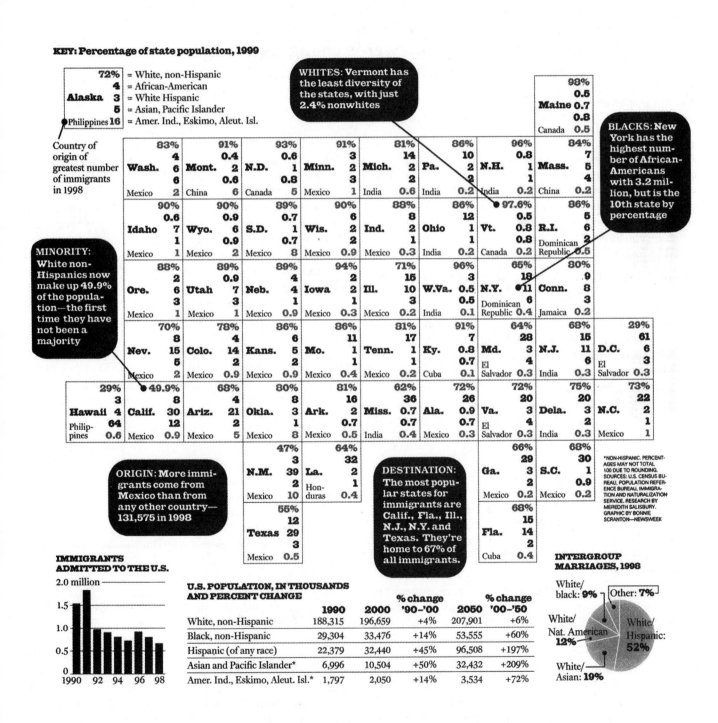

KEY: Percentage of state population, 1999

72%	= White, non-Hispanic
4	= African-American
Alaska 3	= White Hispanic
5	= Asian, Pacific Islander
Philippines 16	= Amer. Ind., Eskimo, Aleut. Isl.

Country of origin of greatest number of immigrants in 1998

WHITES: Vermont has the least diversity of the states, with just 2.4% nonwhites

BLACKS: New York has the highest number of African-Americans with 3.2 million, but is the 10th state by percentage

MINORITY: White non-Hispanics now make up 49.9% of the population—the first time they have not been a majority

ORIGIN: More immigrants come from Mexico than from any other country— 131,575 in 1998

DESTINATION: The most popular states for immigrants are Calif., Fla., Ill., N.J., N.Y. and Texas. They're home to 67% of all immigrants.

State data boxes (percentages top to bottom: White non-Hispanic, African-American, White Hispanic, Asian/Pacific Islander, Amer. Ind., plus country of origin):

- **Wash.** 83% / 4 / 6 / 6 / 2 — Mexico
- **Mont.** 91% / 0.4 / 2 / 0.6 / 6 — China
- **N.D.** 93% / 0.6 / 1 / 0.8 / 5 — Canada
- **Minn.** 91% / 3 / 2 / 3 / 1 — Mexico
- **Mich.** 81% / 14 / 2 / 2 / 0.6 — India
- **Pa.** 86% / 10 / 2 / 2 / 0.2 — India
- **N.H.** 96% / 0.8 / 1 / 1 / 0.2 — India
- **Mass.** 84% / 7 / 5 / 4 / 0.2 — China
- **Maine** 98% / 0.5 / 0.7 / 0.8 / 0.5 — Canada

- **Idaho** 90% / 0.6 / 7 / 1 / 1 — Mexico
- **Wyo.** 90% / 0.9 / 6 / 0.9 / 2 — Mexico
- **S.D.** 89% / 0.7 / 1 / 0.7 / 8 — Mexico
- **Wis.** 90% / 6 / 2 / 2 / 0.9 — Mexico
- **Ind.** 88% / 8 / 2 / 1 / 0.3 — Mexico
- **Ohio** 86% / 12 / 1 / 1 / 0.2 — India
- **Vt.** 97.6% / 0.5 / 0.8 / 0.8 / 0.2 — Canada
- **R.I.** 86% / 5 / 6 / 2 / 0.5 — Dominican Republic

- **Ore.** 88% / 2 / 6 / 3 / 1 — Mexico
- **Utah** 89% / 0.9 / 7 / 3 / 1 — Mexico
- **Neb.** 89% / 4 / 4 / 1 / 0.9 — Mexico
- **Iowa** 94% / 2 / 2 / 1 / 0.3 — Mexico
- **Ill.** 71% / 15 / 10 / 3 / 0.2 — Mexico
- **W.Va.** 96% / 3 / 0.5 / 0.5 / 0.1 — India
- **N.Y.** 65% / 18 / 11 / 6 / 0.4 — Dominican Republic
- **Conn.** 80% / 9 / 8 / 3 / 0.2 — Jamaica

- **Nev.** 70% / 8 / 15 / 5 / 2 — Mexico
- **Colo.** 78% / 4 / 14 / 2 / 0.9 — Mexico
- **Kans.** 86% / 6 / 5 / 2 / 0.9 — Mexico
- **Mo.** 86% / 11 / 1 / 1 / 0.4 — Mexico
- **Tenn.** 81% / 17 / 1 / 1 / 0.2 — Mexico
- **Ky.** 91% / 7 / 0.8 / 0.7 / 0.1 — Cuba
- **Md.** 64% / 28 / 3 / 4 / 0.3 — El Salvador
- **N.J.** 68% / 15 / 11 / 6 / 0.3 — India
- **D.C.** 29% / 61 / 6 / 3 / 0.3 — El Salvador

- **Hawaii** 29% / 3 / 4 / 64 / 0.6 — Philippines
- **Calif.** 49.9% / 8 / 30 / 12 / 0.9 — Mexico
- **Ariz.** 68% / 4 / 21 / 2 / 5 — Mexico
- **Okla.** 80% / 8 / 3 / 1 / 8 — Mexico
- **Ark.** 81% / 16 / 2 / 0.7 / 0.5 — Mexico
- **Miss.** 62% / 36 / 0.7 / 0.7 / 0.4 — India
- **Ala.** 72% / 26 / 0.9 / 0.7 / 0.3 — Mexico
- **Va.** 72% / 20 / 3 / 4 / 0.3 — El Salvador
- **Dela.** 75% / 20 / 3 / 2 / 0.3 — India
- **N.C.** 73% / 22 / 2 / 1 / 1 — Mexico

- **N.M.** 47% / 3 / 39 / 2 / 10 — Mexico
- **La.** 64% / 32 / 2 / 1 / 0.4 — Honduras
- **Ga.** 66% / 29 / 3 / 2 / 0.2 — Mexico
- **S.C.** 68% / 30 / 1 / 0.9 / 0.2 — Mexico

- **Texas** 55% / 12 / 29 / 3 / 0.5 — Mexico
- **Fla.** 68% / 15 / 14 / 2 / 0.4 — Cuba

NON-HISPANIC PERCENTAGES MAY NOT TOTAL 100 DUE TO ROUNDING. SOURCES: U.S. CENSUS BUREAU, POPULATION REFERENCE BUREAU, IMMIGRATION AND NATURALIZATION SERVICE. RESEARCH BY MEREDITH SALISBURY. GRAPHIC BY BONNIE SCRANTON—NEWSWEEK

IMMIGRANTS ADMITTED TO THE U.S.

Bar chart: 2.0 million scale, years 1990, 92, 94, 96, 98

U.S. POPULATION, IN THOUSANDS AND PERCENT CHANGE

	1990	2000	% change '90–'00	2050	% change '00–'50
White, non-Hispanic	188,315	196,659	+4%	207,901	+6%
Black, non-Hispanic	29,304	33,476	+14%	53,555	+60%
Hispanic (of any race)	22,379	32,440	+45%	96,508	+197%
Asian and Pacific Islander*	6,996	10,504	+50%	32,432	+209%
Amer. Ind., Eskimo, Aleut. Isl.*	1,797	2,050	+14%	3,534	+72%

INTERGROUP MARRIAGES, 1998

Pie chart:
- White/black: 9%
- Other: 7%
- White/Nat. American: 12%
- White/Hispanic: 52%
- White/Asian: 19%

What's White, Anyway?

The question is as old as America itself, and as the country's racial barriers erode, the answer is changing yet again—while the advantages of whiteness are murkier than ever.

BY ELLIS COSE

IN ARGENTINA, WHERE HE WAS BORN, MY ACQUAINTANCE had always been on solid taxonomic ground. His race was no more a mystery than the color of the clouds. It was a fact, presumably rooted in biology, that he was as white as a man could be. But his move to the United States had left him confused. So he turned to me and sheepishly asked in Spanish, "Am I white or am I Latino?"

Given his fair complexion and overall appearance, most Americans would deem him white, I replied—that is, until he opened his mouth, at which point his inability to converse in English would become his most salient feature. He would still be considered white, I explained, but his primary identity would be as a Latino. For his U.S.-raised children, the relevant order will likely be reversed: in most circles they will simply be white Americans, albeit of Argentine ancestry, unless they decide to be Latino. At any rate, I pointed out, the categories are not exclusive—although in the United States we often act as if they are.

He said he understood, though something in his manner told me he was more confused than ever. Playing the game of racial classification has a way of doing that to you. For though the question—*who is white?*—is as old as America itself, the answer has often changed. And it is shifting yet again, even as the advantages of whiteness have become murkier than ever.

In the beginning, the benefits were obvious. American identity itself was inextricably wrapped up in the mythology of race. The nation's first naturalization act (passed during the second session of the first Congress in March 1790) reserved the privilege of naturalization for "aliens being free white persons." Only after the Civil War were blacks allowed to present themselves for citizenship, and even then other suspect racial groups were not so favored. Thus, well into the 20th century persons of various ethnicities and hues sued for the purpose of proving themselves white.

In 1922 the case of a Japanese national who had lived in America for two decades made its way to the Supreme Court. Takao Ozawa argued that the United States, in annexing Hawaii, had embraced people even darker than the Japanese—implicitly recognizing them as white. He also made the rather novel, if bizarre, claim that the dominant strain of Japanese were "white persons" of Caucasian root stock who spoke an "Aryan tongue." The high court disagreed. Nonetheless, the following year a high-caste Hindu, Bhagat Singh Thind, asked the same court to accept him as a white Aryan. In rejecting his claim Justice George Sutherland, writing for the court, declared: "It may be true that the blond Scandinavian and the brown Hindu have a common ancestor in the dim reaches of antiquity, but the average man knows perfectly well that there are unmistakable and profound differences between them today." While the children of Europeans quickly became indistinguishable from other Americans, "it cannot be doubted that the children born in this country of Hindu parents would retain indefinitely the clear evidence of their ancestry," concluded Sutherland.

The McCarran-Walter Act, passed in 1952, finally eliminated racial restrictions on citizenship. No longer were East Indians, Arabs and assorted other non-Europeans forced, in a figurative sense, to paint themselves white in order to become Americans.

Today such an exercise seems weird beyond words. But it's worth recalling that even Europeans were not exempt from establishing their racial bona fides. The great immigration debates of the first part of the 20th century were driven in large measure by panic at the prospect of American's gene pool becoming hopelessly polluted with the blood of inferior European tribes. Many of the leading scientists and politicians of the day worried that immigrants from Eastern and Southern Europe—people considered intellectually, morally and physically inferior— would debase America's exalted Anglo-Saxon-Germanic stock. Such thinking was influenced, among other things, by the rise of eugenics. "The Races of Europe," a book published in 1899 by sociologist William Z. Ripley, was a typical text. Ripley classified Europeans into three distinct races: blond, blue-eyed Teutonics (who were at the highest stage of development); stocky, chestnut-haired Alpines, and dark, slender Mediterraneans. No less a personage than Stanford University president David Starr Jordan bought into the scheme, along with some of the leading lights of Congress. And though "undesirable" European races were never flatly prohibited from eligibility for citizenship, American immigration laws were crafted to favor those presumed to be of finer racial stock. While all whites might be deemed superior to those who were black, yellow or brown, all white "races" were not considered equal to each other.

Much of American history has been a process of embracing previously reviled or excluded groups who were deemed genetically suspect.

Gradually America learned to set aside many of its racial preconceptions. Indeed, much of American history has been a process of embracing previously reviled or excluded groups. At one time or another, various clans of Europeans—Poles, Italians, Jews, Romanians—were deemed genetically suspect; but they were subsequently welcomed. They were all, in essence, made white. The question today is whether that process will extend to those whose ancestors, for the most part, were not European.

To some extent it certainly will. That reality struck me some years ago when, in a moment of unguarded conversation, a radio host observed that "white Asians" were in demand for certain jobs. Initially I had no idea what the man was talking about, but as he rattled on I realized he was saying that he considered some Asian-Americans (those with a lighter complexion) to be, for all intents and purposes, as white as himself. In his mind at least, the def-

inition of whiteness has expanded well beyond its old parameters. And I suspect he is far from alone. This is not to say that Takao Ozawa would be better able today than in 1922 to convince a court that he is Aryan; but he almost certainly could persuade most Americans to treat him like a white person, which essentially amounts to the same thing. America's cult of whiteness, after all, was never just about skin color, hair texture and other physical traits. It was about where the line was drawn between those who could be admitted into the mainstream and those who could not.

Those boundaries clearly are no longer where they once were. And even as the boundaries of whiteness have expanded, the specialness of whiteness has eroded. Being white, in other words, is no longer quite what it used to be. So if Ozawa and his progeny have not exactly become white, they are no longer mired in America's racial wasteland. Indeed, even many Americans with the option of being white—those with, say, one Mexican parent or a Cherokee grandfather—are more than ever inclined to think of themselves as something else. And those for whom whiteness will likely never be an option (most blacks and many darker Hispanics, for instance) are freer to enjoy being whatever they are.

Society, in short, has progressed much since the days when Eastern Europeans felt it necessary to Anglicize their names, when Arabs and East Indians went to court to declare themselves white and when the leading scientists of the day had nothing better to do than to link morality and intelligence to preconceived notions of race. But having finally thrust aside 19th-century racial pseudo-science, we have not yet fully digested the science of the 21st, which has come to understand what enlightened souls sensed all along: that the differences that divided one race from another add up to a drop in the genetic ocean.

Recognizing the truth of that insight is only part of society's challenge. The largest part is figuring out what to do with it, figuring out how, having so long given racial categories an importance they never merited, we reduce them to the irrelevance they deserve—figuring out how, in short, to make real the abstraction called equality we profess to have believed in all along.

All White, All Christian And Divided by Diversity

By ELIZABETH BECKER

DUBUQUE, Iowa

MY grandmother Hulda Pieper Willenburg, proper and prim as she was, would have been horrified at a recent description of her home. But there it was, in The Des Moines Register: someone calling Carroll County and two other prosperous farming areas in western Iowa "very nondiverse in their ethnic background and their religious background."

Granted, the three counties are mostly white and mostly Christian. But homogeneity is in the eye of the beholder. Calling them "nondiverse" erases the historic and often ruthless ethnic and religious divisions that created them—and that haven't entirely disappeared.

In the Carroll County of my grandmother's day, it was German against Irish; Catholic against Protestant. The ethnic divisions were sufficiently deep that Germans only married Germans and, at times, differences were settled with bricks thrown through storefront windows.

The comment was made by Thomas Dorr, an Iowa farmer, at a farming conference in 1999, but the newspaper printed it for the first time last month, after Mr. Dorr was nominated to become the Agriculture Department's under secretary for rural development. Because his remarks connected the counties' agricultural success to "something" about their homogeneity, there was a national outcry, particularly from black farmer's groups. But the notion of the three counties' uniformity went unchallenged.

Carroll, my birthplace and the home to three generations of my German-Catholic family, started as something of an arcadia for German Catholics, who began arriving shortly after the Civil War, fleeing the small wars and strife that would eventually lead to the unification of modern Germany. Many entered the United States at New Orleans and went by boat up the Mississippi. Some disembarked here in Dubuque, stocked up wagons and headed west.

A market town, Carroll was laid out by the railroads midway between Des Moines and Omaha, where the flat plains give way to rolling hills. Its German settlers neither spoke English nor professed a Protestant faith. By the late 19th century they had become prosperous farmers who shipped their grain and livestock to the big cities, and they had quietly taken over more and more of the town. They published Der Carroll Demokrat newspaper, patronized German bakeries and taverns and built the grand Germania Verein, later transforming it into a sumptuous opera house, complete with handpainted scenes of the Koblenz Castle overlooking the Rhine.

It didn't take long before these proud German Catholics felt besieged by "outsiders" trying to tamper with their families and their lives. By the 1880's, they were fighting off their fellow immigrants, German Lutherans, who with American Protestants were insisting on "puritan Sundays" that would have banned all alcohol and beer-soaked singing parties, or sangerfests.

And they took extreme measures against the Irish Catholics, who had been holding separate, English-language masses at the Germans' church of St. Joseph.

In 1885, the diocese sent an Irish priest to St. Joseph—a priest who tried to encourage his parish to Americanize by prohibiting the German language. The German parishioners voted with their feet. They demanded and received a cash return for their investment in the church, and within a year raised $18,000 and built Sts. Peter and Paul, the largest church in Carroll, with a gilded 120-foot spire visible for eight miles.

Growing up in an area of Iowa that was hailed as 'nondiverse.'

My grandparents and a few of my great-grandparents, the Beckers and Willenburgs, lived through what they called Carroll's golden age, prospering in America without giving up who they were, speaking German at home, at church, in town and on their farms. Sts. Peter and Paul's new priest, who was from Bavaria, oversaw a building boom, adding a primary school, a hospital, a school of nursing and an all-women's academy. There was no question of their sense of German Catholic superiority—and therefore of the inferiority of the Irish and Protestant neighbors.

Then the United States joined World War I, and Germany was the enemy.

IOWA turned its German communities, defiantly separated by faith, into one entity by enacting some of the strongest anti-German laws in the country, including a complete ban on "foreign languages" in public places. In Carroll, the English speakers banished German from the pulpit and the telephone, as well as from schools and every shop, store and gathering place in town. Bricks started flying into stores that refused to change their names. The Schmidts became Smiths; Der Carroll Demokrat became The Carroll Times.

Fearful of retribution, the Willenburgs hoisted an American flag on their front porch and gave up German overnight. My aunt and uncles were punished if they uttered anything but English, however broken. (When I was young, Grandmother Hulda still acted as if German was forbidden. She prayed in German and taught me numbers and colors, but never when she thought anyone else was around.)

Some of the Irish, watching the bricks fly, became enraged. The war was Europe's, and America's ally, Britain, had been for centuries their homeland's occupier and oppressor. My grandfather Willenburg made some Irish friends. And he went back to St. Joe's.

BY the time the war ended, the Germans of Carroll—Protestant and Catholic—had transformed themselves into Americans. My great-grandfather Ferdinand Becker had become Fred, though he never did master English.

But consequences linger. Thirty years later, when I went to Grandmother Willenburg's on childhood visits, she spoke as if the war had been yesterday and the Germans were still being challenged by outsiders.

Today, German surnames still predominate around Carroll, a county of 576 square miles and 21,000 people scattered in farms and 16 towns and villages. Catholics are still in the majority.

"There is no spot in Carroll County where you can't find a Catholic church within five miles," said Carl Brincks, a third-generation German Catholic farmer.

Mr. Brincks, 35, said he had seen much change in Carroll. The friction may be gone, but the divisions remain. The Irish and the Germans now live in the same neighborhoods, more or less. Carroll was well over 80 percent Catholic when he was growing up, Mr. Brincks said. Now it has what he called "considerable religious diversity": there's a new Baptist church, a new Church of Christ building and another for Jehovah's Witnesses.

Of course, it's still almost all white. An area so fraught with its own brand of ethnic tension was hardly inviting to people who were even more obviously different, like African-Americans and Hispanics.

So when Mr. Dorr suggested that Carroll looks like a cookie-cutter community of white, church-going farmers, Mr. Brincks was not surprised. He is married to a Korean-American woman and his brother has adopted two children from Asia, but he knows how few non-Europeans live in the county.

"I guess I wasn't offended by Tom Dorr's comment, because he was stating the obvious," he said.

From the *New York Times,* June 10, 2001. © 2001 by The New York Times Company. Reprinted by permission.

UNIT 3

Immigration and the American Experience

Unit Selections

Key Points to Consider

• Does attention to historical background and its expression in current culture promote both understanding and tolerance?

• Is understanding ethnic traditions and cultures a necessary component of American education?

• How does an emphasis on historical ethnic studies assist in our study of contemporary issues in race and ethnic relations?

• What is the distinction between the words "immigration," "migration," and "emigration"?

• The U.S. Census reports the number of foreign-born and American-born persons and the ethnicity and/or ancestry of persons. What differentiates these various methods and categories?

• In what respects are historical accounts of America's immigration tradition relevant to contemporary immigration issues and policies? Is immigration history portrayed as a series of success stories that reveal fortitude and talent that overcomes suffering and hardship or as collection of tales illustrative of torments and tears and ongoing exclusion and domination?

• Why do periods of economic crisis appear to exacerbate tensions and strain relations among ethnic groups?

• The clustering of ethnic populations in various regions of America has produced patterns that are worth pondering. Discuss the importance of locality to understanding American ethnicities. Do you think that the immigration question is really a local issue, and not a national concern? Why or why not?

• In what respect do immigrants influence U.S. foreign policy toward the countries from which they and/or their ancestors came?

• What remedies for language diversity are acceptable in a democratic society? Is English becoming the world's second language? What does a second language add to our identity? Our capacity to deal with diversity? Our marketability in an age of globalization?

 **Links: www.dushkin.com/online/**
These sites are annotated in the World Wide Web pages.

Child Welfare League of America (CWLA)
http://www.cwla.org
National Immigrant Forum
http://www.immigrationforum.org
The National Network for Immigrant and Refugee Rights (NNIRR)
http://www.nnirr.org
U.S. Immigration and Naturalization Service (INS)
http://www.ins.usdoj.gov

The history of immigration and ethnic group diversity is embedded in the history of America from its earliest times. Recent archaeological discoveries have considerably extended the time frame and process of the peopling of this continent. These social historical facts have often been ignored or forgotten in contemporary debates about our tradition of being an immigrantreceiving continent.

From the 1850s to the 1870s immigrants to America came predominately from Britain and northern Europe. To these European and perhaps to some Asian immigrants in the American West, America represented freedom to enter the economic struggle without constraints of state-and status-bound societies whose limits could not be overcome except through emigration. Yet this historical pathway to liberty, justice, and opportunity came to be perceived as a "tarnished door" when the deep impulses of exclusion and exclusivity came to the fore. The victims were aliens who, ironically, achieved the American promise but were denied the reward of acceptance and incorporation into the very culture they helped to fashion. The following articles describe the immigrant experience and raise once again the issues that every large-scale multiethnic regime must address: How can unity and diversity be channeled into political, economic, and cultural well-being?

The history of immigration law does not champion American ethnic groups. Immigration laws include the Chinese Exclusion Acts of the 1880s, the National Origins Quota System of the 1920s, the Mexican Repatriation Campaign of the 1950s, and the McCarran-Walter Act in 1952. A new era began with the inclusiveness of the mid-1960s. The findings of the 1990 U.S. Census point to a range of demographic, economic, and social indicators in this most recent era of immigration in the United States. Both the immediate impact of present-day newcomers and the changes in America that can be attributed to the conflicts and contributions of previous immigrants appear to be facets of nearly every contemporary social issue.

The U.S. Census documents the consequences of decades and generations of immigration. It enables us to discern the spectrum of American ethnicities and the regional patterns of ethnic settlement. The stories of new immigrants are aspects of a worldwide drama. The European and American contexts discussed in this unit provide perspectives on immigrant adjustment and their reception in various regimes and cultures. The ongoing issue of cultural formation through language and the political artifices used to heighten or diminish ethnicity as a political factor are explored. The movement of people induces change and growth that poses great potential for well-being and economic development. Nevertheless, the influx of persons and cultures requires awareness of our cultural diversity and common humanity as well as energy, mutual openness to talent, and participation of all in the experience of being and becoming Americans.

Full employment and socialeconomic mobility in countries from which persons are coming to the United States would decrease incentives for migration. Political and religious freedom in other countries would negate another cause for the movement of people from oppressive regimes to democratic and liberal societies.

As the unit articles make clear, immigration not only has an impact on the receiving country but also affects nations that lose the talents, skills, and loyalty of disaffected migrants. Immigration, moreover, contributes to an already complex process of intergenerational relationships and the socialization of persons whose experiences of profound cultural change are intensified by competition, patterns of settlement, options for mobility, and the consciousness of ethnic traditions that conflict with dominant cultural and educational institutions. Michael Piore's assessment of children born to immigrant workers suggests an interesting lens through which the following articles may be read. Dr. Piore writes:

There is nothing in the immigration process that ensures that this second generation will be able to move up to the higher level jobs toward which they aspire. Indeed, historically industrial societies appear consistently to disappoint the expectations of the second generation in this regard. That disappointment has in turn been the source of enormous social tension. The sitdown strikes in the late thirties which sparked the industrial unions movement in the United States may in large measure be attributed to the reaction of the children of pre–World War I European immigrants to their labor market conditions. Similarly, the racial disturbances in Northern urban ghettos in the middle and late 1960s may be looked upon as a revolt of the black migrants against a society bent upon confining them to their parents' jobs.

As a guide for your own study, the U.S. Commission on Civil Rights has noted that increased immigration raises the following issues for both recent arrivals and Americans by birth:

Employment: The areas of occupation selected by or imposed upon various ethnic populations trace ethnic group mobility strategies and ethnic succession in the workplace, especially in manufacturing, hospitals, restaurants, and maintenance and custodial positions. Some ethnic populations appear to have greater numbers of highly educated persons in professional or semiprofessional positions.

Institutional and societal barriers: The job preferences and discrimination against the ethnic enclaves and persons in small communities that are isolated from mainstream Englishspeaking society suggest the value of second-language competencies. Mutual accommodation is required to minimize the effect of inadequate language skills and training and difficulties in obtaining licenses, memberships, and certification.

Exploitation of workers: The most common form is the payment of wages below minimum standards. Alien workers have been stereotyped as a drain on public services. Such scapegoating is insupportable.

Taking jobs from Americans: Fact or fiction? The stunning fact is that immigrants are a source of increased productivity and a significant, if not utterly necessary, addition to the workforce as well as to the consumer power that drives the American economy.

Should immigrants assimilate?

Alejandro Portes and Min Zhou

"My name is Herb / and I'm not poor / I'm the Herbie that you're looking for / like Pepsi / a new generation / of Haitian determination / I'm the Herbie that you're looking for."

A beat tapped with bare hands, a few dance steps, and the Haitian kid was rapping. His song, entitled "Straight Out of Haiti," was performed at Edison High, a school that sits astride Little Haiti and Liberty City—the largest black area of Miami. The lyrics capture well the distinct outlook of his immigrant community. In Little Haiti, the storefronts leap out at the passersby. Bright blues, reds, and oranges vibrate to Haitian *merengue*, blaring from sidewalk speakers. Yet behind the gay Caribbean exterior, a struggle goes on that will define the future of this community. As we will see, it involves the second generation-children like Herbie—who are subject to conflicting pressure from parents and peers, and to pervasive outside discrimination.

Growing up in an immigrant family has always been difficult. Individuals are torn by conflicting social and cultural demands, while facing the challenge of entry into an unfamiliar and frequently hostile world. Yet the difficulties are not always the same. The process of "growing up American" ranges from smooth acceptance to traumatic confrontation, depending on the characteristics that immigrants and their children bring along and the social context that receives them. We believe that something quite disturbing is happening to the assimilation or, if you will, the "Americanization" of the second generation of new immigrants.

Research on the new immigration—that which arose after passage of the 1965 Immigration Act—has focused almost exclusively on the first generation, which is composed of adult men and women who came to the U.S. in search of work or to escape political persecution. Little noticed until recently is the growth of the second generation. Yet by 1980, second-generation immigrants made up 10 percent of the children counted by the U.S. Census. Another survey in the late 1980s found that 3 to 5 million American students speak a language other than English at home.

While there has been a great deal of research and theorizing on post-1965 immigration, it offers only tentative guidance on the prospects and paths of adaptation of the second generation, whose outlook may be very different from that of the first. For example, it is generally accepted among immigration experts that entry-level menial jobs are performed without hesitation by newly arrived immigrants, but that these same jobs are shunned by the immigrants' U.S.-reared offspring. The social and economic progress of first-generation immigrants often fails to keep pace with the material conditions and career prospects that their American children grow to expect.

What literature on second-generation adaptation that exists is based largely on the experience of the descendants of pre-World War I immigrants. The last sociological study of the children of immigrants seems to have been Irving Child's *Italian or American? The Second Generation in Conflict*, published fifty years ago. Conditions at the time were quite different from those that confront settled immigrant groups today. Two such differences deserve special mention. First, the descendants of European immigrants who confronted the dilemmas of conflicting cultures were uniformly white. Even if they were of a somewhat darker hue than the natives, their skin color permitted them to skirt a major barrier to entry into the American mainstream. As a result, the process of assimilation depended largely on the individual's decision to leave the immigrant culture behind and to embrace American ways. This advantage obviously does not exist for the black, Asian and mestizo children of today's immigrants.

Approximately 77 percent of post-1960 immigrants are non- European: 22 percent are Asian, 8 percent are black, and 47 percent are Hispanic. (The latter group, which originates in Mexico and other Latin American countries, poses a problem in terms of classification since Hispanics can be of any race.)

The immigrants of recent years also face economic opportunities different than those in the past. Fifty years ago, the United States was the premier industrial power in the world. Its diversified industrial labor requirements offered the second generation the opportunity to move up gradually through better-paid occupations while remaining part of the working class. Such opportunities have grown scarce in recent years as the result of rapid national de-industrialization and global restructuring. This process has left entrants to the American labor force confronting a growing gap between the minimally paid menial jobs commonly accepted by immigrants and the high-tech and professional jobs generally occupied by college-educated native elites. This disappearance of intermediate opportunities has contributed to the mismatch between first-generation economic progress and second-generation expectations.

ASSIMILATION AS A PROBLEM

We see these processes occurring under particularly difficult circumstances among the Haitians of Miami. The city's Haitian community is composed of some 75,000 legal and clandestine immigrants, many of whom sold everything in order to buy passage to America. Haitians of the first generation are strongly disposed to preserve a robust national identity, which they associate both with community solidarity and with social networks promoting individual success. But in trying to instill in their children national pride and an orientation toward achievement, they often clash with the youngsters' everyday experiences in school. Little Haiti is adjacent to Liberty City, the main black inner-city area of Miami, and Haitian adolescents attend predominantly inner-city schools. Native-born black youth stereotype the Haitian youngsters as docile and subservient to whites, and make fun of the Haitians' French and Creole as well as their accents. As a result, second-generation Haitian children find themselves torn between conflicting ideas and values: to remain "Haitian," they must endure ostracism and continuing attacks in school; to become "American" (black American in this case), they must forgo their parents' dreams of making it in America through the preservation of ethnic solidarity and traditional values.

An adversarial stance toward the white mainstream is common among inner-city minority youth, who instill in the newcomers consciousness of American-style discrimination. Also instilled is skepticism about the value of education as a vehicle for advancement, a message that directly contradicts that from immigrant parents. Academically outstanding Haitian-American students, Herbie among them, have consciously attempted to retain their ethnic identity by cloaking it in black American cultural forms, such as rap music. Many others, however, have followed the path of least resistance and thoroughly assimilated. In such instances the assimilation is not to mainstream culture, but to the values and norms of the inner city. In the process, the resources of solidarity and mutual support within the immigrant community are dissipated.

As the Haitian example illustrates, adopting the outlook and cultural ways of the native born does not necessarily represent the first step toward social and economic mobility. It may, in fact, lead to exactly the opposite. Meanwhile, immigrant youth who remain firmly ensconced in their ethnic communities may, by virtue of this fact, have a better chance for educational and economic mobility.

This situation stands the common understanding of immigrant assimilation on its head. As presented in innumerable academic and journalistic writings, the expectation is that the foreign born and their offspring will acculturate and seek acceptance among the native born as a prerequisite for social advancement. If they did not, they would remain confined to the ranks of the "ethnic" lower and lower-middle classes. This portrayal of the path to mobility, so deeply embedded in the national consciousness, stands contradicted today by a growing number of empirical studies.

A closer look at these studies, however, indicates that the expected consequences of assimilation have not changed entirely, but that the process has become segmented. In other words, the question is to what sector of American society a particular immigrant group assimilates. In the absence of a relatively uniform "mainstream" whose mores and prejudices dictate a common path of integration, we observe today several distinct forms of adaptation. One of them replicates the time-honored portrayal of growing acculturation and parallel integration into the white middle-class; a second leads straight in the opposite direction to permanent poverty and assimilation to the underclass; still a third combines rapid economic advancement with deliberate preservation of the immigrant community's values and solidarity. This pattern of "segmented assimilation" immediately raises the question of what makes some immigrant groups susceptible to the downward route and what resources allow others to avoid this course. In fact, the same general process helps to explain both outcomes. We will advance next our understanding of how this process takes place and how the differing outcomes of the assimilation process can be explained. In the final section, this explanation will be illustrated with recent empirical evidence.

VULNERABILITY AND RESOURCES

While individual and family variables are influential, the context that immigrants encounter upon arrival plays a decisive role in the course that their offspring's lives will follow. This context includes such broad variables as political relations between the sending and receiving countries and the state of the economy in the latter, and such specific variables as the degree to which the immigrant group meets discrimination and finds a pre-existing ethnic community. Thus, Cuban immigrants of the 1960s came under perhaps the best circumstances: they were welcomed by the government, did not meet great prejudice, and soon formed a supportive community. On all three dimensions, the contrast with the Haitians is great.

To explain second-generation outcomes and their "segmented" character, however, we need to consider in greater detail the various paths of assimilation. There are three features of the social contexts encountered by today's newcomers that create vulnerability to downward assimilation: the first is color, the second is location, and the third is the absence of mobility ladders. As noted above, the majority of contemporary immigrants are nonwhite. Although this feature may at first glance appear to be an individual characteristic, in reality it is a trait of the

host society. Prejudice is not invariably suffered by those with a particular skin color or racial type, and indeed many immigrants never experienced prejudice in their native lands. It is by virtue of moving into a new social environment, marked by different values and biases, that physical features become redefined as a handicap.

The concentration of immigrant households in cities and, in particular, central cities, gives rise to a second source of vulnerability because it puts new arrivals in close contact with concentrations of native-born minorities. This leads the majority to identify both groups—immigrants and the native poor—as identical. Even more importantly, it exposes the children of immigrants to the adversarial subculture that marginalized native youth have developed to cope with their own difficult situation. This process of socialization may take place even when first-generation parents are moving ahead economically and, hence, when their children have no "objective" reasons for embracing a countercultural message. If successful, this socialization can effectively block parental plans for intergenerational mobility.

The third source of vulnerability results from changes in the economy that have led to the elimination of occupational ladders for inter-generational mobility. New immigrants form the backbone of what remains of labor-intensive manufacturing in the cities, as well as of the growing personal services sector, but these are niches that seldom offer channels for upward mobility. The new "hourglass economy" created by economic restructuring means that the children of immigrants must cross a narrow bottleneck to occupations requiring advanced training if their careers are to keep pace with their U.S.-acquired aspirations. This "race" against a narrowing middle demands that immigrant parents accumulate sufficient resources to allow their children to cross the bottleneck (and, simultaneously, to believe that they can cross the bottleneck). Otherwise, "assimilation" may be not to mainstream values and expectations, but to the adversarial stance of impoverished groups confined to the bottom of the hourglass.

We have painted the picture in such stark terms for the sake of clarity, although in reality things have not yet become so polarized. Middle-level occupations that require relatively modest educational achievement have not vanished completely. As of 1980, skilled blue-collar jobs (classified by the U.S. Census as "precision productions, craft and repair occupations") had declined by 1.1 percentage points compared to a decade earlier, but still represented 13 percent of the experienced civilian labor force, or 13.6 million workers. Administrative support occupations, mostly clerical, added another 16.9 percent of the jobs. Meanwhile, occupations requiring a college degree increased by 6 percentage points from 1970 to 1980, but still employed less than a fifth of the American labor force (18.2 percent). Even in the largest cities, occupations requiring only a high school diploma were common in the late 1980s. In New York City, for example, persons with twelve years or less of schooling held just over half the jobs in 1987. Yet despite these figures, there is little doubt that the trend toward occupational segmentation has reduced opportunities for upward mobility through well-paid, blue-collar positions. This trend forces today's immigrants to bridge in one generation the gap between entry-level and professional positions, a distance that earlier groups took two or three generations to travel.

At the same time, there are three types of resources that ease the assimilation of contemporary immigrants. First, certain groups, notably political refugees, are eligible for a variety of government programs including educational loans for their children. The Cuban Loan Program, begun by the Kennedy administration as part of a plan to resettle Cuban refugees beyond south Florida, gave many impoverished first-and second-generation Cuban youth a chance to attend college. The high proportion of professionals and executives among Cuban-American workers today, a figure on par with that for native white workers, can be traced, at least in part, to the success of that program. Passage of the 1980 Refugee Act gave subsequent refugees, in particular Southeast Asians and Eastern Europeans, access to a similarly generous benefits package.

In addition, certain foreign groups have managed to escape the prejudice traditionally endured by immigrants. This has facilitated a smoother process of adaptation. Political refugees such as the early waves of exiles from Castro's Cuba, Hungarians and Czechs escaping the invasions of their respective countries, and Soviet Jews escaping religious persecution, provide examples. In other cases, it is the cultural and phenotypical affinity of newcomers to ample segments of the host population that ensures a welcome reception. The Irish who came to Boston during the 1980s provide a case in point. Although many were illegal aliens, they came into an environment where generations of Irish-Americans had established a secure foothold. Public sympathy effectively neutralized governmental hostility in this case, and led to a change in the immigration law that directly benefited the newcomers.

Third and most important are the resources made available through networks in the co-ethnic community. Immigrants who join well-established and diversified ethnic groups have access to a range of moral and material resources well beyond those available through official assistance programs. Educational help for second-generation youth may include not only access to college grants and loans, but a private school system geared to immigrant community values. Attendance at these private ethnic schools insulates children from contact with native minority youth, while reinforcing the authority of parental views and plans.

In addition, the economic diversification of some immigrant communities creates niches of opportunity that members of the second generation can occupy, often without need for an advanced education. Small-business apprenticeships, access to skilled building trades, and well-paid jobs in local government bureaucracies are some of the many ethnic niches documented in the recent literature. In 1987, average sales per firm of the smaller Chinese, East Indian, Korean, and Cuban enterprises exceeded $100,000 per year, and jointly they employed more than 200,000 workers. These figures omit medium-sized and large ethnic corporations whose sales and work forces are much greater. Fieldwork in these communities indicates that up to half of recently arrived immigrants are employed by co-ethnic firms and that self-employment offers a prime avenue of mobility for second-generation youth. Through the creation of a capitalism of their own, some immigrant groups have thus been able to circumvent outside discrimination and the threat of vanishing mobility ladders.

In contrast to these favorable conditions are those faced by foreign minorities who lack a community already in place or co-ethnics capable of rendering assistance. The Haitians in south Florida, cited above, must cope with official hostility and widespread social prejudice, as well as the absence of a strong receiving community. Yet in some cases the existence of a large but downtrodden co-ethnic community may be even less desirable than no community at all. That is because newly arrived youth enter into ready contact with the reactive subculture developed by earlier generations. Its influence is all the more powerful because it comes from individuals of the same national origin, "people like us" who can effectively define the proper stance and attitudes of the newcomers. To the extent this occurs, the first generation's aspirations of upward mobility through school achievement and attainment of professional occupations will be blocked.

THE CASE OF MEXICAN-AMERICANS

"Field High School" is located in a small community in central California whose economy has long been tied to agricultural production and immigrant farm labor. About 57 percent of Field's students are of Mexican descent.

An intensive study of the class of 1985 by M.G. Matute-Bianchi revealed that the majority of U.S.-born Spanish-surname students dropped out by their senior year. Yet of the Spanish-surname students originally classified by the school as Limited English Proficient (LEP), only 35 percent dropped out. (LEP status is commonly assigned to recently arrived Mexican immigrants.) This drop-out rate was even lower than the 40 percent rate for native white students.

Intensive ethnographic fieldwork at the school identified several distinct categories into which the Mexican-origin population could be grouped. "Recent Mexican immigrants" were at one extreme. They dressed differently and unstylishly. They claimed a Mexican identity and considered Mexico their permanent home. The most academically successful of this group were those most proficient in Spanish, reflecting their prior levels of education in Mexico. Almost all were described by teachers and staff as courteous, respectful, serious about their schoolwork, and eager to please, as well as naïve and unsophisticated. They were commonly classified as LEP.

"Mexican-oriented students" spoke Spanish at home but were generally classified as Fluent English Proficient (FEP). They had strong cultural ties with both Mexico and the U.S., reflecting the fact that most were born in Mexico but had lived in the U.S. for more than five years. They were proud of their Mexican heritage, but saw themselves as different from the first group, the *reci'en llegados* (recently arrived) as well as from their native-born Chicanos and Cholos who were derided as having lost their Mexican roots. Students from this group were active in soccer and the *Sociedad Bilingue* and in celebrations of May 5th, the anniversary of the Mexican defeat of French occupying forces. Virtually all the students of Mexican descent who graduated in the top 10 percent of their class were members of this group.

"Chicanos" were by far the largest group of Mexican descent at Field High. They were mostly U.S.-born second- and third-generation students whose primary loyalty was to their in-group, seen as locked in conflict with white society. Chicanos derided successful Mexican students as "schoolboys" and "schoolgirls" or as "wannabes." According to Matute-Bianchi:

> To be a Chicano meant in practice to hang out by the science wing…, *not* eating lunch in the quad where all the "gringos" and "schoolboys" hang out…, cutting classes by faking a call slip so you can be with your friends at the 7–11… sitting in the back of classes and not participating…, *not* carrying your books to class… not taking the difficult classes.., doing the minimum to get by.

Chicanos merged imperceptibly into the last category, the "Cholos," who were commonly seen as "low riders" and gang members. They were also U.S.-born Mexican-Americans, easily identifiable by their deliberate manner of dress, walk, and speech, and other cultural symbols. Chicanos and Cholos were generally regarded by teachers as "irresponsible," "disrespectful" "mistrusting," "sullen," "apathetic," and "less motivated," and their poor school performance was attributed to these traits. According to Matute-Bianchi, Chicanos and Cholos were faced with what they saw as a choice between doing well in school and being Chicano. To study hard was to "act white" and so be disloyal to one's group.

The situation of these last two groups exemplifies a lost race between first-generation achievements and later generation expectations. Seeing their parents and grandparents confined to menial jobs, and increasingly aware of discrimination by the white mainstream, the U.S.-born children of earlier Mexican immigrants readily join a reactive subculture as a means of protecting their sense of self-worth. Participation in this subculture erects serious barriers to upward mobility because school achievement is defined as antithetical to ethnic solidarity. Like the Haitian students in Miami, newly arrived Mexicans are at risk of being socialized into a reactive stance, with the aggravating factor that it is "other Mexicans," not native-born strangers, who convey the message. The principal protection of *mexicanos* against this type of assimilation lies in their strong identification with the home country's language and values, which brings them closer to their parents' cultural stance.

THE CASE OF PUNJABI SIKHS

"Valleyside" is a northern California community in which the primary economic activity is orchard farming. Farm laborers in the area often come from India and are mainly rural Sikhs from the Punjab. In the early 1980s, second-generation Punjabis made up 11 percent of the student body at Valleyside High. Their parents were not only farm laborers; about a third were orchard owners themselves and another third worked in factories in the nearby San Francisco area. An ethnographic study of Valleyside High between 1980 and 1982 by M.A. Gibson revealed a very difficult process of assimilation for Punjabi Sikh students. According to Gibson, Valleyside is "redneck country" and white residents are extremely hostile toward immigrants who look different and speak another language:

Punjabi teenagers are told they stink…, told to go back to India… physically abused by majority students who spit at them, refuse to sit by them in class or in buses, throw food at them or worse.

Despite these attacks and some evidence of discrimination by school staff, Punjabi students performed better than the majority "Anglo" students. About 90 percent of the immigrant youth completed high school, compared to 70 to 75 percent of native whites. Punjabi boys earned above-average grades, were more likely than average to take advanced science and math classes, and often aspired to careers in science and engineering. Punjabi girls tended to enroll in business classes, but were less interested in immediate career plans than in satisfying parental wishes that they first marry. This gender difference reflects the strong influence exercised by the immigrant community over its second generation. According to Gibson, Punjabi parents pressured their children to avoid too much contact with white peers who might "dishonor" the immigrants, and defined "becoming Americanized" as forgetting one's roots and adopting various frowned-upon traits of the majority—such as leaving home at age eighteen, making decisions without parental consent, dating, and dancing, Instead, Punjabi parents urged their children to abide by school rules, ignore racist remarks, avoid fights, and learn useful skills including full proficiency in English.

The overall success of this strategy of "selective" assimilation to American society is remarkable. Punjabi immigrants were generally poor when they arrived and confronted widespread discrimination. They did not benefit from either governmental assistance or a well-established co-ethnic community. In terms of our typology of vulnerability and resources, the Punjabi Sikh second-generation was very much at risk except for two crucial factors. First, immigrant parents did not settle in the inner city nor in close proximity to any native-born minority whose offspring could provide an alternative model of adaptation to white majority discrimination. In particular, the *absence* of a down-trodden Indian-American community composed of children of previous immigrants allowed first-generation parents to influence decisively the outlook of their offspring, including their ways of fighting white prejudice. There was no equivalent of a Cholo-like reactive subculture to offer an alternative blueprint for the stance that "people like us" should take.

Second, Punjabi immigrants managed to make considerable economic progress, as attested by the number who became farm owners, while at the same time maintaining a tightly knit ethnic community. The material and social capital created by this first generation community compensated for the absence of an older co-ethnic group and had a decisive effect on the outlook of the second generation. Punjabi teenagers were shown that their parents' ways "paid off" economically and this fact plus their community's cohesiveness endowed them with a source of pride that counteracted outside discrimination. Through a strategy of selective assimilation, Punjabi Sikhs appear to be winning the race against the inevitable acculturation of their children to American-style aspirations.

THE CASE OF CARIBBEANS IN SOUTH FLORIDA

Miami is arguably the American city that has been most thoroughly transformed by post-1960 immigration. The Cuban revolution had much to do with this transformation, as it sent the entire Cuban upper-class out of the country, followed by thousands of refugees of more modest backgrounds. Over time Cubans in Miami have created a prosperous community. Signs of this prosperity abound: by 1987, Cubans owned more than 30,000 small businesses, which formed the core of the Miami ethnic enclave; by 1989, Cuban family incomes approximated those of the native-born population; the Cuban community has also developed a private school system oriented to its values and political outlook. In terms of the above topology of vulnerability resources, well-sheltered Cuban-American teenagers lack extensive exposure to outside discrimination and have little contact with youth from disadvantaged minorities. Moreover, the development of a Cuban enclave has created economic opportunities beyond those in the narrowing industrial and tourist sectors on which most other immigrant groups in the area depend. Across town, Haitian-American teenagers face exactly the opposite set of conditions.

Among the other immigrant groups in Miami, two deserve mention because they face situations intermediate between those of the Cubans and Haitians. Nicaraguans escaping the Sandinista regime during the 1980s were not as welcomed in the U.S. as Cuban exiles, nor were they able to develop a large and diversified community. Yet Nicaraguans shared with Cubans a common language and culture, as well as a militant anti-communist outlook. This common outlook led the Cuban-American community to extend its resources in support of the Nicaraguans, smoothing their process of adaptation. For second-generation Nicaraguans, this has meant that the pre-existing ethnic community providing a model for their own assimilation is not a downtrodden group, but rather one that has managed to establish a firm presence in the city's economy and politics.

Members of a second group, West Indians from Jamaica, Trinidad, and other English-speaking Caribbean republics, generally arrive in Miami as legal immigrants. In addition, many bring along professional and business credentials as well as the advantage of English fluency. These advantages are diminished, however, by the fact that these immigrants are seen by whites as identical to native-born blacks and discriminated against accordingly. The recency of West Indian migration and its limited numbers have prevented the development of a diversified ethnic community in south Florida. Hence new arrivals experience the full force of white discrimination without the protection of a large co-ethnic group, and with constant exposure to the situation and attitudes of the inner-city population. These disadvantages put the West Indian second generation at risk of bypassing white or even black middle-class models and instead assimilating to the culture of the underclass.

A recently completed survey of eighth and ninth graders in the Dade County (Miami) and Broward County (Fort Lauderdale) schools by the senior author of this article and Lisandro Perez included sizable samples of Cuban, Haitian, Nicaraguan, and West Indian second-generation children. The study defined youth of the "second generation" as those born in the U.S. who have at least one foreign-born parent, and those born abroad who have lived in the U.S. for at least five years. The survey included both inner-city and suburban public schools, as well as private schools and those in which particular foreign-origin groups were known to concentrate. The sample was divided evenly between boys and girls and included children ranging in age from twelve to seventeen.

There were, as expected, large socio-economic differences among the four national groups. Cuban children in private schools had the best educated parents and those with the highest status occupations. Haitians in public schools had parents who ranked lowest in both dimensions. Nicaraguans and West Indians occupied intermediate positions, with parents whose average education was often higher than that of public-school Cubans, but whose occupational levels were roughly the same. While more than half of private-school Cuban respondents defined their families as upper-middle class or higher, only a third of Haitians and Nicaraguans did so.

Most interesting were the differences in ethnic self-identification. Less than one-fifth of the second-generation students identified themselves as non-hyphenated Americans. The proportion was highest among higher-status, private-school Cubans but even among this group almost two-thirds saw themselves as "Cuban" or "Cuban-American." Very few Cubans opted for the self-designation "Hispanic." Nicaraguan students, on the other hand, used this label almost as frequently as "Nicaraguan."

While none of the Latin students identified themselves as "black American," roughly one-tenth of Haitians and West Indians did so. The self-identification of Haitians was similar to that of Nicaraguans in that both attached less importance to the country of origin and more to pan-national identity than did Cubans or West Indians. In total, about half of the Haitian children identified themselves as something other than "Haitian."

Aspirations were very high in all groups. Although there were significant differences in expectations of completing college, at least 80 percent in each group expected to achieve this level of education. Similarly, roughly 70 percent of the students from each nationality aspired to professional or business careers. This uniformity contrasts sharply with the wide variation in socio-economic background and reported experiences of discrimination. The Haitians and West Indians reported discrimination two to three times as frequently as did the Cubans. Majorities of both Haitian and West Indian youth reported having been discriminated against and about 20 percent said that their teachers had done so. In contrast, only 5 percent of Cubans in private school reported such incidents; Nicaraguans occupied an intermediate position, with half reporting discrimination and 13 percent reporting discrimination by their teachers.

Unsurprisingly, Haitian and West Indian teenagers were the most likely to agree that there is racial discrimination in the U.S economy and to deny that non-whites have equal opportunities. Interestingly, they were joined in these negative evaluations by private-school Cubans. This result may reflect the greater information and class awareness of the latter group relative to their less privileged Latin counterparts. However, all Cuban students parted company with the rest of the sample in their positive evaluation of the United States. Roughly three-fourths of second-generation Cubans endorsed the view that "the United States is the best country in the world"; only half of Nicaraguans did so and the two mostly black groups took an even less enthusiastic stance.

The results of this survey illuminate with numbers the "race" between generalized career aspirations and the widely different vulnerabilities and resources created by first-generation modes of assimilation. Aspirations are very high for all groups, regardless of origin; however, parental socio-economic background, resources of the co-ethnic community, and experiences of discrimination are very different. These factors influence decisively the outlook of second-generation youth, even at a young age, and are likely to have strong effects on the course of their future assimilation. The importance of these factors is illustrated by the enthusiasm with which children of advantaged immigrants embrace their parents' adopted country, and by the much less sanguine views of those whose situation is more difficult.

A final intriguing fact about today's second generation as revealed by this survey: the best-positioned group (private-school Cubans) is the one least likely to step out of the ethnic circle in inter-personal relationships, while the group in the most disadvantaged position (Haitians) is the most likely to do so. Overall, the three Latin groups overwhelmingly select friends who are also the children of immigrants and who are mostly of the same nationality. Less than half of Haitians and West Indians do the same.

ASSIMILATION AND THE FUTURE

Fifty years ago, the dilemma of the Italian-American youngsters studied by Child consisted of assimilating to the American mainstream and thus sacrificing their parents' cultural heritage versus taking refuge in the ethnic community and forging the challenges of the outside world. In the contemporary context of "segmented assimilation," the alternatives have become less clear. Children of non-white immigrants may not even have the opportunity to gain access to middle-class white society, no matter how acculturated they become. Yet joining those native circles to which they do have access may prove a ticket to permanent subordination and disadvantage. Remaining securely ensconced in their co-ethnic community may, under these circumstances, be not a symptom of escapism but the best strategy for capitalizing on otherwise unavailable moral and material resources. As the experiences of the Punjabi Sikh and Cuban-American students suggest, a strategy of paced, selective assimilation may prove the best course for immigrant minorities. But the extent to which this strategy is possible depends on the history of each group and its specific profile of vulnerabilities and resources.

Alejandro Portes is the John Dewey Professor of Sociology and international Relations at Johns Hopkins University. Min Zhou is an assistant professor of sociology at Louisiana State University.

Reprinted with permission of the authors and *The Public Interest*, No. 116, Summer 1994, pp. 18-33. © 1994 by National Affairs, Inc.

New Immigrants and Refugees in American Schools: Multiple Voices

Despite the tragedy and anguish that many of these students have suffered, educators can do much to help them improve their lives.

Carolyn B. Pryor

Sumil, a 10-year-old girl wearing a Yemeni headscarf, sits *quietly in a small elementary school classroom furnished with four group worktables and a few desks. A paraprofessional, who speaks Arabic and English, offers encouragement to Sumil and the three other students seated at her table. One is Jordanian, one is Iraqi, and another is Bengali. Each has a different workbook to complete. The resource room teacher, Mrs. Bajic, explains that Sumil is entitled to services in her resource room for two hours a day. The rest of the day, Sumil is supposed to be part of a regular 5th grade classroom. Because she feels so overwhelmed in the regular classroom, however, the school officials agreed to let Sumil stay home each afternoon, until she becomes more acclimated to her new country. Sumil had never held a pencil before she emigrated from Yemen to the United States with her mother and younger brother. While Sumil works at her table, Mrs. Bajic gives individualized instruction and encouragement to students from several other cultural and linguistic backgrounds. She says, "We give them freedom. We reduce their stress. God help us!"*

This classroom scene was encountered during a study of how urban schools are addressing the social and emotional needs of highly diverse newcomers. "God help us!" is likely echoed in thousands of classrooms around the globe. Recent dramatic increases in migration have filled urban classrooms in many countries with students from a wide range of cultures (Glenn, 1992; Kaprielian Churchhill, 1994). Although counting the actual number of refugees and displaced persons is a formidable task (United Nations High Commissioner on Refugees [UNHCR], 2000), recent estimates indicate that more than 22 million international refugees and another 30 million internally displaced people are in the world today (Machel, 1996; Yingling, 1999). Millions of other persons cross national boundaries for political or economic reasons, new adventures, or to reunite with family members.

The children who are part of this massive migration create daunting challenges for schools and communities alike (Mupedziswa, 1997; Perkins, 2000). Teachers and school support staff, limited by inadequate resources, must struggle to meet these students' educational, social, and emotional needs (Gopaul-McNichol & Thomas-Presswood, 1996). Even so, this research demonstrates that despite the tragedy and anguish that many of these students have suffered, educators can do much to help them improve their lives.

This article is based on a study of a small school district that recently incorporated a large number of refugees from the former Yugoslavia. Many studies have reported on educators' views about the schooling of immigrants and refugees (e.g., Dentler & Hafner, 1997; McDonnell, 1993). This study followed a postmodern research paradigm, examining multiple perspectives and giving a voice to marginalized populations

(Gergen, 1985). The primary focus was on the voices of immigrant and refugee parents and children, as well as their neighbors, school administrators, and school support staff; teachers' voices were secondary.

The school district is in a small city that has served for decades as a reception center for immigrants to the United States. It is located in southeast Michigan, near Detroit, where factory jobs and low-cost housing are accessible. The two largest immigrant populations in this small city are Eastern European and Arab. More than 24 different languages are spoken in the homes; 14 percent of the district's students are English-as-a-second-language learners. The research team visited schools and agencies in this community for over a year, interviewing 35 recent immigrant and refugee adults, 40 children of immigrants and refugees (from elementary school through high school), 13 established residents, 15 staff, and 10 community leaders. In addition, helping professionals native to Albania, Poland, and Croatia led focus groups for adult English-as-a-second-language students. Forty-one newcomers participated in a native-language discussion of their family's adjustment experiences, and of their children's social, emotional, and academic needs.

Five themes were explored in the study: 1) family well-being and involvement in schools, 2) children's social and emotional adjustment, 3) second-language learning, 4) community support, and 5) conflict management. This article reports the observations and voices heard for each of these themes, and reviews implications for education practice.

Family Well-Being and Involvement in Schools

At the entrances of the district's elementary schools, signs declare "Welcome, Families." In all of the schools, bilingual parents are hired as paraprofessionals to personally greet newly immigrated families, and serve as interpreters, as needed.

School and Community Leaders' Voices. Despite the school's efforts to involve parents, the results are often discouraging. One of the school social workers explained,

> We've tried many times to get the parents to come to meetings, but we've had very little success. We've tried raffling off $50 worth of groceries to the parents who come, but still few show up. Our parents have too many other burdens and responsibilities to be able to get involved in the school. The parents who do have leadership skills may have children in several buildings, and are stretched too thin. We have not had a parent-teacher organization in our district for years. We would like to be able to do more to help these families, but the number of serious problems they are struggling with is enormous. Having bilingual staff at our school is a great asset. On one occasion, staff learned that a student's father had beaten him with a belt. One of our bilingual parapros helped us to understand that the father was doing this to try to keep his son out of trouble.

Also, she helped the parents understand our laws regarding corporal punishment.

A mental health worker from the Arab and Chaldean Community Service Agency confirmed that many immigrant and refugee parents are overwhelmed with personal problems. In order to get Medicaid, at least one parent has to work 40 hours a week. Many of the families are suffering greatly as a consequence of the Persian Gulf war, and some parents are mentally ill and cannot work. Some escaped from Iraq to Saudi Arabia, and were treated very badly there. Many of them panic if they see a police officer.

Parents' Voices. Interviewers asked parents, "Taking all things together, how happy are you with your life as a whole these days?" Less than 20 percent reported that they are completely happy with their lives; over 70 percent said they are somewhat happy. Their stories revealed that many of them are enduring grueling hours of work, at jobs for which they are overqualified, in the hope that their children's lives will be better. These respondents are the ones most likely to say that they miss their homelands and have not found anywhere to turn for help.

The Albanian focus group members explained that due to an initial lack of information about schools, jobs, and housing, parents may settle into an area, only to learn about a place where they would rather live when it was too late to move. For one thing, their children often have become adjusted to the area and do not want to relocate. This leads to conflicts in the family. The focus group leader suggested,

> Once a month, the principals with the largest number of Albanian children should hold a meeting with the parents about their children's performance in school, assisted by an interpreter. The school should create a committee with outstanding Albanians from the community who can serve as parent mentors and liaisons between new Albanian families and their schools.

Children's Voices. Most of the newcomer children interviewed report that they help their parents with their English. They realize their parents' hopes for the future are focused on them, and they feel determined to succeed. Most hold high aspirations. When asked, "What do you think your life will be like when you grow up?," most envision successful roles for themselves in their new country: a singer, a pilot, a Marine, a basketball player, a computer engineer, a computer programmer, a police officer, a lawyer, a medical doctor, a psychiatrist, a teacher, or even President of the United States. Others talk in general terms:

> I will be a good mother. I'll help my kids speak both languages, and take them to visit Bosnia. I want to be a good American, but not like many of the people here. They don't care about what is happening to other people. I don't want to be like that.

Discussion. Refugee families have suffered much and struggle to maintain themselves with dignity in their host country. They continue to face many challenges and difficulties, however. In the United States, recent changes to welfare laws have made it much more difficult for newcomers to receive benefits (Epenshade, Baraka, & Huber, 1997; Padilla, 1998; Social Security Administration, 1997). Immigrants and refugees can get a good start in schools and communities that have a tradition of welcoming newcomers, but the process often involves humiliation, frustration, loneliness, and loss. One way to help both the parents and the schools is by employing bilingual immigrant and refugee parents as professionals (Comer, 1980).

Children's Adjustment

The school buildings in the studied district are old, crowded, and in need of repair; staff do what they can to make them cheerful. In one elementary building, the stairwell is decorated with flags from many lands. Children's appearance and dress reflect various cultures, and provide colorful variety throughout the school. Although most of the children are appropriately involved in learning, signs of stress occasionally appear. One teacher reported that when the school bell rang, a startled Arab refugee girl darted under her desk; she had been conditioned by the air raid drills she had experienced in her homeland.

School Leaders' Voices. Administrators believe they are doing the best they can, with the resources they have, to meet children's needs. Although each building has some bilingual staff, high school students are sometimes called in to serve as interpreters, due to the number of different languages spoken. Each building has a full-time school social worker, but none is bilingual, and cultural differences sometimes emerge. For example, an attendance officer, who visits homes to determine why children are not coming to school, discovered that girls from conservative Arabic families are not allowed to attend schools with boys once they reach puberty. Many of these girls drop out of school, marry, and then enroll in all-female ESL classes.

Parents' Voices. After the Bosnian focus group meeting, a parent came forward and explained,

> My children in school are doing OK. It's not them I'm worried about. It's my sons who are too old for school that don't have a job or anything to do, but sit around and watch TV. What can be done for them?

In the United States, some immigrant parents live in fear that their children will be corrupted by what they believe to be the materialistic and individualistic dominant culture, become alienated from their families, and fall prey to drugs and promiscuity. Their fears are not unfounded, as research shows that the longer that immigrants live in the United States, the worse their physical and mental health becomes (Escobar, 1998; Hernandez & Charney, 1998; Lamberg, 1996; Vega et al., 1998).

One Jordanian American mother stated,

> I tell my son (who is 8 years old) not to use the restroom in school. I tell him he might catch germs there that he could bring home, and make the whole family ill. I really am afraid he may get drugs from other kids in the restroom.

This parent also is concerned about the celebration of Halloween at school, because she believes it emphasizes diabolical themes. Therefore, she keeps her children home on that day.

Children's Voices. Most of the children interviewed are adjusting well to their new country. When asked how happy they are with their lives as a whole, 47 percent said they were completely happy, another 47 percent said they were somewhat happy, 4 percent said they were neither happy nor unhappy, and 2 percent said they were somewhat unhappy. Most children like their school, feel safe at school, think their teachers are kind and helpful, and have friends. The Bosnian refugees said schoolwork is much easier than what they experienced in their home country. A few are very disappointed by the lack of challenging work, but most enjoy the extracurricular activities. One 8-year-old girl was upset by other pupils' bad behavior: "In Ukraine, the principal would make the child sit in the comer all day. Here, the principal just calls the parents, but it doesn't do any good. Nothing changes." Another girl stated, "Teachers are nicer here. They care about you and what you do after school."

Children were asked questions from the "Childhood War Trauma Questionnaire" (Macksoud, 1990) to determine how many have symptoms of post-traumatic stress disorder (PTSD). The children who experienced war trauma display many of the symptoms—50 percent often talk to others about the traumatic events, 15 percent get scared or upset when they talk about it, 26 percent have dreams about the event, 11 percent feel like the event is happening all over again, and 21 percent startle more than before at loud noises or unexpected things.

Most of the younger children from Bosnia do not have vivid memories of living there, but still they greatly miss their extended family members. They had been sent at an early age to other countries where they had temporary refugee status. Many family members were separated and did not know what had happened to their loved ones. Eventually, it became apparent that the Muslims and those from mixed marriages likely never could go home. At that point, they turned to the United States as their only hope.

On the whole, the children were optimistic about their future in America. (In most other countries, refugees have only temporary status and have no hope of ever becoming equals to the native population.) One 18-year-old Bosnian girl became tearful and emotional when asked about the future. She said she was scared about what it holds for her. When asked what they would wish for, many said that they wished they could go back to their homeland and be reunited with their loved ones.

The children and youths interviewed appreciated having someone take time to listen to them. A girl who experienced war trauma stated, "I enjoyed the interview. I was happy to talk about my life, and happy that someone wants to listen. It's nice to know that people care and want to make our adjustment easier." One high school student, when he learned of this project, wrote up an account of his trauma (see "Anel's Trauma").

Anel's Trauma

I am a Bosnian Muslim, and Serbs attacked my neighborhood. The men were separated from the women, and loaded into buses while the terrified women and crying children looked on. Buses designed to hold 50 to 60 persons were loaded with 100–150 persons piled on top of each other. We were taken to schools barricaded with wire, and anyone who tried to escape was killed in front of the children. For two months we were kept there. We were given no food, only a kind of soup like they just washed their hands in. Many of the children died. Then they put the remaining men and boys in livestock cars, and the train carried us off.

For two days we traveled without any food or water. We were piled on top of each other, and could only relieve ourselves in our pants. At one Serbian village where we stopped, [we] could see through the cars' slats and hear soldiers discussing whether to kill us, and where to put the bodies. Then the train moved on. Three hours later it stopped near a forest, and soldiers took us off. Our initial terror gradually dissolved when these Bosnian soldiers took us to a refugee camp.

Discussion. The effects of war on children are horrendous (Boothby, 1994; Kuterovac, Dyregrov, & Stovland, 1994; Machel, 1996). Many immigrant and refugee schoolchildren suffer from post-traumatic stress disorder, and need assistance (Ajdukovic & Ajdukovic, 1993; Deykin, 1999). Children suffering from PTSD can be identified using screening tools. These children often find it helpful to discuss traumatic experiences with caring adults who will actively listen to them. Younger children may benefit from drawing pictures about their experience, and older children can write or dictate their stories. Schools can be a safe place for them to learn and prepare for responsible citizenship.

Language Learning

In the studied school district, children who qualify for bilingual services may leave their classroom for an hour or two a day to receive services in the language resource room. There, the resource room teachers address their various language backgrounds, while teaching the lesson in English. The middle school uses bilingual teachers and paraprofessionals in the regular classrooms, and the high school provides separate English as a second language (ESL) classes. The morning and evening adult education ESL classes are well attended, as the adults understand they need language skills to obtain good jobs.

In a regular 2nd-grade classroom, an Albanian boy who did not speak English was observed struggling through each assignment. By the afternoon he began to cry. A fellow student who spoke Albanian and English took him to the office; he came

back and reported, "He had a headache. They called his mother to come get him." Perhaps the stress of trying to understand what he was supposed to be doing had proved to be too much.

School and Community Leaders' Voices. The recent diversification of language groups has made it necessary for districts to develop a variety of appropriate strategies for teaching English language learners. Some communities are willing and able to support dual language learning, but others are not. Young children can pick up enough English in one or two years to carry on a conversation and understand what is being said. Experts on bilingual education report that it typically takes four to seven years of bilingual education before an English language learner will understand English literature as well as native speakers of English. Persons from cultures with a strong grounding in literacy will be able to acquire English literacy skills more quickly than those from cultures with primarily oral traditions (Pryor, 1998).

One Russian psychologist stated, "When children learn English more quickly than their parents, it can lead to their taking on somewhat of an adult role in the household. Trouble can arise in the future with things like discipline when the parents learn English and the roles switch back." (See Garcia-Preto, 1996, for a similar view.)

Parents' Voices. In the Polish American focus group, parents reported that their main problem is a lack of fluency in English. "This sometimes leads to ridicule, harassment, and embarrassment in the community," said one parent.

Albanian focus group members with school-age children reported that they find the language barrier particularly disturbing, especially in regard to involvement in their children's homework and assistance with school-related problems. "This barrier leads to closed communication with the school and a lack of information from that source," one parent reported. Parents believe that these barriers weaken their role as natural leaders in their children's lives. When asked "If you could have three wishes, what would you wish for?," one woman replied, "To speak better English, for my children to speak [it] too, and for my daughter to come here."

When asked how to improve the schools, Arab American parents suggested that newcomer classrooms be provided to assist those who need them, and that the number of years in which bilingual students have access to the resource room be extended for as long as the child needs the support.

Children's Voices. When asked "Has learning English been hard for you?," 51 percent of the children interviewed replied affirmatively; 20 percent report that their parents do not speak English; and another 25 percent say their parents speak it "a little." In addition, 84 percent of the children state that they help their parents with their English. Children recognize the importance of learning English. When asked about his future, an 11-year-old from Russia stated, "I'll know the language and I'll go to college if I think it will be good, because I'll know English." Children frequently serve as interpreters and spokespersons for their parents, due to their greater language proficiency.

Discussion. Newcomer adults and children need to learn the language of their host culture rapidly in order to have full access to its opportunities. Teaching parents, as well as the children, the host country's language will help to strengthen families and minimize potential conflicts between generations.

Community Support

Due to the low average income level in this city, community services and financial support for schools are far below that of neighboring suburbs. Community and church agencies serve persons from the major ethnic groups. Many of the schools use old buildings that were formerly parochial schools.

School Leaders' Voices. School administrators work with various cultural organizations and religious leaders in the community to ensure that their practices and programs are culturally sensitive. The schools are careful not to serve culturally inappropriate food in the cafeteria, for example. During Ramadan, schools provide a room where fasting Muslim students can congregate and pray. The high school principal stated,

> Sometimes instead of suspending an Arab student, I have offered the family the option of counseling by an iman (the religious leader). We also have donated furniture to the mosque for their Saturday school. During the Gulf War, adults from the community came in and provided supportive help to the children who were most troubled by it.

The school social workers have found the community health workers from the Arab and Chaldean Community Service Agency to be extremely helpful.

Parents' Voices. In the focus group meetings, the Bosnian refugees were the ones feeling most adrift, with little knowledge of how to find community resources and other help. A father of two had come to the focus group eager for help for his family: "I have a degree in psychology in my country, but what good can it do me here? I must work a factory job to support my family, and I don't have the resources to go back to school to earn another degree." As a class assignment, a graduate student spent a Sunday afternoon visiting this man and his family in his home. She was surprised that the family did not know about the city art museum and other cultural attractions. The man stated, "If only there was someone who could help us and show us around, maybe a senior citizen volunteer. There is so much that we need to know, but we don't know where to begin to get help." The graduate student who interviewed this family later reported her experience:

> I was most impressed by the determination of this family to be mainstreamed and adjust at every level to American culture. Their values and integrity have carried them all through much adversity, sadness, and loneliness. They were so humble, with such dignity. They were so warm and friendly to a total stranger. We laughed and joked; it was such a special experience.

Children's Voices. Some of the children underwent shock when they first arrived in their urban environment, because it is not what they had imagined it would be from movies and television. Typically, they all found things they liked about their new country, but they also found things they greatly missed from their home countries.

> I like the opportunities this country gives to young people. I like it that if you want something bad enough, you can get it through education. You have a choice of going to school and actually becoming something…. I miss the way Bosnia was. The people there were more open to different experiences. People you did not know were friendly people. There was this warm feeling.

Conflict Management

As in other schools across America, the increased threat of violence in society has taken its toll on the students in this district. All but the front doors of school buildings are locked. In the high school, everyone must pass through metal detectors and by a security guard. In the halls, posters stressing intergroup harmony abound: "We love peace." "We all smile in the same language." "Let's be friends." "We celebrate our differences." Posters in an elementary school list "Steps To Be Part of the Peace Movement." Students also can submit requests for mediation.

School Leaders' Voices. One elementary principal described how he tries to help families develop a strong identification with the child's home room and school. Another elementary school set up an Ambassadors of Peace program, whereby community leaders from different cultures speak in classrooms about ways children and adults can promote peace.

In each elementary building, the school social workers and counselors train and supervise teams of 10-13 peer mediators. Pupils experiencing a conflict fill out a request for mediation, and are seen by a pair of peer mediators the next day. The social workers or counselors let the mediators use their office for the mediation, while they oversee the process from the periphery. Pupils are using the process regularly, and the social workers believe it helps students from all backgrounds to communicate effectively and solve interpersonal problems on their own.

Parents' Voices. Established residents who were recommended by the school social workers as representative of the school community at large, including a school secretary and a custodian, were interviewed. They expressed a variety of reactions to the influx of newcomers. One of the established residents said, "I enjoy living in a community with so much diversity. I believe we are seeing here what America will be experiencing in the next 15 to 20 years. We chose to live here so that our children could have this experience." As her children are getting older, however, she is becoming worried that their academic progress may suffer because so much time and energy goes toward the immense needs of the immigrant students. Another parent resented the drain that immigrant and refugee children put on the school, when their parents are not able to contribute significantly to the tax base for the community. One mother stated that the influx of Arabs into her neighborhood made her and her children feel like outsiders. Another said she would move, but added that it was too difficult to find affordable housing elsewhere.

Established residents offered suggestions on how to improve the schools. They wanted more services in schools, such as tutoring, counseling, social skills training, drug and sex refusal skills training, and training in helping people learn to accept and respect others.

Children's Voices. One 16-year-old stated,

> The thing I like about the school is it is so diverse. People come from all different countries. I don't think I would be comfortable going to a school with just one or two races. I went to a school like that in Pennsylvania before we moved here. It was a school that had black and white, some Spanish, some people from Russia, some Arab people. It wasn't like this. There, we were separated. During classes we were friends, but during lunch we were all separated. Here, people [are] from all over the place; you can't really separate them. You want to be friends with everybody, because you want to learn about their country and their culture. I like the fact that the teachers are OK with having to work with kids from all over the place. They don't give anybody a hard time. You have to deal with everybody. I like that. Everybody here gets along. It's amazing. You have people from 30 different countries, and everybody gets along.

When asked what helps people here get along, this student replied,

> I think the teams, like basketball games. We have clubs and councils and people from everywhere come to those clubs and councils, and then you have to work together to make something. Like in a game, they have to work together and put aside their differences in order to win. And in a council, in order for us to make a difference or help the school or help the community, we have to work together.

In the high school, students on the Multicultural Council successfully petitioned the school board to establish a peace education course. Students in the course discuss current issues related to peace and justice in the world at large and in their own community. They study the teachings of historical figures who have committed their lives to peace. They established a peace garden and distributed a booklet celebrating the local diversity. They hung a large banner in the school hallway proclaiming, "We are fighting injustice…. Is there anything else worth fighting about?" The students' own experiences taught them not to turn a blind eye to society's problems, but rather to tackle oppression and injustice head-on through nonviolent activism. To this end, they launched a statewide campaign to have a peace studies curriculum in every school. Their sponsor stated, "We try to get people together and to learn about each other. If we learn about each other, it's easier for us to live together."

Discussion. Although schools and communities may aspire to celebrate diversity, some values and views are bound to clash (Clabaugh, 2000; Mayadas & Illiott, 1992; Pryor, 1992a). Schoolwide programs that teach young children to resolve problems by listening to each other's point of view, understanding how each feels, and selecting mutually agreeable solutions lay the groundwork for future cooperation. Immigrant and refugee youths are becoming strong advocates for peace education in all schools.

Implications for Educational Practice: Classroom, School, and District

Based on the voices heard in this study, several recommendations for educators emerged:

Classroom Strategies. Listen to newcomers and help them tell their stories. The children and adults interviewed found that sharing their stories was enjoyable, cathartic, and affirming. Personal stories of immigrants and refugees are also educational and beneficial for other children to hear. (For suggestions on eliciting and sharing valuable stories, using guided imagery, see Allan & Toffoli, 1989.) Storytelling and listening also can be a schoolwide project.

Honor the child's concept of family and cultural traditions. Immigrant and refugee children greatly miss their homeland and the relatives left behind. Teachers can help children deal with homesickness by encouraging them to keep in touch with living extended family members, or to preserve their memories of those who died. Teachers also can incorporate celebrations and lessons about various cultures that will help newcomers feel valued and at home. (See resource list.)

Building-wide Strategies. Welcome all families into the educational process. Educators need to recognize the tremendous time and economic pressures the parents are under, their difficulty learning a second language, their problems with stress, and their lack of knowledge about how to be involved effectively with schools. Parents' suggestions for mentors and parent-involvement orientation programs in the newcomer parents' native language should be valued.

Newcomer parents want to be involved in their child's education in a comfortable context. By collaborating with helping professionals who are native-language speakers and know the newcomers' culture, educators can find out about parents' hopes, fears, values, and aspirations (National Coalition of Advocates for Students, 1993). A careful needs assessment should be conducted. The Success for All Foundation's Family Support Team Model, which uses incremental steps to bring alienated parents into schools, can be adapted effectively for newcomer parents (Kelen, 1999).

Develop School-to-School Partnerships. A middle school in the studied district has a cultural exchange day with middle school students from an affluent suburban school district. The suburban students help newcomers write their stories and publish them in a booklet. Partnerships between schools with refugee students and those without can provide valuable connections and mutual learning opportunities (Pryor, 1992b). Published works by and about refugee children can be used to prepare students for this experience when such linkages are not possible. (See resource list.)

District-wide Strategies. School districts can take steps to promote family literacy programs, and help immigrant families maintain their native languages. Teaching parents, and their children, the host country's language will help to strengthen families and minimize potential conflicts between generations. Using native language instruction keeps newcomer students from falling behind academically (National Clearinghouse for Bilingual Education, 1996). Some students need full-time intensive support initially, ideally in newcomer "reception" classrooms (Friedlander, 1991). Ongoing language support in a resource room, or through a bilingual classroom assistant, should be provided for as long as a child needs it. Maintaining the native language reinforces family bonds. It keeps children connected with extended family members, thereby reducing risks to their physical and mental health (Cummins, 2000).

Pay attention to newcomers' pleas that something be done to help their older children. Childhood educators should be prepared to direct parents with older children to persons in the community who can respond to their concerns. Nearby community colleges and universities may be sources of help.

Immigrant and refugee parents want to know how to gain access to cultural, recreational, employment, medical, counseling, transportation, shopping, and higher education opportunities. To improve delivery of culturally and linguistically appropriate services, develop a network of community agencies and schools serving immigrant and refugee families. By working with others, school personnel can promote more services for parents, connect families with existing resources, and get new ideas for educating their students. Community volunteers also should be recruited to assist in the acculturation of newcomer families and effectively link them to schools, cultural programs, and other community resources. Regional networks of services need to be established. Urban districts alone cannot be expected to do the task of educating immigrants and refugees.

Promote Diversity Appreciation, Conflict Resolution, and Peace Education in All Schools. A strong commitment to celebrating differences and solving conflicts peacefully can help students from a wide variety of cultures work and play in harmony (National Coalition of Advocates for Students, 1994). Newcomer students can be among the most committed to promoting peace education. When given support by teachers, administrators, and the school board, they can turn ideas into action. Many resources are available to help schools develop diversity appreciation and conflict management programs (see list); the newcomer students themselves are among the most important resources.

Summary

In conclusion, this research study, with its postmodern approach, yielded many useful perspectives. While immigrant and refugee students need to learn from us (McDonnell, 1993), they also have much to teach us about other countries, customs, and peoples. They can inspire us to strengthen family ties, overcome tragic losses, and endure hardships for the sake of a better future. They can join with us to improve schools and communities. The potential impact of this experience is captured well in the words of a peace studies teacher:

> I was sitting in cafés in my suburban hometown reading about multiculturalism but not applying it to anything real. But there is something about sitting across the table from a teen-aged war refugee that changes your life forever. Working here is the ultimate expression for the kind of work I want to do. My students have taught me they don't want buck-passing. They want to face life head-on.

The experiences of those who have worked successfully with immigrants and refugees show that much can be done with caring, commitment, and a willingness to listen and respond. Children, for the most part, are resilient, and teachers can make a tremendous difference in their lives. Pupils like Sumil and teachers like Mrs. Bajic may have their prayers answered when they listen to each other, engage the support of their community, and together promote learning and peace.

References

Ajdukovic, M., & Ajdukovic, D. (1993). Psychological well-being of refugee children. *Child Abuse & Neglect*, 15, 843–854.

Allan, J., & Toffoli, G. (1989). *Guided imagery: Group guidance for ESL students*. Toronto: Lungus.

Boothby, N. (1994). Trauma and violence among refugee children. In A. Marsella, J. Bornemann, S. Ekblad, & J. Orley (Eds.), *Amidst peril and pain: The mental health and well-being of the world's refugees* (pp. 239–259). Washington, DC: American Psychological Association.

Clabaugh, G. K. (2000). Teaching the new immigrants: How "multicultural" an educator are you prepared to be? *Educational Horizons*, 78, 55–57.

Comer, J. P. (1980). *School power: Implications of an intervention project*. New York: Free Press.

Cummins, J. (2000, April 6). *Brave new schools. District-wide inservice training program*. Dearborn, MI: Dearborn Public Schools.

Dentler, R. A., & Hafner, A. L. (1997). *Hosting newcomers: Structuring educational opportunities for immigrant children*. New York: Teachers College Press.

Deykin, E. Y. (1999). Posttraumatic stress disorder in childhood and adolescence: A review. *Medscape Mental Health, 4*(4). Available http://psychiatry.medscape.com

Epenshade, T. J., Baraka, J. L., & Huber, G. A. (1997). Implications of the 1996 welfare and immigration reform acts for United States immigration. *Population and Immigration Review, 23*, 769–801.

Escobar, J. 1. (1998). Immigration and mental health: Why are immigrants better off? *Archives of General Psychiatry, 55*, 781–782.

Friedlander, M. (1991). *The newcomer program: Helping immigrant students succeed in U.S. schools*. Washington, DC: National Clearinghouse for Bilingual Education.

Garcia-Preto, N. (1996). Puerto Rican families. In M. McGoldrick, J. Giordano, & J. K. Pearce (Eds.), *Ethnicity & family therapy* (2nd ed., pp. 183–199). New York: Guilford.

Gergen, K. J. (1985). The social constructionist movement in modern psychology. *American Psychologist, 49*, 266–275.

Glenn, C. L. (1992). Educating the children of immigrants. *Phi Delta Kappan, 73*, 404–408.

Gopaul-McNichol, S., & Thomas-Presswood, T. (1996). *Working with linguistically and culturally different children: Innovative clinical and educational approaches*. Boston: Allyn & Bacon.

Hernandez, D. J., & Charney, E. (Eds.). (1998). *From generation to generation: The health and well-being of children in immigrant families*. Washington, DC: National Academy Press.

Kaprielian-Churchhill, I. (1994). *The pulse of the world: Refugees in our schools*. Toronto: OIEE Press.

Kelen, J. (1999, October). *Voices of immigrant children: Innovations for school social workers and counselors*. Paper presented at the Western Alliances of School Social Work Organizations 6th Annual Conference, Jackson Hole, WY.

Kuterovac, G., Dyregrov, A., & Stovland, R. (1994). Children in war: A silent majority under stress. *British Journal of Medical Psychology, 67*, 363–375.

Lamberg, L. (1996). Nationwide study of health and coping among immigrant children and families. *Journal of the American Medical Association, 276*, 1455–1456.

Machel, G. (1996). *Impact of armed conflict on children*. New York: UN/UNICEF. Full text available at www.unicef.org/graca/

Macksoud, M. (1990). *Childhood war trauma questionnaire*. New York: Project on Children and War, Center for the Study of Human Rights, Columbia University.

Mayadas, N. S., & Illiott, D. (1992). Integration and xenophobia: An inherent conflict in international migration. In A. S. Ryan (Ed.), *Social work with immigrants and refugees* (pp. 47–62). New York: Haworth.

McDonnell, L. M. (1993). *Newcomers in American schools: Meeting the educational needs of immigrant youth*. Santa Monica, CA: RAND (ERIC Document Reproduction Service No. ED 362 589).

Mupedziswa, R. (1997). Social work with refugees: The growing international crisis. In M. Hokenstadt & J. Midgley (Eds.), *Issues in international social work* (pp. 110–124). Washington, DC: NASW Press.

National Clearinghouse for Bilingual Education. (1996). *Why is it important to maintain the native language?* Available from http://www.ncbe.gwu.edu

National Coalition of Advocates for Students. (1993). *Achieving the dream: How communities and schools can improve education for immigrant students*. Boston: Author.

National Coalition of Advocates for Students. (1994). *Delivering on the promise: Positive practices for immigrant students*. Boston: Author.

Padilla, Y. C. (1998). Immigrant policy: Issues for social work practice. *Social Work, 42*, 595–606.

Perkins, L. M. (2000). The new immigrants and education: Challenges and issues. *Educational Horizons, 78*, 67–71.

Pryor, C. B., with A. Ginn-Clark, K. Kostrzewa, D. Asher, R. Palmer, & M. Gaba. (1998). *Integrating immigrant and refugee children into urban schools*. Detroit, MI: Wayne State University, Skillman Center for Children, Occasional Paper.

Pryor, C. B. (1992a). Building international relations for children through sister schools. *Phi Delta Kappan, 73*, 399–403.

Pryor, C. B. (1992b). Integrating immigrants into American schools. *Social Work in Education, 14*, 153–159.

Social Security Administration. (1997). *Impact of welfare reform on qualified aliens*. Retrieved from http://www.ssa.gov

United Nations High Commissioner on Refugees. (2000, April). Statistics. Retrieved from www.unhcr.ch/statist/ main htm

Vega, W. A., Kolody, B., Aguilar-Gaxiola, S., Alderete, E., Catalano, R., & Caraveoo-Anduaga, J. (1998). Lifetime prevalence of DSM-III-R psychiatric disorders among urban and rural Mexican Americans in California. *Archives of General Psychiatry, 55*, 771–782.

Yingling, P. (1999). Chair's report (introduction to special issue on refugees). *Peace and Freedom: Magazine of the Women's International League for Peace and Freedom, 49* (4), 3.

Acknowledgments

Support for this research was provided by a grant from the Hewlett Foundation, through the Program for Mediating Theory and Democratic Systems, Wayne State University. Dr. Marija Dixon, a psychotherapist who works with refugees, proposed the collaborative research project on which this article is based, helped with the research design and literature review, and led the Bosnian focus group session. Many other professionals donated time to the project, and more than 60 graduate students assisted with the data collection. Thanks also go to Navaz Bhavnagri for encouraging the submission of this article to *Childhood Education* and for providing helpful editorial suggestions. Above all, thanks go to the children, youth, and adults who told us their stories and gave us ideas for improving our schools and communities.

Resources

Classroom Strategies

Stories By and About Immigrant and Refugee Children

Anti-Defamation League of B'nai B'rith, http://www.adl.org (See section on children's stories.)

Ashabranner, B., & Ashabranner, M. (1987). *Into a strange land*. New York: Dodd. (True experiences of Southeast Asian refugees, written for a teenager audience.)

Criddle, J. K., & Teeda, B. M. (1987). *To destroy you is no loss: The odyssey of a Cambodian family*. New York: Little, Brown/Atlantic Monthly. (grades 10–12)

Marx, T., & Karp, C. (2000). *One boy from Kosovo*. New York: Harper for Children. (grades 5–8)

UNICEF. (1994). *I dream of peace: Images of war by children of former Yugoslavia*. New York: HarperCollins.

Helping Children Recover From Trauma and Loss

International Save the Children Foundation. *Promoting psychosocial well-being among children affected by armed conflict and displacement: Principles and approaches*. Retrieved 4/9/00 from http://www.savechildren.or.jp/alliance/confl5.html

Multicultural Families and Traditions

Arab World & Islamic Resources and School Services, 2137 Rose St., Berkeley, CA 94709; 510-704-0517.

Birmingham Public Schools-Detroit Interfaith Round Table. (1997). *A resource guide about religion* (3rd ed.). Birmingham, MI: Birmingham Public Schools.

Michigan State University Extension Multicultural Resource Guide (updated annually). Copies may be ordered through pizanad@msue.msu.edu, or by calling 517-265-5304.

Building-wide Strategies

Multicultural Family Involvement

National Coalition of Advocates for Students. (1988). *New voices: Immigrant students in U.S. public schools*. Boston: Author.

Parents for Unity. www.4children.org/news/50001dre.htm

Success for All Foundation, 200 West Towsontown Blvd., Baltimore, MD 21204-5200; 800-548-4998. www.successforall.net

School-to-School Partnerships

School-to-school Connections Bulletin Board, for Educators. www.askasia.org/for_educators/school_to_school_connection/bulletin_board/list.cgi

District-wide Strategies

Culturally and Linguistically Appropriate Community Services

Center for Multicultural Human Services, 701 West Broad Street, Suite 305, Falls Church, VA 22046; 703-533-3302. http://www.cmhsweb.org

Kretzmann, J. P., &McKnight, J. L. (1993). *Building communities from the inside out: A path toward finding and mobilizing a community's assets*. Chicago: ACTA Publications.

Lipson, J. G., Dibble. S. L., & Minarik, P. A. (Eds.). (1996). *Culture & nursing care: A pocket guide*. San Francisco: University of California/San Francisco Nursing Press.

Family Literacy Programs and Bilingual Education

Center for Applied Linguistics. http://www.cal.org/pubs/ncrepubs.htm

National Clearinghouse for Bilingual Education. http://www.ncbe.gwu.edu

Office of Bilingual Education and Minority Language Affairs. http://www.ed.gov/offices/OBEMLA

Diversity Appreciation, Conflict Resolution and Peace Education

Anti-Defamation League of B'nai B'rith. 212-490-2525. A World of Difference Institute, 823 United Nations Plaza, New York, NY 10017; 212-967-0779. Free catalogue of resources to promote diversity and tolerance: http://www.adl.org

Center for Peace and Conflict Studies, Wayne State University. http://www.pcs.wayne.edu

Children's Creative Response to Conflict, Box 271, Nyack, NY 10960 USA; 914-353-1796.

Educators for Social Responsibility. www.esrnational.org

Facing History and Ourselves. http://www.facing.org

Grace Contrino Abrams Peace Education Foundation. http://www.peaceed.org

National Coalition of Advocates for Students. (1994). *Looking for America, Volumes I & II*. Boston: Author.

National Conference for Community and Justice. http://www.nccj.org

National Conflict Resolution Education Network. http://www.crenet.org

National School Safety Center. http://www.nsscl.org

Carolyn B. Pryor is Associate Professor Emeritus, Wayne State Universtity, Detroit, Michigan.

From *Childhood Education,* Annual Theme 2001, pp. 275-283. Reprinted by permission of Carolyn B. Pryor and the Association for Childhood Education International. © 2001.

Surveying the Backgrounds of Immigration Scholars: A Report

By Rubén G. Rumbaut

Who studies immigration in the United States? Where do they come from? In 1998 the International Migration Program of the Social Science Research Council sponsored the National Survey of Immigration Scholars, a project which I designed and carried out while at the Russell Sage Foundation. We mailed a survey in early 1998 to 1,189 scholars in immigration studies; the list was drawn from the lists of members of formal professional organizations in immigration within the disciplines of history, anthropology, political science and sociology. Recent applicants for fellowships in the SSRC's International Migration Program were also queried. A total of 753 completed forms were returned (of 411 members of the Immigration and Ethnic History Society who were surveyed, 282 or 69% responded; 61% of 385 members of the American Sociological Association's International Migration Section responded; and 64% of the 120 surveyed from the anthropologists' Committee on Refugees and Immigrants responded). The resulting sample consisted of immigration scholars not only in a wide range of disciplines but at all stages in their careers. More scholars had earned their highest degree in sociology (33%) than in any other discipline; they were closely followed by history (28%), anthropology (12%), and political science and economics (9%). Other researchers had doctoral training in psychology, education, public health, urban planning, public policy, area studies, ethnic studies, and other disciplines. The survey offered some interesting answers.

Table 1 provides a profile of the characteristics of these immigration scholars, cross-tabulated by when they earned their highest degree (a doctorate in 90% of the cases). By generations in the United States, almost half (48%) of the total are of immigrant stock themselves; that is, 30% are foreign-born (first-generation immigrants), and 18% are U.S.-born children of immigrants (second-generation). By comparison, 10% of the U.S. population generally are foreign-born, and 10% are second-generation. Of the immigration scholars, another 29% are third-generation, having one or more foreign-born grandparents, while less than a fourth (23%) reported no foreign-born grandparents (fourth-generation or more).

There were more than 150 different responses to the question on ethno-national self-identity; Table 1 reports these only in aggregate form. About one-tenth (12%) reported an Asian ethnicity or national origin, mostly Chinese, Korean, Japanese, Filipino, and Indian. Another tenth (10%) were of Latin American or Caribbean origin, mainly Mexicans, Cubans, Puerto Ricans, and Jamaicans, although 3% claimed a "Hispanic" or "Latino" pan-ethnic identity. More numerous (over 40%) were scholars of European origin, mainly Irish, German, Italian, and Polish; 100 (13%) reported they were Jewish (of varying origins). A fifth of the sample (21%) claimed a plain "American" or "white" identity; the remaining 8% indicated various kinds of mixed ethnicity or gave other responses.

This group of scholars is relatively young. A third (34%) had earned their highest degree in 1995 or after, and another 27% got their degree between 1985 and 1994. Over half got their doctorates in the 1990s. Only 7% had earned their degrees before 1965, with 17% in the 1965–74 decade, and 16% during 1975–84. By professional status, 21% were full professors. Substantial numbers were advanced graduate students or scholars employed in research, administrative, or other positions; 5% were retired.

The immigration field has been transformed in various ways over the past few decades. There has been a dramatic reversal in the proportion of male and female researchers. Among scholars who had earned their degrees before 1965, 92% were men and only 8% were women; but the proportion of women has grown consistently, so that among the youngest cohort of scholars, 62% are women

Table 1.

Characteristics of Immigration Scholars, by Year They Received Their Ph.D. or Highest Degree

Characteristics	Discipline of Highest Degree					
	Pre-1965	1965-74	1975-84	1985-94	Post-1995	Total
(% within columns)	(N=52)	(N=127)	(N=119)	(N=200)	(N=255)	(N=753)
Gender:						
Female	7.7	26.0	37.8	57.0	62.4	47.1
Male	92.3	74.0	62.2	43.0	37.6	52.9
Generation:						
(Foreign-born) First	17.3	18.9	25.2	36.0	34.9	29.7
(U.S.-born) Second	36.5	16.5	16.0	13.5	19.6	18.1
Third	30.8	37.8	37.0	29.5	19.6	28.8
Fourth+	15.4	26.8	21.8	21.0	25.9	23.4
Ethnicity or national origin of researcher:						
Asian	-	4.7	7.6	14.5	17.3	11.7
Latin Am., Caribbean	-	3.9	7.6	14.0	12.9	10.0
African	-	0.8	2.5	4.5	3.1	2.8
Jewish	25.0	15.0	15.1	11.0	11.0	13.3
Irish	9.6	11.8	8.4	4.5	10.2	8.6
Other European	21.2	33.9	26.9	22.5	15.3	22.6
"American," white	26.9	22.0	21.0	19.0	20.0	20.7
Mixed, other	17.3	7.9	10.9	10.0	10.2	10.4
Current position:						
Professor	44.2	60.6	37.0	7.0	-	21.0
Associate Professor	-	8.7	21.8	23.0	0.4	11.2
Assistant Professor	-	-	1.7	26.5	15.7	12.6
Instructor	15.4	1.6	5.0	5.0	11.0	7.2
Research	-	12.6	12.6	11.5	12.2	11.3
Student, other	-	1.6	3.4	11.5	53.7	22.0
Administrative, other	1.9	7.1	15.1	14.0	7.1	9.8
Retired	38.5	7.9	3.4	1.5	-	4.9
Immigration-related dissertation:						
Yes	28.1	25.7	43.7	58.2	77.2	55.4
No	71.9	74.3	56.3	41.8	22.8	44.6

NOTE: Figures are column percentages, i.e., within "year of Ph.D."; for each variable, columns add up to 100%.

and 38% are men. Generational changes also have taken place, roughly paralleling the larger national patterns of immigration to the United States in this century. There has been a sharp increase in the proportion of first-generation immigrants, basically doubling from the 18% or so who earned their degrees before 1975 to the 36% or so who have gotten their degrees since 1985. These generational patterns, in turn, are reflected in the changing ethnic composition of immigration researchers. Until the early 1980s, the percent of these scholars who were of Asian, African, Latin American or Caribbean origin was minuscule: virtually none among those who earned their doctorates before 1965, merely single-digit percentages among degree recipients in the 1975–84 decade. But those proportions have climbed along with immigration, especially among Asian-origin scholars, who collectively made up 17% of the most recent degree recipients, and Latin-origin scholars, who make up another 13%. By contrast, the proportion of Jewish scholars has dropped from 25% to 11% over time, as has that of scholars of other European ethnicities.

These changes by gender, generation, and ethnicity, in turn, have been accompanied by a notable shift in research foci. Particularly remarkable is the change in the proportion of scholars whose dissertation research was related to immigration. Among scholars who earned their highest degree before 1975—during an era when immigration had not re-emerged as a significant public issue—only about a fourth wrote immigration-related dissertations, especially in history; but among younger scholars who have earned their degrees since 1995, that proportion has tripled to 77%. The patterns point to a heightened degree of specialization in the immigration field in graduate school, in contrast to older scholars who appear to have switched to immigration research after having first focused on other topics.

Three out of four (77%) indicated that they specialized in a particular immigrant or ethnic group. By cross-tabulating their own ethnicity with that of the groups they study, it is possible to classify the scholars, at least preliminarily, as ethnic "insiders" vs. "outsiders," that is, as members or non-members of the ethnic groups which they research (see Robert Merton's classic discussion in "Insiders and Outsiders: A Chapter in the Sociology of Knowledge," American Journal of Sociology 77[1972]: 9–47; and Herbert Gans, "Toward a Reconciliation of 'Assimilation' and 'Pluralism,'" International Migration Review 31[1997]: 875–892). By this measure, 37% of the sample were classified as insiders, 39% as outsiders, and the remaining 23% of the cases did not focus on particular ethno-national groups (hence are also non-insiders).

There has clearly been a change in the ethnicity or national origin of the groups that are now the focus of research attention. Among scholars who earned their degrees before 1975, only about a fifth focus on immigrants from Asia, Latin America or the Caribbean, compared to 38% of those who got their doctorates during 1975–84, 48% of the 1985–94 cohort, and 57% of the most recent degree recipients. At the same time, the proportion focusing research attention on European-origin groups has declined over time. Not surprisingly, these changes have combined to increase the proportion of ethnic "insiders" among immigration scholars from 25% among the

older cohort with pre-1965 doctorates to about 40% among younger cohorts with post-1985 degrees.

Table 2 provides a breakdown of key social and professional characteristics by the major disciplines surveyed: history, sociology, anthropology, and political science and economics (combined because of their smaller sample size and commonality of patterns), and all other social sciences. First, there are significant disciplinary contrasts by gender. Males comprise almost two-thirds of the historians (65%) and the majority of the political scientists and economists (55%), while females are in the majority among the anthropologists (57%). The sociologists break down exactly even by gender. Generational differences by discipline are even more pronounced. There are more foreign-born (first-generation) scholars of immigration in sociology (42%) than in any other discipline, and fewest among the historians, only 14% of whom are immigrants themselves. By contrast, far more historians are third-generation scholars (45%) than is the case among any of the other disciplines, with sociologists having the fewest members of the third generation (18%). Perhaps, one might surmise, taking a page from Marcus Lee Hansen, the sociologists' grandchildren will grow up to become historians!

As would be expected, there are significant differences among disciplines in ethnic composition as well. Among sociologists of immigration, 35% are of Asian, Latin American or Caribbean backgrounds, compared to only about a tenth of the historians and anthropologists, and a fourth of the political scientists and economists. Jewish scholars and others of European ancestry predominate among historians, while scholars who identify as plain "Americans" or "whites" prevail proportionately among the anthropologists, political scientists and economists. These patterns, in turn, are partially reflected in the ethnicity of the groups of these scholars' current research interest. Thus, among the sociologists, 60% report that they focus on Asian, Latin American and Caribbean groups in their research, as do 66% of the anthropologists, whereas relatively few historians focus on any of these populations. Instead, historians of immigration look back to the earlier waves of mass immigration from Europe, with over 60% among them focusing on European-origin groups in their scholarship. That is a far greater proportion than is found among other social scientists, who pay very little attention to Europeans in the contemporary U.S. immigration context. Indeed, by far the highest proportion of ethnic "insiders" is found among the historians (55%), compared to 33% among the sociologists, and about 20% among the anthropologists, political scientists and economists.

Still, a breakdown of "insiders" and "outsiders" among immigration researchers—as classified above in the context of individuals' ethnic identity and research interest—shows a pattern of decreasing insiderness with successive generations. That is, among foreign-born scholars 50% were classified as insiders, as were 48% of the second generation, 31% of the third generation, and 19% of fourth or higher gener-

Table 2.

Characteristics of Immigration Scholars, by Discipline of Ph.D. or Highest Degree

Characteristics (% within columns)	Discipline of Highest Degree					
	History (N=207)	Sociology (N=246)	Anthropology (N=93)	Pol. Sc. Econ. (N=66)	All others (N=141)	Total (N=753)
Gender:						
Female	35.3	50.0	57.0	45.5	53.9	47.1
Male	64.7	50.0	43.0	54.5	46.1	52.9
Generation:						
(Foreign-born) 1st	14.0	41.9	23.7	33.3	34.0	29.7
(U.S.-born) 2nd	22.2	15.0	14.0	24.2	17.0	18.1
3rd	45.4	18.3	34.4	22.7	22.0	28.8
4th+	18.4	24.8	28.0	19.7	27.0	23.4
Researcher's ethnicity or national origin:						
Asian	6.8	17.1	7.5	12.1	12.1	11.7
Latin Am., Carib.	3.9	16.7	4.3	13.6	9.2	10.0
African	2.4	2.0	5.4	4.5	2.1	2.8
Jewish	19.3	8.5	12.9	13.6	12.8	13.3
Irish	14.0	5.7	5.4	4.5	9.9	8.6
Other European	33.3	16.3	19.4	9.1	26.2	22.6
"American," white	13.0	20.3	30.1	28.8	22.7	20.7
Mixed, other	7.2	13.4	15.1	13.6	5.0	10.4
Ethnicity of group under research:						
Asian	7.7	26.0	37.6	9.1	26.2	21.0
Latin Am., Carib.	6.8	33.7	28.0	25.8	19.9	22.3
African	3.9	3.3	17.2	6.1	5.0	5.7
Jewish	12.6	2.4	3.2	3.0	6.4	6.1
Irish	12.6	0.8	1.1	-	3.5	4.5
Other European	36.7	6.5	4.3	3.0	21.3	17.0
Other, or N.A.	19.8	27.2	8.6	53.0	17.7	23.4
Insider/outsider ethnicity of researcher:						
Insider	54.6	33.3	19.4	21.2	37.6	37.2
Outsider	25.6	39.4	72.0	25.8	44.7	39.4
N.A. or N.D.	19.8	27.3	8.6	53.0	17.7	23.4

NOTE: Figures are column percentages, i.e., within "discipline"; for each variable, columns add up to 100%.

ations. In general, except for the historians, the more distant the scholars from the time of immigration, the greater the proportion of ethnic outsiders. The decisive break appears to occur at the third (and higher) generations; the difference between first- and second-generation scholars in the proportion of insiders is small and not significant.

The proportion of insiders and outsiders also varies with the main topics of current or planned immigration research. Low insiderness is seen in political and economic research, in the mostly anthropological subjects such as refugee issues, transnationalism and diasporas, and also in education, religion, and health. The highest proportion of co-ethnic insiders were found among those scholars whose research focuses on gender and immigrant women, identity, media and popular culture. Intermediate between these are research topics concerning generations, children of immigrants, family, social mobility and stratification, chosen mostly by sociologists and historians.

The field of immigration studies will be advanced, among other things, through our knowledge of its social bases. There is value in making immigration research itself the object of systematic and reflexive scrutiny, and analyzing it from the vantage point of the sociology of knowledge. Unlike the nascent scholarship on immigration at the turn of the past century, the present era has seen many immigrants themselves become leading scholars of immigration in certain disciplines, while children and especially grandchildren of immigrants are prominent immigration scholars in others. The finding that almost half of today's immigration scholars are themselves of immigrant stock—including the majority of the sociologists, and over a third of the historians—underscores the profound impact of immigration on the field itself. Simply put, immigration is producing many of the scholars who study it and who will tell its story.

Rubén G. Rumbaut is Professor of Sociology at Michigan State University. He has written a longer discussion of the survey, with additional data and tables: "Immigration Research in the United States: Social Origins and Future Orientations," American Behavioral Scientist 42 (1999): 1285–1301. *A revised version of that article will appear in late 2000 in the volume* Immigration Research for a New Century: Multidisciplinary Perspectives *(Russell Sage), edited by Prof. Rumbaut, Nancy Foner and Steven J. Gold.*

Following the Chain: New Insights into Migration

By Jon Gjerde

In a field that regularly utilizes metaphors, "chain migration" is a metaphor that is both one of the most useful, and yet most overused, by scholars of immigration and ethnicity in the United States. As far as I can tell, the term was coined in 1964 with the publication of John and Leatrice McDonald's study of migration and social networks in the formation of ethnic communities. Since then scholars have built upon the metaphor. Two scholars of Italian migration to North America, for example, have entitled their work, "Forging the Chain" and "Inside the Chain," whereas a study of Indochinese refugees has been called "Links in a Chain." And scholars in general, as I shall point out below, have sought ways to preserve use of the metaphor, yet make it a more accurate representation of human migration behavior.

"Chain migration," then, is not a cute turn of phrase, but rather a useful concept in understanding the behavior of migrants. Simply put, a chain migration occurs when a linkage or "chain" develops that connects the migrants' point of origin to their destination. Initial migrants who move to a new location initiate the process. Once they establish a foothold, these pioneers assist subsequent migrants by sending information and capital home. This in turn encourages further migration from the originating area to the new colony and a migration chain is thus forged. Once migrants from specific locations in the sending area are linked to distinct destinations, migrants move into what scholars term "migration fields," or destinations in specific areas. Scholars have contended that chain migrations are especially common in long-distance international migrations because reliable information about possible destinations is less available and migrants tend to rely to an even greater degree on family and friends.

Significantly, chain migration is a process that has been identified in a variety of migration experiences by scholars in a range of disciplines. Although this overview will focus on international migration, it bears emphasizing that the chain migration concept has also been critical in understanding long-distance internal migration. African American migrants in the Great Migration from the South in the twentieth century were often part of a migration chain.

Because there has been so much research using the concept of chain migration, I am able to focus only on a few representative works. Hence this discussion can at best be suggestive of chain migration studies as a whole. I will outline the work of a few historians, geographers, and anthropologists on topics of international migration to destinations in North and South America.

Two exemplary studies of the European migration to North America published in the 1980s are historian Walter D. Kamphoefner's *The Westfalians: From Germany to Missouri* (1986) and geographer Robert C. Ostergren's *A Community Transplanted: The Trans-Atlantic Experience of a Swedish Immigrant Settlement in the Upper Midwest, 1835–1915* (1988). Kamphoefner details the high levels of chain migration that linked communities in Westphalia to two counties in Missouri and thereby created a remarkable ethnic cohesion among these people in the United States. As a geographer, Ostergren is even more cognizant than Kamphoefner of spatial arrangement in his study of the migration from the Swedish region of Dalarna to Minnesota. With painstaking precision, he first considers the diffusion of emigration within Dalarna and the complex relationships of kinship and spatial proximity that knit the migrants to one another. Ostergren then illustrates the striking linkages of migration that resulted in tightly knit rural communities in Minnesota. Significantly, the communities that were forged out of these migrations were not static relics of Swedish life, but places that were forced to adapt to a challenging new environment. The chain migration created the basis for commonality, but it did not negate cultural adaptation.

Scholars of the European migration to South America also have been aware of the power of chain migration. Jose C. Moya's *Cousins and Strangers: Spanish Immigrants in Buenos Aires, 1850–1930* (1998) is a richly detailed work that examines patterns of migration to and creation of Spanish communities in Argentina's capital city. Rather than "forging a chain," Moya argues that a more satisfactory metaphor is "weaving the net." Immigrants were not part of a simple two-dimensional chain; rather, the chain migration created multiplier effects that caused the origins of immigrants to branch out, creating a net-like array. Moya also notes provocatively that the chain migration could lie dormant for some time and then be renewed at a later date.

In migrations that contain a substantial remigration, the chain migration can work in both directions, a fact that is illustrated particularly well in studies of recent international migrants. Madeline Y. Hsu, in her recent study of migrants from Taishan to the United States (*Dreaming of Gold, Dreaming of Home: Transnationalism and Migration Between the United States and South China, 1882–1943* [2000]), for example, stresses the dynamism created in local communities due to migration and return. Building on earlier work on the Chinese diaspora, Hsu both depicts the strategies of survival utilized by migrants and their kin and the profound effects of return migration and infusion of capital into the local Chinese community.

Migration networks in these cases strengthen the chain as they link back and forth across oceans and national borders.

Similar themes of transnational communities linked by chain migrations are observed in Nina Glick Schiller *et al. Towards a Transnational Perspective on Migration* (1992). This collection of essays, many of which are authored by sociologists and anthropologists, typically focus on chain migrations between specific transnational sites. To cite only two examples, Roger Rouse focuses on challenges faced by male immigrants from Michoacán to the San Francisco Bay area, while Eugenia Georges considers the experiences of women who moved from a village in the Dominican Republic to New York City. Methodologies employed include field work in the sending and receiving areas, and interaction with subjects in ways not possible in historical research. These scholars focus on the altered strategies to improve economic well-being and the changing gender relationships expressed by their respondents. Knowledge of behavior both at home and in the migrants' destinations is thus pivotal in making the case for cultural change resulting from migration. Again, people moving in a chain migration fashion undergird the research design.

How does the concept of chain migration enlarge our understanding of migrants and their experience? On the one hand, in the case of international migration, it forces scholars to consider the premigration experiences of their subjects. To understand the patterns of migration from a region, scholars must examine the origins of the migration itself; this usually demands a grasp of the home community and the selection of the migrants. Moreover, pondering fields of migration demands that scholars think about networks that are created through space and across national boundaries. It is no accident that a growing interest in the chain migration phenomenon has been accompanied by an increased interest in transnational migrations.

On the other hand, scholars have reflected on the impact of chain migrations on the ethnic communities themselves. Because chain migrations privilege local ties from the places of origin, they are instrumental in fostering the maintenance of cultural forms and social conventions. It has been repeatedly observed that members of chain migrations tend to marry people of local origins, retain regional dialects, and construct immigrant institutions based on sub-national foundations. This fact not only gives us greater understanding of the process of adjustment for immigrants, but also complicates the process of ethnicization when local identities endure. The ways in which immigrants navigate between local ties carried from home and protean ethnic identifications in relation to life in a different nation-state are pivotal issues that colored the study of immigrant groups in the United States.

Despite the significance of chain migration, we must be cautious in its use for a variety of reasons. First, what about those who were not a part of an easily identified chain migration? Or, put differently, what proportion of immigrants were individuals who did not enjoy the succor of friends and family, and how might their story be different? Does the study of the chain migration privilege and thereby overstate cultural retention? One way to finesse this problem is to stress the cultural change that occurred in tightly knit communities stemming largely from chain migrations. If cultural change occurs there, as Ostergren argues in his study of Swedish Minnesotans and as Rouse illustrates in his work on Michoacán, one might argue that it is even more common in heterogeneous communities. In rare cases, we can determine the degree to which an entire migration is contained within a migration chain. When I was able to examine the destinations of every immigrant to the United States from a region in Norway, I discovered that 79.8% of the earliest immigrants moved first to three rural destinations. However, the intensity of the chain migration waned, so that only a little over two-fifths of the latest immigrants made one of these three locations their first home in the United States.

Yet one might argue that this Norwegian case in itself is atypical; which leads us to another caution in examining chain migration: it might occur more frequently in populations with specific traits. Unfree migrants, for example, are less likely to be chain migrants simply because their migration was not by choice. In contrast, literate migrants seemingly would be more able to dispense information than the illiterate would, and thus would be more likely to be part of a chain migration. The wealthy could more easily pay for dissemination of information than poorer migrants. And one might think that more recent immigrants would be more likely to enjoy the connections with kin because of the decreasing costs and increasing facility of keeping in touch with people in the home country. In sum, we need to be careful both not to assume that the chain migration pattern is the norm and to consider those who might be able or willing to profit from moving in a chain migration fashion.

These caveats notwithstanding, scholars in a variety of disciplines likely will continue to use chain migrations as a basis for future research. Historians and geographers, as they link people through space, will both be able to stress the significance of the chain migration in informing adaptation in the new locale and in examining cultural change in communities fostered by chain migrations. Likewise, anthropologists will continue to work on the migration fields which are created through chain migrations and which will enable them to conduct fieldwork that will localize larger migration patterns. And whether they are examining Dominicans migrating to metropolises in the twenty-first century or Swedes to rural locales in the nineteenth, they will be focusing on common human behavior.

Jon Gjerde is Professor of History at the University of California, Berkeley. In 1985 he published From Peasants to Farmers: The Migration from Balestrand, Norway to the Upper Middle West *(Cambridge University Press). His 1997 book* The Minds of the West: Ethnocultural Evolution in the Rural Middle West, 1830–1917 *(Univ. of North Carolina Press) received both the Theodore Saloutos Award from the IEHS and the (separate) Theodore Saloutos Book Award from the Agricultural History Society.*

From *The Immigration and Ethnic History Newsletter,* May 2001, pp. 1, 8. © 2001 by The Immigration and Ethnic History Newsletter. Reprinted with permission of the author, Jon Gjerde.

Ellis Island finds an immigrant wave online

By Gregg Zoroya
USA TODAY

PHOTO BY ROBERT DEUTSCH, USA TODAY

The Great Hall: The giant room at the Ellis Island Museum, now crowded with tourists, saw the arrival of more than 22 million immigrants from 1892 to 1924.

NEW YORK—Dot Ratigan tried until the wee hours without success to dig into her immigrant family past, working from her Macintosh up in Cape Elizabeth, Maine.

Exasperated that Ellis Island officials had placed an unprecedented pool of migrant data on the Internet, only to see her access barred because of overwhelming public response, Ratigan fired off an angry e-mail.

"My parents arrived at Ellis Island with less aggravation and frustration than I have had getting on this site," she wrote. "Let me know when you are up to snuff."

Six weeks and 300 miles later, the first-generation American is here on the very island in New York Harbor where her family landed, in the same famous French Renaissance building where those tired, poor and huddled masses queued for freedom nearly a century ago in the

Great Hall. She's poring over the ship's manifest that shows her mother, then a teenager, freshly arrived from Ireland on April 16, 1915.

"I'm like a dog with a bone. I will not give it up until I get what I want out of it," says the 65-year-old grandmother.

It's estimated that 40% of Americans today can trace a relative back to Ellis Island during what was the greatest migration in modern history. When the Statue of Liberty-Ellis Island Foundation took the fruits of a seven-year and $22.5 million effort to transcribe ship passenger manifests for the Port of New York between 1892 and 1924 and placed that information on the Web (www.ellisisland-records.org) April 17, officials expected heavy traffic.

They had no idea.

Jupiter Media Metrix, which tracks Internet use, says the site immediately filled with more than 80,000 people logging on. In the first few days, an estimated half million others, like Ratigan, were turned away. Interest has eased in recent weeks, though traffic remains steady at 40,000 to 60,000 visitors a day.

The solution to the Internet gridlock was easy: Officials scrambled to double, then triple, online capacity. Today, nearly everyone who tries to access their family's Ellis Island immigrant records can get online. Harder to explain was what drove the unusually heavy response. Why would so many people clamor to find a dusty set of facts about someone, in many cases, they never knew? Why do they spend an average of 15 to 20 minutes in the site, a virtual lifetime in a cyberworld notorious for short attention spans?

Genealogists suspect the reason is simpler than we like to admit: shedding light on our ancestors brings greater focus on our favorite subject—ourselves.

At the same time that the foundation placed its database on the Internet, it opened the American Family Immigration History Center. Just down the stairwell from the Great Hall of the original 100,000-square-foot processing center for the immigrants—today the Ellis Island Immigration Museum—people line up to seek their family history. In a matter of minutes, they are ushered to a cubicle with a computer terminal that links them to the past and, in a way, to the present and to themselves, experts say.

"We need to know who came before us and what they were like in order to know who we are," says Stephen Brigante, president and CEO of the Statue of Liberty-Ellis Island Foundation.

Genealogists estimate that six in 10 Americans are, in one form or another, researching family history.

"When you do it in the context of family, it gives you more of a sense of completeness for yourself," says Wayne Metcalf, a director in the family and church history department for the Church of Jesus Christ of Latter-day Saints. The Mormons, who believe that tracing family history is part of their religious mission, volunteered

some 12,000 church members to transcribe the passenger manifests for the Ellis Island project.

To be sure, when first-, second- and third-generation Americans struggle to explain this compulsion for gathering Ellis Island information, the motivations tumbling out are much the same: pride in an ancestor's life-altering decision, the desire to assemble a lasting family history, a gnawing hunger for detail.

"There's just a feeling, some kind of need. I don't know if closure is the word. But we feel the need to get this information. We want to know as much as we can," says John Reynolds, 35, a morning radio host for WYMG in Springfield, Ill. He spent hours at his Compaq computer in the basement of his home each day trying to access information about his grandfather, Giovanni Albertano, who arrived on Ellis Island from northern Italy in 1920, at age 18, to work in the copper mines in Calumet, Mich.

Reynolds says he was particularly moved to discover that his grandfather arrived at Ellis Island the same date, Oct. 9, that Reynolds was born in 1965.

"It was startling when I saw that. And they named me after him," he says. (Giovanni is John in English.)

Others accessing the Ellis Island records also make it an inward-looking issue.

Jami Becker, 32, a computer game designer from San Francisco, loves the family legend of how her grandfather, Isador Becker, a Jewish immigrant, jumped into the ocean shortly before docking in America. He was trying to retrieve his windblown hat so he would be properly attired arriving in his new home. Working to call his name up on a computer at the Ellis Island family history center here, she talks of melting pots, the search for identity, the need to feel connected to a family history.

"I was really shocked at how emotional it was for me to come here today," she says.

At another computer screen, Indianapolis architect Eugene Brese, 59, eager to leave his three daughters with a greater appreciation of what he sees as his family's work ethic. He searches for the manifest of Polish immigrant grandfathers who arrived in Ellis Island, one to work in the steel mills of Lackawanna, N.Y. and the other to work in a cement plant there.

"It makes you enjoy your life a little more just knowing how far you've come," says Mike DiFranco, 23, of Jacksonville, Fla., a photographer's mate aboard the USS John F. Kennedy aircraft carrier. He is here printing out a suitable-for-framing photograph of the steamer, Moltke, on which his great-great-grandmother arrived from Naples.

"I mean, how cool is that? I just sailed up here on the ferry and she pretty much saw the same thing on that boat in 1906," he says. "It's kind of wild."

Lauren MacArthur put it in the plainest terms.

The 8-year-old from South Mountain Elementary in Millburn, N.J., is on a class outing to Ellis Island. Her father, Richard, 45, helps pull up the records of Lauren's great-grandfather, who arrived from Scotland.

"He is Scottish, just like me," Lauren says. "So that's something about me."

BY ROBERT DEUTSCH, USA TODAY

Field trip: Emily Nissum, 8, Daniel Levine, 8, Rick Macarthur and daughter Lauren, 8, and teacher Dana Townsend, from South Mountain Elementary in Millburn, N.J., do a family search at the Ellis museum.

For Ratigan, the grandmother from Maine, who arrives this day with her sister, Joan Wald, 68, of Tarrytown, N.Y., efforts here are just a small step on a journey that has lasted years and taken her to Ireland to search ancient municipal birth-and-death records.

Ratigan has already seen these Ellis Island records. A former nurse who started four businesses, she is a single-minded woman with a firm handshake who kept trying the Ellis Web site until she got in. And she has returned to it dozens of times.

Pulling up the now-familiar manifests, she points out anomalies in the record that could be clues to her family's resourcefulness.

Her mother, Margaret Carberry, was 16 when she arrived from Liverpool, England, in the company of her older sister, Delia, 27. Knowing they would be asked if they had a place to stay America, both gave an address in New York that just happens to be the same as the woman, a stranger, who is in line ahead of them.

"My aunt went up, she looked over the shoulder, got the information, went back and told my mother what to say," she says. "They were cheating."

The other oddity is that absence of any record of her father's arrival. Austin Tierney, a year younger than Ratigan's mother, met and married Margaret in America. The youngest of three sons, he was the only survivor after his older brothers were killed in World War I. Facing conscription, he vanished from Ireland and suddenly turned up in New York.

"I do think that they smuggled him in somewhere," Ratigan says. "We'll probably be thrown out of the country, Joan, by the time I finish this."

"It's a mystery," her sister says later. "She loves a mystery."

Archive-quality images and other information

A search at Ellis Island starts by entering your ancestor's name in an orientation kiosk to determine whether arrival records are on file.

For $5, a computer station can be used to access the data. As with the Internet access, which is free, the records here offer 10 categories of information: name, ethnicity, last residence, date of arrival, age, gender, marital status, ship, port of departure and the line where the immigrant is listed on the manifest. Depending upon the year of arrival, other information may be available, such as the immigrant's destination in America or how much money he or she carried.

Access to the database here, unlike the Internet, is guaranteed. A computerized voice-over walks the novice through a search ("Let's try to get closer by adding another piece of information ..."). If a name can't be found, the software offers other possible spellings. (Officials recommend that you bring any detailed information you have about your relative, such as the year of arrival at Ellis Island.)

Archival-quality images can be made of a summary of one passenger's records or the actual manifest page containing that information. A photograph of the ship also can be obtained. The passenger summary print is free; images of the manifest page or the ship cost $10 to $35, depending upon the size requested. Within weeks, these will be available for purchase over the Internet.

For a $45 contribution, you can join the Statue of Liberty-Ellis Island Foundation and access a research area where you can compile documents and photographs into a family scrapbook.

Ellis Island and the Statue of Liberty are open daily, except Christmas, from 9:30 a.m. to 5 p.m., with extended summer hours. Tickets for both sites are $7 for adults, $6 for seniors (62 and up) and $3 for children ages 3 to 17; younger kids get in free.

Information: 212–363–3200. Ferry information: 212-269-5755 or http://www.statueoflibertyferry.com/.

UNIT 4

Indigenous Ethnic Groups

Unit Selections

22. **As Others Abandon Plains, Indians and Bison Come Back**, Timothy Egan
23. **Culture Corrosion in Canada's North**, DeNeen L. Brown
24. **Inside the Arctic Circle, an Ancient People Emerge**, Warren Hoge

Key Points to Consider

- Novel approaches toward the peaceful reconciliation of conflict should be explored more thoroughly. For example, unlike conflict among ethnic groups in the United States, conflict between the United States and Native Americans is regulated by treaties. The struggle over claims regarding the rights of nations and the interests of the U.S. government and its citizens is no longer at the margin of public affairs. Does the definition of this conflict as an issue of foreign and not domestic policy provide a meaningful distinction? Should the claims of ethnic groups in defense of culture, territory, and unique institutions be honored and protected by law and public policy? Why or why not? Is sovereignty an issue? Defend your answer.

- How should commitments to the self-determination of people be ensured and enforced? What value conflicts, if any, are beyond compromise?

- What are the most compelling issues that face indigenous ethnic communities? Economy? Culture? What social, economic, and political conditions will affect the next indigenous ethnic generation?

- Will the strides of the current Native American community allow the next generation to enter the middle class mainstream of America? Should that be a goal? Does improving economically and in terms of other quality-of-life indicators mean the denial of traditional cultural values and practices?

- How much devolution of authority to Native Americans are state legislatures willing to negotiate? What role should the national government play—an advocate for Native Americans or states or an honest broker? Does the role depend on the issue? Water? Casinos? Mining? Taxation? What about cultural rights?

 **Links: www.dushkin.com/online/**
These sites are annotated in the World Wide Web pages.

American Indian Science and Engineering Society (AISES)
http://spot.colorado.edu/~aises/aises.html

The contemporary issues of Native Americans as well as the descendants of all conquered indigenous peoples add their weight to the claims for cultural justice, equal protection, and due process in our hemisphere, but in fact this is a worldwide phenomenon. The United Nations provided a media forum for attention to indigenous populations, NGOs (nongovernmental organizations) committed to human rights, and to address global economic interests regarding the protection of human and physical ecologies. The post–World War II end of colonialism and the emergence of new nations in Asia and Africa pointed to the development of new states, but also to the problems of nationbuilding in contexts of extreme ethnic variety. Even the Soviet Union became engaged in the plethora of nations and ethnic populations of Central Asia and Eastern Europe. Only during the last decade have social and political scientists been able to view these widespread phenomena from a perspective that enables us to see the full implications of ethnic and race relations as a foundational issue for political and economic order.

Relationships between indigenous peoples in the United States were marginated and isolated. Their cultures were articulated in folkloric and touristic ways when interaction with mainstream America occurred. Such traditional relations were challenged during the civil rights era. Moreover, the celebration of the bicentennial of the American Revolution in 1976, the empowerment of Native Americans, and their victories in the courts and in legislative authority produced a new threshold from which the renegotiation of relationships could begin. With new cultural confidence and economic capacity, most notably in the gaming industry, the descendants of native peoples entered a new epoch of American pluralism. Some may argue that the reclamation and revival of tradition and power are unique social and political events. A wider view suggests that they are but another manifestation of an ethnic group's articulation of its power and the pursuit of its agenda within the contexts of the American legal and economic order. Acute popular consciousness of indigenous peoples was heightened when attempts to celebrate the 500th anniversary of Christopher Columbus's voyage of discovery encountered strong resistance from advocates of Native Americans.

On the international level another front of resistance emerged in the struggle against apartheid in South Africa. While many Americans viewed the South African situation through the simplistic lens of color consciousness, its impact on the larger arena has become apparent. The development of a new South African regime increased awareness of indigenous peoples. The exploration of roots and new remedies for the conquest that turned many into a permanent underclass has awakened indigenous people, and a code of international conduct in protection of cultural rights has entered international law.

The following articles represent a cross section of the current experience of indigenous ethnic groups, their forced accommodation of a high-tech world, the environmental and cultural effects of rapid change, and the challenges to a renewal of their identifying traditions. The indigenous ethnic populations invite us

to recall their struggles and to find ways of shaping and sharing the new sense of pluralism offered within the American experience and the spiritual sources of ethnic identity that people encounter as the legitimacy of ancient practices widens.

Indigenous ethnic communities have encountered a complex array of historical, social, cultural, and economic forces. As a result, in the late twentieth century, the traditions of indigenous ethnic groups were renegotiated by yet another generation. The North and South American economies and pluralistic cultures as well as those of other continents, are at a challenging stage of their quest for self-sufficiency. Current indigenous ethnic leaders challenge past perceptions. Some find interaction easy, but others avoid striking a balance between traditional values and new demands. Native Americans have increasingly interfaced with the American legal system at the state level on issues of land use and gaming, which represent part of this current redefinition. Finally, however, they are challenging themselves to be themselves, and examples of indigenous selfhelp reveal insights into how personal leadership and service to the community weave the social fabric of civil society.

Ethnicity is built upon the truth and strength of a tradition. A sense of family and community and an unwillingness to give up claims have led to standoffs with many forces within America. From this perspective, this unit details ways in which an ethnic group retrieves its rights and heritage to preserve an ancient culture from extinction.

The expansion and profitability of Native American gambling casinos, their attendant impact on state and local economies, and the tax exemptions enjoyed by these ventures appear to be headed toward controversies that may spill over into new issues of public order. On the international level, the discussion of human and cultural rights of peoples guaranteed in the United Nations charter and the traditional mode of state sovereignty indicates that a fragile accommodation between indigenous people and the mainstream societies at whose margins they exist may be entering a new phase. Their unequal relationship began with the consolidation of large territorial political and economic regimes. Under scrutiny are personal rights and group rights, pluralistic realms that ensure transnational solidarity, and cultural and religious challenges to those in authority fueled by the passion for power at those intersections between modernity and tradition—the large-scale institutional versus the local and culturally specific community.

As Others Abandon Plains, Indians and Bison Come Back

By TIMOTHY EGAN

FORT YATES, N.D. In writing the obituary of the Great Plains, social historians have looked out at the abandoned ranches, collapsed homesteads and dying towns huddled against the wind in a sea of grass and seen an epic failure.

And the numbers do tell a compelling story. More than 60 percent of the counties in the Great Plains lost population in the last 10 years. An area equal to the size of the original Louisiana Purchase, nearly 900,000 square miles, now has so few people that it meets the 19th-century Census Bureau definition of frontier, with six people or fewer per square mile. And a large swath of land has slipped even further, to a category the government once defined as vacant.

But something else is under way from the Badlands of the Dakotas to the tallgrass fields of Oklahoma: a restoration of lost landscape and forgotten people, suggesting that European agricultural settlement of big parts of the prairie may have been an accident of history, or perhaps only a chapter.

As the nearly all-white counties of the Great Plains empty out, American Indians are coming home, generating the only significant population gains in a wide stretch of the American midsection. At the same time, the frontier, as it was called when it was assumed that the land would soon be spotted with towns and farms, is actually larger than it has been since the early 20th century.

These changes have been under way for decades. But they have reached a point—108 years after Frederick Jackson Turner suggested that the American frontier was closed, with the buffalo herds wiped out and native populations down to a few tribes—that there are now more Indians and bison on the Plains than at any time since the late 1870's.

"What's happening is really quite astonishing," said Patricia Locke, a Lakota and Chippewa elder and a MacArthur Foundation fellow who returned to the Standing Rock Sioux Reservation here several years ago. "It's like an evacuation one way, and a homecoming in the other."

Indians, of course, are still a fraction of the overall Plains population, making up just under 8 percent of the population in the state, Oklahoma, where they have the biggest population, 272,601 people.

But while many Plains counties lost 20 percent or more of their population, the overall Indian population grew by 20 percent in North Dakota, 23 percent in South Dakota, 18 percent in Montana, 20 percent in Nebraska and 12 percent in Kansas. Some of this can be attributed to better counting and higher birthrates, but tribal officials say there has been steady in-migration dating to the mid-1980's.

In North Dakota alone, 47 of the 53 counties lost population. Among the handful that gained people were three counties populated primarily by Indians.

In South Dakota, half of the counties lost people. But the second-fastest-growing county, Shannon, is in the heart of Indian country, on the Pine Ridge Reservation, a county that is 94 percent Indian and grew by 26 percent in the last census.

And much of Montana is nearly as open today as it was when Lewis and Clark explored there nearly 200 years ago. All but four of the counties in the flat eastern part of the state lost population; of those with gains, three contain Indian reservations.

"All of these numbers suggest that the experiment on much of the northern Plains with European agricultural settlement may soon be ending," said Myron Gutmann, a University of Texas professor who is an authority on Plains population trends.

As Indians have moved home, on or near reservation lands, whites have fled the counties that were opened to homesteading in the last of the great Western land rushes in the early 20th century.

The whitest county in the nation, Slope County, N.D., is down to 767 people; all but three of its residents are white. By contrast, in 1915, six years after the prairie was opened to ranchers and farmers through the Enlarged Homestead Act, Slope County was bustling, with 4,945 people. Now the county seat, Amidon, has 25 people, and the population density, less than one person per square mile, is well below the 19th-century Census Bureau definition of land that is vacant or wilderness.

Much of North Dakota has a ghostly feel to it: empty homesteads and occasional schoolhouses litter the land, with caved-in roofs and grass growing where

Population Shifts

Though counties across the Great Plains have lost population, the number of American Indians has risen.

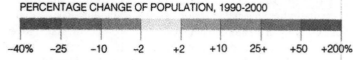

PERCENTAGE CHANGE OF POPULATION, 1990-2000

-40% -25 -10 -2 +2 +10 25+ +50 +200%

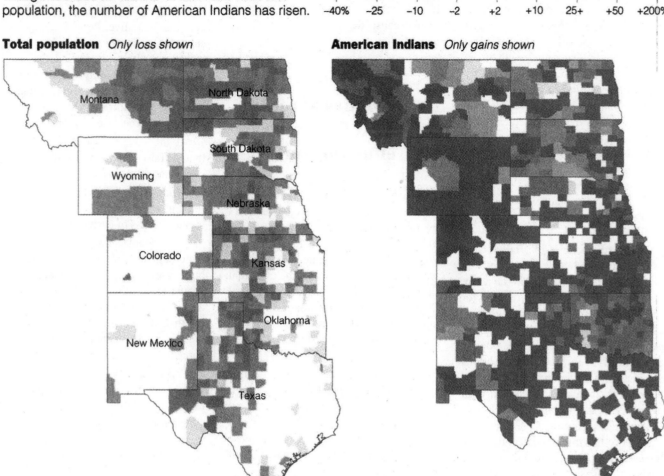

Total population *Only loss shown*

American Indians *Only gains shown*

THE NEW YORK TIMES

Source: Analysis of Census data by Andrew A. Beveridge, Queens College Sociology Department

there used to be front porches. The wind blows so hard that a cup of coffee brought outside develops whitecaps.

Cattle ranching and farming of wheat, barley and corn still prevail, especially on large corporate farms in the middle and southern plains. But in Slope, Hettinger, Adams, Grant, Burke, Divide, Garfield or any of the hundreds of other plains counties that seem to have one foot in the grave, land is being left to the wind and sparse rain.

In publicly owned prairie land, the native grasses and wildflowers have returned, and species like prairie dogs, black-footed ferrets, burrowing owls and bison have made comebacks. Much of this land will never be plowed again, for a third of the nation's 3.7 million acres of

national grassland is designated roadless under a measure started by President Bill Clinton over the objections of many in the region's Congressional delegation. Other parts are managed by private groups like the Nature Conservancy, which has been buying up ranches and homesteads.

"I'm an old prairie guy, and it does my heart good to see so much of the Plains greening up again with native species," said Greg Schenbeck, a wildlife biologist with the grasslands division of the Forest Service. "And I tell you, people who come to visit are really excited—they talk about the expansiveness, the openness, the grass stretching to the horizon."

At the turn of the century, only a few hundred buffalo were left in the West.

Now there are 300,000, and more than 30 tribes in the northern Plains are controlling large herds on land where bison, unlike cattle, need no help to flourish. A third of the nation's 31 accredited Indian colleges offer bison management.

"Just having these animals around, knowing what they meant to our ancestors, and bringing kids out to connect to them has been a big plus," said Mike Faith, who manages the bison herd on the Standing Rock Sioux Reservation here, not far from where Sitting Bull was killed.

Indians have the highest rate of diabetes in the nation. Part of the overall restoration of the Plains is an effort to get bison meat, which is low in cholesterol and fat, back into the Indian diet.

"We're probably one of the few ethnic communities that have been blessed with a God-given creature to help restore us," said Donald Lake, director of the Inter-Tribal Bison Cooperative of Rapid City, S.D., a nonprofit group that works to repopulate Indian country with bison.

Mr. Lake, a Santee Sioux from Nebraska, has returned to the Plains after living for years in Los Angeles. He likes the slower pace, the connection to other Indians, the low prices. He winces at the description that the historian Turner used to describe frontier land as it became populated with Europeans. It was, Turner wrote, "the place where civilization meets savagery."

Many Indians have moved back to reservations because of jobs in the casinos, the so-called new buffalo, which have been the main economic salvation. On the Standing Rock Reservation, for example, the casino is the county's biggest job provider, employing 376 people, and it has expanded six times since it opened in 1993. But Indian reservations remain among the poorest places in the nation, with high unemployment, high out-of-wedlock birthrates and chronic drug and alcohol abuse.

Still, life has improved. Tourism has increased. People come to look at bison, tribal officials say; others pay up to $2,500 for the right to hunt them. People interested in the Plains tribes' history are also drawn to the prairie.

"Sitting Bull is one of the biggest names in the world, and he still has family here," said Elaine McLaughlin, the Standing Rock tribal secretary. "A lot of people in state government seem surprised when people show up from all over because they want to know more about Indians."

The nearly white counties of the Great Plains are emptying out.

The re-emergence of a Great Plains of Indians and bison was foretold in 1987 by two Rutgers University professors, Frank J. Popper and his wife, Deborah E. Popper. They said white depopulation would accelerate, as it became clear that farming and building towns on the arid Plains was "the largest, longest-running agricultural and environmental miscalculation in American history."

They proposed a "Buffalo Commons" in the empty counties, an open range populated by the species that once thundered over the land. People throughout the prairie scorned their idea, and the Poppers became the objects of intense hatred. But their idea has been revived of late, with little rancor.

While the Poppers may ultimately be proved right in several respects, they were wrong in one major sense: In their vision, government would be the driving force, buying land and bringing buffalo back, then turning some of it over to Indians to manage.

Now, in a twist, it is government that keeps the white farming and ranching communities alive, through annual subsidies of more than $20 billion. Many historians have long argued that white settlement, particularly of the northern Plains, was largely government-induced from the start, through subsidies to railroads and homesteaders.

"If the government ever pulled out, the Buffalo Commons would come on like a storm," Mr. Popper said.

Indians and bison have returned by self-initiative and free enterprise, helped by the success of casinos.

"The people coming back, they get their degrees and they start their own businesses, or take jobs as teachers here on the reservation," said Anita Blue of the Turtle Mountain Reservation in North Dakota, where the population in the Indian-dominated county grew 7.1 percent.

The idea of Manifest Destiny in reverse is scoffed at by many people, especially in the dying counties.

But a sense of irrevocable change pervades the northern Plains. "There is a lot of that Buffalo Commons idea that's probably true," said Gov. John Hoeven of North Dakota, a Republican elected on a pledge to revitalize the state. "It's never going to look like it did before, when all the farms and ranches were healthy."

Culture Corrosion in Canada's North

Forced Into the Modern World, Indigenous Inuit Struggle to Cope

By DeNeen L. Brown
Washington Post Foreign Service

PANGNIRTUNG, Nunavut—The elders still speak of it, the time when the old world shifted. The change came, they say, like a storm they could not read in the clouds or in a ring around the sun. It came in the form of an attempt to "civilize" them. Against the wind, the people first had to brace themselves, then they had to adapt, then they had to try to stop the wind.

With violent images like these, the Inuit recall their introduction to *qallunaat*, the "non-Inuit," and to a money economy.

Jamaise Mike was born in 1928 in an igloo, but now he is sitting in a Kentucky Fried Chicken restaurant in Pangnirtung, Nunavut, three miles from a fjord. A Jennifer Lopez song is playing on the sound system. Urban pop has reached this far. The restaurant is surrounded by mountains, a vast, hard, white desert and sea ice, a region of myths, where Mike grew up.

"Most elders were born and raised on the land," Mike said, through an interpreter, speaking in the Inuktitut language. "Everything people needed to survive surrounded them on the land. Today it is different, living in a community with a store. Everything is different from when you had to do everything yourself to survive. You depended on yourself. Now, you need money."

Modern history offers countless examples of indigenous cultures coming under siege from the industrialized world. But few have experienced change with the speed and intensity that struck the Inuit, the native people who inhabit Canada's far northern reaches.

Only a generation ago, the Canadian government forced many of them out of the Arctic wilderness and into artificial communities like this one on Baffin Island. In some places, elders say, the government systematically killed many of the dogs that pulled their sleds, giving people no choice but to come in from the land. Children were put in Christian boarding schools.

"White people from the south," said Mike, "were more terrifying than polar bears." Change happened so fast that today people born in the Arctic "stone age," without machines or electricity or a sense of the hours, live side-by-side with teenagers bred on cable television and hip hop.

Often the two cultures rub against each other with tragic consequences. Rates of alcoholism in this once alcohol-free society now are among Canada's highest. The same is true for suicide.

THE WASHINGTON POST

Unemployment is endemic, with people relying on a stream of government subsidies from the south.

Yet Mike and his generation are determined that the qallunaat wind will not prevail. Indeed, safeguarding Inuit ways is the defining issue of the politics of the north. It was why Inuit leaders persuaded the Canadian government to turn this part of the country in 1999 into a homeland, the vast territory of Nunavut, population 27,000. Nunavut means "our land."

The Inuit argue that they will maintain their traditional lifestyle, "even if we spend as much time surfing the Internet as checking the fishing nets," wrote John Amagoalik, former chief commissioner of the Nunavut Implementation Commission, in a book about the territory. "We live in wooden houses, drive Jeep Cherokees, and fly in jumbo jets all over the world. But we are still Inuit. It is our spirit, our inner being, that makes us Inuit."

So today the 1,240 people of Pangnirtung walk between two cultures, belonging fully to neither. And each of these individuals is a different mix of the two.

A Loss of Memory

Margaret Nakashuk is sitting in a caribou skin house. Its rafters are whale bones. The Inuit were inventive. Whale bones were used for utensils and needles. She is explaining the heating system, how seaweed was dipped into whale blubber, seal oil or caribou fat and how it was the woman's job to keep dipping the seaweed into the stone bowl to keep the fire going. She is explaining how they made seal-skin boots and the women chewed the hide to make it soft.

She is reciting this from memorization. She has never lived in such a house. Nakashuk, 29, manager of the visitor center in Pangnirtung, is a member of the first generation of Inuit to be born not on the land but in a community. She is sitting in a skin house that is on display in the museum.

"There are two different worlds we live in," she says. "My father, now 65, he was telling us when they were young they lived in a… house like this, living on the land. When he was young, his grandmother told him one day you will live in the white man's world. You will have a house. You will drive a vehicle. You will have material clothes. He laughed because he couldn't imagine."

Now she laughs because the grandmother's omen has come true. But it is not an easy life. Nakashuk worries a lot about how to get enough money to support her family. Her husband cannot find a job and she has a mortgage and she has to buy food.

The change to a money economy was rapid. For many people here it brought debt, want and depression. Now, there are tragic stories walking around the sea ice like ghosts, people caught between a traditional culture and a money culture, trying to make ends meet.

"I have a daughter who is 8. I have a daughter who is 12. I had a son," says Sheila Kunilusie, 34, who works in a restaurant. "He went hunting with my husband. They never came back."

Then she pauses. It is not a dramatic pause for sympathy, just one to catch her breath enough to tell the rest of the story.

Her husband, a young man of the new generation, didn't really know how to hunt. He'd been taught the skills out of respect for tradition, as an attempt to keep the old ways alive. Perhaps he did not learn enough about surviving in the brutal environment beyond the settlement's boundaries.

He could not find a job. The family needed food. So he decided to try his luck with a gun. He and the boy departed. "After three or four days, I got worried," she says. "A helicopter searched for them. They finally found them on the beach." Their boat had capsized.

"They were frozen. I really wanted to see my son one last time," Kunilusie is saying. She pulls her black hair off her face. "But I couldn't. His face was eaten by ravens."

Suicide Plagues Youth

Steven Kunilusie, 28, a janitor, is walking across water. He is headed toward the floe edge, the point at which still water meets moving water. "I lost a friend in that shack," he says, pointing to a small wooden tool shed on the shore. "He was 14. He hung himself. His mother found him. He said he wanted to be alone. But no one knew he would do it."

Nunavut's suicide rate is five times the national average. People say the cause is a combination of long, dark winters of black sun, with nothing to do, no reason to go out and hunt now that there are stores, and money from the south.

In 1999, 58 of Nunavut's 27,000 people committed suicide. Fifty-two were by hanging, six by firearm. Fifty-seven of them were Inuit.

Suicide is accepted as an almost routine part of life. In the old days, it was generally only the elders who did it, during times of starvation, in the belief they were becoming too much of a burden for their families. They would take a lone suicide walk into the cold.

Now, most of the suicides are committed by the young, between the ages of 15 and 29.

Kunilusie, who is not related to Sheila Kunilusie, says he feels trapped in a land where elders once used most of their energy just trying to survive. Now that his generation does not have to worry so much about heat or food, boredom has set in. There is little to do, and depression seems to catch hold of people.

What Kunilusie wants most in the world is to go to Iqaluit, the biggest town in Nunavut, or way south to Ottawa or Toronto. "I would leave," he says, "but I have no money." He works part time because that is as much work as he can get. He thinks he could have a better life down south.

Alcohol would be an escape, Kunilusie says, but it is hard to come by in this community, where drinking caused such problems in the past that alcohol has been banned.

"No one knew he was going to do it," said Kunilusie, talking again of the long-dead friend. "He just said he wanted to be alone."

No Need to Graduate

Up an icy hill, Ann Kullualik and her three friends are playing near a graveyard. Joshua Nakula, 14, is riding a Honda four-wheeler. He spins, doing doughnuts in the snow. The girls giggle. They are part of the newest generation, so far removed from the land. They wear baggy pants and listen to rap.

They are proud to be Inuit but they are eager to fit in with pop culture from the south. What teenager in the world wants to be different?

"The qallunaat think we don't listen to music," says Ann. "They think we are so different than them. They think we live in igloos." She is writing something in the snow. "I went to Winnipeg once and they kept asking me, 'Are you Eskimo?'" which is considered a derogatory term here. "I was like, 'Holy Cow! No! I'm Inuit.' Everybody here listens to rap. I grew up going hunting. But I don't like it now. I guess I grew out of it."

Now, they are heading to a dance at the high school, where the dropout rate is high. Eighteen students were in the class of 2001 in the sixth grade; only six graduated this year.

People are flocking to the school tonight, because "Much TV," a Canadian television program, has come to town and is throwing a party. Teenagers in black jeans and black mascara crowd the steps of the school, waiting for things to start. They say they like Tupac and Brandy but not Britney Spears.

The doors finally open, and inside the music thumps, echoing in an empty gymnasium with slick wooden floors. The dance floor is empty, just like in any gymnasium in any high school in the south, where students come to a high school dance and cling to the walls.

A teacher is talking about how difficult it is to keep students in school, and how easy it is for them to drop out. Their parents are of the generation that was forcibly sent away to boarding schools; to them, school is something to be fled.

Teachers worry about this generation most. They are caught between the tendons of the wind. Even the smartest girl in the senior class might not stay on to graduate, because she sees no need.

Outside, two children are playing in the snow. Steven Shoapik, 14, is sliding on a sled. "I quit school," he says. "It was boring. My parents said nothing." Steven says he wants to stay at home and watch "Arthur" or the "Magic School Bus."

Following 'White Ways'

Up the icy road, Mike takes a walk. He is pointing out the new way and the old way: The wooden houses here are tied down by wire ropes, anchored into the permafrost so they will not blow away. Traditional houses did not need those ropes.

On the edge of a cliff is an old Hudson's Bay store, which brought trade to this area. The doors are now nailed shut. There are new stores in town that sell cosmetics and wolf scarves.

Mike is still walking. This walk is nothing compared to when he had to walk carrying a caribou on his back. His house, made of dark brown wood, has the old life and the new. Out front is a snowmobile, a power saw, a harpoon and a frozen seal he caught a month earlier.

Inside, he takes the remote control and turns off the television. A soap opera was playing to an empty house. His wife died several years ago. Now he lives alone. He looks at the clock. He used to know the time by the location of the stars. Then, time didn't matter.

Everything is changing, he says. He is not angry, simply worried. His way of life is in danger of dying. A couple of years ago an anthropologist came and recorded his story. It was an attempt to keep his words alive.

"On the land in the Inuit way, you follow the elders. The elders would have a meeting and the elder would tell a person what to do and what not to do.... These days, younger guys follow the white ways. Some kids think they know more than elders just because they go to school.

"Now they say, 'Your culture is not useful.'"

At the edge of town, there are two crates, shipments of food from the south. Dogs tethered with lashes in a team are howling. Ravens are flying above the water tower. The night is coming and the wind has shifted.

From the *Washington Post,* July 16, 2001, pp. A1, A11. © 2001 by The Washington Post. Reprinted by permission.

Inside the Arctic Circle, an Ancient People Emerge

By WARREN HOGE

KARASJOK, Norway—They are the indigenous people of Europe, a tribe that spent centuries quietly keeping to themselves in the dark and frozen expanse across the continent's roof but who are now raising their voices to get the attention of the people who live below.

Known as Samis, they are making themselves heard quite purposefully in their own language, a tongue once forbidden in Norway, which they feel defines and sustains them as a separate and lasting culture.

In this town 250 miles north of the Arctic Circle—less than 10 miles to Finland, 100 miles to Sweden or Russia—the Samis have just inaugurated a stirring symbol of their presence, a silvery larchwood and stainless steel complex, part of which rises out of the snow in the shape of a lavvu, the Sami tepee. It houses a parliament that Norway has set up to indicate the Samis right to cultural protection and their status as an ethnic minority.

On a morning in late February, the temperature outside is a numbing minus 31 degrees Fahrenheit, and the sun, which makes its daily passage just above the horizon for only six hours, casts a light so weak it produces only shades of gray. Inside, though, the soaring hall of blond Norwegian wood glows from light bulbs suspended from the ceiling, and the men and women of the Sami parliament fill the halls and corridors with a warming blur of color from the blue, red, green and yellow patterns of their clothing.

So far, the assembly's power is limited to counseling the Norwegian Parliament in Oslo on issues of particular importance to the Samis, like education, conservation, farming, land and reindeer herding, the profession that still occupies 10 percent of Samis. But the assembly's meaning to them goes deeper.

"People come up to me and take my hand and say, 'Thank you for what you have done,'" said Ole Henrik Magga, 54, the Sami parliament's first president. "It has to do with a deep-rooted negative thing that governed then for so long and made them unable to stand up and say, 'I am a Sami.'"

Johann Mikkal Sara, 47, a member of the parliament said, "O.K., you can say this is just symbolic, but when Norway built this building, they accepted the Samis as people, and that's supremely important to us."

Long known as Lapps, a term they now disdain as colonial, the Samis are an ancient people who form the ethnic minority in Norway, Sweden and Finland. Their total number is estimated at 80,000, with more than half of them in Norway. An additional 2,000 live on the Kola Peninsula in Russia. Their land has been partitioned by national borders so unceasingly that they have often found themselves paying taxes to several countries at once.

Walter Gibbs for The New York Times

The Sami parliament building is a silvery larchwood and stainless-steel complex, part of which rises out of the snow in the shape of a lavvu, the Sami tepee.

They believe they were here before the Swedish, Finnish or even Viking culture had developed, and that their land, long classed by Norway as "ownerless," is rightfully theirs.

Researchers have found they have no genetic resemblance to any other people. "The Samis are about language and culture, they are not about a tribe wandering in from the East," said Audhild Schanche, an anthropologist at the Nordic Sami Institute in Kautokeino.

While they are members of international indigenous people's organizations and consider themselves akin to the Indians and the Inuit of the Americas, they have not experienced the same historic levels of violence and repression, do not feel the kind of deep antagonism that some native peoples do toward colonizers and have been less demanding in pressing their cause.

"For people like Indians who have been really oppressed in their lands," Mr. Magga said, "they can't understand how we can have friendly meetings with representatives of the Norwegian government."

In addition, Samis don't have skin color or facial features that make them stand out from Norwegians. "I went to Canada and met Indians, and they didn't believe I was one of them," said Nils Gaup, 45, a sandy-haired, pale-skinned film director whose Sami-language movie "Pathfinder" was an Academy Award nominee for best foreign-language film in 1987.

The New York Times

North Sami is the language of the assembled lawmakers in Karasjok.

Sami complaints have centered on disputes with farmers and other settlers about ownership and land use and about Norway's efforts, however well intentioned, to blend them into its culture. An official policy of assimilation gained force in the 19th century and resulted in laws banning the instruction or speaking of the Sami language and outlawing the sale of land to people who spoke Sami at home.

Over the years, many Samis blended in with Norwegian society, abandoning their language and sometimes changing their last names to disguise their origins.

"In some ways, our looks and appearances were a curse for us because it enabled Samis to stay hidden," said Tove Anti, 35, a staff officer with the parliament. "If we looked different, it would have been easier for us to win back the people we lost through assimilation. It would have been easier to band together."

The Samis are pacific by nature. "We don't even have a word for war in our language," said Ms. Anti. But a dispute in 1979 over a Norwegian plan to construct a dam on the Alta River 100 miles north of here that would inundate the Sami town of Masi and lay roads through prime reindeer grazing and calving areas made them suddenly aggressive.

For three years, the Samis engaged in civil disobedience, picketing the site and the national Parliament in Oslo and attracting young supporters to the cause.

"For my generation of Norwegians, the Sami struggle for indigenous rights became our issue, and we all got into our vans and went up to Alta," said Thomas Hylland Eriksen, 39, a professor of anthropology at the University of Oslo. "It was more than just trying to save a river," Mr. Gaup said. "It was a major cultural moment."

A commission was appointed to study Sami land claims, and it concluded that the Samis were "a people, with a people's special history, language, culture and visions of the future." The 1984 document recommended that a Sami parliament be created, saying, "The state of Norway was formed on the territory of not one, but two peoples: "Norwegians and Samis."

By 1989, the assembly was created—with the goal being the development of a model for Sami autonomy within the Norwegian state.

The parliament meets for a week four times a year. There are 39 lawmakers from 13 constituencies, and they represent 5 political groupings. They are elected every four years on the same day as the national Parliament in Oslo is chosen, and voters can qualify by proving that recent ancestors spoke Sami. The number of voters has risen in each election.

The Samis treat their overlapping national status in a characteristically nonconfrontational way. "We never say, 'We are going to Finland,'" Ms. Anti said. "We say, 'We are going to the Finnish side of the border. We also don't call this the Norwegian Sami parliament, we call it the parliament of the Samis in Norway. It's important because words have a lot of power."

Their language is related to Finnish and Estonian and is broken down into three broad dialects by region, with the majority speaking North Sami, the language of the parliament. There are now Sami book publishers, newspapers, radio stations, television channels and recordings of yoiks, poetic chants that Samis associate with healing and travel to spiritual realms.

For centuries, Samis who lived by the sea worked as fishermen, while those inland led nomadic lives, following their reindeer herds around winter pastures in the interior to lands near the coast in summer.

"Samis believe the earth is a living thing," said Mr. Gaup. "Norwegian culture, like the rest of Western culture, believes the earth is more like a machine. You didn't have to live in a tent to share in that belief that earth is a living thing. I was ashamed, for instance, if I took too many fishes form the lake, and I had the same attitude toward hunting."

He summed it up with a phrase emblematic of the culture. "You took," he said, "just what you needed."

UNIT 5
Hispanic/Latino Americans

Unit Selections

Key Points to Consider

- In what regards do Cuban refugee issues provide material for a case study in ethnic politics?

- On December 10, 1996, the Mexican government passed a law allowing dual citizenship for persons living in the United States. What does this policy portend for the relationship between Mexico and the United States? At present, is this law of citizenship a threat to or an opportunity for ethnic group relations? Does the election of President Vincente Fox and the defeat of PRI in Mexico forecast the renegotiation of relations between Mexico and the United States?

- When do ethnic and racial issues foster understanding? Does the charge of racialism within the Hispanic/Latino community expose the limits of solidarity? How about the existence of color consciousness that is present in the population? Does the historical anti-immigrant position of African Americans explain this matter or does such an argument simply fuel allegations of discrimination?

- What are the strengths and weaknesses of strong bonds within ethnic communities? What role does ethnic media play in the formation and continuity of community? Can ethnic media cross over to wider audiences?

- In what respects is Hispanic/Latino American culture becoming part of mainstream American culture? What can be expected for relationships between Hispanic ancestry populations and the newest immigrants from Spanish-speaking countries?

- Are Hispanic voters in California, Texas, Florida, and New York the crucial electoral difference for presidential elections? Explain.

- Attention to and discussion of specifically ethnic entertainment and the paucity of ethnic entertainers in mainstream programming has entered a new level of concern: the development of crossover roles for Hispanic actors and actresses has emerged on the agenda. Does this pathway of expressing ethnic group interests suggest that assimilation and ethnic particularity need not be exclusive? Is this perspective an example of pluralism that expresses personal freedom and the endorsement of options that are open to persons with more than one cultural competency?

 **Links: www.dushkin.com/online/**
These sites are annotated in the World Wide Web pages.

Latino On-Line News Network
http://www.latnn.com
National Council of La Raza (NCLR)
http://www.nclr.org

The following collection of materials on Hispanic/Latino Americans is a composite of findings about ethnicities. The clustering of these ethnicities and nationalities, as well as their relationship to the Spanish language, seem to be sufficient evidence of the commonalties that constitute the shared expression of this complex of past and contemporary politics. Yet the use of the terms "Hispanic" and "Latino" that differentiates them from Anglo-American foundations, and their social expression as they search for a cultural and political terrain, are but the surface of the process of intergroup dynamics in the United States. Are Portuguese-speaking groups Hispanic?

The articles in this unit propose angles of vision that enable us to view the process of accommodation and change that is articulated in political practice, scholarship, advocacy, and art. The issues presented provocatively shift traditional perspectives from the eastern and midwestern mindset toward the western and southwestern immigration to the United States.

The Immigration Act of 1965 induced a process not unlike the period of large-scale eastern and southern European immigration between 1880 and 1924. This immigration includes scores of various ethnic groups. Cultural/geographic descriptions are not the clearest form of ethnic identity. Hispanic/Latino Americans are not a single ethnic group. The designation of various ethnic populations whose ancestry is derived from Spanish-peaking countries by the words "Latino" and "Hispanic" is a relatively recent phenomenon in the United States.

Hispanic was used in the 1970s and Latino was added to the U.S. Census in 1990. The cultural, economic, and political differences and similarities among various Hispanic/Latino communities, as well as the wide dispersal of these communities, suggest the need for care in generalization about Latino and Hispanic American populations. Does geographic location in the United States significantly influence personal and group issues?

The realities of these groups—whether they are political refugees, migrant workers, descendants of residents settled prior to territorial incorporation into the United States, long-settled immigrants, recent arrivals, or the children and grandchildren of immigrants—present interesting and varied patterns of enclave community, assimilation, and acculturation, as well as isolation and marginalization. Hispanic/Latino American linkages to Central and South American countries and Spain, the future of their emerging political power, and their contributions to cultural and economic change within the United States are interesting facets of the Hispanic/Latino American experience.

The Hispanic/Latino experience is a composite of groups seeking unity while interacting with the larger arena of ethnic groups that constitute American society. Convergent issues that bridge differences, as well as those that support ideological and strategic differences, bode a future of both cooperation and conflict.

What issues bind Hispanic or Latino groups together? What values cause cleavages among these populations? What does bilingualism mean? Is bilingualism a freedom-of-speech issue? Is bilingualism a concern of non-Spanish-speaking persons in the United States? What are the implications of establishing an official public language policy?

Competition and conflict over mobility into mainstream leadership positions are aspects of American society that may be exacerbated by the misuse of ethnic indicators. Nonetheless, indicators of social cohesion and traditional family bonds are apparently noncompetitive and nonconflictual dimensions of robust ethnic experiences. Thus, fears that Hispanic/Latino Americans may not relish competitive pressures are assuaged by the capacities of family and community to temper the cost of any such failure. This complex dynamic of personal and group interaction is a fascinating and fruitful topic for a society seeking competitiveness and stronger community bonds. Cast in this fashion, the American dilemma takes on a new and compelling relevance.

HISPANIC DIASPORA

Drawn by jobs, Latino immigrants are moving to small towns like Siler City, North Carolina, bringing with them new diversity—and new tensions.

BY BARRY YEOMAN

THE DAY OF THE RALLY, Ruth Tapia awakes with a feeling of disgust. It's a drizzly, overcast morning in February, and all is quiet on the street outside her small, white brick home in Siler City, North Carolina. But Tapia knows that a platoon of white supremacists is already gathering under the leafless willow oaks at City Hall, preparing to listen to David Duke rail against the influx of thousands of Latinos to Siler City. And she knows that when the former Klansman is introduced to the crowd, she has to be there. "I want to look him in the eye," she thinks. "I'm not scared of him. This is my country."

Five years earlier, Tapia had moved to Siler City so her husband Israel, a Mexican-born Baptist preacher, could minister to the immigrants who were pouring into this Southern town of chicken factories and textile mills. It was nothing like the Texas Panhandle where Tapia grew up. Latinos were still a novelty here, and locals didn't know how to react to the newcomers crowding into apartment complexes and trailer parks throughout the town of 8,000. At a health clinic one day, a well-meaning employee approached Tapia and asked very slowly, "Do you speak-ee English?" "No, I don't speak-ee," Tapia shot back. "I *speak* English."

As the immigrants continued to arrive, eventually comprising 40 percent of the population, the reactions grew more hostile. Last year, when Tapia tried to renew her driver's license, a clerk accused her of forging her U.S. birth certificate and threatened to have her arrested. Tapia, big and tough-talking, arrived home in tears.

Now David Duke is holding a rally less than a mile from her home, and Tapia knows most of her Latino neighbors are too terrified to go. Immigrants from Mexico, Guatemala, and El Salvador, many arrive without proper documents and live in constant fear of arrest and deportation. They are drawn by the promise of work—difficult and often dangerous factory jobs that pay less than $15,000 a year—and by a friendly, slow-paced life that reminds them of the rural communities they left behind. But they worry that the racial resentment that hounded them in places like Los Angeles and Houston has followed them to their new home in Siler City.

As soon as Tapia arrives at the rally, she starts trembling. Cordoned off with yellow police tape, organizers are unloading dozens of carefully lettered signs. "To hell with the wretched refuse," says one. "No way, José!" says another. As they distribute the pickets, Tapia takes out her camera and starts documenting the hate surrounding her.

A man in a black suit takes the podium and lashes out at the local factories recruiting Latino workers. "Ladies and gentlemen, you all are here today because you share a deep feeling about what is happening to your city," declares Sam van Rensburg, a leader of a neo-Nazi group called the National Alliance. "Your city is being sold out for a quick buck by unscrupulous corporations, who are willing to ruin the town your fathers founded. Folks, there is no such thing as cheap labor. You and I will pay for this labor for the rest of our lives."

As van Rensburg goes on about "mongrels" and the "sewer of immigration," Tapia drives home to fetch her husband. Enraged, she vents about what she has heard downtown. "Ruth, calm down. I'm not going if you're like that," Israel tells her. As they drive back to City Hall, he warns, "Don't yell anything out." But when David Duke starts speaking, Tapia can't restrain herself.

"Siler City is at a crossroads," says the former grand dragon and Louisiana state representative. "Either you get the INS to kick the illegal aliens out, or you'll lose your community and your heritage."

Tapia yells, "We're staying!"

Behind her, a man shouts, "Go back to your own country!"

"I was born here," she snaps back.

One immigrant stages a more civil protest, hoping to model for Duke and his followers the Christian values they claim to hold dear. When the former Klansman finally winds down his hour-long speech, he raises his arms in a wave and walks toward the crowd of almost 500 people. Above the cheers comes an accented voice: "Mr. Duke! Mr. Duke! David!" The white supremacist leader looks around until he sees a large Mexican man with brushed-back hair and a jutting jaw. The man has inserted himself between Duke and his admirers—a defiant and risky stance—and his arms, too, are raised. "Mr. Duke," says Israel Tapia. "Jesus loves you."

UNTIL RECENTLY, Siler City was best known to fans of "The Andy Griffith Show" as a shopping destination for the citizens of Mayberry. A village of Protestant churches and tractor dealerships, it's where Frances Bavier, the actress who played Aunt Bee, retired in 1972 because it so much resembled her fictional hometown. A decade ago, when Bavier died, Siler City was a study in black and white, with no colors in between. But today the town, like scores of others throughout the South and Midwest, is being reworked in shades of brown. Disillusioned by high rents, low wages, and racist backlash in border states like California and Texas, many immigrants have set off for communities where Spanish surnames were rarities 10 years ago.

The immigrants are being welcomed—and often actively recruited—by meatpacking and poultry companies. Hoping to avoid unions, both industries have set up shop in rural areas, but cannot attract enough local workers with the low wages they offer. Blue-collar Latinos from the border states, by contrast, are eager for the pay—and less likely to seek medical care or protest dangerous working conditions. "I don't want them after they've been here a year and know how to get around," one supervisor at a North Carolina meatpacking company told a worker advocate recently. "I want them right off the bus."

The transformation has been rapid and widespread. Workers from Mexico and Central America now debone chickens in North Carolina, Arkansas, and Delaware and slaughter cattle and pigs in Kansas, Nebraska, and Iowa. Over the last decade, census figures show, 800,000 Latinos left California for other states; the state experiencing the fastest influx is Arkansas, where the Latino population has soared by 149 percent. And the trend is just beginning: By 2025, the Hispanic populations of

Arkansas, Delaware, Georgia, Kansas, Maryland, Nebraska, and North Carolina are expected to grow 70 percent or more, compared to overall growth rates of less than 20 percent.

"It's a very massive and very sudden growth," says University of Pennsylvania sociologist Ruben Hernandez-Leon. "We call this phenomenon a diaspora not only because people are moving from the Southwest, but also because people are joining that flow from Latin America, mainly women and children. These destinations are becoming sites for family reunification."

In Siler City and elsewhere, many of the new residents say their new hometowns resemble the communities they left behind in Latin America: rural, family-oriented, religious, without the eight-lane freeways and rush-rush lifestyle that make places like Southern California such a discordant experience. "This is my promised land, Nebraska," says Jacinto Corona, a Mexican immigrant who left California in 1994 and drove four days through a winter storm until he reached Grand Island, population 40,000. "Here, we have great opportunities to find a good job, good pay, cheaper houses," says Corona, who spent his first three years in Nebraska packing gizzards in a turkey processing plant. "More important, the families here have great values. In the cornfields, man, those 11- and 12-year-olds really work hard."

But as the number of immigrants has soared, many have become walking targets for crime and exploitation. In one of the most outrageous cases, private security guards in Nashville are accused of systematically terrorizing Latino residents of several apartment complexes they were supposed to be protecting. The guards allegedly entered apartments, handcuffed residents, held guns to their heads, and ransacked their belongings. They kicked residents in the ribs, maced their genitals, and warned, "I'm going to throw your Spic ass out of the country." According to the weekly *Nashville Scene*, the owner of the security firm encouraged the assaults. "I'm bored," he told his staff on one occasion. "Let's go down to taco city and fuck with the Mexicans."

Even where violence hasn't erupted, hostility has often trumped hospitality. Not far from Siler City, county commissioners in Burlington, North Carolina, unanimously called for a halt to all immigration—legal and illegal. In Bybee, Tennessee, more than two-thirds of the town's residents tried to block the opening

of a Head Start center for Latino children. In Lexington, Kentucky, residents circulated a petition opposing efforts to make the city "a safe place for Hispanics." And in one poll, 79 percent of white North Carolinians said their neighbors would oppose living among Latinos.

Such sentiments don't surprise Lewis Phillips, police chief in Siler City for the past 17 years. "I've been asked how long it will take for people to accept them," he says. "It's not going to happen anytime soon. A lot of the older people here, they will never accept them."

UN SALUDO PARA *Chirilagua! ¡Un saludo para Veracruz!*" Wilfredo Hernandez lugs a video camera on his broad shoulders, filming a succession of immigrants sitting on park benches. A bulky, 36-year-old Salvadoran with a perpetually calm demeanor, he calls out a litany of Latin American towns as he pans from one face to another. "A greeting for Aguascalientes," he says in Spanish, facing a parishioner from that Mexican town. "A greeting for Tránsito."

On this cloudless summer morning, members of the Loves Creek Hispanic Baptist Mission are gathered at Jordan Lake, just down the road from Siler City. Today, Israel Tapia will immerse three of Hernandez's relatives in the Jordan, namesake of the river where Christ was baptized. "Here, in nature, is where God is," says Tapia. It will be a celebration of individual salvation, but it will also mark the growth of the church and the entire community. Nine Spanish-speaking congregations now serve Hispanics in Siler City, from mainstream Catholics to storefront Pentecostals—a testament to the community's almost-overnight development. In 1990, there were only 147 Hispanics among the town's 4,808 residents. Since then, more than 3,000 Hispanics have settled in Siler City.

As the Baptists gather at the water's edge, Hernandez puts the camera down and joins the congregation in hymns whose melodies are borrowed from the rhythms of tropical music and bolero. An ecstatic smile fills his face. Six years ago, Hernandez was just squeaking by in Southern California, trying to support his family on a cook's paycheck. Today he owns a mobile home and makes $11 an hour building trailers for other Latinos moving to town.

Hernandez had been pondering a move to Siler City for years. Fleeing civil war in El Salvador, he had arrived in Los Angeles in 1981. "From what I had heard, California was a wonderful land, a place for opportunities," he says. But those opportunities proved scarcer than Hollywood images had led him to believe. Hernandez found a $3.35-an-hour job washing dishes from 5 p.m. till 3 a.m. In the mornings he walked 45 minutes to a language school—he couldn't afford a bicycle—and stayed awake as long as he could in class. He shared a house with 13 others.

Things improved when he married Blanca, a fellow Salvadoran, and the couple moved into a one-bedroom apartment and started a family. But even with two incomes, they could barely afford the $525 rent. And when their oldest girl entered elementary school, Wilfredo had new concerns. "I worried about my daughter," he says, "that she'd try to get involved in gangs in order to survive."

Meanwhile, his relatives had moved to Siler City and were singing its praises with a missionary zeal. Every weekend, the phone would ring in Los Angeles, and it would be his mother, extolling the plentiful jobs and the safety of her new community. "When can you come here?" she would ask.

The question was answered in 1994, when the mammoth Northridge earthquake hit Los Angeles. Hernandez and his family were among 30,000 left homeless by the disaster. So Blanca and the girls rode a Greyhound bus for three days until they reached Siler City, where they moved into her mother-in-law's house. Wilfredo followed a month later in the family Honda. As with other immigrants, the move represented a shift in thinking as well as location. "California might have been the promised land 20 or 30 years ago," Hernandez says. "Not anymore."

When Hernandez, a lifelong city dweller, arrived in North Carolina, Siler City seemed like a ghost town. Even today, five years into the influx of Hispanics, Siler City looks at first glance like a typical Southern town. A four-lane highway runs from east to west, studded with McDonald's, Kentucky Fried Chicken, Golden Corral, and a brand-new Wal-Mart. Off the main road, nondescript ranch homes mingle alongside gracious two-story houses with wraparound front porches. Punctuating the landscape are the poultry plants and textile mills, low-slung concrete and metal buildings whose hunger for workers has fueled the town's rapid transformation.

It's only downtown that the demographic changes become apparent. The window of an insurance agency sports two flyers for the town's spring cleanup, one in English and the other in Spanish. Nearby, a business called Latin American Services promises help with plane fares, income tax forms, and traffic tickets. On a side street, Tienda Diana sells rice flour and dried fish, saffron and Salvadoran cheese. Colorful cardboard posters on telephone poles advertise Latin dances at a nightclub in Greensboro, 35 miles away. Like many small-town business districts, this one was dying a decade ago. Now it's springing back to life in two languages.

"The reason is plain and simple: jobs," says Ilana Dubester, director of the Hispanic Liaison, a nonprofit organization that helps immigrants make the transition to American life. "Local industries were desperate for labor. Word got out—let's put it that way—that they needed workers. The word from clients is that there are signs on the border that say, 'Come to Siler City.'"

Poultry companies are recruiting immigrants to fill dangerous jobs that pay less than $15,000 a year.

Like many of the town's new arrivals, Blanca Hernandez found a job on the midnight shift at the Townsend poultry plant. For $250 a week—more money than she had ever made—she stood on an assembly line, cutting and deboning chickens as they came by on a conveyor belt. The cavernous room was cold and noisy, but at least she could usually work at a manageable pace. But then the plant would fall behind in production, and the line would suddenly speed up. "When they really needed the chickens quickly, they just turned the button and the belt would go faster," she says. Sometimes the carcasses would pile up in front of her. Her arms hurt much of the time.

Poultry jobs are notoriously debilitating, which is one reason the industry is so desperate for employees. According to the Department of Labor, 9 percent of poultry workers suffer serious injuries or illnesses each year, three times the average for private industry. (The only manufacturing sector with a higher rate is meatpacking, which also has a large immigrant workforce.) By repeating the same action for hours at a stretch—often in extreme temperatures—workers develop painful disorders like carpal tunnel syndrome, which make it difficult to perform even simple tasks like picking up car keys. Some, too crippled to work, have been forced to return to Latin America. Others have undergone surgery to relieve the excruciating pain in their hands and wrists.

"Sometimes I couldn't sleep at night," recalls Javier Gutierrez, a Mexican immigrant who says he was injured by the repetitive motion of cutting and packing chicken wings at the Townsend plant. The company, which was cited for 40 serious health and safety violations during its last complete state inspection, refused to speak with *Mother Jones* about worker injuries.

After a year, Blanca Hernandez quit the poultry plant and took a job sewing panties at a local textile mill, where again she repeats the same motion over and over. The plant is noisy, and she and her co-workers pass the time by shouting over the din, catching up on gossip and talking about food and cosmetics. This spring, she was forced to go on light duty: The cumulative effect of repetitive factory work caught up with her, and she underwent surgery to relieve the pain in her wrist from carpal tunnel syndrome.

FOR MANY NEWCOMERS, the dangerous working conditions in Siler City are offset by the low rent and bite-your-tongue politeness of rural North Carolina. "Here, we have a more united relationship," says poultry worker Lidia Lopez, who moved from Guatemala by way of Los Angeles. "I go to the street to get the mail, and an old man comes and greets me and says, 'How are you?' There is a policeman, a young man, who talks to my husband when he's mowing the grass. When I go out, I try to talk, even though my English is not good. I feel they want to be friendly."

But in recent years, the reception has grown cooler—and sometimes violent. Thieves realized that many Latinos, wary of banks, often carried their savings in their pockets. That brought a rash of street robberies, in Siler City and throughout North Carolina. Walking to work at six o'clock one morning, Wilfredo Hernandez's father was attacked and robbed by two men who struck him in the face. "I was angry that I couldn't do anything about it," Hernandez says.

Local officials have also contaminated the town's race relations. The Hispanic

Task Force, which had no Hispanic members, published a brochure warning immigrants that it is illegal "to have chickens and goats inside the city limits" and "for a man to beat his wife or children." Those who break the law, the pamphlet warned, "will be arrested and face criminal proceedings."

Other officials took the threatening tone a step further. Last summer, police officers approached Rick Givens, a Democratic county commissioner, to complain about problems they faced during traffic stops. Coming from countries with different driving laws—and often afraid to visit government offices—some immigrants were driving without valid licenses or insurance. "Can you do anything about it?" Givens says one officer asked him. A retired pilot and Harley rider who is unafraid to speak his mind, Givens responded by dashing off a letter that essentially invited the Immigration and Naturalization Service to come in and clean house. "More and more of our resources are being siphoned from other pressing needs so that we can provide assistance to immigrants who have little or no possessions," Givens wrote the INS with the approval of his fellow commissioners. "Many of these new needy, we believe, are undocumented or have fraudulent paperwork. We need your help in getting these folk properly documented or routed back to their homes."

It seemed to Givens a simple solution. "I said, 'Screw 'em,'" Givens says. "If we have people who are here illegally, why can't we have these people sent home?"

The letter, which was quickly reprinted in Spanish, filled the town's newest residents—even those with legal documentation—with fear of mass arrests. Latino leaders tried to reassure immigrants over the airwaves, in Spanish-language newsletters, and from the pulpit. "We don't come to take away jobs," Israel Tapia preached in an emotional Saturday night sermon. "We come here to make Siler City the No. 1 town it is becoming, and I want to tell you the church is here to protect you and fight for you."

But his words did little to reassure residents, many of whom feared what they saw as a government-sanctioned call for a purge. "Some people were afraid to get out of their homes, because they didn't know if there was going to be a raid at the supermarket, a raid at work," says Ilana Dubester of the Hispanic Liaison. "Would they be put in jail, and their children would be abandoned? If you're from Latin Amer-

ica, you're used to seeing children on the street, just like abandoned dogs and cats."

The feds never did show up—but it didn't take the arrival of INS officials to poison the atmosphere. As if his constituents were taking their cue from Givens, acts of discrimination increased dramatically after the commissioner wrote his letter. Ruth Tapia had her run-in with the driver's license clerk. Several residents reported being threatened with deportation during traffic stops. Local businesses were suddenly demanding that Hispanic customers produce identification. And last fall, the hostility blew into the open when longtime residents packed a meeting and demanded that the county Board of Education do something about the growing number of Latino students in Siler City's schools. Even though the children quickly learn English, that didn't seem to satisfy residents like Kay Staley, who complained that her granddaughter began the year as one of only two white children in her elementary school class. "These two little girls were devastated and scared to death because no one spoke their language," Staley told the school board.

AS THE TENSIONS ROSE, educators at the University of North Carolina sponsored a weeklong trip to Mexico to give local leaders a better understanding of immigration issues. Among those invited to attend was Rick Givens. Suspicious of what he calls "all these die-hard liberals trying to give the world away," he agreed nonetheless to go along.

From the moment he arrived in Mexico, Givens felt himself growing uncomfortable with his own long-held assumptions. He met the parents of emigrants, visited a health clinic struggling to pay for medical supplies, and witnessed poverty firsthand. The breaking point came when he went to a school outside Puebla, where children attended classes in handmade tents. There, as a disabled teenager read an essay about how much his education meant to him, Givens began to cry. By the day's end he and his fellow travelers had started a fund to further the boy's education.

"Sometimes along the way, you forget what humble means," says Givens, the son of a railroad switchman. "You forget where you come from. It put me right back where I belong." On the plane home, the commissioner announced that he would disavow his earlier invitation to the INS. "I'm going to eat a lot of crow," he told his colleagues. "I still think our government's

immigration policy stinks, but I'm not going to make a big deal over legal or illegal. I'm going to help these people acclimate into our community and let the government sort out the work visas."

A decade ago, Siler City was a study in black and white. Today it is being reworked in shades of brown.

By the time he returned to Siler City, however, the poison spread by his original letter was already growing more toxic. A local white supremacist named Richard Vanderford had received a permit to hold the anti-immigration rally at City Hall. It would not be a first in the South: In 1998, organizers of a similar event in Culliman, Alabama, burned a Mexican flag while 60 people looked on. But with David Duke as the featured speaker, the Siler City demonstration was designed to be the first of a series of rallies across the South and Midwest. "We're focusing on how this is affecting Middle America," explains Vince Edwards, a spokesman for Duke. "The Southwest is almost lost to us."

The day of the rally, nearly 500 people turned out—some to gawk, a few to counterprotest, and many to show their support for Duke. Clyde Jones, a 63-year-old tobacco farmer who blames larger operations that rely on cheap imported labor for driving him out of business, donned a Confederate-flag jacket and drove in from the next county. "Mexicans took my job and my family's starving," said Jones. "My ancestors fought for this country, and they took it away without a shot." He turned to his son, who was wearing a matching jacket, and smiled. "Nice-looking Aryan people here," the father said.

With the county commissioner recanting his INS letter, protesters had a new enemy. "Recall the race traitor Rick Givens," said one picket sign. In his speech, Duke referred directly to Givens' new commitment to help Latinos integrate into the community. "We're not going to solve the problems of Mexico by turning America into another Mexico," Duke said. "Siler City is a symbol of what's happening in America. If you don't do something now, you're going to be outnumbered and outvoted in your own country."

Three days later, Duke followed up with a warning letter to Givens. "Our message to you is simple," he said. "Either change your policies and enforce the law of the land, or we will be forced to organize a recall effort and remove you from office."

Givens fired off a response. "I know that illegal immigration is wrong," he wrote the former Klansman. "But if the government of the United States can't deal with the illegal problem, then what makes

me a God or who appointed you?" Explains the commissioner: "I didn't want to be an asshole. But I didn't want to cow down to the Hooded Wonder."

Others were cowed. Several Latino families moved away after the rally, fearful of the spotlight being focused on Siler City. "They just weren't willing to take the risk of something happening in this town, as far as Immigration coming," says Dubester. "Why would you stay if you know there's work elsewhere?"

But hate rallies and racial animosity are unlikely to stop the immigration to towns

like Siler City. Work is plentiful, housing is cheap, and local white supremacists can't match the clout of anti-immigrant leaders in states like California and Texas. In these new border towns, few people are looking for paradise. Just survival.

"All I wanted to do was have a job, have a decent life, and be able to give everything that I wanted to my family," says Wilfredo Hernandez, sounding like generations of immigrants who have come before him. "I never wanted anybody to like me because of the color of my skin. I just want to have a job and go on with my life."

Specific Hispanics

Morton Winsberg

SUMMARY Los Angeles, New York, Miami, Chicago, and Houston are well-known Hispanic markets. But just below the big five are dozens of smaller Hispanic centers. This first-ever look at 12 Hispanic groups reveals the top towns for Colombians, Brazilians, and others. The rapid growth of specific Hispanic groups is destined to attract attention from marketers.

Most marketers are familiar with the three biggest Hispanic-American groups. Since the U.S. census first counted Hispanics in 1970, those who identify Mexico, Puerto Rico, and Cuba as their country of origin have comprised about three-fourths of the total U.S. Hispanic population. Hispanics from other Latin-American nations and cultures are less well-understood, but they constitute one-quarter of an estimated $170 billion consumer market. And because Hispanics of all kinds often live together in small areas, each country of origin can form a visible and desirable target market.

Among all Hispanics, the share of Mexicans has fallen from 62 percent of all U.S. Hispanics in 1970 to 61 percent in 1990. The Puerto Rican and Cuban shares have remained at about 12 percent and 5 percent, respectively. Hispanic Americans who don't have origins in these three countries are a small share of the nation's total Hispanic population, but they have been growing. Their numbers grew by slightly more than 2 million between 1970 and 1990. Immigrants of the new wave have been fleeing civil wars in Nicaragua, El Salvador, Guatemala, and Colombia. Others come for jobs or to rejoin family members already here.

The 1970 and 1980 censuses identified just four categories of Hispanics: Mexican, Puerto Rican, Cuban, and "other." The 1990 census provides much more detailed information, identifying 12 nations of Hispanic origin, as well as "other" Central Americans and "other" South Americans. These data provide the first opportunity to understand where specific Hispanic groups live.

> **Immigrants have always settled in America's largest cities, and today's immigrants are not much different.**

Many of the smaller Hispanic subgroups never show up on marketers' computer screens. Language barriers and the lack of large ethnic neighborhoods can make it hard to reach them with specially designed messages. Also, many Hispanic immigrants do not plan to become U.S. citizens or permanent residents. But rapid growth will inevitably lead more businesses to target Hispanic diversity. In ten years, America's Little Havanas will get a lot bigger.

BELOW THE BIG FIVE

Immigrants have always settled in America's largest cities, and today's immigrants are not much different. Six of the 12 Hispanic subgroups identified in the 1990 census have more than 80 percent of their populations in the nation's 20 largest cities, and 3 others have between 70 and 79 percent.

Mexican Americans are the only exception to the urban rule, because many of their ancestors never immigrated. Many Mexicans became U.S. citizens in the 19th century following the acquisition of Mexican territory by the United States. Almost all of this land was and still is rural or small cities. Many Mexicans who immigrated to the U.S. in recent years have settled in these same southwestern states. Here they normally reside in cities both large and small, as well as in rural areas.

Hispanics, like immigrants who came earlier, tend to concentrate in one or two major urban areas. New York City and Los Angeles early became a popular destination for Hispanics, but more recently, many have chosen Miami, Washington, D.C., and San Francisco. An example of an unusually high concentration of a Hispanic group in one city is the 77 percent concentration of people of Dominican origin in the New York urbanized area. Greater New York also has 60 percent of the nation's Ecuadorians and 44 percent of Puerto Ricans. Los Angeles has 49 percent of the nation's Guatemalans and 47 percent of its Salvadoreans. Miami is home to 53 percent of Cuban Americans.

Several U.S. places have Hispanic populations that rival or even surpass the largest cities in their countries of origin. New York's Puerto Rican population is now more than double that of San Juan. New York also has the second-largest urban population of Dominicans in the world, and the third-largest Ecuadorian population. The Mexican, Salvadorean, and Guatemalan populations of urban Los Angeles are surpassed only by those of their respective capitals: Mexico City, San Salvador, and Guatemala City.

Eighteen percent of all Hispanic Americans live in Los Angeles, and 12 percent live in New York. These two urban areas rank among the top-5 for 11 of the 12 Hispanic groups. Miami is on the top-5 list for 9 Hispanic groups, Washington, D.C., for 6, San Francisco for 5, and Houston and Chicago for 4.

TWELVE FLAGS

Hispanics of all types cluster in New York

Central Americans in San Francisco, Colombians

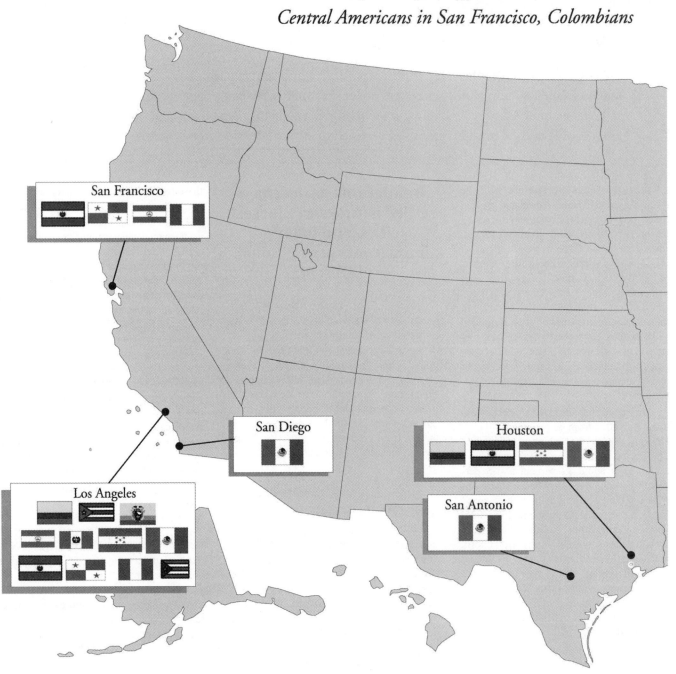

(top-five urbanized areas for Hispanics by country of origin, 1990)

OVER AMERICA

and Los Angeles. But you can also find lots of
in Chicago, and Peruvians in Washington

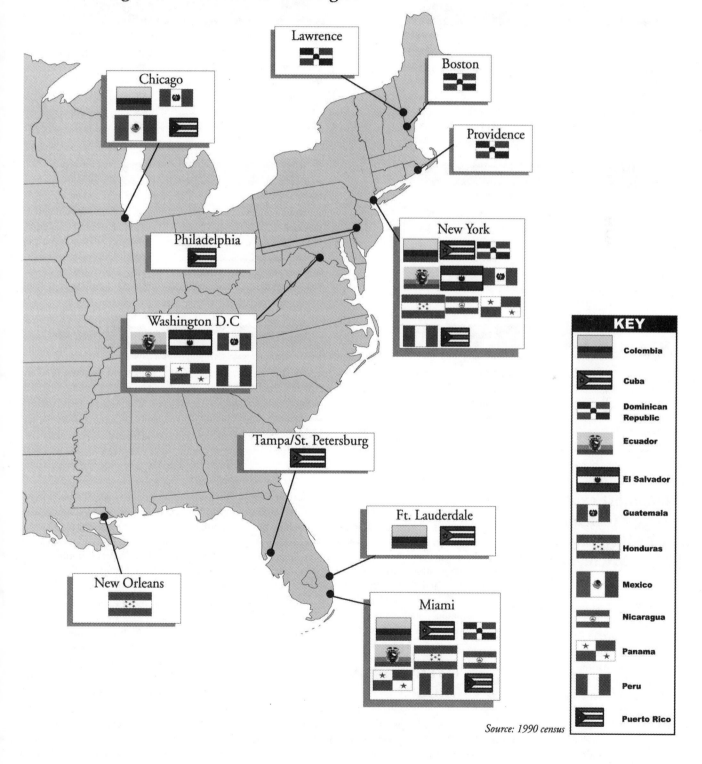

KEY

	Colombia
	Cuba
	Dominican Republic
	Ecuador
	El Salvador
	Guatemala
	Honduras
	Mexico
	Nicaragua
	Panama
	Peru
	Puerto Rico

Source: 1990 census

Little Quitos and Little

Mexico		
top-five urbanized areas	population	share
U.S. total	13,393	100%
Los Angeles	3,066	23
Chicago	538	4
Houston	528	4
San Antonio	524	4
San Diego	414	3

El Salvador		
top-five urbanized areas	population	share
U.S. total	565	100%
Los Angeles	265	47
New York	62	11
Washington, DC	52	9
San Francisco	43	8
Houston	39	7

Puerto Rico		
top-five urbanized areas	population	share
U.S. total	2,652	100%
New York	1,178	44
Chicago	1,464	6
Philadelphia	107	4
Miami	68	3
Los Angeles	51	2

Dominican Republic		
top-five urbanized areas	population	share
U.S. total	520	100%
New York	403	77
Miami	23	5
Boston	16	3
Lawrence, MA	12	2
Providence, RI	9	2

Cuba		
top-five urbanized areas	population	share
U.S. total	1,053	100%
Miami	559	53
New York	154	15
Los Angeles	55	5
Tampa-St. Petersburg	32	3
Ft. Lauderdale	24	2

Colombia		
top-five urbanized areas	population	share
U.S. total	379	100%
New York	152	40
Miami	53	14
Los Angeles	27	7
Ft. Lauderdale	12	3
Houston	10	3

The most exotic place where Mexicans cluster may be Bay City-Saginaw, Michigan.

The census also reveals many smaller areas with large and growing populations of specific Hispanics. For example, San Antonio and San Diego have the fourth- and fifth-largest Mexican-American communities in the nation, and Philadelphia has the third-largest Puerto Rican population. Tampa and Fort Lauderdale have the fourth- and fifth-largest concentrations of Cubans, and the Massachusetts areas of Boston and Lawrence have the third- and fourth-largest Dominican groups.

Chicago is the only midwestern urban area to come up on any of the top-5 lists, but it comes up a lot. Chicago has the country's second-largest Puerto Rican population, the second-largest Mexican population, and the third-largest Guatemalan and Ecuadorian populations. As a whole, Chicago has the fourth-largest Hispanic population of any urban area, at 4 percent of the national total.

TWELVE HISPANIC GROUPS

Laredo, Texas, is not big as urban areas go, with 99,258 people in 1990. But 94 percent of Laredo residents are Hispanic, and the

overwhelming majority are of Mexican origin. The census count of Hispanics, also mainly Mexican, is 90 percent in Brownsville and 83 percent in McAllen, two other Texas border towns. Several border towns in other states have equally high shares of Mexican Americans.

Perhaps the most exotic place where Mexicans congregate in large numbers is in the Bay City-Saginaw metropolitan area in Michigan. Mexicans first came to Bay City-Saginaw to work on the local cucumber farms. The descendants of these farm laborers now hold urban jobs, many in the local foundries.

Puerto Ricans began immigrating to the U.S. after World War II, and now they are a significant presence in the industrial

San Juans

Mexicans are by far the largest Hispanic-American group, but 77 percent of Dominican Americans live in one urban area.

(top-five urbanized areas for Hispanics by country of origin, population in thousands; and share of segment, 1990)

Guatemala

top-five urbanized areas	population	share
U.S. total	269	100%
Los Angeles	133	49
New York	27	10
Chicago	15	6
San Francisco	11	4
Washington, DC	9	4

Peru

top-five urbanized areas	population	share
U.S. total	175	100%
New York	54	31
Los Angeles	27	15
Miami	16	9
Washington, DC	11	7
San Francisco	9	5

Nicaragua

top-five urbanized areas	population	share
U.S. total	203	100%
Miami	74	37
Los Angeles	37	18
San Francisco	25	12
New York	14	7
Washington, DC	8	4

Honduras

top-five urbanized areas	population	share
U.S. total	131	100%
New York	33	25
Los Angeles	24	18
Miami	18	14
New Orleans	9	7
Houston	5	4

Ecuador

top-five urbanized areas	population	share
U.S. total	191	100%
New York	115	60
Los Angeles	21	11
Chicago	8	4
Miami	8	4
Washington, DC	5	3

Panama

top-five urbanized areas	population	share
U.S. total	92	100%
New York	27	29
Miami	7	7
Los Angeles	6	6
Washington, DC	4	4
San Francisco	2	2

cities of New York and southern New England. When older residents of these cities had achieved middle-class status and moved to the suburbs, they left behind entry-level jobs in manufacturing and service, and low-cost housing. The Puerto Ricans who took those jobs established the barrios of New York City.

While less affluent Puerto Ricans came to the U.S. for jobs, many middle-class Cubans fled their native country for political reasons. Cubans soon became closely identified with southeastern Florida, but now they are found in several other Florida towns. In the university towns of Gainesville and Tallahassee, for example, many second-generation Cuban Americans live as students.

Dominicans are a major Hispanic force in New York City and several New England industrial towns. They are only 2 percent of the nation's 1990 Hispanic population, but they are 15 percent of Hispanics in New York, 22 percent in Providence, and 35 percent in Lawrence, Massachusetts. Dominicans are flocking to the Northeast for the same reason Puerto Ricans did several decades ago: jobs. Hondurans and Nicaraguans, who have also immigrated largely for economic reasons, are settling in more bilingual areas on the Gulf of Mexico.

Hondurans are most numerous in New York, Los Angeles, and Miami, and Nicaraguans are most common in Miami, Los Angeles, and San Francisco. But both groups are dwarfed by the enormous numbers of other Hispanics in these large urban areas, so their largest concentrations emerge in unexpected places. Although Hondurans are less than 1 percent of the nation's Hispanic population, they are 20 percent of Hispanics in New Orleans. Nicaraguans are also well-represented among New Orleans Hispanics, and they are visible in nearby Baton Rouge and Port Arthur. Salvadoreans are just 3 percent of the nation's Hispanic population, but 25 percent of Hispanics in Washington, D.C.

Panamanians are perhaps the most geographically diverse of any Hispanic group. They are disproportionately represented in the local Hispanic population in towns near large military installations such as Fayetteville, North Carolina (Fort Bragg);

Columbus, Georgia (Fort Benning); Clarksville, Tennessee (Fort Campbell); Killeen, Texas (Fort Hood); Seaside, California (Fort Ord); and naval installations in Norfolk, Virginia; and Tacoma, Washington. Many who identified their ethnic origin as Panamanian in the 1990 census were military personnel once stationed in the former Panama Canal Zone.

People of South-American origin began moving in large numbers from New York City or coming directly from their homelands to coastal Connecticut towns during the 1980s, attracted to a growing number of service jobs that were not being filled by the local population. Housing was also more affordable than in New York City.

The affluent Connecticut town of Stamford is particularly attractive to South Americans. Its Hispanic population includes large proportions of Colombians, Ecuadorians, and Peruvians. In nearby Norwalk, Colombians are 20 percent of the city's Hispanic population.

MARKETING ATTENTION

So far, few U.S. corporations have paid attention to the special needs of "other" Hispanics. Mainstream marketers "are resistant enough to work with Hispanic marketing in total," says Nilda Anderson, president of Hispanic Market Research in New York City. "They are not going to do focused marketing."

One problem is a lack of marketing information. Recent census results and private research have improved the data on smaller Hispanic groups, says Gary Berman, president of Market Segment Research in Coral Gables, Florida, but few data were available until the 1990s.

Another problem is that Hispanic immigrants are less likely than previous generations of immigrants to live in ethnic-specific neighborhoods. In Miami, for example, newly arrived Cubans are often neighbors to Nicaraguans, and Nicaraguans may live next to Venezuelans. The city's celebrated "Little Havana" neighborhood is defined by its Cuban-owned businesses, but census data do not show an extreme overrepresentation of Cubans living in the area adjacent to those businesses.

Whatever their nation of origin, most Hispanic immigrants quickly acquire two basic American tools: a car and a telephone. Miami's Cubans may go to Little Havana to shop, socialize, and eat, just as Miami's Nicaraguans go to the Sweetwater district to buy copies of *El Diario La Prensa* and loaves of *pan Nicaraguense.* But when the trip is over, they return to homes scattered all over the city.

The affluent Connecticut town of Stamford is particularly attractive to South Americans.

Another problem is that many Hispanic immigrants are not interested in owning a home, buying a new car, or otherwise participating as full-fledged American consumers. New York City is home to about 10,000 foreign-born Brazilians, for example. But "most Brazilians are in New York only to save money for the return to Brazil," says Maxine L. Margolis, an anthropology professor at the University of Florida in Gainesville. In her book *Little Brazil,* Margolis tells the story of a local television news program called "TV Brasil." When it began, Brazilian-owned businesses were eager to sponsor it. But the ads failed to attract new customers, she says, because many Brazilians spend only what they must and save everything else.

Perhaps the biggest problem is the size of "other" Hispanic groups. "TV Brasil's" producers tried to persuade the Coors Brewing Company to advertise by claiming that 200,000 Brazilians lived in New York City, according to Margolis. But Coors turned them down anyway, claiming that the market was too small.

These obstacles may scare most businesses away, but the few that do target "other" Hispanics are rewarded with a growing source of loyal customers. As the airline of Colombia, Avianca focuses its U.S. advertising on Colombians, says Alberto Gil, a marketing analyst for the airline in New York City. The city's five boroughs are home to about 86,000 Colombians, according to demographer Frank Vardy at the Department of City Planning.

Avianca advertising runs primarily on Spanish-language television, radio, and in newspapers circulated in New York. "We don't care so much about whether the [medium] has a high rating for all Hispanics, but for Colombians," he says. The airline gauges Colombians' interests by asking its customers to name their favorite publications, radio stations, and TV shows.

The airline also focuses on a 20-block area in North Queens that is the geographic heart of Colombian settlement in New York City. Travel agents in that neighborhood receive special attention from the airline, says Gil. "We are a symbol for [Colombians]," he says. "We are Colombia in the United States."

Colombian politicians are well aware that New York-based expatriates form a powerful voting bloc. In past elections, polling places for Colombian elections have been established at the Colombian consulate and in Queens, says Javier Castano, a reporter for the Spanish-language newspaper *El Diario.* Colombian presidential candidates occasionally travel to New York City at election time, and politicians from many countries buy advertising in *El Diario* and other New York media.

Immigrants follow well-worn paths when they come to the United States, and these paths do not change rapidly. If immigration from Latin America continues at its current rapid pace, America's Little Havanas, Little San Juans, and other Hispanic enclaves will eventually grow to the point where targeting "other" Hispanics makes sense to mainstream marketers. Investing small amounts of time and money on specific Hispanics today could yield big payoffs tomorrow.

—*Additional reporting by Patricia Braus*

Behind the Numbers This study examines 1990 Hispanic populations in urbanized areas, defined by the U.S. Census Bureau as "one or more places (central place) and the adjacent densely settled surrounding territory (urban fringe) that together have a minimum of 50,000 persons." In 1990, the census identified 397 urbanized areas. For more information, contact the author at (904) 644-8377 or the Census Bureau at (301) 763-4040.

Morton Winsberg is professor of geography at Florida State University in Tallahassee.

The Blond, Blue-Eyed Face of Spanish TV

Activists Decry Shows as Lowbrow, Stereotypical—and Absent Afro-Latinos

By MICHAEL A. FLETCHER
Washington Post Staff Writer

Malin Falu has long been among New York's most beloved Spanish-language radio personalities. The region's huge Latino community has showered her with awards and has compared her to Barbara Walters and Oprah Winfrey because of the renowned figures she has interviewed and her intimate on-air style.

Falu, 54, studied theater in London, pursued modeling in New York and has hosted a version of the "Soul Train" music show in her native Puerto Rico. But whenever she has tried to capitalize on her experience by landing work on Spanish-language television in the United States, she has been stopped dead in her tracks.

A seemingly sure-fire endorsement deal fell apart after she met face-to-face with its sponsors. A television station lost her audition tape after she tried out for a news anchor's job. Also, two segments she had shot for a national morning show were killed.

Falu says those rejections are evidence of the rigid racial hierarchy that holds sway on Spanish-language television in the United States. Quite simply, she says, the whiter you are, the better your chances to be a star.

"I think this is all about race," said the brown-skinned Falu. "Professionally, there is no other reason for me not to be hired."

Falu's view is shared by an increasingly vocal corps of activists, actors and broadcast personalities who are critical of what they call a kind of racial caste system that gives Spanish-language television an almost exclusively Caucasian face.

Not only are few Afro-Latinos or indigenous people cast in Spanish-language television shows, they say, but the few that are most often play demeaning roles.

Latinos span the racial spectrum, with some being blond and blue-eyed and others having African features. A majority of those in the United States are of mixed race, indigenous or African stock. But that reality is not reflected in the offerings on the two networks that dominate Spanish-language television in this country, Univision and Telemundo.

Few darker-skinned personalities deliver the networks' domestically produced news shows. On the wildly popular telenovelas, the soap operas that are a programming staple of both networks, the starring roles are almost always filled by white Latino actors who typically play members of the upper class. Darker-skinned people, meanwhile, most often portray maids, gardeners, chauffeurs or dabblers in witchcraft.

"These shows stereotype the hell out of people," said Juan A. Figueroa, president and general counsel of the Puerto Rican Legal Defense and Education Fund. "If you looked at the soap operas without knowing better, you would think they came from Scandinavia or somewhere like that with all the blond, blue-eyed people you see. Meanwhile, the few people of color are relegated to the subclasses."

The racial images offered on Spanish-language television have been a source of dissatisfaction among Latino leaders for years, but the issue rarely has surfaced in public as activists have chosen to focus on increasing opportunities for Latinos on the major U.S. television networks and on film.

But that is beginning to change with the explosive growth of Spanish-language television. The four major television networks have seen their audience share shrink in recent years, but the Spanish-language audience has grown. In several major cities, including Miami, Houston and Los Angeles, Spanish channels are now the most watched among key demographic groups.

"There is a reluctance, more than a reluctance, in our community around this issue," Figueroa said. "It is considered taboo to even bring it up. But that is part of the challenge we face now in breaking that barrier."

Last year, Latino activists led a brief boycott of the four major U.S. networks for what they called a "brownout" of Latino characters from prime-time programming. The protest prompted ABC, NBC, CBS and Fox to add Latino characters to their shows.

But even as they took on the big four networks, many activists quietly seethed at the offerings available on Spanish-language television as well as the lack of racial diversity on the networks. Just as some African Americans have taken on BET, the nation's only major black-oriented cable television network, for a programming lineup they call lowbrow and stereotypical, some Latinos say Spanish-language television offers too many sexist portrayals of women, a mind-numbing array of formulaic telenovelas and, most of all, a lack of racial diversity.

"When we challenged the networks on the lack of diversity, it raised the question of what was going on with Spanish television," said Marta Garcia, co-chair of the National Hispanic Media Coalition. "And we have been very clear on the fact that both Univision and Telemundo need also to clean up their acts when it comes to diversity and how they portray dark-complected people."

Garcia met recently with Henry G. Cisneros, the president of Univision, to complain about the images on the network, which dominates Spanish-language television in the United States and has grown to be the nation's fifth-largest television network. Coalition officials have also raised similar concerns with Telemundo executives.

Meanwhile, activists are pushing the Puerto Rican Legal Defense and Education Fund to consider a lawsuit against the two major Spanish-language networks challenging their depiction of darker-skinned people.

A Telemundo spokesman acknowledged that black and indigenous people may be underrepresented in the network's shows. But, he added, Telemundo is working to improve the diversity of its offerings but is limited because it purchases much of its programming from Latin American producers. Likewise, Univision buys the bulk of its programming from the Venezuelan television company Venevision and Mexico's Grupo Televisa. And in both Mexico and Venezuela, darker skinned people are rarely seen on television.

"People who are really militant about this might exaggerate the situation," said Ted Guefen, the Telemundo spokesman. "But they say those images are underrepresented; they do have a point."

Guefen pointed out that one of the hottest new shows on Telemundo is "Xica," a novela based on the life of historical figure Xica Da Silva, a 19th-century slave who won her freedom with her lovemaking prowess. The Brazilian-made show is noted for its steamy scenes featuring young actress Tais Araujo, who is called the first black woman to be cast in the leading role of a Latin American telenovela.

Univision officials did not respond to repeated requests for comment. Several phone calls to the network's public relations officials resulted in promises to contact programming executives. But no Univision executive offered comment. Similarly, e-mails sent to both Cisneros and his administrative assistant brought no response.

Activists who have met with Cisneros say they have been promised improvements, particularly as Univision moves toward producing more of its own shows.

"Latino programming in all of its genres has a hard time accepting as a critical part of its identity [our] mestizo, mulatto origins," said Felix R. Sanchez, president of the National Hispanic Foundation for the Arts. "We have to reach a point where we say mestizo, mulatto is beautiful, much like the turning point for African Americans in the 1960s, when they said black is beautiful."

Roland E. Roebuck, a D.C. government employee and self-styled Afro-Latino activist, has written to Cisneros and several Latino civil rights groups to complain about the racial images on Univision and Telemundo.

"Much of the programming is filled with these Clairol ladies trying to accentuate their European tendencies," Roebuck said. "It seems that everyone uses Clairol to tint their hair and become instantly blond" even though they are Latino.

A survey of 4,000 Latino members of the Screen Actors Guild by the Tomas Rivera Policy Institute recently found that Latino actors preferred the opportunities offered by English-language productions to those offered in Spanish television. A majority of the respondents felt that Spanish-language productions provided greater opportunities for fair-skinned Latino actors, with the opposite being true for darker-skinned Latinos.

"It's true. There are many actresses who could not get work in [Latin America] because of their skin tone," said Tony Plana, star of the new Showtime series "Resurrection Boulevard," which has broken new ground with its all-Latino cast and won kudos for its depiction of a Latino family in Los Angeles. "They tend to want to have a blond, blue-eyed, upper-class character."

Analysts say the lack of racial diversity on Spanish-language television is rooted not as much in the attitudes of the programming executives here as it is in the racial attitudes that prevail in Latin America. That attitude, they say, is particularly evident in the telenovelas, which are a global phenomenon and air in more than 100 countries. The melodramas, which typically run for several months, often feature a love story in which a woman is trying to make the leap to the upper classes by getting a rich man to fall in love with her.

"There is a class phenomenon in Latin America where you think of upper class and upper-middle class being more European, and the black and indigenous population being more in poverty," said Harry P. Pachon, president of the Rivera Institute, a Latino research organization in Claremont, Calif. "And it seems that Spanish-language television has taken this to heart."

Elpidia Carrillo, a Mexican-born actress who through the years has played in American films alongside mega-stars, including Jack Nicholson, Richard Gere and Arnold Schwarzenegger, said that in Mexico, her stunning but decidedly non-white look was a barrier to getting many acting roles.

"It seems that I was always being cast as a *campesina* [farm worker], or a prostitute," said Carrillo, who lives in Los Angeles. "It has only been a little better here. It was very difficult for me to try to get a job in Mexico. There are not many stories written for Latin-looking actresses…. [The Latin American film industry] is very racist that way."

Jerry G. Velasco spent eight years as an actor in Mexican telenovelas. He has been a taxi driver, a chauffeur and an organized crime hoodlum. Only once did he land what he considers a classier role, when he played a historical character who was the vice president of Mexico.

Velasco, now a film industry activist in Los Angeles, said the parts he got during his Mexican television career had nothing to do with his limitations as an actor. Instead, he said, they were the result of his olive-colored skin, something he and many other Latinos in the television and movie business say defines their opportunities.

"I'll tell you this," he said. "I would never be the one who gets to take the leading blond girl home."

Latino, White Students Cling to Own Social Circles

By Emily Wax
Washington Post Staff Writer

Dawson is acting too weird this time.

His thin, blond hair is coiffed a little too high and a little too long. And he's spouting a lot of melodramatic nonsense, using all his big SAT words, going on and on about life and love and high school. Dawson has everything. A creek. A girlfriend, depending on the episode. A decent, even sizable, inheritance. And friends with some really cool dreams and some really complex "issues."

His image glows every Wednesday at 8 p.m. in this comfortable Arlington living room, where 10 to 20 Washington-Lee High School students sprawl out on the large, puffy sofas to watch the teen soap opera "Dawson's Creek." They call it "Creek Night." They watch, they laugh, sometimes they hurl things at the television.

Creek Night is a ritual for these teenagers, a time to unwind from the rigors of classes, sports, college applications. Most of the people who attend here are seniors in Washington-Lee's academically challenging International Baccalaureate program. Most grew up in Arlington, attending the same elementary schools and middle schools. They are the student government leaders; all of them plan to go to college.

And all of them are white.

Which is notable, because 66 percent of Washington-Lee's enrollment is made up of minority students—37 percent Latino, 15 percent Asian American and 14 percent black. Yet a white student who takes IB classes, works on the yearbook, hangs out at the mall with friends and goes to a school baseball game might as well be attending a majority-white school.

"It's something I have thought about when I wonder why our student clubs aren't more diverse," says Beth Skelton, a friendly girl with a big, curly ponytail who has been hosting Creek Night since sophomore year. "It's not that we don't want to be friends."

Beth says she is glad to be attending a diverse high school, as are many of her friends. And yet in the three years that she has hosted Creek Night, she has never personally invited a Latino student.

"Creek is with people who I have classes with, and there are no Hispanic students in my classes, and for W-L that's just incredible, I know," says Beth.

"There's an open invitation for anyone to come, and I would welcome them if they came. But I haven't done a whole lot of seeking people out."

High School Is High School

In the hallways of Washington-Lee, there are teenagers from dozens of countries. And yet, the abiding truth about being in high school is still this: Similar kids hang out together.

"We don't really know each other," says senior Chrissy Ambrose. There's nothing mean about it, she emphasizes. It's just that she has known Lindsay Stagna and Beth, as she puts it, "since she was born."

High school is the time when teenagers figure out who they are and then reinforce it by spending time with people who act and dress as they do, who listen to the same music. As America's schools become more diverse, this self-selection is a growing national concern.

"You see this social separation happening at many high schools," says Dana Moran, a high school teacher in Berkeley, Calif., who has been studying student life since 1998 as part of a diversity project with the University of California. "It's a part of high school life, and at diverse schools like our school, it can end up leaving Latino students outside of many social activities that are going on."

Certainly, progress has been made. At suburban schools like Washington-Lee, multiculturalism is hip, and racial slurs are on their way out. But in the end, students from different backgrounds simply ignore each other.

"It's unrealistic to say, 'Okay, kids, shake hands, be best friends,'" says Marsha Dale, who runs "A World of Difference" peer training workshops several times a year at Washington-Lee as part of a national program run by the Anti-Defamation League. "That's not human nature."

On workshop days, throughout the school—in the orchestra room, in the library—students of all shades and accents and wearing all brands of jeans and sneakers form small groups and try to connect with each other.

For one exercise, the students are asked to pick several words to describe themselves.

Chris Jones, 17, says he may look black but he is half Latino. "I would totally describe myself as a minority," he says.

When the immigrant students speak up, their countries of origin are the first things they mention. They are Bolivian, Salvadoran, Ethiopian.

The white students start off with their interests—they love music, they're techies, they're dreamers and writers. One jokes that he is "your boring white guy."

The immigrant students list their religion as their second description; the white students are quiet on this subject. "I know it's one of my biggest flaws, but I don't like religion," admits Nicole Koglin, a white student who is a diversity peer trainer. "So it's true—it's hard for me to relate."

Other white students say they are ill at ease when they see Hispanic classmates with "Jesus Loves El Salvador" on their backpacks and large crosses around their necks. For them, religion is a more private experience.

"People say: 'You are so religious. Why?'" Gaby Florido says. "Sometimes people think, 'Don't you have anything better to do than go to church?'"

Some white and Latino students also describe themselves as good dressers, and that brings up the issue of what "good" means to different groups in the halls of Washington-Lee. Jewelry, cars, hair-styles—everything's different. The students toss the words "classy" and "trashy" around when referring to name-brand vs. discount stores, respectively.

"It's like some kids are happy if they have clothes just to cover their bodies so they aren't naked," says Gaby.

Chris poses a different question: Have you ever seen one group exclude another at Washington-Lee?

Kyle Curd says it's not that simple—it's just that it's too uncomfortable to roam outside your own circle of friends.

"Me being white, I mean, it's not that I can walk into the Spanish crowd at lunch," Kyle says. "It would be harder for me to fit in."

At one point, a white student in diversity training becomes frustrated when some Latino students start speaking Spanish to each other. "We are in America. Now speak English," she says.

The students in the room call out, "Ouch!" That's what the instructions tell them to do when someone says something hurtful.

All these differences are tossed around candidly in the workshop. Here and there, an insight emerges.

"I used to think people were dumb if they couldn't speak English," says Kristen Wagner, a white student who lived in Tanzania when her father worked for the Peace Corps. "I was too quick to judge."

Adds Steve Atlas, 18, a white student who is going to Brown University in the fall: "I do have sympathy for them. A lot of the Latino students have to work jobs and have harder lives. That's why maybe they are going to community college instead and don't have a lot of money for clothes. It's a lot different."

Next year, the school has decided to make the workshop an official class, for credit.

Scene From a Mall

On a Friday night at Ballston Common Mall, Sarah Zeballos, Nick Trujillo, Gaby Florido and Lizeth Marin are polishing off steak fajitas at Chevys. They are Latino friends at Washington-Lee, popular kids in their own circle.

They're downing basket after basket of chips when Sarah spots some of the students from the Creek Night crowd—Lindsey and Katy Maher and Beth—across the restaurant.

Sarah, a soft-spoken, dark-haired girl, is one of just a handful of Latinos in the senior class who is in the full IB certificate program. That means she will graduate with the same kind of diploma Beth will have.

She considers whether she should go over and say hi. She's wearing her small circular glasses and jeans; they're wearing makeup and skirts. But she works up her courage and goes for it anyway.

"Hi, you guys," she says, ambling over.

Beth smiles warmly and says hello. The other girls are involved in their own conversation and don't notice.

"How are you?" Sarah asks. "I haven't seen you in so long."

"I'm good," Beth says. "What's up? How are you?"

"Fine, good," Sarah says.

Then there is silence.

"See you Monday," Sarah says. And back she goes to Gaby and her other friends. The encounter lasts less than a minute.

"The same people have been in the same classes for years," Sarah says. "They learn to respect you, but it's hard to make friends with them. Sometimes, you just want to fit in. But you can't go and say, 'I am going to be your friend.' They already know each other."

Sarah came to the United States when she was 12. She and her three sisters and parents lived in a three-room apartment. She enrolled in summer school and made friends with many of the students from her country who were spending those months learning English.

It wasn't until school started that fall that she fully realized that her school life in America would be very different from summer school. In high school, she noticed something about the white students: "They turn in their homework on time, yes, but I also noticed they are different from us. They go and drink and have fun and go back and study," Sarah says quietly. "We

don't really have that luxury. We can't take the risk of slacking off too much."

Bianca Zurita, a Bolivian student, volunteers: "White nerds are more perky than Spanish nerds."

Latino kids laugh at that statement. But Bianca just shrugs, as if the statement is as plain and as true as the time or the temperature.

"Maybe 'cause the Spanish kids know they have to try harder in life," she explains.

Just last year, when Sarah was in a math class with Beth, the divide didn't seem so vast. A few of the IB students came to Sarah's 17th birthday party, ate her mother's homemade *saltenas*. Sarah taught them how to salsa dance.

"I'm not a very good dancer at all," says Beth, giggling. "But going over there was so much fun, and some of the other girls from Creek now go salsa dancing every week."

Though universities want diverse enrollments, the achievement gap in test scores, high school grade-point averages and extracurricular activities makes the pool of equally qualified Latino and white students vastly different in size. Factor in financial difficulties, immigration status and cultural issues, and the divide grows.

For instance, late in their junior year, Sarah and Beth discovered that they had both been accepted to Cornell University's pre-college summer program, where high school kids live in dorms, take classes for college credit and meet current students. The program costs $6,000.

But Sarah couldn't go. She didn't get the scholarship money she hoped for, and besides, she needed to work all summer to pay for her braces, which cost $3,400. So she took a job as a hostess at Rio Grande Cafe. All summer, she seated people and smiled at them through her braces.

You see some of the white kids and you know they don't have to pay for their braces," she says.

Still, Sarah says her *ganas*—her desire—keeps her going. She is careful to tell friends that she is not a victim just because she has had different circumstances.

"Having less makes you try harder," Sarah says. "Ganas means you still work hard and do well and you try not to let the other stuff bother you."

Sarah's parents have moved the family three times since arriving in the United States, each time trying to find a larger apartment they could afford. Sarah's mother, who received a college degree in business in Bolivia, has switched jobs several times, from cleaning offices to working in the kitchen of a fast-food restaurant to baby-sitting. Her father received an accounting degree in Bolivia, but here, he works as an electrician.

Beth's parents are divorced, but money has not been a big worry for her family. Beth's father works for the federal government; her mother works for the Arlington schools developing science curricula.

Beth attended the Cornell program because her parents paid, but she was troubled that Sarah could not join her.

"It kind of feels weird that there are these differences, like, that I would be able to do one thing and she wouldn't," says Beth. "I'm very fortunate in many ways. It was hard to think that she couldn't go. She is just as qualified as me, probably more so."

This year, Beth and Sarah aren't in any classes together. They still smile at each other in the halls. Their budding friendship has faded, but they still care about one another: Beth invited Sarah to her small graduation party.

Standing Out in Class

For many students, the system segregates them first. Then they separate themselves.

The IB program has stopped white flight, many teachers say in private, and although the program is wildly popular and academically praised, some believe that it creates more division within the school.

During a recent morning in Tom Shelstrat's advanced IB social anthropology class, students rush in with highlighters in hand and take seats in a circle. Before class starts, soft music plays in the background.

Of the class of 15 students, two are Hispanic—Luz Carera and Milady Rodriguez. Shelstrat says this is an improvement over past years, a sign that the school is starting to include more Hispanics, and indeed wants to.

Milady and Luz both wanted to be in the class very badly; Luz entered the class late in the year. She wanted it so much that she stayed after school to have Shelstrat tutor her. They are doing well in the class.

Right now, they are studying "In Search of Respect: Selling Crack in El Barrio," a book about life in a poor Latino neighborhood in East Harlem. During a recent session, Shelstrat asked Milady to talk about the role of women and issues of oppression in her native El Salvador.

Shelstrat is overjoyed to have these students in his class. "It's like gold when you get a minority student who can relate to things you are studying and can talk about their experience, their culture," Shelstrat says. "Those are really magic moments."

Both Luz and Milady say that it's nice that the teacher respects their experiences and that many of the issues discussed help to debunk stereotypes. But it can be awkward being the only Latinos.

"It's good that we are here," says Luz, who is deeply shy and rarely speaks in class. "But in other ways, you think, 'Oh, I am representing Spanish people.'" And aside from the work itself, the first few months of being in the class is just intimidating."

"One day I walked in, I was like, 'Wow!'" says Milady, a thin girl who came here six years ago. "It was so many white students."

In Lynn Russo's "regular" social studies class, the demographics are the opposite of those in the IB class. There are two or three white students, and the rest are minorities. Before Russo starts class, kids chatter in Spanish, Arabic and Urdu.

Caroline Bell-Luehrs, who is white, says she likes being in the class because the teacher is really good and she does not want to "live in a bubble," like some of the IB students.

"Some of those kids would die if you put them in a room with Spanish kids," says Caroline, shrugging her shoulders. "Sometimes you feel that those kids are in their own school."

Sitting in her office, where red Persian-style rugs make the room seem less institutional, IB program coordinator Marilyn Leeb says she is aware of that criticism but that she works hard to make all classes more diverse.

She says she allows students of all levels to sample the program, letting them take one, two or three IB classes. And she has been encouraging Latino students to take advanced science classes and an advanced Spanish class for fluent speakers.

"It's challenging and hard for all of these reasons," Leeb says. "But I think it's the right thing to do—to really try and hope things change."

Moving more Latinos into advanced classes is an important goal of the principal's and the superintendent's. Still, they realize how complex it can be.

"Sometimes, children don't want to be in those classes because of the isolation they will feel when they think they have to represent their entire race," Principal Marion D. Spraggins says. "That's a tremendous responsibility. But that just means we need to do more."

This year, Spraggins told teachers to select high-performing students and send them to her office. She sat the teenagers down and said: "Listen, guys: Your teacher thinks you can do this work. What can we do to help you take these classes?"

College Dreams Diverge

During senior year, the obsession with college becomes a palpable divide at Washington-Lee.

Nick Trujillo wants to go away to school, maybe to Florida Tech. He wants a new, more independent life. Nick's mother died in Venezuela when he was 8. His aunt and uncle, who raised him, can't imagine why he would leave home. They think he should live at home and study at Northern Virginia Community College.

His sister Carolina, 19, feels torn.

"We have always been all together—always," Carolina says one evening before dinner in their high-rise apartment. Nick rolls his eyes and interrupts.

"I say I should go where it's better for me. I want to study psychology," he says.

"I think they have to let him go, but we have always been here together, through so much together, since our mom died in Venezuela," Carolina says. "I try to tell them he needs to live his own life, to go to the best school for his major. But they don't like the idea of him to go away. It's not his fault that the best universities are so far away."

Carolina attends Nova.

For the white middle-class students, however, there is little debate. Most of the IB students want to go far away, to big universities. The University of Virginia, for instance, is too close to home to carry much cachet in these discussions.

On a Wednesday night, the Creek crowd has gathered at the Lost Dog Cafe in Arlington. They discuss where they've applied as if they are listing awards they have won. The list becomes an extension, a symbol, of their identity.

Many have spent weekends visiting colleges. They come back with sweat shirts and stories of leafy campuses and parties at fraternity houses.

Beth prefers a small liberal arts school, so she has applied to William and Mary, Kenyon and the College of Wooster in Ohio, her top choice.

After they eat, they pile into cars and head to Beth's for Creek Night. Slowly, friends gather, and the laughter grows louder than the television.

Tonight's episode is about vandalism at school. Joey—one of the show's main female characters—paints a mural with Chinese characters to convey the word "possibility."

A white student sprays paint on the mural and tells the principal that it was an eyesore.

The principal responds, "Possibility— is that offensive to you?"

The student answers, "I am white and rich and that's all the possibility I need."

Beth and her friends roll their eyes.

"Silly," Chrissy says. "I am glad I go to Washington-Lee," Russ Evans, 17, says. "We don't have people like that."

Everybody agrees and laughs and starts other conversations.

The show goes to a commercial. When it continues, Joey asks Dawson this question: "What unifies us as a school? Nothing, really."

The kids at Creek Night fall quiet.

Postscript

Most of the seniors have gotten their college acceptance letters by now. Beth Skelton is going to her first choice— Wooster College in Ohio.

Sarah Zeballos got a full-tuition scholarship to American University.

Gaby Florido will go to Virginia Commonwealth University, where she plans to study pre-medicine. She was accepted at several other schools, but because she is not a citizen, only VCU offered her financial aid.

Nick Trujillo will attend Nova. He had hoped to transfer to Florida Tech, where he was also accepted. But because of money and his family's desire for him to stay close to home, he is now thinking about going to Virginia Tech.

Faces in the Hallways

Chris Jones, 17
A student of two worlds

Jones is a mixed-race student. He looks black, and because he is also half Latino, he wants to be friends with both groups of students at school. He tries to sit at different lunch tables. Sometimes friends think it's strange how easily he slips between the groups.

"No one realized that I am half Spanish," said Jones. "They wonder why I hang out with everybody. I just try to ignore that. I sometimes sit at a table with all Spanish kids, and the next day I could sit at a table with all black kids. I like doing that."

Russ Evans, 17
Only white student on varsity soccer team

Curly-haired Russ Evans has always loved soccer. But when the 17-year-old first came to Washington-Lee, he didn't try out for the team. He saw that most of the team was primarily Latino and that the coach sometimes ran the games in Spanish. But soon he decided that his worries were silly and went out for the team.

"They are really good players, and if you treat them right, you can make friends," said Evans. "Sometimes you just have to take a sense of humor about being the only white student and just have fun. When you hear what these students have been through, it really is humbling."

Susan Ward
Parent volunteer in school library

At first, Ward and her husband wanted their daughter, Erin, to attend a private Catholic school. Then the upper-middle-class couple heard about the school's International Baccalaureate program, which they thought would be academically rigorous for Erin, who is a bright student with excellent grades.

"What makes it a struggle for the school is not the ethnic background of the students. It's the economics," Ward said. "They don't have the educational background that a lot of the American-born families do. They are deprived of things that we don't even understand. My daughter is in a different world in this school, and poverty is what separates those worlds."

UNIT 6
African Americans

Unit Selections

Key Points to Consider

- Does the exposure of race profiling by law enforcement agencies and the end of affirmative action in educational policy indicate that public governmental programs are not responsive to the needs and desires of African Americans?

- Is racebased violence increasing? Defend your answer.

- Can any Democrat be elected President without massive electoral support of African Americans? Does a Republican presidential candidate need the support of African American voters to win? Explain.

- What are the most compelling issues that face African American communities? Is location an important variable in the formulation of your answer? What role will new African immigrants play in the African American community?

- What social, economic, and political conditions have supported the expansion of an African American middle class?

- What explains the persistence of an African American underclass? In what respect is this question related to integration? In what respect is attention to education an answer to economic and social integration of African Americans?

- Does the name "African Americans" augment the development of pluralism? Discuss in terms of Afrocentrism and integration.

- What effect will the Supreme Court's de-emphasis on remedies for segregation and on other initiatives that use racial preferences have on race and ethnic relations?

 **Links: www.dushkin.com/online/**
These sites are annotated in the World Wide Web pages.

National Association for the Advancement of Colored People (NAACP)
http://www.naacp.org

The 2000 U.S. Census appears to be heading toward a substantive redefinition of racial and ethnic diversity in as much as respondents were able to select multiple racial/ethnic identities. Thus, the last vestige of the official separation of white and black demographics will emerge from the crucible of America's primordial problem of overcoming slavery and color consciousness.

A 1988 *New York Times* editorial suggests an appropriate introductory focus for the following collection of articles about an ethnic group that traces its American ancestry to initial participation as "three-fifths" of a person status in the U.S. Constitution and to its later exclusion from the freedoms of this polity altogether by the U.S. Supreme Court's *Dred Scott* decision. The editors of the *Times* wrote in the article "Negro, Black and African American" (December 22, 1988):

The archaeology is dramatically plain to older adults who, in one lifetime, have already heard preferred usage shift from *colored* to *Negro* to *black*. The four lingual layers provide an abbreviated history of civil rights in this century.

The following glimpses of the African American reality, its struggles for freedom, its tradition and community, its achievements, and the stresses of building bridges between worlds reveal a dense set of problems. More importantly, they suggest pieces of authentic identity rather than stereotype. Becoming a healthy ethnic society involves more than the end of ethnic stereotyping. The basis of ethnic identity is sustained by authentic portrayals of positive personal and group identity. The cultivation of ethnicity that does not encourage disdain for and selfhatred among members and groups is an important psychological and social artifice.

Progress on issues of race involves examination of a complex of historical, social, cultural, and economic factors. Analysis of this sort requires assessment of the deep racism in the American mentality, that is, the cultural consciousness and the institutions whose images and practices shape social reality.

Prior to the information explosion, discrimination and prejudice based on skin color were issues rarely broached in mainstream journals of opinion. Ethnic and racial intermarriage and the influence and impact of skin hue within the African American community raise attendant issues of discrimination and consciousness of color. This concern began in eighteenth- and nineteenth-century laws and practices of defining race that shaped the mentalities of color consciousness, prejudice, and racism in America. Other dimensions of the African American experience can be found in this unit's accounts of African American traditions and experiences of self-help and the family. New perspectives on the civil rights era can be gained from reflective accounts of the leaders who influenced the direction of social change that reconfigured race and ethnic relations in America.

As this debate continues, patterns of change within African American populations compel discussion of the emerging black middle class. The purpose and influence of the historically black university, the reopening of the discussion of slavery and the separate-but-equal issue, and the renewed attention to Afrocentric education are clear evidence of the ambivalence and ambiguity inherent in the challenges of a multicultural society. Earlier dichotomies—slave/free, black/white, poor/rich—are still evident, but a variety of group relations based on historical and regional as well as institutional agendas to preserve cultural and racial consciousness have complicated the simple hope for liberty and justice that was shared by many Americans. Issues of race and class are addressed in this section. Various approaches to Afrocentrism are explained and contrasted.

Questions on the future state of American ethnic groups raise profound issues. For example, an understanding of the changing structure of the African American family has stubbornly eluded researchers and parents who confront the realities of pride and prejudice. Does the continual discovery of prejudice and discrimination in corporations have implications for public policy? Should public policy sustain an ethnic model of family or direct the formation of family life that is consonant with public purposes and goals?

The civil rights movement has been over for more than 20 years, but many African Americans still face challenges in housing, employment, and education. Changing circumstances within the larger American society and the civil rights agenda itself have been affected by success and failure, and onceclear issues and solutions have taken on more complex structural, economic, and philosophical dimensions. The growing gap between blacks and whites in terms of education, financial status, and class and the growing crime and death rates of young black men paint a daunting picture of past policies and of this population's future. According to scales of mortality, health, income, education, and marital status, African Americans have emerged as one of the most troubled segments of American society.

To be sure, African Americans have made advances since the civil rights movement of the 1960s. They have made dramatic gains in education, employment, and financial status. Unfortunately, they still are portrayed as being part of an urban underclass when only onethird of their population is actually in this group. While not all African Americans are poor, those who are poor are in desperate situations. Will help come from the African American population that now constitutes part of the middle and upper classes of American society?

Scholarly differences of opinion concerning the composition of the urban underclass do not minimize the hardships that many endure. The growth of the underclass, its isolation from society, and society's inability to help it are tremendous obstacles that face our nation. Concrete strategies for improving this situation call upon both the public and the private sectors in areas of education, employment, and training. Suggestions for meeting future needs of this population and pragmatic policy responses also will help the general population.

The issues of race in the workplace and remedies for discriminating practices have been raised in the debate regarding the Civil Rights Act of 1991. Exploring ethnic and racial mobility and developing strategies that foster the breakdown of discrimination engage us in a web of baffling arguments and social, political, and institutional procedures.

10 Most Dramatic Events In
African-American History

Lerone Bennett Jr.

1. The Black Coming

A YEAR before the arrival of the celebrated *Mayflower*, 244 years before the signing of the Emancipation Proclamation, 335 years before *Brown* vs. *Board of Education*, a big, bluff-bowed ship sailed up the river James and landed the first generation of African-Americans at Jamestown, Va.

Nobody knows the hour or the date of the official Black coming. But there is not the slightest doubt about the month. John Rolfe, who betrayed Pochohontas and experimented with tobacco, was there, and he said in a letter that the ship arrived "about the latter end of August" in 1619 and that it "brought not anything but 20 and odd Negroes." Concerning which the most charitable thing to say is that John Rolfe was probably pulling his boss' leg. For no ship ever called at an American port with a more important cargo. In the hold of that ship, in a manner of speaking, was the whole gorgeous panorama of Black America, was Jazz and the spirituals and the black gold that made American capitalism possible.[*] Bird was there and Bigger and King and Malcolm and millions of other Xs and crosses, along with Mahalia singing, Duke Ellington composing, Gwendolyn Brooks rhyming and Michael Jordan slam-dunking. It

was all there, illegible and inevitable, on that day. A man with eyes would have seen it and would have announced to his contemporaries that this ship heralds the beginning of the first Civil War and the second.

As befitting a herald of fate, the ship was nameless, and mystery surrounds it to this day. Where did this ship come from? From the high seas, where the crew robbed a Spanish vessel of a cargo of Africans bound for the West Indies. The captain "ptended," John Rolfe noted, that he needed food, and he offered to exchange his cargo for "victualle." The deal was arranged. Antoney, Pedro, Isabella and 17 other Africans with Spanish names stepped ashore, and the history of Africans in America began.

And it began, contrary to what almost all texts say, not in slavery but in freedom. For there is indisputable evidence that most of the first Black immigrants, like most of the first White immigrants, were held in indentured servitude for a number of years and then freed. During a transitional period of some 40 years, the first Black immigrants held real property, sued in court and accumulated pounds and plantations.

This changed drastically in the sixth decade of the century when the White founding fathers, spurred on by greed and the unprotected status of African immigrants, enacted laws that reduced most Africans to sla-

very. And so, some 40 years after the Black coming, Black and White crossed a fatal threshold, and the echo of that decision will reverberate in the corridors of Black and White history forever.

2. The Founding of Black America

W HEN on a Sunday in November 1786, the little band of Black Christians arrived at Philadelphia's St. George's Methodist Episcopal Church, the sexton pointed to the gallery. The Blacks paused and then started up the rickety stairs with downcast eyes and heavy hearts. To the leaders of this group, Richard Allen and Absalom Jones, this was the ultimate indignity—to be shunted from the first floor to the gallery in a church Black men had helped build.

The group had barely reached the top of the stairs when a voice from the pulpit said, "Let us pray." Without thinking, the men plopped down where they were—in the *front* of the gallery. Allen was praying as hard as he could when he heard loud voices. He opened his eyes and saw a White sexton trying to pull Absalom Jones from his knees.

"You must get up; you must not kneel down here!" the White sexton said.

"Wait until the prayer is over," Jones replied.

The voices echoed through the church, and people looked up and beheld the incredible scene of a Black Christian and a White Christian wrestling in the house of the Lord over the color of God's word.

"Get up!" the sexton said. "Get up!"

"Wait until the prayer is over," Jones replied wearily, "and I will not trouble you any more."

Four or five White Christians rushed to the sexton's aid, and the struggle spread over the gallery. Before the issue was resolved, the prayer ended. The Black men stood up then and, without a word, streamed out of the church in the first mass demonstration in Black American history.

Richard Allen added a mournful postscript:

"... And they were no more plagued by us in the church."

They were no more plagued by Blacks in a lot of places. For the Philadelphia demonstration was the focal point of a national movement that created the foundations of Black America. On April 12, 1787, Richard Allen and Absalom Jones created the Free African Society which DuBois called "the first wavering step of a people toward a more organized social life."

Similar societies were formed in most major Northern cities. And on this foundation rose an intricate structure of independent Black churches, schools and cultural organizations. The movement climaxed in the 1820s and 1830s with the founding of Freedom's Journal, the first Black newspaper, and the convening of the first national Black convention.

3. Nat Turner's War

GOD was speaking, Nat Turner said later.

There was, he remembered, thunder and lightning and a "loud voice" in the sky. And the voice spoke to him, telling him to take up the yoke and fight against the serpent "for the time was fast approaching when the first should be last and the last should be first."

Nat Turner was numbered among the last. And although he was a slave in Southampton County, Va., it would be said of him later that he "made an impact upon the people of his section as great as that of John C. Calhoun or Jefferson Davis." A mystic with blood on his mind and a preacher with vengeance on his lips, he was an implacable foe of slaveholders. He had believed since he was a child that God had set him aside for some great purpose. And he decided now that God was calling him to rise up and "slay my enemies with their own weapons."

To this end, Turner, who was about 30 years old, chose four disciples and set his face towards Jerusalem, the county seat of Southampton.

On Sunday morning, Aug. 21, 1831, the disciples gathered on the banks of Cabin Pond on the property of Joseph Travis, who had married the widow of Turner's last master and who had therefore inherited Turner and death. Nat, who appreciated the value of a delayed and dramatic entrance, appeared suddenly late in the afternoon and announced that they would strike that night, beginning at the home of his master and proceeding from house to house, killing every man, woman and child.

At 1 a.m., Nat Turner and his army crept through the woods to the home of the luckless Joseph Travis. They were seven men, armed with one hatchet and a broadax. Twenty-four hours later, they would be seventy and at least fifty-seven Whites would be dead.

When, on Monday morning, the first bodies were discovered, a nameless dread seized the citizens. Men, women and children fled to the woods and hid under the leaves until soldiers and sailors arrived from Richmond and Norfolk. Some Whites left the county; others left the state.

Defeated in an engagement near Jerusalem, Turner went into hiding and was not captured until six weeks later. On Nov. 11, 1831, the short Black man called the Prophet was hanged in a field near the courthouse. Before climbing the gallows, he made one last prophecy, saying there would be a storm after his execution and that the sun would refuse to shine. There was, in fact, a storm in Jerusalem on that day, but Turner was not talking about the weather—he was predicting a major disturbance in the American psyche. The storm he saw came in the generation of crisis that his act helped precipitate.

4. Free at Last!

TO Felix Haywood, who was there, it was the Time of Glory when men and women walked "on golden clouds."

To Frederick Douglass, it was a downpayment on the redemption of the American soul.

To Sister Winny in Virginia, to Jane Montgomery in Louisiana, to Ed Bluff in Mississippi, to Black people all over the South and all over America, it was the Time of Jubilee, the wild, happy, sad, mocking, tearful, fearful time of the unchaining of the bodies of Black folks. And the air was sweet with song.

Free at last!
Free at last!
Thank God Almighty!
We're free at last.

W.E.B. Du Bois was not there, but he summed the whole thing up in phrases worthy of the ages. It was all, he said, "foolish, bizarre, and tawdry. Gangs of dirty Negroes howling and dancing; poverty-stricken ignorant laborers mistaking war, destruction, and revolution for the mystery of the free human soul; and yet to these Black folk it was the Apocalypse." And he added:

"All that was Beauty, all that was Love, all that was Truth, stood on the top of these mad mornings and sang with the stars. A great human sob shrieked in the wind, and tossed its tears upon the sea—free, free, free."

Contrary to the common view, the emancipation of Blacks didn't happen at one time or even in one place. It started with the first shot fired at Fort Sumter. It continued during the war and in the Jubilee summer of 1865, *and it has not been completed.* For the slaves, who created the foundation of American wealth, never received the 40 acres of land that would have made freedom meaningful.

It was in this milieu that African-Americans embarked on a road called freedom. As the road twisted and turned, doubling back on itself, their enemies and their problems multiplied. But they endured, and endure.

5. *Booker T. Washington vs. W. E. B. Du Bois*

THERE was a big parade in Atlanta on Wednesday, Sept. 18, 1895, and a huge crowd gathered in the Exposition Building at the Cotton States Exposition for the opening speeches. Several Whites spoke and then former Gov. Rufus Bullock introduced "Professor Booker T. Washington." The 39-year-old president of Tuskegee Institute moved to the front of the platform and started speaking to the segregated audience. Within 10 minutes, reporter James Creelman wrote, "the multitude was in an uproar of enthusiasm—handkerchiefs were waved… hats were tossed into the air. The fairest women of Georgia stood up and cheered."

What was the cheering about?

Metaphors mostly—and words millions of Whites wanted to hear. Washington told Blacks: "Cast down your buckets where you are." To Whites, he offered the same advice: "Cast down your bucket [among] the most patient, faithful, law-abiding and unresentful people the world has seen…."

Suddenly, he flung his hand aloft, with the fingers held wide apart.

"In all things purely social," he said, "we can be as separate as the fingers, yet [he balled the fingers into a fist] one as the hand in all things essential to mutual progress."

The crowd came to its feet, yelling.

Washington's "Atlanta Compromise" speech made him famous and set the tone for race relations for some 20 years. One year after his speech, the Supreme Court rounded a fateful fork, endorsing in *Plessy* vs. *Ferguson* the principle of "separate but equal."

Washington's refusal to make a direct and open attack on Jim Crow and his implicit acceptance of segregation brought him into conflict with W.E.B. Du Bois and a group of Black militants who organized the germinal Niagara Movement. At its first national meeting at Harpers Ferry in 1906, the Niagara militants said, "We claim for ourselves every single right that belongs to a freeborn American, political, civil, and social; and until we get these rights we will never cease to protest and assail the ears of America."

So saying, the Niagara militants laid the foundation for the National Association for the Advancement of Colored People which merged the forces of Black militancy and White liberalism.

6. *The Great Migration*

HISTORY does not always come with drums beating and flags flying.

Sometimes it comes in on a wave of silence.

Sometimes it whispers.

It was like that in the terrible days of despair that preceded the unprecedented explosion of hope and movement that is called The Great Migration.

This event, which was the largest internal migration in American history and one of the central events of African-American history, started in the cracks of history, in the minds

and moods of the masses of Blacks, who were reduced to the status of semi-slaves in the post-Reconstruction period. Pushed back toward slavery by lynchings, segregation and the sharecropping systems, they turned around within themselves and decided that there had to be another way and another and better place. The feeling moved, became a mood, an imperative, a command. Without preamble, without a plan, without leadership, the people began to move, going from the plantation to Southern cities, going from there to the big cities of the North. There, they found jobs in wartime industries and sent letters to a cousin or an aunt or sister or brother, saying: Come! And they came, hundreds and hundreds of thousands. The first wave (300,000) came between 1910 and 1920, followed by a second wave (1,300,000) between 1920 and 1930, and third (500,000) and fourth (2,500,000) waves, even larger, in the '30s and '40s.

In the big cities of the North, Blacks emancipated themselves politically and economically and created the foundation of contemporary Black America.

7. *Brown vs. Board of Education*

THE marshal's voice was loud and clear.

"Oyez! Oyez! Oyez! All persons having business before the Honorable, the Supreme Court of the United States, are admonished to draw near and give their attention, for the Court is now sitting."

The marshal paused and intoned the traditional words:

"God save the United States and this Honorable Court!"

It was high noon on Monday, May 17, 1954, and the Supreme Court was crammed to capacity with spectators. Among the dozen or so Blacks present was Thurgood Marshall, chief counsel of the NAACP, who leaned forward in expectation.

Cases from four states (South Carolina, Virginia, Delaware, Kansas) and the District of Columbia were before the Court, which had been asked by Marshall and his associates to overturn the *Plessy* vs. *Ferguson* decision and declare segregation in public schools unconstitutional. All America awaited the long-expected decision which would come on a Monday. But which Monday? No one knew, and there was no sign on the faces of the justices that the issue was going to be settled on this day.

The Court disposed of routine business and announced decisions in several boring cases involving the sale of milk and the picketing of retail stores. Then Chief Justice Earl Warren picked up a document and said in a firm, quiet voice: "I have for announcement the judgment and opinion of the Court in No. 1—*Oliver Brown et al. v. Board of Education of Topeka.* It was 12:52 p.m. A shiver ran through the courtroom, and bells started ringing in press rooms all over the world.

Warren held the crowd in suspense, reviewing the history of the cases. Then, abruptly, he came to the heart of the matter:

"Does segregation of children in public schools solely on the basis of race, even though the physical facilities and other 'tangible' factors may be equal, deprive the children of the minority group of equal educational opportunities?" Warren paused and said: "We believe that it does." The decision was unanimous: 9–0.

The words raced across the country and were received by different people according to their different lights. Southern diehards like Herman Talmadge issued statements of defiance and promised a generation of litigation, but the implications of the decision were so enormous that many Americans were shocked into silence and wonder. In Farmville, Va., a 16-year-old student named Barbara Trent burst into tears when her teacher announced the decision. "We went on studying history," she said later, "but things weren't the same and will never be the same again."

8. Montgomery and the Freedom Movement

IT was a quiet, peaceful day in Montgomery, Ala., the Cradle of the Confederacy—but it was unseasonably hot for December 1.

The Cleveland Avenue bus rolled through Court Square, where Blacks were auctioned in the days of the Confederacy, and braked to a halt in front of the Empire Theater. There was nothing special about the bus or the day; neither the driver nor the passengers realized that a revolution was about to begin that would turn America and the South upside down.

Six Whites boarded the bus at the Empire Theater, and the driver stormed to the rear and ordered the foremost Blacks to get up and give their seats to the White citizens. This was an ancient custom, sanctioned by the peculiar mores of the South, and it excited no undue comment. Three Blacks got up immediately, but Rosa Parks, a mild-mannered seamstress in rimless glasses, kept her seat. For this act of defiance, she was arrested. Local leaders called a one-day bus boycott on Monday, Dec. 5, 1955, to protest the arrest. The one-day boycott stretched out to 381 days; the 381 days changed the face and heart of Black America, creating a new leader (Martin Luther King Jr.), and a new movement. There then followed in quick succession a series of movements (the Sit-ins and Freedom Rides) and dramatic events (Birmingham, Selma, Watts, the March on Washington) that constituted Black America's finest hour and one of the greatest moments in the history of the Republic.

9. Little Rock

THE GIANT C-119 flying boxcars circled the field, like grim birds.

One by one, they glided into the Little Rock, Ark., airport and debouched paratroopers in full battle gear. There were, in all, more than 1,000 soldiers, Black and White; and they were in Little Rock to enforce the orders of a federal court. For the first time since the Reconstruction era, the United States of America was deploying federal troops to defend the rights of Black Americans.

Escorted by city police cars, a convoy of olive-drab jeeps and trucks sped to Central High School where a howling mob had prevented the enrollment of nine Black students. The troops deployed on the double to block all entrances to the schools, and signalmen strung telephone lines and set up command posts.

Wednesday morning, Sept. 25, 1957, dawned bright and clear, and nine Black teenagers gathered at the ranch-style home of Daisy Bates, president of the Arkansas NAACP. At 8:50 a.m., there was a rumble of heavy wheels. The teenagers rushed to the window.

"The streets were blocked off," Daisy Bates recalled later. "The soldiers closed ranks... Oh! It was beautiful. And the attitude of the children at that moment: the respect they had. I could hear them saying, 'For the first time in my life I truly feel like an American.' I could see it in their faces: Somebody cares for me—America cares."

At 9:45, U.S. soldiers with drawn bayonets escorted six Black females and three Black males into Central High School, and the Rev. Dunbar H. Ogden, president of the Greater Little Rock Ministerial Association, said: "This may be looked back upon by future historians as the turning point—for good—of race relations in this country."

10. Memphis and the Triumph of the Spirit

THERE had never been a moment like this one.

Time stopped.

Everything stopped.

And every man and woman living at that terrible time would be able to tell you until the end of their time what they were doing and where they were on Thursday, April 4, 1968, when word came that Martin Luther King Jr. had been assassinated on the balcony of the Lorraine Motel in Memphis, Tenn.

The response in Black and White America was tumultuous. Performances, plays, meetings, baseball games were cancelled, and men and women walked aimlessly through the streets, weeping.

There were tears, rivers of tears, and there was also blood. For Black communities exploded, one after another, like firecrackers on a string. Some 46 persons were killed in uprisings in 126 cities, and federal troops were mobilized to put down rebellions in Chicago, Baltimore and Washington, D.C.

To counteract this fury, and to express their sorrow, Americans of all races and creeds joined forces in an unprecedented tribute to a Black American. President Lyndon B. Johnson declared a national day of mourning and ordered U.S. flags to fly at half-mast over U.S. installations at home and abroad. On the day of the funeral—Tuesday, April 9—more than 200,000 mourners followed King's coffin, which was carried through the streets of Atlanta on a wagon, borne by two Georgia mules.

Eighteen years later, the spirit and the truth of Martin Luther King Jr. triumphed when he became the second American citizen (with George Washington) to be celebrated in a personal national holiday.

*The Shaping of Black America

Academic Haven for Blacks Becomes Bias Battleground

By CRAIG TIMBERG
Washington Post Staff Writer

ETTRICK, Va.—Most of the professors at what was once called Virginia State College for Negroes have ancestors who came to this country in a slave ship. Not Godwin Mbagwu. He came here as a young, Nigerian academic seeking opportunity, in an airliner.

The distinction was lost on Mbagwu for many years as he made Virginia State University his professional home, first as a student, then as a top researcher and chemistry professor. But it was not lost, he says, on the leaders of this historically black campus, where he learned that to be an African in America is not necessarily to be an African American.

The quest to keep VSU an academic haven for U.S.-born blacks, says Mbagwu, 54, led university officials to thwart his research efforts, block his promotions and hold down his annual evaluations and raises, even as he won state and national awards for excellence. Fed up, he borrowed a tool long used by African Americans facing discrimination: Mbagwu sued and won.

A federal jury in Richmond awarded Mbagwu $231,000 in compensatory and punitive damages last year. U.S. District Judge Robert E. Payne followed up in May by awarding the lawyers for Mbagwu and a second foreign-born professor,

Fathy Saleh of Egypt, $1.3 million in legal costs.

Among the evidence Payne cited was a comment that university President Eddie N. Moore Jr. allegedly made to Jean R. Cobbs, a fellow African American and department chairwoman, shortly after Moore's arrival in 1993. Cobbs recalled Moore saying that "there were too many foreigners in [the] Life Sciences [department], and he planned to do something about that."

Moore forcefully denied that comment and the other allegations against him and the other university officials. But Payne issued an injunction against further discrimination and declared that "reprehensible national origin discrimination" existed "at the highest levels of VSU."

"The injunction secured by Mbagwu likewise will serve to notify those who run universities, public and private, that they will be branded as discriminators, a loathsome appellation, if, as did the defendants here, they discriminate against members of their faculty," Payne wrote.

Saleh won $117,000 on his claim that the university retaliated against him for publicly charging discrimination against white and foreign-born professors in 1995. Three other foreign-born professors who have

sued VSU with similar discrimination claims have won lucrative settlements out of court. The university's tab for damages, legal fees and settlements from the suits by these five professors already tops $2.4 million.

University officials flatly deny the charges and vow to win the Mbagwu and Saleh case on appeal. "This case shows how diversity in the workplace can be used as a weapon against the boss," said university lawyer Bradley B. Cavedo. "That's all it shows."

It also shows how the same laws that attacked discrimination at traditionally white colleges can be turned against officials at historically black ones. Discrimination suits by white professors have been won at Cheyney University outside Philadelphia, Albany State College in Georgia and, during the early 1980s, at Howard University in the District. Meanwhile, the number of predominantly black colleges has fallen to about 100 as some historically black schools have become majority white.

Reginald Wilson, a senior scholar emeritus at the American Council on Education, said historically black colleges remain an enormous source of pride and academic opportunity for African Americans, but university officials can violate civil rights laws if they try to keep their colleges black.

"Presidents of these universities, in trying to keep their students and faculty black and their universities black, are making some egregious choices," said Wilson, who has no direct knowledge of the cases at VSU. "They're making a decision that historically makes some sense, but they're making a decision that in the year 2000 may be illegal."

Virginia State was founded in 1882 across the Appomattox River from the central Virginia city of Petersburg. Since then, 20,000 students—the overwhelming majority African American—have earned degrees there, making it vital to Virginia's black middle class. Today, nine out of 10 students at VSU are black.

The faculty is more mixed, with both foreign-born and white professors significant minorities. The university doesn't track the national origins of its faculty, but of the 172 professors last year, 43 were white and 107 black; the latter number includes Mbagwu and other black Africans.

Students at VSU say the foreign-born professors, particularly the Africans, are an asset to the university, bringing enthusiasm and broad perspectives to their classes.

"Most of the foreigners come from Africa," said Antoine Wongus, 19, who's studying to become an architect. "Being that I'm an African American, that's like connecting me back to my past."

But students also say that some of the foreign-born professors are hard to understand—something that university officials pointed to in marking down Mbagwu's performance—and there is, students add, an inevitable culture clash on campus as well.

"You see it every day," said Cornell Turner, 19, of the attitudes toward foreign-born professors. "'He's foreign. Why don't they go back over there?'"

Similar tensions can be heard in the words of Florence S. Farley, an African American department chairwoman, in July 1995. It was a week after Saleh and a second professor publicly alleged that university officials were discriminating against white and foreign-born professors.

"We ought to be the majority here, the descendants of the slaves in this country ought to be," Farley told the faculty council, according to a transcript of the meeting. "Now it doesn't mean that anybody should dominate anybody just because they're descendants of slaves, but we shouldn't be absent. And when we start being absent here, I'm going to be concerned."

The allegations of discrimination at VSU focus on the arrival in 1993 of university President Moore, until then the state treasurer under the administration of then-Gov. L. Douglas Wilder. Tensions had long existed among the various factions at VSU, say the foreign-born professors, but with Moore's arrival, that became outright discrimination.

Moore, 52, is a former Army officer, oil company executive and comptroller of the College of William and Mary. He has led a major building program and fundraising campaign at VSU while overseeing improvements in SAT scores and graduation rates.

But he has also clashed with professors, who have chafed at his management style and financial reforms, including a system tying faculty pay raises to annual evaluations of their performance as teachers and researchers.

University officials say this change has caused the weaker professors to retaliate under the guise of civil rights law. But Mbagwu and others say the annual evaluations were a tool used to elevate African Americans while holding foreign-born professors down.

Moore angrily denies that there is discrimination on his campus.

"I have seen what I consider to be discrimination in my life," he said. "Speaking for myself and my values, no, it's not [discrimination], especially with regard to me and my actions."

Mbagwu, who has been a VSU professor since 1981, said he recalls an encounter with Moore in the first months of his administration. The day was Oct. 1, independence day in his homeland of Nigeria. It was also the day that a grant proposal representing the culmination of years of his cancer research—including a year while a visiting professor at Harvard—was due at the offices of the National Institutes of Health in Bethesda.

Mbagwu said that two weeks earlier, he had submitted the grant proposal, worth nearly $500,000 in money and equipment to VSU. But Moore refused to sign until 2:30 on the afternoon of the due date. Mbagwu raced up the highway to NIH headquarters in Bethesda, more than 140 miles away, but found it closed, missing the deadline.

"It was such an excruciating experience, so frustrating," Mbagwu recalled. "At the time, I couldn't understand why someone would want to interfere with my project."

Moore disputes that account. Mbagwu, according to Moore, submitted his proposal to the VSU administration late and ran up against his heightened scrutiny of all fiscal matters—not a desire to discriminate.

"Nothing that had to do with the review of that grant had to do with where he was born," Moore said.

The heart of Mbagwu's case is his annual evaluations and resulting raises under Moore's administration.

In 1995, Mbagwu won a national teaching and research award called "Giants in Science," given to five professors each year by the Quality Education for Minorities Network, based in Washington. In 1996, Mbagwu won the "Outstanding Faculty Award," given to 11 Virginia professors each year by the State Council of Higher Education for Virginia.

To bolster Mbagwu's application for that award, Moore wrote: "Dr. Mbagwu is a leading research scientist and an outstanding educator....

His teaching is considered first-rate by students and faculty."

Meanwhile, in the VSU Chemistry Department of four professors—two black, one white and Mbagwu —he received the worst evaluations and the smallest raises every year from 1994 to 1998 except for one, when his was the second-lowest raise. In evaluations and later explanations, the department chairman said that Mbagwu spent too little time on campus and sometimes started class late, and that some students had trouble understanding his accent.

"I felt very betrayed," Mbagwu said, "because these actions were occurring in a university that was originally founded on the principles of justice, equality and fairness to everyone. It was a very wrenching, depressing experience."

Moore said he had no personal role in the evaluations and perhaps overstated Mbagwu's skills as a teacher in supporting his application for the "Outstanding Faculty" award. In court, the university has stood behind the evaluations as fair and accurate representations of Mbagwu's work in those years. School officials have noted that the awards covered achievement throughout Mbagwu's career, not just one year.

The department chairman "just didn't see Dr. Mbagwu the way Dr. Mbagwu saw Dr. Mbagwu," Cavedo said.

Appeals by both sides are scheduled to be heard by the 4th U.S. Circuit Court of Appeals in Richmond this fall.

Meanwhile, neither VSU nor the administration of Gov. James S. Gilmore III (R) has formally investigated the discrimination complaints at the university. The complaints and the mounting bills for defending against them have, however, caught the attention of the panel on the House Appropriations Committee that oversees spending at Virginia's public colleges. Some lawmakers are demanding an explanation.

"For them not to allow foreign-born professors the same opportunity as native-born professors is outrageous," said Del. John A. "Jack" Rollison III (R-Prince William), a member of the panel. "I thought that the days of discrimination were behind us in Virginia."

As for Mbagwu, he has recently applied for the position of associate dean at VSU. Asked whether he expects a fair hearing from the same administrators he sued, Mbagwu replied, "I hope so."

LAYING DOWN the BURDEN *of* RACE

BY WARD CONNERLY

NOT LONG AGO, after I'd given a speech in Hartford, Connecticut, I saw a black man with a determined look on his face working his way toward me through the crowd. I steeled myself for another abrasive encounter of the kind I've come to expect over the past few years. But once this man reached me he stuck out his hand and said thoughtfully, "You know, I was thinking about some of the things you said tonight. It occurred to me that black people have just got to learn to lay down the burden. It's like we grew up carrying a bag filled with heavy weights on our shoulders. We just have to stop totin' that bag."

I agreed with him. I knew as he did exactly what was in this bag: weakness and guilt, anger, and self-hatred.

I have made a commitment not to tote racial grievances, because the status of victim is so seductive and so available to anyone with certain facial features or a certain cast to his skin. But laying down these burdens can be tricky, as I was reminded not long after this Connecticut meeting. I had just checked into the St. Francis Hotel in San Francisco to attend an annual dinner as master of ceremonies. After getting to my room, I realized that I'd left my briefcase in the car and started to go back to the hotel parking garage for it. As I was getting off the basement elevator, I ran into a couple of elderly white men who seemed a little disoriented. When they saw me, one of them said, "Excuse me, are you the man who unlocks the meeting room?"

I did an intellectual double-take and then, with my racial hackles rising, answered with as much irritation as I could pack into my voice: "No, I'm *not* the man who unlocks the rooms."

The two men shrank back and I walked on, fuming to myself about how racial profiling is practiced every day in subtle forms by people who would otherwise piously condemn it in state troopers working the New Jersey

Turnpike. As I stalked toward the garage, I didn't feel uplifted by my righteous anger. On the contrary, I felt crushed by it. It was a heavy burden, so heavy, in fact, that I stopped and stood there for a minute, sagging under its weight. Then I tried to see myself through the eyes of the two old men I'd just run into: someone who was black, yes, but more importantly, someone without luggage, striding purposefully out of the elevator as if on a mission, dressed in a semi-uniform of blazer and gray slacks.

I turned around and retraced my steps.

"What made you think I was the guy who unlocks the meeting rooms?" I asked when I caught up with them.

"You were dressed a little like a hotel employee, sir," the one who had spoken earlier said in a genuinely deferential way. "Believe me, I meant no insult."

"Well, I hope you'll forgive me for being abrupt," I said, and after a quick handshake I headed back to the garage, feeling immensely relieved.

IF WE ARE TO LAY THIS BURDEN DOWN for good, we must be committed to letting go of racial classifications—not getting beyond race by taking race more into account, as Supreme Court Justice Harry Blackmun disastrously advised, but just getting beyond race period as a foundation for public policy.

Yet, I know that race is a scar in America. I first saw this scar at the beginning of my life in the segregated South. Black people should not deny that this mark exists: it is part of our connection to America. But we should also resist all of those, black and white, who want to rip open that scar and make race a raw and angry wound that continues to define and divide us.

Left to their own devices, I believe, Americans will eventually merge and melt into each other. Throughout

Photo: Ward Connerly/Encounter Books

My Grandfather Eli Soniea was an ambitious man with a feel for business. He was also a no-nonsense type who didn't like anyone, especially his own kin, putting on airs.

our history, there has been a constant intermingling of people—even during the long apartheid of segregation and Jim Crow. It is malicious as well as unreasonable not to acknowledge that in our own time the conditions for anger have diminished and the conditions for connection have improved.

We all know the compelling statistics about the improvements in black life: increased social and vocational mobility, increased personal prestige and political power. But of all the positive data that have accumulated since the Civil Rights Act of 1964—when America finally decided to leave its racial past behind— the finding that gives me most hope is the recent survey showing that nearly 90 percent of all teenagers in America report having at least one close personal friend of another race.

My wife Ilene is white. I have two racially mixed children and three grandchildren, two of whose bloodlines are even more mixed as a result of my son's marriage to a woman of half-Asian descent. So my own personal experience tells me that the passageway to that place where all racial division ends goes directly through the human heart.

Not long ago, Mike Wallace came to California to interview Ilene and me for a segment of "60 Minutes." He seemed shocked when I told him that race wasn't a big topic in our family. He implied that we were somehow disadvantaging the kids. But Ilene and I decided a long time ago to let our kids find their way in this world without toting the bag of race. They are lucky, of course, to have grown up after the great achievements of the civil rights movement, which changed America's heart as

much as its laws. But we have made sure that the central question for our children, since the moment they came into this world, has always been *who* are you, not *what* are you. When we ignore appeals to group identity and focus instead on individuals and their individual humanity, we are inviting the principles of justice present since the American founding to come inside our contemporary American homes.

I WON'T PRETEND THIS IS always easy. While a senior at college, I fell in love with an effervescent white woman named Ilene. When Ilene's parents first learned how serious we were about each other, they reacted with dismay and spent long hours on the phone trying to keep the relationship from developing further. Hoping for support from my own relatives, I went home one weekend and told Mom (the grandmother who had raised me) about Ilene. She was cold and negative. "Why can't you find yourself a nice colored girl?" she blurted out. I walked out of the house and didn't contact her for a long time afterward.

Ilene and I now felt secretive and embattled. Marrying "outside your race" was no easy decision in 1962. I knew that Ilene had no qualms about challenging social norms, but I was less sure that she could deal with exclusion by her family, which seemed to me a real possibility. Nonetheless, she said yes when I proposed, and we were married, with no family members present.

I called Mom the day after and told her. She apologized for what she'd said earlier. Ilene's parents were not so quick to alter their position. For months, the lines of communication were down. Sometimes I came home from work and found Ilene sitting on the couch crying.

Finally her parents agreed to see her, but not me. I drove her up to their house and waited in the car while she went in. As the hours passed, I seethed. At one point I started the engine and took off, but I didn't know the area and so, after circling the block, came back and parked again. When Ilene finally came out of the house, she just cried for nearly the entire return trip.

Today, people would rush to hold Ilene's parents guilty of racism.

But even when I was smoldering with resentment, I knew it wasn't that simple. These were good people— hard working, serious, upstanding. They were people, moreover, who had produced my wife, a person without a racist bone in her body. In a sense, I could sympathize with my new in-laws: there were no blacks in their daily life, and they lived in a small town where everyone knew everything about everyone else. Our marriage was a leap nothing in her parents' lives had prepared them to take.

But their reaction to me still rankled. After having to wait in the car that afternoon I vowed never to go near their house again.

For a long time we didn't see Ilene's parents. But we did see her Aunt Markeeta and Uncle Glen. They were wonderful people. Glen, dead now, was a salt-of-the-

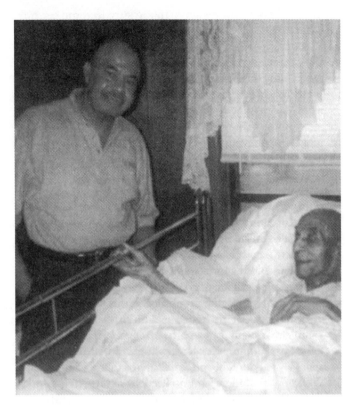

Photo: Ward Connerly / *Encounter Books*

My father's unintended deathbed gift to me was the relevation that it is not the life we're given, but the life we make of the life we're given that counts.

earth type who worked in a sawmill, and Markeeta had a personality as piquant as her name. They integrated us into their circle of friends, who became our friends too. In those healing days, we all functioned as an extended family.

If I had to pick the moment when our family problems began to resolve themselves it would be the day our son Marc was born.

Not long after, we were invited to come for a visit. This time I was included in the invitation. I remember sitting stiffly through the event, which had the tone of the recently released film, *Guess Who's Coming to Dinner?* I was supremely uncomfortable, but I also sensed that the fever had broken. And indeed, a peace process was in place. The visits became more frequent. The frigid tolerance gradually thawed into welcome.

There was no single dramatic moment that completed the reconciliation; no cathartic conversation in which we all explored our guilt and misconceptions. Instead, we just got on with our lives, nurturing the relationship that had been born along with my son. It grew faster than he did. Within a year we were on our way to becoming what we are now—a close-knit, supportive family. Today, my relationship with my in-laws could not be better. I love them very much, and they let me know that the feeling is mutual.

The moral is clear. Distance exaggerates difference and breeds mistrust; closeness breaks down suspicion and produces connection. My life so far tells me that our future as a nation is with connection.

MOST PEOPLE CALL ME A BLACK MAN. In fact, I'm black in the same way that Tiger Woods and so many other Americans are black—by the "one drop of blood" rule used by yesterday's segregationists and today's racial ideologues. In my case, the formula has more or less equal elements of French Canadian, Choctaw, African, and Irish American. But just reciting the fractions provides no insight about the richness of life produced by the sum of the parts.

A journalist for the *New York Times* once described my bloodline as being right out of a Faulkner novel. He was right. And my family was always trying to understand how the strands of DNA dangling down through history had created their individual selves. They had their share of guilty secrets and agonized over the consequences of bad blood, whatever its racial origin. But in their actions, they, like Faulkner's characters, treated race and other presumed borders between people as being permeable.

I grew up with my mother's people. My maternal grandfather was Eli Soniea, a mixed-blood Cajun born in the tiny Louisiana town of Sulphur. He eventually settled in Leesville, not far from the Texas border, a sleepy town with hazy foothills stretching behind it like a movie backdrop.

Eli died ten years before I was born, and I never knew him. But photographs of him have always intrigued me. He was light skinned, had straight black hair, and a serious look. I've been told he spoke a pidgin French and English and was an ambitious man. He worked as a carpenter, sometimes ran a construction gang, and amassed enough money to buy some land and build a restaurant and bar in Leesville. He was evidently a no-nonsense type who didn't like anyone, especially his own kin, putting on airs.

Eli's wife, my grandmother Mary Smith—or "Mom" as I always called her—was half Irish and half Choctaw. This latter element was clearly evident in her high cheekbones and broad features, and in the bloom of her young womanhood she was sometimes referred to as an "Indian Princess." Mom was born and raised in Texas. She married Eli Soniea as a result of an "arrangement" brokered by her parents, after which he brought her to Louisiana.

In their early life together, the two of them lived in that part of Leesville known as "Dago Quarters" because of the large number of Italian immigrants. After Eli's early death—when I was growing up you didn't ask why or how someone died; the mere fact of it ended all discussion—Mary's only income was from the restaurant and bar he had built, which she leased to people who did business with the servicemen from the nearby Army base.

Because money was tight, she moved the family to a less expensive neighborhood, the predominantly black "Bartley Quarters."

The complexions of Mom's own six children ranged from light to dark. (William, for instance, was always known as "Red" because of his Indian look and coloring.) But whatever their exact coloration or facial characteristics, they all had "colored" on their birth certificates. In Louisiana in those days, being "colored" was not just a matter of blood; it was also a question of what neighborhood you lived in and what people you associated with. "Colored" is on my birth certificate.

The Sonieas' race problem came not only from whites but from blacks too. Leesville's social boundaries were reasonably porous, but if you were falling down through the cracks rather than moving up, as the Sonieas were doing after Eli died, you attracted notice. My grandmother often recalled how her new neighbors in Bartley Quarters called her and her children "high yellers," a term coined by white Southern racists but used with equal venom by blacks too. In fact, Mom's kids had so much trouble that officials tried to convince them to transfer out of the school to escape the racial animosity. This experience left some of my relatives with hard feelings that never really went away. During the campaign for California's Proposition 209, for instance, when I was being accused of selling out "my people," my Aunt Bert got annoyed one day and said, "When we lived back in Leesville, they didn't want to be our 'brothers and sisters'; they didn't own us as 'their people' then; so why do they think we owe them something now because of skin color?"

My biological mother Grace, Bert's little sister, was the youngest of Mom's children. I wish I had more memories of her. I have only one sharp image in my mind: a face resting in satin in a casket. Old photographs show my mother as a beautiful woman with a full, exotic face. But she wasn't beautiful lying there with a waxy, preserved look, certainly not to a terrified four-year-old dragged up to the front of the church to pay his last respects. I still remember standing there looking at her with my cousin Ora holding my hand to keep me from bolting as the pandemonium of a Southern black funeral—women yelling, crying, fainting, and lying palsied on the floor—rose to a crescendo all around me.

ACCORDING TO FAMILY LEGEND, she died of a stroke. But I suspect that this claim was really just my family's way of explaining away something infinitely more complex. Two other facts about my mother's life may have had something to do with her early passing. First, she had been in a serious car accident that left her with a steel plate in her head. And secondly, she had been physically abused by my father.

I didn't find this out until I was in my fifties. The information accidentally escaped during a conversation with my Aunt Bert, who said, when the subject of my father came up, "You know, your Uncle Arthur once said, excuse the expression, 'That son of a bitch once took out a gun and shot at me!'"

I asked her why.

"Because Arthur told your father that if he ever beat your mother again he'd kill him, and your father got out a gun."

I guess Roy Connerly was what they called a "fancy man" back then. Judging from his photos, he was quite handsome, with light skin and a wicked smile, and a reputation as a gambler, a drinker, and a womanizer. He worked odd jobs, but it seems that his real profession was chasing women. I've been told so many times about the day he got tired of me and my mother and turned us in at my grandmother's house that it has come to feel like my own legitimate memory.

He arrived there one afternoon with the two of us and with his girlfriend of the moment, a woman named Lucy. My Aunt Bert was watering the lawn when he walked into the yard.

"Is Miss Mary here?" my father asked.

Bert said yes.

"Go get her," he ordered.

Bert went in to get Mom, who appeared on the porch wiping her hands on her apron.

"I'm giving them back to you, Miss Mary," Roy said, gesturing at my sobbing mother and at me, the miserable child in her arms. "I want to be with Lucy."

Always composed in a crisis, Mom looked at him without visible emotion and said, "Thank you for bringing them."

A few days later he brought my red wagon over. Then Roy Connerly vanished from my life.

Later on I learned that Roy Connerly eventually got rid of Lucy and, at the age of 39, entered a relationship with a 15-year-old girl named Clementine and had a couple of kids by her. But nothing more than that for over 50 years. Then, just a couple of years ago, a writer doing a profile on me for the *New York Times* called one day.

"Are you sitting down?" he asked melodramatically.

I asked him what was up. He said that in his research about my background he had discovered that my father was still alive, 84 years old, and living in Leesville. The writer gave me his phone number.

I didn't do anything about it for a long time. Then, in the fall of 1998, I was invited to debate former Congressman William Gray at Tulane University in New Orleans. One of the things that made me accept was how close it was to Leesville. But I didn't actually decide to go there until after the speech. I came back to the hotel, rented a car, and got directions from the concierge.

It was a four-hour drive in a dreary rain. I warned myself not to surrender to counterfeit sentiment that would make a fool of both me and my father.

I stopped on the outskirts of town and called from a convenience store. My father's wife Clementine answered. I told her who I was and asked if I could come by and see him. There were muffled voices on the other end of the line, then she came back on and said that I should stay put and she'd send someone out to lead me to the house.

A few minutes later, a couple of young men in a beat-up blue car came by and motioned at me. I followed them down the main street and over railroad tracks to a run-down neighborhood of narrow houses and potholed roads without sidewalks.

We got out of the car and went into a tiny, shuttered house whose living room was illumined only by a small television set. I introduced myself to Clementine, and we talked about my father for a minute or two. She emphasized that the man I was about to meet was very old, quite ill, and easily confused.

When she led me into the bedroom, I saw him, sunk down in the mattress, a bag of bones. His hands and feet were gnarled and knobby with arthritis, but in his face I saw my own reflection.

I touched his arm: "How are you feeling today?"

He looked up at me uncomprehendingly: "All right."

"You know who I am?"

Seeing that he was lost in a fog, Clementine said, "It's Billy," using my childhood nickname. He looked at her, then at me.

"Oh, Billy," the voice was thin and wavering. "How long you're staying?"

I told him I couldn't stay long.

There was an awkward silence as I waited for him to say something. But he just stared at me. We looked at each other for what seemed like a very long time. Finally, a lifetime's worth of questions came tumbling out.

"Did you ever care how I was doing?" I asked him.

"No," he replied uncertainly.

"Did you ever try and get in touch with me?"

"No," he looked at me blankly.

"Did you ever even care what happened to me?"

"No."

At this point Clementine intervened: "I don't even think he knows what you're asking."

I stood there a moment, resigning myself to the situation. I would never get an explanation for his absence from my life. Then Joseph, one of the young men who'd guided me to the house and who I now realized was my half-brother, beckoned me out of the room. In the hallway, he asked if I'd like to visit some of my other relatives living nearby. I said yes and he took me outside. We crossed the street to a narrow house where an elderly woman was waiting for us. Joseph introduced her to me as my Aunt Ethel. She cordially invited us in.

Ethel had married my father's brother and served as the family's unofficial archivist and historian. As we talked, she asked if I knew anything about my father's family. I said no. Ethel showed me some photos. She told me that his mother, born in 1890, was named Fannie Self Conerly, and that they spelled it with one *n* then. She said that Fannie's mother was Sarah Ford Lovely, who had died at the age of 98, when I was a boy. This woman, my great-grandmother, had been born a slave.

After I walked back to my father's house and sat for a while beside him, I stood and said, "I've got to be going. You take care of yourself."

"You too," he said to me. "You ever coming back this way again, Billy?"

I smiled and waved and left without answering, and without asking him the one question that was still on my mind: Did you beat my mother like they say? Did you hasten her death and thus deprive me of both of you?

On the drive back to New Orleans I thought about my discoveries—this sickly old man who was my life's most intimate stranger; the fact that his blood and mine had once been owned by another human being. I felt subtly altered, but still the same. My father's gift to me, if you could call it that, was a deeper realization that it is not the life we're given that counts, but the life we make of the life we're given.

Ward Connerly is a businessman and regent of the University of California.

From *The American Enterprise*, a publication of the American Enterprise Institute, June 2000, pp. 36-40. Excerpted from *Creating Equal: My Fight Against Race Preferences* by Ward Connerly. © 2000 by Encounter Books. Reprinted by permission.

Reparations For American Slavery

The following letter was published in *The Freedmen's Book*, a collection of African-American writings compiled by the abolitionist Lydia Maria Child in 1865. The letter is a response to a slave owner who has written to his former slave at the war's end, asking him to return to work in Tennessee.

To my old Master, Colonel P. H. Anderson, Big Spring, Tennessee.

Sir. I got your letter, and was glad to find that you had not forgotten Jourdon, and that you wanted me to come back and live with you again, promising to do better for me than anybody else can. I have often felt uneasy about you. I thought the Yankees would have hung you long before this, for harboring Rebs they found at your house. I suppose they never heard about your going to Colonel Martin's to kill the Union soldier that was left by his company in their stable. Although you shot at me twice before I left you, I did not want to hear of your being hurt, and am glad you are still living. It would do me good to go back to the dear old home again, and see Miss Mary and Miss Martha and Allen, Esther, Green, and Lee. Give my love to them all, and tell them I hope we will meet in the better world, if not in this. I would have gone back to see you all when I was working in the Nashville Hospital, but one of the neighbors told me that Henry intended to shoot me if he ever got a chance.

I want to know particularly what the good chance is you propose to give me. I am doing tolerably well here. I get twenty-five dollars a month, with victuals and clothing; have a comfortable home for Mandy,—the folks call her Mrs. Anderson,—and the children—Milly, Jane, and Grundy—go to school and are learning well.... We are kindly treated. Sometimes we overhear others saying, "Them colored people were slaves" down in Tennessee. The children feel hurt when they hear such remarks; but I tell them it was no disgrace in Tennessee to belong to Colonel Anderson. Many darkeys would have been

proud, as I used to be, to call you master. Now if you will write and say what wages you will give me, I will be better able to decide whether it would be to my advantage to move back again.

As to my freedom, which you say I can have, there is nothing to be gained on that score, as I got my free papers in 1864 from the Provost-Marshal-General of the Department of Nashville. Mandy says she would be afraid to go back without some proof that you were disposed to treat us justly and kindly; and we have concluded to test your sincerity by asking you to send us our wages for the time we served you. This will make us forget and forgive old scores, and rely on your justice and friendship in the future. I served you faithfully for thirty-two years, and Mandy twenty years. At twenty-five dollars a month for me, and two dollars a week for Mandy, our earnings would amount to eleven thousand six hundred and eighty dollars. Add to this the interest for the time our wages have been kept back, and deduct what you paid for our clothing, and three doctor's visits to me, and pulling a tooth for Mandy, and the balance will show what we are in justice entitled to. Please send the money by Adams's Express, in care of V. Winters, Esq., Dayton, Ohio. If you fail to pay us for faithful labors in the past, we can have little faith in your promises in the future. We trust the good Maker has opened your eyes to the wrongs which you and your fathers have done to me and my fathers, in making us toil for you for generations without recompense.... Surely there will be a day of reckoning for those who defraud the laborer of his hire.

In answering this letter, please state if there would be any safety for my Milly and Jane, who are now grown up, and both good-looking girls. You know how it was with poor Matilda and Catherine. I would rather stay here and starve—and die, if it come to that—than have my girls brought to shame by the violence and wickedness of their young masters. You will also please

state if there has been any schools opened for the colored children in your neighborhood. The great desire of my life now is to give my children an education, and have them form virtuous habits.

Say howdy to George Carter, and thank him for taking the pistol from you when you were shooting at me.

From your old servant,
Jourdon Anderson

TIMELINE OF REPARATIONS FOR AMERICAN SLAVERY

1865 General William Tecumseh Sherman issues Special Field Order #15, providing forty-acre tracts of captured land along the Atlantic coast, from South Carolina to Florida, for 40,000 former slaves.

Congress establishes the Freedmen's Bureau in March to oversee the distribution of land.

President Andrew Johnson reverses the "forty acres and a mule" provision, ordering the Freedmen's Bureau to return the land to the pardoned Confederate landholders. Later, the claim of forty acres and a mule is, oddly, dismissed in many mainstream standard history books as myth. For example, the most recently revised edition of *The Civil War Dictionary* begins its entry with this phrase:"Legend that sprang up among the newly-freed slaves..."

1866 Congress passes the Southern Homestead Act to provide freedmen with land in southern states at a cost of $5 for eighty acres. Act fails dismally; only 1,000 freedmen receive homesteads.

1867 Republican Representative Thaddeus Stevens proposes H.R. 29, a slave-reparations bill, which promises each freed adult male slave forty acres of land and $100 to build a dwelling. "[The freedmen] must necessarily... be the servants and the victims of others unless they are made in some measure independent of their wiser neighbors," Stevens argues.

1915 Treasury Department is sued for $68 million in remuneration for labor performed under slavery. The government dismisses the case on grounds of sovereign immunity.

1955 Activist Queen Mother Audley Moore founds the Reparations Committee of Descendants of United States Slaves after reading "in an old Methodist encyclopedia" that "a captive people have one hundred years to state their judicial claims against their captors or international law will consider you satisfied with your condition."

1962 Queen Mother Moore's reparations committee files a claim in California.

1969 James Forman, a radical activist and member of SNCC, interrupts Sunday services at Manhattan's Riverside Church and presents his "Black Manifesto" demanding that American churches and synagogues pay $500 million in reparations.

1987 National Coalition of Blacks for Reparations in America (N'COBRA) established to seek reparations from the federal government in the form of a domestic "Marshall Plan" for black Americans.

1989 Representative John Conyers proposes H.R. 3745, the first of several unsuccessful proposals for the formation of a commission to study reparations for American slavery.

1994 Florida agrees to pay $2.1 million in reparations to the survivors of the 1923 Rosewood massacre.

1995 The Ninth Circuit Court of Appeals rules in *Cato v. United States*, holding that the claim for $100 million in reparations and an apology for slavery lacks a "legally cognizable basis," and concluding that the "legislature, rather than the judiciary, is the appropriate forum" for such claims.

1999 Representative Conyers proposes H.R. 40, seeking a formal apology for slavery and providing for a commission to study reparations.

2000 Representative Tony Hall proposes H.R. 356, a formal resolution to acknowledge and apologize for slavery.

A LEGISLATIVE AND JUDICIAL HISTORY OF AMERICAN SLAVERY AND ITS AFTERMATH

1619 Twenty Africans sold as bond servants in Jamestown, Virginia.

1621 Dutch West India Company given a monopoly of the American slave trade.

1662 Virginia's general assembly determines that "[c]hildren got by an Englishman upon a Negro woman shall be bond or free according to the condition of the mother," effectively sanctioning the breeding of slaves by slaveholders.

1663 Maryland provides that African slaves shall serve for the duration of their lives.

1664 Maryland declares that baptism does not alter slave status.

1672 King Charles II charters the Royal African Company with exclusive rights to provide the colonies with Africans, putting England at the vanguard of the slave trade by century's end.

1688 Quakers in Germantown, Pennsylvania, draft an antislavery resolution.

1705 Virginia confers upon blacks the status of real estate.

1717 Maryland legislates that if "any free negro or mulatto" marries a white man or woman, he or she becomes a slave along with their children. Whites and mulattoes born of white women who intermarry, however, are consigned to seven years' servitude.

1724 New Orleans establishes the Black Code, with fifty-five articles designed to regulate the behavior of slaves.

1777 Vermont becomes the first American territory to declare slavery illegal.

1778 Virginia outlaws the trafficking of slaves into the commonwealth.

1779 The Virginia Assembly passes Thomas Jefferson's "A Bill Concerning Slaves," restricting the movements of slaves and requiring white women who bear mulatto children to leave the commonwealth with their children.

1780 The state constitution of Massachusetts declares colored persons descended of African slaves to be citizens.

1783 Maryland forbids further importation of slaves.

1787 The Constitutional Convention determines that for the purposes of representation and taxation slaves will be counted as three fifths of a free man.

1790 The first census of the United States records 757,000 black Americans, composing 19 percent of the population. More than 697,000 of them are slaves.

1791 Free Negroes of Charleston, South Carolina, protest severe legal disabilities and request to be treated as citizens.

1792 Construction begins on the White House in Washington, D.C., requiring an influx of slaves to lay the foundation.

1793 Congress passes the Fugitive Slave Act, which allows slave owners to seize runaways in any state or territory and sets fines for the harboring of fugitive slaves at $500.

Three slaves are executed in Albany, New York, for antislavery activities.

1797 Congress rejects the North Carolina Slave Petition, the first recorded petition for an end to slavery by freed blacks.

1800 Boston refuses to support black schools.

1804 Underground Railroad begins when a Revolutionary War officer purchases a slave and takes him to Pennsylvania. The slave's mother later escapes and follows her son north.

Virginia forbids all evening meetings of slaves.

1808 Congress prohibits further importation of slaves.

1810 Maryland denies free blacks the right to vote.

1817 The American Colonization Society is established to send freed blacks to Africa.

1820 The Missouri Compromise, admitting Missouri as a slave state and Maine as a free state, prohibits slavery in the rest of the Louisiana Purchase north of the 36th parallel.

1822 The American Colonization Society establishes the Liberian colony on the west coast of Africa.

1827 New York enacts gradual emancipation law.

1831 Nat Turner leads a slave rebellion in Southampton County in Virginia, killing fifty-five whites. One hundred twenty blacks are killed in retaliation in less than two days. Mississippi law declares that it is "unlawful for any slave, free Negro, or mulatto to preach the Gospel." Violators receive thirty-nine lashes upon their naked back.

1832 Alabama law declares that "any person or persons who shall attempt to teach any free person of color or slave to spell, read or write, shall, upon conviction thereof by indictment, be fined in a sum not less than $250, nor more than $500."

1836 Congress passes a resolution ceding authority over slave laws to the states.

1847 Liberia declares independence.

1850 The Compromise of 1850 results in a new Fugitive Slave Act strengthening slaveholders' ability to capture runaways in the northern free states.

1857 The Supreme Court rules in *Dred Scott v. John F. A. Sanford*, declaring that the Missouri Compromise is unconstitutional, that blacks are not citizens, and that a slave does not become free upon entering a free state.

1862 Congress abolishes slavery in the District of Columbia and the territories.

1863 President Abraham Lincoln issues the Emancipation Proclamation, freeing slaves in the Confederate states.

1865 The Thirteenth Amendment is ratified, abolishing slavery in the United States.

1866 Congress passes the Civil Rights Act on April 9, granting citizenship and equal rights to black Americans.

The Fourteenth Amendment is passed, guaranteeing to all U.S. citizens due process and equal protection under the law.

1867 Congress grants black citizens the right to vote in the District of Columbia and the territories.

The first of several Reconstruction Acts places Confederate states under federal military rule.

1869 The Fifteenth Amendment is passed, guaranteeing black Americans the right to vote.

1875 The Civil Rights Act of 1875 passed, guaranteeing equal rights to black Americans in public accommodations and in service on a jury.

Mississippi elects the first black, Republican Blanche Kelso Bruce, to the United States Senate for a full six-year term.

1877 The Compromise of 1877 ends Reconstruction.

1881 Tennessee segregates railroad cars. Other southern states follow suit.

1883 The Supreme Court declares the Civil Rights Act of 1875 unconstitutional, holding that the Fourteenth Amendment forbids states, but not citizens, from discriminating against blacks.

1890 The Mississippi Plan requires black voters to pass literacy and "understanding" tests, leading the effort by southern states to disenfranchise black citizens.

1896 Supreme Court rules in *Plessy v. Ferguson*, establishing the separate-but-equal doctrine.

1909 The National Association for the Advancement of Colored People (NAACP) is established to advocate for civil rights for black Americans.

1910 Baltimore approves the first city ordinance designating the boundaries of black and white neighborhoods.

1913 President Woodrow Wilson institutes federal segregation of workplaces, restrooms, and lunchrooms.

1917 Marcus Garvey establishes a Universal Negro Improvement Association branch in the United States and launches the "Back to Africa" movement.

1934 Costigan-Wagner Antilynching Bill defeated in Congress.

1948 Supreme Court rules in *Shelley v. Kraemer*, one of several housing-discrimination cases, that enforcement of restrictive covenants by state courts is unconstitutional.

President Harry S. Truman integrates the armed forces.

1954 Supreme Court ruling on *Brown* v. *Board of Education of Topeka, Kansas* strikes down the separate-but-equal doctrine.

1957 Congress passes the Civil Rights Act of 1957—the first since Reconstruction—creating a Civil Rights Division in the Justice Department and the Civil Rights Commission to study all aspects of segregation.

1960 The Civil Rights Act of 1960 outlaws interference with desegregation orders and voter rights. The Supreme Court declares segregation in bus and railway terminals unconstitutional in *Boynton* v. *Virginia*.

1964 The Civil Rights Act of 1964 creates the Equal Employment Opportunity Commission and prohibits discrimination by businesses and employers.

1965 The Voting Rights Act is passed to enforce the Fifteenth Amendment. 250,000 blacks register to vote by the end of the year.

1968 The Civil Rights Act of 1968 prohibits discrimination in housing.

1978 Supreme Court ruling in *Regents of the University of California v. Bakke* strikes down quota system in university admissions.

1995 The Regents of the University of California vote to end affirmative action in university admissions.

1996 California votes in favor of Proposition 209 to ban affirmative action in government employment and college admissions.

1998 Washington citizens vote to ban affirmative action in government employment and college admissions. Similar efforts follow in Florida.

1999 After an investigation reveals that black drivers on the New Jersey Turnpike were five times more likely than white drivers to be stopped by New Jersey State Police, the Justice Department appoints a state monitor.

RACISM ISN'T WHAT IT USED TO BE

But not everyone has noticed

Ed Marciniak

A new vocabulary is surfacing to assess the state of race relations in the United States. The operative words and approaches signal remarkable changes.

In the 1960s our racial language was dominated by "civil rights," "integration," "desegregation," "prejudice," "discrimination," "colored," and "Negroes." Nowadays, the comparable words and ideas have become: "racism," "diversity," "hate crimes," "racial profiling," "redlining," "reparations," "blacks," and "African Americans."

We are in transition, striving to find a racial vocabulary appropriate to today's society and culture. This is a touchy, controversial endeavor.

The 1960s, furthermore, emphasized equality of treatment—in employment, voting, housing, and government services. In the new millennium the stress has shifted to equality of results. Now the assumption of some is that ethnic and racial groups should be proportionately represented in occupations, incomes, wealth, college graduations, achievements, and failures. On the other hand, black athletes now dominate the nation's sports, such as track, basketball, football, and baseball (almost). Inequality is not the same as inequity.

The variations in language reflect the notable developments in race relations since 1963 when Martin Luther King Jr. gave his "I Have a Dream" speech to two hundred thousand people, culminating the March on Washington. Or since 1964 when Congress enacted the U.S. Civil Rights Act. Consider only a few of the changes:

In 1966, 42 percent of American blacks had incomes below the official poverty line. Recently, the U.S. Census Bureau reported that 24 percent of the nation's blacks were under that poverty line. At the same time, the poverty rate for whites was 8 percent.

Nationwide, the count of black elected officials zoomed from some 100 in the 1960s to 9,000 in the new millennium. In political jurisdictions where the voting majority is of one race, candidates of another continue to gain office.

We now have a national holiday in January honoring a black minister who preached and practiced nonviolence. And it can no longer be claimed that 11 A.M. on Sunday is the nation's most segregated hour of the week.

Affirmative-action programs originally intended for blacks now embrace Hispanics, Asians, women, and/or gays. Some university affirmative-action programs give priority to students in poverty.

The reading public has come to realize that Toni Morrison is black and a writer. But she is not a black writer.

Hispanics will soon overtake blacks as the largest "minority." Meanwhile, efforts to create ongoing coalitions among blacks, Hispanics, and Asians have not been successful.

A growing number of blacks who have "made it" want to be seen as having arrived there by their own ability rather than affirmative action. In California, Florida, Michigan, and Texas, for example, affirmative-action programs based on race in college admissions have been challenged by whites, and also by some blacks.

These racial changes since the 1960s—and others too numerous to highlight—have encouraged a new generation of black leaders to recommend that priority also be given to those social problems that only tortuously can be linked solely to racism. They point, for example, to the prevalence of black-on-black crime, absentee fathers, the disproportion of AIDS among blacks compared to whites, the large number of single-parent black households in public-housing projects, and the poorly performing public schools in those neighborhoods. The victims of black crime are predominantly black.

That is why in Chicago last year, U.S. Representative Bobby Rush (D-Ill.) convened a summit on black-on-black crime and asked the attendees to "find alternatives to the culture of gun violence. It is critical we teach by example the true method of conflict resolution… " At about the same time, James T. Meeks, vice president of Jesse Jackson's Rainbow/Push coalition, appealed to fellow blacks: "Let's stop blaming everybody else for the problems of black men and start doing something for ourselves. Yes, white folks have treated us wrong. Yes, there is an injustice, but we're doing a whole lot of stuff to ourselves. To black America, if you want to help, we've got to start in our own house."

Several years ago, the need for such self-scrutiny was dramatically summarized in the *Economist* (March 7, 1998):

> Black unemployment in desperate ghettos is not obviously the result of racism. Most of the worst-stricken cities are run by black mayors, after all; and social services that might once have ignored the plight of blacks are also run by blacks. Black entrepreneurs as well as white ones have fled the inner cites for the suburbs…. A bigger cause of black poverty is that 70 percent of all black children are born out of wedlock…. During the Depression, poverty was acute but families were more cohesive.

In spite of an era of high prosperity, the persistence of child poverty among blacks (and whites), can be attributed, in the main, to the decline in marriage and to the tide of single-parent households. Statistics for 1999 from the U.S. Census Bureau confirmed this conclusion: 50 percent of black children under six in families without a father lived in poverty, while only 9 percent of those in a two-parent family were poor.

While the new black leaders may echo the *Economist*'s devastating overview, they do not deny that racism exists. For them, however, racism as *the* reason for the durability of black poverty has become more difficult to substantiate. Consequently, they search for new ways to eradicate disparities in income, seeking additional means of uprooting black poverty. They struggle to have their voices heard and their proposals implemented. In doing so, they play down white guilt and black helplessness.

On the other hand, the racial gains since the 1960s, the disturbing social conditions within some black communities, and the calls for self-help initiatives have put traditional civil-rights leaders on the defensive. Disinclined to air "dirty linen" in public, they continue viewing the world through the prism of race. As a result, the civil-rights establishment now strives even harder to keep racism high on the nation's agenda and conscience. How? By shunning the more favorable data about black achievement. They publicize instead anecdotal data about racism's presence to garner support for their contention that the nation's 34 million blacks are still the victims and that racism is omnipresent.

In their eagerness, hyperbole often suffuses their arguments. Alabama's Southern Poverty Law Center recently claimed in a fund-raising letter: "I'm sure that you are well aware that our schools are racked with racial strife and intolerance against those who are different. Some call it a national crisis. Our communities are seething with racial violence. African Americans, Hispanics, and Asian Americans are assaulting each other."

In their tug of war with the venerable civil-rights establishment, new—and increasingly influential—black leaders no longer seek to divide (victimizers vs. victims). Instead, they hope to unite blacks and whites so that together they will address the serious social problems that beset inner-city neighborhoods. Their first priority goes to reducing urban poverty. In the new millennium, a new civil-rights agenda is being fashioned to promote two-parent families, curb street violence, improve public schools, reduce dependency on drugs, and uproot poverty. These objectives may prove to be more difficult to achieve than the equal-opportunity goals of the civil-rights movement in the 1960s, but they are no less worthy of pursuit.

Ed Marciniak *is president of the Institute of Urban Life at Loyola University, Chicago.*

Don Wycliff

Ed Marciniak is absolutely right when he says we are struggling for a new way to talk intelligently and usefully about race. But what inhibits such conversation, I think, is less the lack of a new vocabulary than the persistence of an old one: the vocabulary of racial guilt and innocence. Our whole racial "dialogue" has become a contest to establish or escape guilt, and, as a result, is shot through with dishonesty.

Most white people—or what appears to me to be most—seem intent mainly on establishing their personal innocence: innocence of racial bias, of discrimination, of any connection to or benefit from slavery. Not only is this beside the point, it's also impossible. One cannot escape the personal implications of membership in a society, no matter how personally blameless one may be. Where race in America is concerned, there are no innocents.

For their part, black people—or at least black leaders—seem more intent than ever on pressing the issue of white personal guilt: for slavery, for segregation, for lingering discrimination, for whatever deficits African Americans still suffer. More than three decades into the nation's effort to pay off that promissory note Martin Luther King Jr.

spoke of in his "I Have a Dream" speech, black leaders seem intent on denying that anything at all has changed, determined not to "let the white man off the hook." As a black man, a Christian, and a person who has required the forgiveness and forbearance of others more than once in his life, I am deeply troubled by this particular gambit. The notion of acting as moral prosecutor and judge of a fellow human being strikes me as odious. I take seriously the scriptural admonition against judging others, "for the measure by which you measure is the measure by which you will be measured." There is nothing more foolish and unbecoming, it seems to me, than to go about peering into the eyes of others in search of motes.

(I am reminded in this connection of an e-mail sent me by a black friend of about my age, fifty-four, after the recent deadly school shooting in San Diego. It was a newspaper column in which the writer, a white man, urged other whites to face up to the fact that this kind of behavior was a white kid's malady. My friend underscored that point in his accompanying note. I didn't reply to him, but if I had I would have told him you could bet that, before this terrible phenomenon runs its course, there'll be a black kid somewhere who will do the same thing. There is no racial immunity to the sort of demons that possess children and propel them to such murderous lunacy. To think such immunity exists is to succumb to the pride that goes before a fall—and an embarrassment.)

Not only is such moral prosecution foolish and unbecoming, it's ineffective. Increasingly over the last two decades, white people have given evidence that they have hardened to this sort of thing, that they're through feeling racial guilt—whether they ought to be or not. Obviously, not all take this attitude, but a growing number that now seem to be a majority do. This refusal of guilt first manifested itself in the election of Ronald Reagan and has continued ever since—even through the two Clinton administrations. Paralleling this change has been another: the loss by blacks of the moral high ground that goes along with victim status. Frankly, given the very real and dramatic progress African Americans have made over the last three and one-half decades, it is hard to sustain the argument that we remain, as a group, victims of a relentless and unyielding societal racism. To be sure, racism persists and continues to distort lives. Probably in no area is its effect greater than in law enforcement and criminal justice. The ruinous rates of black unwed motherhood to which Marciniak refers are not unrelated to the depressing rates of arrest and incarceration of black men, so many of whom are thereby rendered "unmarriageable."

But to contend, as some black spokesmen do, that racism remains the defining fact of black life in this country, that "a black man just can't get ahead," is simply, demonstrably false. There are too many exceptions, too many success stories, for that to be true. Such exceptions are now, arguably, the rule. But it wasn't just a general perception of steadily increasing black progress that eroded the notion of blacks as victims and changed the moral equation on race. Had that been the case, I don't think there would be the raw edginess to race relations that is so much in evidence now. No, there was one very specific and singular event that, I believe, sealed the change. That event was the trial of O.J. Simpson and the reaction of black people to it.

It appeared to many whites—and I hear this every time a hot racial issue is aired in the newspaper—that a black man got away with murder in this high-profile case by portraying himself as a victim of police racism. Not only did blacks on the Simpson jury let him get away, but the black community at large applauded it, demonstrating thereby that racial solidarity was more important than justice. Or so the thinking goes. I don't think it was fully appreciated at the time what a watershed in race relations the Simpson verdict was. Indeed, grotesque as the idea may seem, the Simpson case is emblematic of what many white and black conservative critics consider the grievous defect of affirmative action and other programs of racial redress: a black man escaped responsibility for the killing of two white persons so that society could make redress for his supposed victimization by a social institution, the police. Take away the homicidal element and these critics see the same principle at work in, for example, the University of Michigan affirmative-action cases: In an attempt to redress historical social wrongs, less-deserving minority applicants are favored over more-deserving white ones. It's an argument that, it appears, the Supreme Court is ready to buy.

So if there is unfinished business in the area of racial equality and the old vocabulary of racial guilt and innocence have become impediments, what's to be done? We could do far worse, I think, than go back to Martin Luther King Jr. for instruction and example. King and his "dream" are invoked so frequently and wantonly nowadays that I have almost grown tired of them. I know that's heresy, but there is a treacly quality to so much of the talk about King and his dream that it is like an overdose of candy. However, the fact is that King preached hard truths and he was not a man to take the easy road. He entered by the narrow gate—the gate of nonviolent direct action. You almost never hear anyone talk about that anymore. The genius of his approach was manifold. It involved direct action, an active challenge to injustice. But it was nonviolent, a refusal to use what he considered immoral means to achieve a moral end. It put the onus on those maintaining the system of injustice to respond—and to live with themselves afterward. It forced them to confront their consciences, not to listen to moral harangues.

That last fact is critical, especially in our over-the-top, in-your-face, finger-wagging age, when nobody feels any compunction about calling attention to the faults and failures of others. King had the grace and the good sense not to go about acting as moral prosecutor of his fellow humans—even if he may privately have considered them monsters. That may have been a tactical decision—like leaving room in a diplomatic negotiation for one's rival to gracefully back down, to save face. I like to think his belief in nonviolence was an expression of real grace, the result of King's having received forgiveness for his sins and thereby being inclined to forgive others. But whether King's attitude was tactical or something more—or something else entirely—I don't see any contemporary black leader who behaves that way. And that's a real loss because King's approach is the only way whites can be rendered receptive again to the need to exert themselves to rectify what remains of racism in American society.

We in the United States have made an amazing racial revolution over the last three and one-half decades. There may be another nation that has done as much, but if there is, I don't know of it. We must tell our people—black, white, brown, red, yellow—all about that revolution. We need to give ourselves a big round of applause. Then we must challenge ourselves—without condemning—to finish the job. And we must do it in terms that will cause people to nod "yes" instead of turning away in disgust. I personally am fond of those words from the preamble to the Constitution, the ones about creating "a more perfect union." Where is the Martin Luther King of our age, or the Abraham Lincoln, or the Lyndon Johnson, or the Cesar Chavez, who can speak those words in a way that will move us to the next stage of the struggle for American union?

Don Wycliff *is public editor of the* Chicago Tribune.

From *Commonweal*, June 1, 2001, pp. 12-14. © 2001 by Commonweal Foundation. Reprinted by permission. For subscriptions, call toll-free: 1-888-495-6755.

UNIT 7
Asian Americans

Unit Selections

Key Points to Consider

- Public attention to the activities of Asian Americans associated with campaign finance scandals and alleged espionage related to nuclear armament has fostered public perceptions of this ethnic group that has caused considerable concern within Asian American communities. Discuss and explain the relationship of persons and groups that is illustrated by such media and governmental action.

- The public passions generated during World War II have subsided, and anti-Japanese sentiment is no longer heard. Do you agree or disagree with this statement? Why?

- How can inclusiveness as an American value be taught? What approaches are most promising?

- What can be learned from examining Asian Americans' educational performance excellence and economic and cultural success in the United States? Asian Indians have surfaced in a plethora of cases related to courtship and marriage. In what respect are communitarian and nuclear approaches to family relationships a source of cultural benefits and burdens?

 **Links: www.dushkin.com/online/**
These sites are annotated in the World Wide Web pages.

Asian American Resources
    http://www.ai.mit.edu/people/irie/aar/

The Asian and American contexts discussed in this unit provide perspectives on immigrant adjustment and their reception in various regimes and cultures. The ongoing issue of cultural formation through language and the political artifices used to heighten or diminish ethnicity as a political factor are explored.

The following collection of articles on Asian Americans invites us to reflect on the fact that the United States is related to Asia in ways that would seem utterly amazing to the world view of the American founders. The expansion of the American regime across the continent, the importation of Asian workers, and the subsequent exclusion of Asians from the American polity are signs of the tarnished image and broken promise of refuge that America extended and then revoked. The Asian world is a composite of ethnicities and traditions ranging from the Indian subconti-

nent northeastward to China and Japan. The engagement of the United States beyond its continental limits brought American and Asian interests into a common arena now called the Pacific Rim. The most recent and perhaps most traumatic episode of this encounter was the conflict that erupted in 1941 at Pearl Harbor in Hawaii. Thus, examining the Asian relationship to America begins with the dual burdens of domestic exclusion and war. The cultural roots and current interaction between the United States and Asia form a complex of concerns that are explored in this unit's articles. Understanding the cultural matrices of Asian nations and their ethnicities and languages initiates the process of learning about the Asian emigrants who, for many reasons, decided to leave Asia to seek a fresh beginning in the United States.

The growth of Asian American population since the immigration reform of 1965, the emergence of Japan and other Asian nations as international fiscal players, and the image of Asian American intellectual and financial success have heightened interest in this ethnic group in the United States. The variety of religious traditions that Asian immigrants bring to America is another dimension of cultural and moral importance. In what respect are non-Judeo-Christian-Islamic faith traditions issues of consequence? The aftermath of conflict and resulting analysis have riveted attention on the ethnic factor.

The details of familial and cultural development within Asian American communities compose worlds of meaning that are a rich source of material from which both insights and troubling questions of personal and group identity emerge. Pivotal periods of conflict in the drama of the American experience provide an occasion for learning as much about ourselves as about one of the newest clusters of ethnicities—the Asian Americans.

One of the first large-scale interactions between the United States and Asia was with the Philippine Islands and its population. This experience of war and empire and the attendant century-long process of military and defense relationships, as well as the exportation of institutions and cultural change, have forged a unique international-intercultural symbiosis. The role of the ethnic Chinese diaspora and the emergence of economic strength and political change in Asia suggest the globalization of the ethnic factor. Even the name of this American ethnic population has changed, as has its relationship to the islands and its ancestry. There is new politicization of the future of both an Asian homeland and the diasporic remnant. Its aspiring leaders are fashioning a new consciousness that is meaningful for its time and is inspiring actions that will articulate a most worthy future.

Misperceived Minorities

'Good' and 'bad' stereotypes saddle Hispanics and Asian Americans

Pamela Constable

Washington Post Staff Writer

Richard Lopez, 29, a fourth-generation Mexican American businessman from San Bernardino, Calif., grew up in what he called a "Brady Bunch" suburb, and learned Spanish only to communicate with his great-grandmother. He is mystified when Hispanic newcomers complain of discrimination and angry when whites assume he needed special help to move up in American society.

"Nobody ever put a roadblock in front of me. I earned my way into college, and it offended me when people asked if I was receiving affirmative action," he says in a telephone interview. "I think a lot of the whining about discrimination is blown out of proportion. The biggest thing holding a lot of Mexicans back here is their resentment against those who succeed."

Ray Chin, 46, an insurance agent in New York's Chinatown, spent his teenage years washing bathrooms and delivering groceries in the city after his parents fled Communist China in the 1950s. Today he has earned the stature that often leads Asian Americans to be called the "model minority," a phrase he views as more curse than compliment.

"Yes, we can successfully join the mainstream, but once we reach a certain level, we're stifled by that glass ceiling," Chin says amid the din of a crowded Chinese restaurant. "People think we Asians can take care of ourselves, and they don't see the need to help us. But it's not true. We are still not included in things and we have to work three times harder to get to the same level as our co-workers."

No matter how much personal success they achieve, Hispanics and Asian Americans say they must fight stereotypes that can undermine their confidence or limit their potential. Whether "negative" or "positive"—the lazy, welfare-dependent Hispanic or the shy, technically oriented Asian American—

such perceptions can be equally harmful and unfair, members of both groups say.

Worse, they say, is that ethnic minorities in the United States sometimes come to accept others' stereotypes about them, even when the facts and their experiences do not support those biases. For that reason, they may remain extremely sensitive to discrimination even when they have matched or surpassed white Americans in income and education.

Such contradictions—both in the views of other Americans toward Hispanics and Asian Americans and, at times, in the views of those groups about themselves—appeared throughout a nationwide telephone poll of 1,970 people conducted by The Washington Post, the Kaiser Family Foundation and Harvard University.

Yet there is also enormous diversity of opinion and experience within these two ethnic categories, other surveys and interviews show. The perceptions of Hispanics and Asian Americans about their opportunities and obstacles vary dramatically depending on their class, community and country of origin.

"It's very misleading to talk about the views of whites versus the views of minority groups like Latinos, because you cannot assume commonalty within those groups at all," says Rodolfo de la Garza, a professor of government at the University of Texas in Austin. He says it is crucial to know what language people speak, where they were born and how long they had been in the United States to accurately assess their views.

In a recent nationwide survey of 1,600 Hispanics by the Tomas Rivera Center in Claremont, Calif., for example, 71 percent of Hispanics from Central America said they believe that U.S. society discriminates against Hispanics, but only 42 percent of Cuban Americans agreed. Just over half of Mexican American respondents, by far the largest group of Hispanics in the United States, shared that view.

Poverty rates vary widely within both the Hispanic and Asian American communities, often depending on when, and from what country, members emigrated. In Los Angeles, unemployment is only 4 percent among Korean Americans, who flocked to the United States in the 1960s, but it is 21 percent among newly arrived Cambodian refugees. In New York, 32

Poll

HOW HISPANICS, ASIANS SEE THEMSELVES AND HOW OTHERS SEE THEM

*P*oll respondents were given a list of things some people have mentioned as reasons for the economic and social problems that some Hispanics and Asian Americans face today and were asked if each one is a major reason for those problems.

Is this a major reason for Hispanics' problems?	Hispanics who said 'yes'	Whites who said 'yes'	Blacks who said 'yes'	Asians who said 'yes'
Lack of jobs	68%	42%	74%	53%
Language difficulties	66%	56%	59%	59%
Lack of educational opportunities	51%	46%	63%	53%
Breakup of the Hispanic family	45%	28%	38%	22%
Past and present discrimination	43%	31%	58%	29%
Lack of motivation and an unwillingness to work hard	41%	25%	19%	32%

Those polled were asked the same question about Asians:

Is this a major reason for Asians' problems?	Asians who said 'yes'	Whites who said 'yes'	Blacks who said 'yes'	Hispanics who said 'yes'
Language difficulties	44%	44%	52%	37%
Lack of jobs	34%	31%	46%	43%
Past and present discrimination	20%	24%	41%	31%
Lack of educational opportunities	17%	18%	31%	31%
Breakup of the Asian family	14%	16%	27%	35%
Lack of motivation and an unwillingness to work hard	10%	22%	23%	20%

Polling data comes from a survey of 1,970 randomly selected adults interviewed in August and September, including 802 whites, 474 blacks, 352 Asian Americans and 252 Hispanics. The minority groups were oversampled to obtain large enough subsamples to analyze reliably. Margin of sampling error for the overall results is plus or minus 3 percentage points. The margins of sampling error for the four subsamples ranged from 4 percentage points for the white subsample to 7 percentage points for the Hispanic subsample. Sampling error is only one of many potential sources of error in public opinion polls.

percent of Dominican Americans are poor, but only 11 percent of Colombian Americans are.

For Hispanics or Asian Americans who live in the cocoon of urban ethnic enclaves, it may take a foray into other regions to make them appreciate the prejudice faced by others. Juan Santiago, 30, an office manager in the Bronx, N.Y., whose parents emigrated from the Dominican Republic, says he never experienced discrimination growing up in his heavily Dominican neighborhood. Then he went out to New Mexico as a foreman on a construction job.

"All the workers were Mexican, and the white owners had no respect for them. The work was very hard, the pay was very low, and there was no overtime," he recounts. "They tried to exploit me, too, but I knew my rights and I wouldn't let them. Until, then, I never really understood what discrimination was."

BUT LIFE INSIDE ETHNIC GHETTOS ALSO CAN CONfine and isolate, discouraging immigrants from joining American society at large and reinforcing others' misperceptions about them. In interviews, many foreign-born Hispanics and Asian Americans said they cling to immigrant communities, speaking to bosses and salesclerks in their native tongues and rarely meeting white Americans.

Yu Hui Chang, 35, a waitress in lower Manhattan, N.Y., says she and her husband work 12 hours a day in Chinese restaurants and rarely see their young son. Speaking through an interpreter in the cramped office of a Chinatown labor union, the Shanghai-born woman says she feels trapped in her community but is determined to succeed in her new country.

"It is very hard to be a woman in Chinatown," says Chang, who emigrated in 1982. "My life is nothing but working, working all the time. In China, I thought America was full of gold, and I still have the dream of taking that gold back home, but I can never save any."

Like Chang, the great majority of Asian Americans and Hispanics who responded to the Post/Kaiser/Harvard poll said they believe strongly in the American dream, but 46 percent of Asian Americans and 55 percent of Hispanics said they are farther from achieving it than they were a decade ago.

Both groups singled out hard work and family unity as keys to success here, and both singled out the same major obstacles: lack of good jobs, crime and violence, high taxes and the gap between their incomes and the rising cost of living. All agreed that learning English is crucial.

"You have to learn the language of the enemy to survive," says Juan Garcia, a Dominican-born man who manages a discount clothing shop in Washington Heights, a largely Hispanic section of Manhattan. "I've been here 13 years and my English is still poor, so I can't always defend myself," he adds in Spanish, describing his humiliation at being turned away from a fast-food counter when he could not explain his order.

Nonetheless, Garcia says he would not want to give up the comforts of American life. His son, 16, is studying computers and dreams of becoming a doctor. "Once you become civilized, you don't want to go back to a village with no lights or running water," he says.

Nationwide, the poll suggested that Asian Americans as a group think they have done much better economically than Hispanics think they have done. Asian Americans also have a far more optimistic view of their chances for success. Eighty-four percent of Asian Americans guessed that the average Asian American is at least as well off as the average white American, and 58 percent said they have the same or better chance of becoming wealthy.

Hispanics, on the other hand, tended to be more pessimistic and to believe others' critical views of them. In the poll, 74 percent of Hispanics said the average Hispanic is worse off than the average white, and 41 percent cited low motivation and unwillingness to work as a reason for their lack of advancement. Yet studies show that Hispanics have an unusually high level of participation in the work force.

"We are very susceptible to what others think about us, so we absorb those negative stereotypes in defiance of the facts," says Cecilia Munoz, Washington director of the National Council of La Raza, a Hispanic advocacy group. A 1994 survey by the council found that Hispanics have been most often depicted on TV and in films as "poor, of low status, lazy, deceptive, and criminals."

In the Post/Kaiser/Harvard poll, only one-quarter of white Americans cited unwillingness to work as a major obstacle for Hispanics; many more agreed with Hispanics that language problems and lack of educational opportunities are their biggest problems. In assessing the status of Asian Americans, whites cited only language difficulties as a major problem, suggesting that whites believe that Asian Americans face fewer barriers than Hispanics face.

More Hispanics say they thought they face the most discrimination as a group, but despite their relative economic success, more Asian Americans say they and their relatives and friends had experienced prejudice personally.

A majority of both groups agree that minorities should work their way up without special government help but also insist that government should protect their rights, for example by enacting tougher laws against workplace discrimination. And in interviews, many Hispanics and Asian Americans expressed deep concerns about a rising tide of anti-immigrant feeling.

Some specialists say the recent political furor over illegal immigrants has exacerbated a false impression that hordes of foreigners are arriving on U.S. shores. In the poll, the respondents guessed that 65 percent of Hispanics in the United States were born in foreign countries. According to the National Council of La Raza, only 33 percent of Hispanics were born in foreign countries.

"I see many Latinos trying to distance themselves from their roots as they react to the wave of anti-immigrant sentiment," says Harry Pachon, who directs the Tomas Rivera Center. "But I keep asking, how does an Anglo driving down the street pick out which Latino is native-born, which is a refugee, which is undocumented?"

IN OTHER WAYS, THE POLL SUGGESTED THAT MOST respondents are not especially hostile to either ethnic minority.

Three-quarters said it "wouldn't make much difference" to the country if the number of Hispanics or Asian Americans were to increase significantly. Less than one-quarter said it would be a "bad thing" if either group were to grow substantially.

Yet the perception of growing xenophobia has created tensions between foreign-born and more established Hispanics and Asian Americans. Even in a community such as Jackson Heights, in Queens, N.Y., where Korean, Cuban, Vietnamese and Colombian immigrants live in tolerant proximity, second-generation residents expressed concern in interviews that illiterate or illegal newcomers are creating a negative image of all ethnic minorities.

"People have this idea that we are coming here in industrial quantities to invade America and go on welfare. The truth is that most of us were born here, we are working hard or going to school," says Mario Vargas, 22, a college student whose parents emigrated from Colombia. "But these days, the stereotypes are making it harder for the rest of us."

Arranged Marriages, Minus the Parents

For Some South Asians, Matrimonial Sites Both Honor and Subvert Tradition

By REENA JANA

HARSHA KUMAR, a 29-year-old technology officer for an e-commerce company in Westborough, Mass., wanted to find a wife. And Mr. Kumar, who was born in India and educated in the United States, wanted to begin his search in a way that blended both Old and New World sensibilities.

"I knew I wanted to marry an Indian or Indian-American woman, but arranged marriage seemed unnatural to me," Mr. Kumar said. "Meeting someone online seemed more natural to me, maybe because I work in e-commerce and am on the Internet and using e-mail a lot already."

In January 1998, Mr. Kumar signed up with Internet Matrimonials (matrimonials.com), a service for people of South Asian heritage. Traditionally, many South Asians have arranged marriages through relatives or "marriage bureaus," paid matchmakers sometimes called bride brokers. In addition, publications like India Abroad and The Times of India have carried classified ads usually placed by parents looking for serious prospective brides and grooms. But in the last few years, matrimonial Web sites have offered an alternative.

Internet Matrimonials says that it receives nearly 40,000 visits a month. The site charges customers $30 apiece to advertise themselves to potential spouses by indicating their religion, occupation, cultural background and location.

Through Internet Matrimonials, Mr. Kumar began sending e-mail to a law student in Bombay named Hema Sastry twice a day, once in the morning and once at night. They found that beyond having compatible biodata— the term used for the résumé-like summaries used in each matrimonial ad for each person's caste, education and physical attributes—they also shared an interest in Indian music.

They soon exchanged photographs by mail. In February 1999, Mr. Kumar decided to make the trip to India to meet Ms. Sastry in person. They became engaged and in

December 1999 were married in India. Mr. Kumar's wife then moved to the United States.

"Some people might think it's crazy that we began our relationship via e-mail," Mr. Kumar said. "But I think we communicated more than some people who date one another once a week. We probably even communicated more than we do now, living in the same house as a husband and wife who get too busy caught up with work and errands."

Matrimonial Web sites seem to strike a compromise between ancient South Asian social traditions and the contemporary attitudes of many Indian- and Pakistani-Americans by cutting out the intermediary of arranged marriages: the family. Just as online trading is starting to cut out the middleman in the investing business, the Web is being used to help arrange marriages without help from relatives or marriage bureaus. The sites can be particularly useful for South Asians abroad; in 1998 alone, 36,500 Indians and 13,100 Pakistanis moved to the United States.

Technology simplifies the search for suitors of certain castes or religions.

Mr. Kumar said his parents had not been put off by his lack of interest in a traditional arranged marriage.

"They got what they wanted and I got what I wanted, and the match was even better, I think, than either an arranged marriage or a 'love marriage,'" Mr. Kumar said, using a term for unarranged marriages that result from dating. Love marriages are still looked down upon by some conservative South Asian families, both in this country and abroad.

Mr. Kumar's experience was so positive that he recommended the Internet Matrimonials site to his sister, Reshma, who also lives in the United States. She met her husband through the same service.

The most popular of the hundreds of matrimonial sites on the Web include Internet Matrimonials, A1 Matrimonials (www.a1im.com), IndianMarriages (www.indianmarriages.com) and Suitable Match (www.suitablematch.com). Most sites offer some free services, like letting people search their bride and groom databases, and allow users to post photos and descriptive paragraphs about themselves for prospective marriage partners only.

A1 Matrimonials explicitly states that "no dating ads will be allowed." IndianMarriages invites individuals and parents as well as marriage bureaus to log on. The site offers simple, advanced and keyword searches. Users enter or search for information in fields like "age" and "caste," but they can also search for more detailed information like "wears turban." A "deluxe" paid account allows users to use e-mail to get in contact with those whose ads are posted. People can peruse the database free.

Marriage sites cater to a technologically sophisticated population. According to Forrester Research, 69 percent of Asian-American households are online, compared with 43 percent of the general population.

"We feel like we're helping Indians and Indian-Americans help qualify or reject potential mates faster than ever before," said Nahrain Bhatia, who founded Suitable Match, a heavily visited site with 10,000 registered members. He came up with the idea for the site after he realized that his American-born daughters were of marriageable age and that he was not sure where they might find Indian-American husbands.

"I think there's a real transition occurring in the way people of Indian descent find their spouses," Mr. Bhatia said. "They are generally busy professionals. They need the process to become more efficient and more effective. Plus, most of the Indian-Americans who are online are young and educated—quite an attractive pool of marriage candidates."

Bharat Manglani, an Indian immigrant and the president of Asian Matches (www.asianmatches.com), which also runs the Suitable Match site, says that online services can streamline the marriage process. Mr. Manglani's own parents spent three years finding a wife for him. When they finally found her through a newspaper ad, it took six months for the families to arrange to introduce the future bride and groom to each other in person.

"If we can reduce a six-month process to six days, think of how much easier we can make finding a mate," Mr. Manglani said. "I mean, a successful marriage is all about sheer luck. Wouldn't it be better to be up front about whether or not a bride or groom won't work as quickly as possible? Then our clients could move on and

just get that much closer to finding the right person, get married and get on with their lives."

Achla Sagal, 30, a second-generation Indian-American lawyer in Dayton, Ohio, had considered an arranged marriage, but after seven years of her parents' hunting in vain for her ideal groom, she grew frustrated. Ms. Sagal surfed the Web until she found two free sites, A1 Matrimonials and IndianMarriages, and placed ads with them. Ms. Sagal said her parents were eager to see their daughter married and support her online quest for a husband.

"I figured that without parental buffers, I might be able to more easily find an Indian-American who genuinely wanted to get married to another Indian-American," Ms. Sagal said. She had tired of offline meetings with marriage candidates who, after formal introductions with both sets of parents and other relatives in the same room, would admit that they were there only out of obligation to their families.

"Online, the contact between me and a potential groom is much more direct," said Ms. Sagal, who has yet to find a groom. She has had responses from more than 25 potential grooms and has corresponded with 10.

The online options for finding a mate might seem very modern, but they represent an acceptance of the prejudices of previous generations. Looking for a spouse through such strict criteria as caste or subcaste, graduate degrees or even lightness of complexion (common fields on most matrimonial sites) echoes the strict categories that traditional South Asian parents and marriage bureaus have used for centuries.

"In the end, I feel like using online matrimonial sites is hypocritical," said Koki Jhumra, a 22-year-old Pakistani-American who works as a Web site developer in Cambridge, Mass. "Basically you're engaging in a meat hunt, like you would in a bar, even though that's what you're theoretically trying to avoid." Ms. Jhumra said she had tried a matrimonial site and had been disappointed when a potential mate she met online decided that she was too young.

"And it's funny," Ms. Jhumra said, "because at the same time you're trying to meet people online by pre-screening them by the same biases—like someone's age, education, social status or wealth—used by your parents and marriage bureaus alike, rather than finding out if you have things in common and communicate well."

Still, Kirin Narayan, a professor of anthropology and languages and cultures of Asia at the University of Wisconsin at Madison, said that South Asian matrimonial Web sites could catch on.

"Marriages to an appropriate person of the right religion, region, caste, subcaste and so on used to be arranged through the intermediaries of elders and match-makers who were linked in local networks," Professor Narayan said. "In more impersonal settings, like cities, matrimonial advertising through newspapers could forge new links and expand the range of available prospects beyond existing networks."

That view was echoed by Anne Monius, an assistant professor at the Center for South Asian Studies at the University of Virginia who lectures on arranged marriage.

"Indian parents who are immigrants might not have the network in the States necessary to arrange a marriage easily," she said. "These Web sites can help because they offer a controlled environment, in terms of a somewhat screened community."

Even operators of reputable marriage bureaus are turning to the Web to reach unattached South Asians and South Asian-Americans. Falguni Mehta, who has run a marriage bureau that bears her name in Bombay for more than 12 years and says she has arranged more than 5,000 marriages, started her own Web site (www.falgunimehta.com) in 1997. Since going online, she said, she has arranged five to seven marriages a month via the Web. Most clients have been Indian-Americans.

Mrs. Mehta posts information only on clients whose backgrounds she has checked. "I make the first inquiry about a bride or groom's background," Mrs. Mehta said, "and I've built up a trustworthy reputation with a traditional marriage bureau over the years. But on these other sites, people can manipulate the truth quite easily, and there is no one who can monitor that."

Although his parents weren't pressuring him to marry, Manish Vij, the 27-year-old founder and vice president for marketing at Pointera, a Silicon Valley company, posted an ad with Internet Matrimonials out of curiosity.

Mr. Vij noticed that certain terms kept surfacing in the ads placed by divorced women. "Issueless divorce," he deduced, stands for "no children," while "innocently divorced" means "still a virgin." Both terms can easily be searched for on most sites.

Mr. Vij said he would prefer meeting his wife offline. "I'd rather feel chemistry," he said, "which one might experience meeting a woman not only at a party but also in an arranged meeting set up by relatives."

Wartime Hysteria

Reviewed by PETER IRONS

**BY ORDER OF THE
PRESIDENT FDR
and the Internment of Japanese
Americans**
By Greg Robinson
Harvard Univ. 336 pp. $27.95

**FREE TO DIE FOR THEIR
COUNTRY
The Story of the
Japanese American Draft
Resisters in World War II**
By Eric L. Muller
Univ. of Chicago. 256 pp. $27.50

**LAST WITNESSES
Reflections on the Wartime
Internment of Japanese
Americans**
Edited by Erica Harth
Palgrave. 293 pp. $24.95

Two months after Japanese forces launched a "sneak attack" on Pearl Harbor, President Franklin D. Roosevelt authorized the evacuation and internment of "all persons" of Japanese ancestry from the West Coast. Forced to leave their homes on a week's notice, more than 110,000 people—two-thirds of them native-born American citizens—were shipped by bus and train to "relocation centers" ringed with barbed wire and guarded by Army troops. The residents of what Roosevelt himself described as "concentration camps" endured their internal exile as punishment for what one young man, Fred Korematsu, said was the crime of "looking like the enemy."

Korematsu was one of a handful of Japanese Americans who refused to obey the military curfew and evacuation orders that followed Roosevelt's edict, and whose criminal convictions the Supreme Court upheld in 1943 and 1944. In 1983, a federal judge vacated Korematsu's conviction, ruling that government lawyers had deliberately lied to the Supreme Court in justifying the internment. Standing proudly in the East Room of the White House in January 1998, Korematsu received the Medal of Freedom from President Bill Clinton, who lauded the former convict as "a man of quiet bravery" who deserved the nation's "respect and thanks for his patient pursuit to preserve the civil liberties we hold dear."

One of the guests at the White House ceremony was Norman Mineta, who spent three years of his childhood in the Heart Mountain internment camp in Wyoming and who now serves in President Bush's cabinet as transportation secretary. Mineta's role in protecting America's airports and travelers after the "sneak attack" on the World Trade Center and the Pentagon highlights the irony of calls for the internment of Americans of Arabic ancestry. Already, it is highly likely that government lawyers are reviewing the Supreme Court decisions in the Japanese-American internment cases to see whether President Bush can invoke "pressing military necessity" as justification for restricting the movements of members of another ethnic minority.

These recent events provide a contemporary relevance to three books that have joined the growing literature on the Japanese-American wartime experience. One deals with President Roosevelt's decision to authorize the internment program, one recounts the trials of the young men who resisted the military draft while in the camps, and a third offers 17 essays of personal recollection and historical reflection. Greg Robinson, a fellow in history at George Mason University, narrows his focus on the internment to one man, finding it "especially perplexing that such an ac-

tion could have taken place during the administration of Franklin Roosevelt, a President justly celebrated for his attachment to human rights and his dedication to creating government programs to serve the needs of ordinary Americans."

By Order of the President traces FDR's suspicions of Japan's intentions in the Pacific back to his service as assistant Navy secretary during Woodrow Wilson's presidency. Roosevelt viewed all Americans of Japanese ancestry as "foreigners" and responded to intense pressure from West Coast politicians and the Hearst press in authorizing the internment. He also displayed a cavalier attitude toward the Constitution, brushing aside arguments that the forced relocation of American citizens would violate that charter's promise of "due process of law" for those of every racial and ethnic background. In these respects, FDR differed little from earlier wartime presidents, including Lincoln and Wilson, who approved the mass detention of "disloyal" elements such as Confederate or German sympathizers.

Robinson shows that Roosevelt played an active role in the internment policy, but fails to note that he was most often simply approving the proposals of his Cabinet members and staff. It is unlikely that the president spent more than a few hours, over a three-year period, actually discussing the internment question with his subordinates. Robinson concedes that FDR's decision to authorize the program "was made casually, with no consideration or weighing of the racial or constitutional implications of that action." This point could certainly have been made, and its implications explored, without the weight of 45 pages of footnotes.

Robinson is right to conclude that FDR "deserves censure for not providing moral and constitutional leadership" on this issue. But the nation as a whole, not just one man, failed to prevent or protest this grave injustice to fellow Americans who "looked like the enemy." In *Free to Die for Their Country*, Eric L. Muller of the University of North Carolina law school provides a fascinating, chilling account of the punishment imposed on some 300 young men who refused to obey draft orders served on them in the internment camps. They chose, in effect, to transfer from one kind of prison to another. These Japanese-American draft resisters have largely been ignored by historians, who focus on the bravery of the men who joined the segregated Army units that suffered heavy losses in hand-to-hand combat with German troops in Italy. One such veteran, who lost an arm to a German grenade, is Sen. Daniel Inouye of Hawaii, who has written the foreword to Muller's book.

Muller weaves government records, trial transcripts and the recollections of a dozen surviving draft resisters—now in their seventies and eighties—into a compelling story of young men thrown together by wartime, another "band of brothers" who fought for principle. They faced vengeful prosecutors, federal judges

who called them "traitors," small-town jurors who had never met anyone of Japanese ancestry, and the hostility of many fellow Japanese Americans eager to prove themselves through hyper-patriotism. Muller pins the label of "callous racists" on the federal judges in Wyoming and Idaho who ran production-line trials and sentenced resisters to prison for three to five years. Their openly contemptuous treatment of American citizens they called "Japs" makes this label quite apt. Only one judge, Louis E. Goodman in California, broke ranks with his colleagues, dismissing the indictments of 26 resisters on grounds that their harsh treatment was "shocking to his conscience."

Muller worries that Judge Goodman's approach leaves open the question of "whose conscience will be the benchmark?" In the end, he sides with Goodman in the "unique case of moral outrage" presented by the Japanese-American draft resisters, but his appreciation of the tough legal questions raised by their stand makes his book a model of engaged scholarship.

Erica Harth, who teaches at Brandeis, spent a year of her childhood in the Manzanar, Calif., internment center, where her

mother worked in the camp administration. Most of the essays she collected for *Last Witnesses* are by writers and political activists, some born in the camps and some the children and grandchildren of camp residents. They vary in style and in their distance from the internment experience, but all testify to the lasting impact of that traumatic experience on the succeeding generations of Japanese Americans.

One pair of essays, by Mitsuye Yamada and her daughter Jeni, sensitively explores the "legacy of silence" that made Mitsuye wait until her daughter was a teenager to tell her that she had been interned. All three of these new books help to "move beyond silence" and illustrate the conflict between wartime passions and the rights of people who "look like the enemy."

Peter Irons teaches at the University of California, San Diego, and is the author of "Justice at War: The Story of the Japanese American Internment Cases."

UNIT 8

The Ethnic Identity: The Experience and Persistence of Diversity

Unit Selections

Key Points to Consider

- The post-Nixon and post-Watergate era of ethnic data collection began with the 1980 Census. A considerable shift toward self-identification began, which allowed persons to claim specific and/or multiple categories. Does the earlier scheme of designating groups have any scientific or political merit? Does personal identification trump all other considerations? How does ethnicity of an earlier era suggest the tension between worlds of meaning discussed in this section?

- When the U.S. Commission on Civil Rights held hearings on issues related to eastern and southern European ethnic groups in the United States, leaders of these groups objected to the names EuroEthnic and EuroAmerican. They preferred specific ethnicities such as Polish American and Italian American. Does this extend to being a hill-billy?

- Does "Whiteness" provide a cultural legacy comparable to an ethnic heritage and culture? If so, what texts are central to this culture and tradition? Comment on the idea that the legacy of multiple ancestral origins and ethnic identities of European Americans derived from an earlier era of immigration reveals a lack of relevancy and the marginality of these ethnic populations to the central ethnic issues of our time. Who decides that your ethnicity is meaningless?

- What is a central ethnic issue? By what criteria do we decide the importance and preferential protection of one ethnic group vis à vis another group?

- What lessons can be learned from the experiences of eastern and southern Europeans?

 **Links: www.dushkin.com/online/**
These sites are annotated in the World Wide Web pages.

American Ethnic Studies
http://www.library.yale.edu/rsc/ethnic/internet.html
American Indian Ritual Object Repatriation Foundation
http://www.repatriationfoundation.org
Center for Research in Ethnic Relations
http://www.warwick.ac.uk/fac/soc/CRER_RC/
The International Center for Migration, Ethnicity, and Citizenship
http://www.newschool.edu/icmec/

Personal reflections on the relevance of ethnicity to one's self-concept and the search for clearer expressions of group identity are included in this unit. The article from What Ethnic Americans Really Think presents the reader with findings from an inaccessible body of ethnic-specific opinions about public issues and values. Readers may be interested in using the social distance and group affinity questionnaire provided in that article as a tool for testing and discovering patterns of race and ethnic relations within their local reach. Recent concerns of ethnic groups include language preservation, fair hearings for homeland interests, enclave neighborhoods, inclusion in ethnic studies, and their articulation of historical American expressions of fairness, justice, and equity, as well as the collection of accurate data from all ethnic groups in America. These values are thoroughly patterned into their world view and their appropriation of the expansive promise of the American icon—the Statue of Liberty. Ethnicity is often associated with immigrants and with importation of culture, language, stories, and foods from foreign shores. Appalachian, western, and other regional ethnicities are evidence of multigenerational ethnic cultural development within the American reality. The persistent, ongoing process of humanities is expressed locally in unique and intriguing folkways, dialects, languages, myths, festivals, food displays, and other enduring monuments and visible signs of the past and of the public dimension of cultural consciousness that constitutes ethnicity. As this unit's articles illustrate, ethnic experiences may be less foreign and alien than most imagine them to be.

Mediterranean and eastern European immigrants and their religious traditions entered an industrializing economy that required their labor, much like plantation production in an earlier period required the indentured servant and the slave. But they also met a cultural and political climate of potent challenges and denials of their integrity and existence.

Moynihan and Glazer, in *Beyond the Melting Pot* (1964), the report of the Kerner Commission, and findings of the National Center for Urban Ethnic Affairs confirmed that ethnicity was a salient factor. The descendants of Mediterranean and eastern European immigrants, even into the fourth generation, were just barely moving toward the middle class, absent in the professions, and rarely admitted to prestigious universities or colleges. More specifically, Italian and Polish people, like blacks and Hispanics/Latinos were found to be excluded from the executive suites and boardrooms of America's largest corporations, publicly regulated utilities, and philanthropies.

The emergence of interest in retracing the pathways of these immigrant groups and assessing their participation in intergroup relations in America are topics of many scholarly disciplines. The inclusion of the following articles is but a peek behind the curtain of this neglected dimension of race and ethnic relations in America. Apropos of the selection of articles and our attempt to understand current attention to this persistent cluster of ethnic Americans (the descendants of Mediterranean and eastern European groups, which have been ignored and neglected, mislabeled white-ethnics and/or Euro-ethnics) is Noel Ignatiev's provocative book, *How the Irish Became White.* Irish immigrants, though not a Mediterranean or an eastern European American ethnic group, had a similar experience in America of

being different from and perceived as racially apart from the American regime, owing to their conquered status in the British empire. Irish American freedom and participation in American life was the prototype of the American Dream.

After all, it was this American promise that resonated in their hearts and minds in 1965, when a coalition of Mediterranean and eastern European Americans in the national government, such as Emmanuel Cellers, Jacob Javits, Peter Rodino, John Brademas, Abraham Ribicoff, and ethnic, Catholic religious leaders, such as Msgr. Geno Baroni and Rev. Theodore Hesburgh, joined Protestant and secular organizations in support of the immigration reform proposed by President John Kennedy that ended the quota system and in support of the 1965 Voting Rights Act that ensured fair elections for the disenfranchised, especially Negroes in the South. This legislative coalition accomplished, through deliberative democracy, not by the mandate of the Supreme Court or the edict of administrative regulation, a fundamental change that significantly altered the terms of race and ethnic relations.

The massive migration of peoples during the past 30 years, which has included significantly large Mediterranean and eastern European populations, has reengaged the immigrant factor in American politics and the ethnic factor among all Americans. Should ethnic populations be denied their distinctiveness through absorption into the mass of modernity, or can their distinctiveness accompany them into mainstream modern American identities? This is the pivotal issue of American pluralism.

Please Ask Me Who, Not 'What,' I Am

My ethnicity isn't obvious on first glance. But why should it matter to people I've just met?

By JORDAN LITE

I'VE BEEN THINKING A LOT ABOUT that "Seinfeld" episode where Elaine is dating this guy and it's driving her nuts because she doesn't know "what" he is. They ultimately discover that neither is exotic enough for the other and they're so disappointed that they stop seeing each other.

It's the story of my life these days. Each new guy I meet, it seems, is fascinated by my ostensible failure to fall into an obvious racial category. Last year we could opt out of defining ourselves to the Census Bureau, but that option doesn't seem to have carried over into real life. I've lost track of how many flirty men have asked me what I am.

The first time, I was in Iowa and snobbishly dismissed the inquiry as rural provincialism. Then it happened again while I was on a date in San Francisco, a city that prides itself on its enlightenment.

Isn't it rude to ask "what" someone is when you've just met? Common courtesy would suggest so. But many people seem to feel uncomfortable if they can't immediately determine a new person's racial or ethnic background.

Of course, I've mused over "what" a stranger might be. But it's never occurred to me that asking "What are you?" of someone I've just met would elicit anything particularly revealing about him. I ask questions, but not that one.

So when a potential boyfriend asks me "What are you?" I feel like he wants to instantly categorize me. If he'd only let the answer come out naturally, he'd get a much better sense of what I'm about.

Perhaps acknowledging explicitly that race and ethnicity play a role in determining who we are is just being honest. But I'm not sure that such directness is always well intended. After I grouchily retorted "What do you mean, 'What am I?'" to one rather bewildered date, he

told me his dad was African-American and his mom Japanese, and that he ruminated all the time over how to reconcile such disparate influences. I realized then that he believed my being "different" would magically confer upon me an understanding of what it was like to be like him.

If you're looking for your soulmate, maybe it's only natural to want a person who has shared your experience. But for some people, "What are you?" is just a line. "You're exotic-looking," a man at a party explained when I asked him why he wanted to know. In retrospect, I think he probably meant his remark as a compliment. As a Hispanic friend pointed out, when all things Latin became the new craze, it's trendy to be exotic. But if someone wants to get to know me, I wish he would at least pretend it's not because of my looks.

Still, this guy's willingness to discuss my discomfort was eye-opening. He told me that he was part Korean, part white. Growing up in the Pacific Northwest, he wasn't the only biracial kid on the block. One could acknowledge race, he said, and still be casual about it.

Although I spent my childhood in a town lauded for its racial diversity, discussing race doesn't often feel easy to me. Maybe my Japanese classmate in the first grade could snack on seaweed without being hassled, but I can readily recall being 11 years old and watching a local TV news report about a pack of white boys who beat, then chased a terrified black teen onto a highway, where he was struck by a car and killed. The violence on TV silenced me. It seemed better not to risk asking questions that might offend.

Years after we graduated from our private high school, one of my good friends told me how out of place she felt as one of the few black students. Her guardedness had kept me from probing; but there's a part of me that wonders if talking with her then about her unease at school would have made me more comfortable now when people ask me about my place in the world.

But as it is, I resent being pressed to explain myself upfront, as if telling a prospective date my ethnicity eliminates his need to participate in a real conversation with me. "What are you?" I am asked, but the background check he's conducting won't show whether we share real interests that would bring us together in a genuine give-and-take.

In a way, I enjoy being unclassifiable. Though there are people who try to peg me to a particular ethnic stereotype, I like to think others take my ambiguous appearance as an opportunity to focus on who I am as a person. So I haven't figured out why being myself should kill any chance of a relationship. Not long ago, a man asked me about my background when we met for a drink.

"Just a Jewish girl from New Jersey," I said truthfully.

I never heard from him again.

LITE *recently worked in Ghana as an AIDS educator.*

WHO ARE WE?

In many parts of the U.S. the image persists of Italian Americans as largely blue-collar workers with little education and large families. But current research reveals a more accurate sociological portrait of the estimated 26 million Americans of Italian heritage.

By RAYMOND A. BELLIOTTI

IN the last census of 1990, Italian Americans constituted the fifth largest ethnic group in this country after Germans, British, Irish and African Americans. Myths and stereotypes of these Italian Americans abound because we have relatively little empirical research on their attitudes, attributes, and lifestyles. Four years ago, however, a comprehensive study of Italian Americans was released, although its findings were largely ignored by the national media.

A Profile of Italian Americans

In 1992, the National Italian American Foundation commissioned the National Opinion Research Center (NORC) at the University of Chicago to undertake a research project on Italian Americans. The study that resulted was called "A Profile of Italian Americans: 1972–1992." It compared Italian Americans to 14 other ethnic racial, and religious groups in the United States including Asians, African Americans, Jews, Hispanics and other Europeans. The 15 ethnic groups were compared in 80 categories, including education, income, politics, social habits, values, attitudes, and general psychological well-being.

Photo of the Italian Catholic Society of Washington D.C. in 1919. Even today, Italian Americans remain largely Roman Catholic. Nevertheless, the number of Catholics among them has declined over the last twenty years, from 81 percent to a present 70 percent.

The NORC report revealed that the average Italian American still lives in the city he or she was raised in, has attended at least one year of college and has an average family income of about $33,000 a year. These facts indicate that Italian Americans slightly exceed the average when it comes to education and occupational prestige, and rank sixth out of the 15 ethnic groups in terms of average family income.

The Family

The NORC study also revealed that the contemporary Italian-American family differs considerably from the traditional, large and patriarchal stereotype of it in the popular mind. In its structure, stability and birth rate, today's Italian-American family resembles a modern American middle-class family more than it does a traditional southern Italian one.

Compared to the other 14 ethnic groups in the NORC study, Italian Americans are raised in more stable families, mainly because of relatively fewer deaths, involuntary separations and divorces. From the 1970s to the 1990s, between 79 and 83 percent of the Italian Americans surveyed grew up in homes with both parents present.

The NORC study also found that, since the 1970s, the proportion of Italian Americans with unmixed ancestry (that is, with ancestors only from Italy) has fallen from 81 percent to 69 percent. Of the married Italian Americans in the study, only 33 percent had an Italian-American spouse, down from 68 percent before 1920. Nevertheless, the study found that Italian Americans still ranked fourth after Jews, Asians and Hispanics among those who married people of their own ethnic background.

When they do marry, Italian Americans tend to have fewer children than other minorities—one or two children—giving them the lowest birth rate (after Jews) of the 15 groups. This finding conflicts with the image of large Italian-American families, but corresponds to actual family patterns even for the parents of today's Italian-American adults, who were raised in smaller families than most other groups—about 3 children compared to the overall average of 4.0.

In their social interactions (spending social evenings with friends or parents), Italian Americans rank higher than average—fifth among all groups. Most strikingly, they rank first in percentage of members who said they spend at least one evening a year in a bar, and second in percentage of drinkers. Traditionally, this high use of alcohol has not been a problem of Italian Americans because their alcohol consumption is culinary and social. Therefore, Italian Americans have manifested relatively high rates of alcohol use, but low rates of drinking problems. Recent trends, however, suggest that problem drinking among Italian Americans has reached or slightly exceeded national averages. In the late 1970s, 19 percent of the Italian Americans in the NORC survey reported that they sometimes drink more than they think they should. In the 1990s, this percentage moved up to 27 percent.

Politics

The NORC report found that Italian Americans, like Americans in general, have moved to the right over

A gathering of the Rossi and Scarboro families, founders of the successful Italian Swiss Colony wineries in California. Although the image of large and patriarchal families persists in the popular mind, the families of present-day Italian Americans actually differ considerably.

the last two decades. "In the early 1970s, only 17 percent [of Italian Americans] were Republicans," the report notes. "This number has doubled to 35 percent presently. Most of this increase has been at the expense of the Democrats. In the early 1970s, 45 percent of Italian Americans were Democrats. This number has since fallen to 32 percent. Likewise, the identification as Independents also slipped slightly, from 36 percent to 33 percent," the study found.

In terms of political ideology, Italian Americans increasingly identify themselves as conservatives. This political shift to the right has brought Italian Americans to the center of the political spectrum, midway between liberal Democratic groups such as Jews and Blacks, and conservative Republican groups such as British and German Americans.

Values and Attitudes

Despite a tendency toward conservative politics, Italian Americans strongly support liberal social causes. They are more permissive on sexual matters than other Americans, somewhat more approving of nontraditional roles for women, and less likely to approve corporal punishment for children. Eighty-nine percent of the Italian Americans in the NORC survey said they would vote for a woman as president; 55 percent were pro-choice; and more than 60 percent thought that the U.S. government should spend more on health, education, and the poor.

The picture of Italian Americans that emerges differs radically from a popular and firmly established perception of Italian American families as partriarchal, authoritarian, and insular.

Psychological Well-Being

The NORC survey also found that between 1972 and 1987 Italian Americans consistently expressed significantly less general happiness than the correlated national norms. They are less likely than other Americans to report that their lives are exciting, currently ranking next to the bottom among all groups, above only African Americans.

Since 1984, Italian Americans have expressed great satisfaction with friends, ranking first among the 15 ethnic groups in this category. Since 1972, Italian Americans have not differed much from the national averages on expressions of satisfaction with their families.

The overall conclusion that emerges is that while Italian Americans do not differ greatly from other groups in terms of earning power, professional stature, and family profile, their psychological well-being tends to be lower, except for their high satisfaction with friendships.

Religious Attitudes

Italian Americans still report the second highest percentage of Roman Catholic affiliation among all groups, although the figures have dropped from 81 percent to 70 percent over the past 20 years. Their strength of religious identification and church attendance are well below national norms. Italian-American Catholics are also somewhat more likely than other Americans to express so-called "progressive and compassionate" images of the Supreme Being, seeing him as a friend rather than as a king.

Two street scenes in New York's Little Italy in the 1970s: men conversing around a table as in a village in the "old country" and a bread delivery on Mulberry Street. Italian neighborhoods like this one, in big cities, are shrinking rapidly as more and more families leave in pursuit of social and economic betterment.

The overall picture suggests that Italian Americans are not more traditionalist, authoritarian, and patriarchal than other Americans in their religious beliefs, nor are they strong traditionalists in their faith.

Summary of the NORC Study

Tom Smith, who compiled the NORC report, concluded that Italian Americans are distinctive in various ways. "In many social, family, and religious attitudes, Italian Americans are moderate liberals, not patriarchs, traditionalists, or conservatives. This shows up in their sup-port for equal treatment of women, sexual tolerance, and other progressive values. They also favor government spending for human services. In particular, Italian Americans are strong backers of governmental health care programs," Smith said.

Smith also noted that Italian Americans valued fulfilling friendships, were more satisfied with their friends, and more likely to socialize with them than any other group.

A superficial reading of the NORC survey results may lead to the conclusions that the distinctive features of Italian-American ethnicity have vanished. One might note a few interesting, marginal differences between Italian-Americans and national norms but conclude that Italian Americans on the whole have assimilated mainstream American norms.

Certainly when we examine two cardinal indicators of social position, education and occupation, we see that Italian Americans meet or slightly exceed national norms. Such indicators are important when assessing a group's qualifications for places in the labor market, the extent to which mainstream culture has successfully instilled dominant American values, and correlations with income and wider social prestige.

This obvious interpretation is persuasive, but it may hinder a fuller understanding of who we are. First, it ignores how ethnic groups not merely internalize dominant norms, but also influence them. Second, it obscures class differences. We are never fully identified merely by our ethnicity. Socioeconomic class, gender, religion, occupation, generation, and primary leisure-time projects, among other things, also make us who we are.

The data in the NORC survey were not broken down by generation, socioeconomic class, and gender. They may paint a broad picture of contemporary Italian Americans, but they fail to address numerous questions: What social differences, if any, exist between working-class Italian Americans and professional Italian Americans? Between Italian Americans who are city dwellers and those who live in small towns? Is the only remaining robust marker of Italian-American ethnicity the blue-collar culture we see caricatured drearily in the media?

We would expect that Italian-American ethnicity would be more obvious among members of earlier generations, older cohorts, inhabitants of the remaining Little Italys in the northeast, and recent arrivals to the United States. But the foregoing data obscure our full understanding of possible differences among Italian Americans because the information is presented, understandably, at the highest level of generality.

Preserving Our Heritage

What do we have to do to keep our Italian-American heritage alive? At a minimum, we must initiate and participate in group and family events that remember, celebrate and transmit our cultural legacy. Such events permit us to keep faith with the past and reinforce solidarity.

Other appropriate ethnic behavior can include such commonplace actions as preparing and eating our traditional dishes, participating in specific holiday rituals, studying and speaking Italian, or even spicing English speech with Italian and dialect words and phrases, teaching our children about their ethnic history and background, practicing our customs and traditions, subscribing to an Italian-American magazine, newspaper, or newsletter; going to Italian-American films and plays; and attending Italian-American festivals and celebrations.

Less common but more ethnically intense actions include residing in an Italian-American neighborhood; producing an Italian-American newspaper, magazine or play; teaching or enrolling in an Italian-American studies course; engaging in concerted ethnically based political action; partaking in Italian-American religious societies; and participating in ethnic social and cultural clubs.

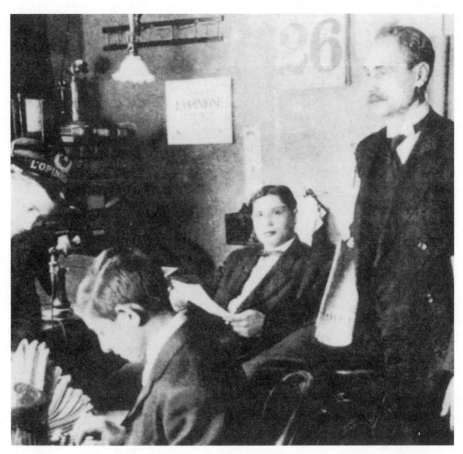

The editorial office of the Philadelphia newspaper, L'Opinione. Like the use of the Italian language, the once numerous Italian-language newspapers are largely a thing of the past. But Italian-American magazines and newspapers do exist today, and subscribing to them helps keep our ethnic heritage alive.

Ethnic social structures, such as families, neighborhoods, cultural clubs, and political organizations sustain a vital ethnic identity that does not degenerate into weak symbolic ethnicity or mere passive acceptance of Italian-American ethnicity. Such robust ethnic behavior recognizes certain debts of gratitude and obligations of legacy to those who preceded us, who lived the immigrant experience, who fought to survive and flourish, and who paved the way for us in today's American society.

Raymond A. Belliotti is a professor of philosophy at State University of New York at Fredonia. This article is based on his most recent book, Seeking Identity: Individualism versus Community in an Ethnic Context *(University Press of Kansas, 1995), with permission of the publisher.*

From *Ambassador,* Number 29/30, 1996, pp. 18-21. Reprinted courtesy of Ambassador magazine, a publication of the National Italian American Foundation in Washington, DC.

Where We Stand on Issues

Politically, large majorities of African Americans, Hispanics and American Jews are Democrats. Asian Americans tend to be independent, while Italian and Arab Americans are evenly split between the two major parties.

Nevertheless, it appears from our polling that neither party identification nor stated political philosophy alone is enough to predict how individuals in the various ethnic communities will define their stances on several important issues.

In our survey, we covered 28 key policy questions and found the results to be quite revealing. For example, in seven areas, large majorities in all of the groups agree with positions that have traditionally been viewed as *liberal*. They agree on:

- Allowing patients to sue HMOs
- Using the federal surplus to provide health insurance for un-insured
- Increasing of the minimum wage by $1 in two years
- The need for new gun control laws
- The United States unilaterally banning nuclear weapons
- The United States paying back dues to the United Nations
- The federal government imposing strict regulations and fines on polluters

On several other issues, however, majorities in almost all of the groups agree with what have been described as *conservative* positions. There is wide agreement on:

- The policy of school vouchers
- Parental notification of girls under 17 who seek an abortion
- Treating children 14–16 as adults if they commit a crime involving a gun
- The need for the death penalty
- Opposition to racial preferences in hiring and college admissions
- Favoring states setting education policy, not the federal government
- Allowing individuals to invest part of their payroll taxes in retirement accounts

There are other areas where there are differences among the six ethnic groups surveyed. (For a closer look at where the six groups stand on some of the major issues of the day, see Table 33).

Issues

a. Providing parents with school vouchers so their children can attend any school they choose.

Providing school vouchers to parents is a very popular issue among Hispanic Americans. More than 80% say they support providing parents with school vouchers. Close to 75% of Asian Americans are for vouchers. Also, almost 70% of African Americans, Italian Americans and Arab Americans support the voucher system. Slightly over 50% of Jewish Americans are in support.

b. There should be a law allowing patients to sue their HMO (health maintenance organization) if they are denied treatment.

Jewish Americans, along with Hispanic Americans, are most supportive of this empowerment for patients, with 90% favoring this position. Close to 89% of Arab Americans, 86% of Italian Americans, and 85% of African and Asian Americans agree that there should be laws allowing patients to sue their HMOs.

c. Using the government surplus to provide health insurance for the working poor and children.

There is a broad consensus on this issue. Close to 93% of Hispanic Americans, more than 90% of African Americans, and almost 90% of Asian Americans favor using the budget surplus to provide healthcare coverage for the poor. Nearly nine in ten Jewish and Arab Americans, along with 85% of Italian Americans are also in favor of the government using the surplus to take care of the healthcare needs of the working poor and children in America.

d. Increasing the minimum wage by $1 an hour over the next two years.

An increase in the minimum wage is a top priority of all the groups with more than four in five supporting an increase.

166

Table 33. Issue Support (Agreement)

Issue	Italian	African	Hispanic	Jewish	Asian	Arab
School vouchers	67.0	70.0	**83.0**(2)	*52.0*(3)	74.0	69.0
Allow patients to sue HMO	86.0	86.5	**89.5**	**90.0**	*74.5*	**89.0**
Use surplus for health insurance (4)	84.0	93.5	93.5	86.5	89.5	86.5
Increase minimum wage by $1 in 2 years	82.5	94.0	92.5	85.0	88.0	80.5
Treating 14–16 year-olds as adults if used a gun	85.0	74.0	78.5	81.5	80.0	83.0
$1,000 campaign contribution limit	70.5	63.0	*58.5*	**75.0**	66.0	69.5
New gun control laws	*69.5*	78.0	82.0	83.5	**88.0**	76.0
Death penalty	**78.5**	*64.0*	73.0	67.5	75.5	71.5
Flat tax	**55.5**	43.0	47.5	*34.5*	40.0	50.0
School boards can restrict subjects taught	27.5	32.0	26.0	*19.5*	**41.0**	36.0
Racial preferences in hiring/college admissions	*11.0*	**32.0**	26.0	17.0	20.5	21.0
U.S. unilaterally ban testing of nuclear weapons	66.5	65.0	70.0	68	72.5	65.5
Government impose strict regulations/fines on polluters	93.5	92.0	95.5	92.5	92.5	92.5
Strengthening Social Security and Medicare	94.5	96.0	95.0	94.0	91.5	92.0
Allow individuals to invest part of payroll taxes	84.3	79.0	78.5	76.0	82.5	81.0
Active U.S. participation in global trade	71.0	*69.5*	83.0	76.5	**84.0**	79.5

(2) Bold numbers indicate groups that support a position to a much greater degree than other groups.

(3) Italicized numbers indicate the groups whose support for a particular issue is significantly lower than the other groups.

(4) Shaded categories are those where a near consensus exists among the groups.

e. Prosecuting teenagers 14 to 16 as an adult if they have committed a violent crime using a handgun.

Again, there is broad agreement on this issue. Italian, Arab, and Jewish Americans are slightly more likely than the other three groups to want tough laws when dealing with 14 to 16 year-old offenders who use a gun when committing violent crimes. Also, 80% of Asian Americans, 78% of Hispanic Americans, and 74% of African Americans favor tough prosecution of teenagers.

f. Putting a limit of $1,000 on campaign contributions in all elections.

Jewish Americans lead the other ethnic groups in supporting limits on campaign contributions. Three in four (75%) support a $1,000 cap on campaign contributions. They are closely followed by 71% of Italian Americans and 70% of the Arab Americans. More than 65% of Asian Americans, 64% of African Americans and 58% of Hispanic Americans also support the cap on contributions.

g. Passing new gun control laws.

There is significant support across the board for new gun control laws from all groups. Asian Americans are most in favor, while Italian Americans are least in favor.

h. Imposing the death penalty for particularly heinous crimes.

More than three in four (78%) Italian and Asian say they are in favor of using the death penalty as a punishment for terrible crimes. They are followed by about 70% of Jewish, Arab, and Hispanic Americans also in support. Although African Americans did show support for the death penalty, they are the least supportive, with less than 65% agreeing with this method of punishment.

i. Revising the income tax code so that every individual pays a flat tax regardless of his/her income.

Close to 60% of Jewish Americans are opposed to a flat tax. More than half of Asian Americans, 48% of Hispanic Americans, and 40% of African Americans are also opposed to a flat tax. More than half of Italian Americans are in support.

Table 34. Abortion Position

	Italian	African	Hispanic	Jewish	Asian	Arab
Pro-choice in all instances	29.0	40.5	23.5	**61.5**	39.0	28.5
Pro-choice except for late-term abortion	24.0	12.5	10.0	17.5	12.0	16.5
Pro-life in all instances	8.5	8.5	**16.5**	3.5	7.5	7.0
Pro-life except for rape and incest	18.0	13.0	13.5	5.0	11.0	16.0
Pro-life except for life of mother	18.0	22.5	35.0	10.0	25.5	29.5
Total "pro-life"	46.5	54.0	**64.5**	18.5	43.5	52.0
Total "pro-choice"	53.0	53.0	34.0	**79.0**	51.0	45.5

j. Local school boards have a right to restrict the teaching of topics, such as evolution.

Localizing the authority over what topics are taught at the school board level is not a popular issue with these ethnic groups. More than 75% of Jewish Americans oppose allowing local school boards deciding what can and cannot be taught in schools. A majority of all other groups agree.

k. Racial preferences in hiring or college admissions

Close to 70% of Hispanic Americans and more than 64% of African Americans oppose taking into account racial preference when hiring or admitting students to a college. In addition, 87% of Italian Americans, 80% of Jewish Americans, 76% of Asian Americans and 75% of Arab Americans are also opposed to racial preferences.

l. The United States should unilaterally ban underground testing of nuclear weapons.

Asian Americans and Hispanic Americans are most in support of a unilateral ban of nuclear weapons testing. More than 67% of Jewish Americans, 65% of Italian, Arab, and African Americans also support a unilateral U.S. nuclear test ban.

m. The government should impose stricter regulations and tax penalties on factories that release harmful pollutants into the air.

There is overwhelming support across the board for getting tougher with polluters, with more than nine in ten in each group supporting stricter regulations and penalties.

n. Strengthening the Social Security and Medicare system.

More than 90% of all groups showed strong support for a federal focus on these two important retirement benefits. Af-

rican Americans and Jewish Americans are among the most supportive.

o. Allowing individuals to invest a portion of their Social Security pension in personal retirement accounts.

Again, there is strong support across the board for allowing private investment of Social Security funds.

p. Active United States participation in the global free trade agreements

Asian (84%), Hispanic (83%) and Arab Americans (80%) are most supportive of U.S. participation in global free trade agreements. They are followed by Jewish (76%), Italian (70%), and African Americans (69%).

The Question of Abortion

Jewish Americans are the most pro-choice, with more than 60% saying that it should always be up to the woman whether she should get an abortion. Least pro-choice are Hispanic Americans.

The group with the most pro-life attitude is Hispanics—16.5% are opposed to abortion in all cases, and 64.5% define themselves as "pro-life" in particular cases. Between 43%–54% of Asian, Italian, Arab and African Americans term themselves pro-life. Only 18.5% of Jewish Americans would describe themselves as such.

a) Banning all abortions, except for the life of the mother.

Table 35. Exceptions to Supporting Abortion

Issue	Italian	African	Hispanic	Jewish	Asian	Arab
Ban abortion except for life of mother	47.0	44.0	61.0	20.5	47.0	53.5
Notify parent if under 18 wants abortion	77.5	77.5	82.5	49.5	79.5	78.5

More than 60% of Hispanic Americans are supportive of a ban on abortion, except in cases where the life of the mother is in danger. About 50% of Arab Americans support the ban, except for life of mother.

More than 75% of Jewish Americans are opposed to a ban except in cases of risk to the mother, followed by 50% of Italian Americans. Almost half (48%) of African Americans and 47% of Asian Americans are also opposed.

b) A physician should be legally required to notify parents of a girl under the legal age who requests an abortion.

More than four in five (82%) Hispanic Americans, close to 80% of Arab and Asian Americans, and 77% of African and Italian Americans all support the notion that a physician be legally required to notify the parents of a girl under the legal age who is seeking an abortion. Less than half of Jewish Americans support it.

Chapter Three from *What Ethnic Americans Really Think: The Zogby Culture Polls,* James J. Zogby, 2001, pp. 30-38. © 2001 by Zogby International. Reprinted by permission.

UNIT 9

The Ethno-Religious Factor: Challenges in an Era in Search of Order

Unit Selections

Key Points to Consider

- Do regional organizations and/or international organizations such as the United Nations have the capacity and the rightful authority to intervene in ethnic group conflicts and/or to prevent the wholesale destructions of ethnic groups within countries? Why or why not? Are there human rights that are beyond the claims of sovereignty? Explain.

- Are such judgments and mobilizations of military power influenced by concerns that are measurable in terms of economic and strategic benefits or are human and cultural rights as important as traditional criteria used in international relations? Defend your answer.

- Explain how the relationship of ethnic Americans to changes and challenges in the world arena provides strength or liability to American interests. Does conflict between ethnic interests and national interests present real or imaginary fears about U.S. activities in international affairs? Explain.

- How will increased immigration, technological advances, and a more competitive world market affect the relationships between religious and ethnic groups?

- Should the claims of ethnic groups in the United States in defense of culture, territory, and unique institutions be honored and protected by law and public policy? Why or why not?

 **Links: www.dushkin.com/online/**
These sites are annotated in the World Wide Web pages.

Africa News Online
http://www.africanews.org
Cultural Survival
http://www.cs.org
Human Rights and Humanitarian Assistance
http://www.pitt.edu/~ian/resource/human.htm
The North-South Institute
http://www.nsi-ins.ca/ensi/index.html
U.S. Agency for International Development
http://www.info.usaid.gov/

Since the breakup of the Soviet empire, ethnicity has reoriented the international arena. New national claims as well as the revival of ancient antagonisms are fragmenting Europe. War, the systematic expression of conflict, and its aftermath are also occasions for the use and misuse of ethnically charged political rhetoric. The presence of a politically relevant past and the invocation of religious warrants for group conflict have indicated the need for new approaches to peacekeeping and educational strategies for meeting and transcending group differences.

Ethnic relations have erupted into warfare in Africa, where conflicts have shattered emerging states and thus challenged the hopeful myth of postcolonial renewal as well as the racial/ethnic myth of black solidarity. But Africa's emerging countries are not alone: the Middle East, central Europe, Canada, Northern Ireland, and the Balkans are additional venues of destructive conflict. Each of these simmering cauldrons—not melting pots—illustrates the stakes and consequences of unresolved conflict and distrust concerning land, religion, culture, leadership, and economic production and distribution. Each also shows the rewards and recognitions that fuel human passions, ambitions, and the will to dominate and to govern the affairs and destinies of various peoples that cohabit contiguous regions.

The winds of political change in the Middle East and eastern and central Europe reveal the saliency of religion and ethnicity and the varied textures of group relations. In America the ongoing affinity of ethnic populations to the nations of their origin is expressed in subtle as well as obvious ways. The articles in this unit explain the transmission of ethnic tradition and suggest linkages between religion and ethnicity. The story of the interaction of ethnicity and religion is curiously exposed in the etymology of the Greek word *ethnikos* (i.e., the rural, Gentile, or pagan people of the ancient Mediterranean world). Though such philological roots no longer drive our principal understanding of ethnicity, the experience of social affinity and cultural affiliation elaborated in the following articles deepens our awareness and understanding of ethnicity—a changing yet persistent aspect of human identity and social cohesiveness.

The process of better understanding the multiethnic character of America and the world involves the coordinated efforts of formal and informal education, which are influenced by public and private institutions and the community-based voluntary associations that are the building blocks of society. This collection of articles addresses resistance to the challenges that are embedded in passionately held and politically potent traditions of ethnic opposition. The persistence of confusion, uncertainty, insensitivity, and violence toward and among ethnic groups is a sobering and stunning fact. Strategies for dealing with the tension and reality of bias are examined in this unit. Hatred and prejudice are frequently based on conscious manipulation of powerful images that profoundly shape personal and group identity. Even on the most basic level of public perception, most agree that progress has been made toward a society of equality and social justice, with increased hopes for decreased segregation in schools and neighborhoods. Yet differing views among ethnic and racial groups indicate that uniformity and a shared sense of the past and present are not generally common. Attempting to overcome such gulfs of misunderstanding before they lead to more serious forms of conflict is among the great challenges of the present.

Thus, the dramas of regional ethnic struggle and the growth of worldwide ethnic challenges to the constitution of human order itself are increasingly marked by episodes of blatant bigotry, intolerance, fanaticism, and zealotry. For those who can embrace the mystery of diversity, however, there is hope for the human condition in the twenty-first century.

A City That Echoes Eternity

For billions, Jerusalem is not just sand and stone but sacred—a place of the world, and beyond it.

BY KENNETH L. WOODWARD

ONE MAN, JESUS WARNED, CANNOT SERVE TWO MASTERS. Yet Jerusalem is sacred stone and soil to Jew and Christian and Muslim alike. A place on the map like any other city, Jerusalem exists more vividly, more powerfully, more *dangerously* within the longitude and latitude of the religious imagination. In that fertile region of the mind, what has already occurred in time past—the building of Solomon's temple, the crucifixion of Christ, the ascension of the Prophet Muhammad—is also promise of what is to come, "when time shall be no more." Among all the cities of the earth, only Jerusalem is seen as the locus of redemption and final judgement. For that reason alone, it inspires the fanatic. It is a burden no merely civil administration should ever have to bear. But short of that eschatological moment, Jerusalem seems to be always searching for respite from political tension, that it might live up to the meaning of its name: City of Peace.

To know what Jerusalem means to the three great monotheisms is to realize that politics alone can bring only a provisional kind of peace. Jews have the oldest identification with the city—and the Bible, which mentions Jerusalem 667 times, for their witness. In the background is God's promise of land and progeny to Abraham, His obedient servant. In the Book of Exodus, that promise takes the specific form of Canaan—the Holy Land—for the wandering tribes of Israel, King David made Jerusalem his capital and there, some 30 centuries ago, Solomon built the first temple. The exile of the Jews to Babylon only made the yearning for Jerusalem more intense. "If I forget you, O Jerusalem," wrote the Psalmist, "let my right hand wither." A second temple was built by King Herod, only to be destroyed in A.D. 70 by the Romans. What remains of the Western wall is now Judaism's holiest shrine. Jerusalem, wrote Abraham

Joshua Heschel right after the Israeli occupation of the city in 1967, is "a city of witness, an echo of eternity." It is also a city of waiting, the place where the messiah, when he comes, will rebuild the temple. To die in Jerusalem, pious Jews believe, is to be assured of atonement.

For Christians, the messiah has already come and atonement has been accomplished in the person of Jesus. Jerusalem is where he suffered, died and rose again in glory—and where he will return to judge the living and the dead. It is also the city where the Last Supper was celebrated and where, at Pentecost, the church itself was born. As a place of Christian pilgrimage, Jerusalem has no equal. Medieval maps place it at the center of the universe (as did Dante), and paintings show medieval Jerusalem descending as the heavenly city to come. Today pilgrims can touch the rock where Jesus was crucified and, under the same church roof, the tomb where he was buried. The cross is gone, but in the Christian iconography, it continues to be the *axis mundi* connecting earth with heaven in the sacred drama of redemption.

For Muslims, Jerusalem is the third holiest place, after Mecca and Medina. To Muhammad, it was the city of the holy prophets who had preceded him. And so, before Mecca became the center of the Islamic universe, Muhammad directed all Muslims to bow for prayer toward Jerusalem. According to later interpretations of a passage in the Qur'an, Muhammad himself made a mystical "night flight" to Jerusalem aided by the angel Gabriel. From there, on the very rock where Abraham had offered his son as a sacrifice (now the shrine of the Dome of the Rock, atop the Temple Mount), Muhammad ascended a ladder to the throne of Allah. This ascension confirmed the continuity between Muhammad and all previous prophets and messengers of God, including

Jesus, in a lineage going back to Adam. It also established a divine connection between Mecca and Jerusalem.

Thus, for billions of believers who may never see it, Jerusalem remains a city central to their sacred geography. This is why the future of the city is not just another Middle Eastern conflict between Arabs and Jews. From a purely secular perspective, of course, the shrines dear to Jews, Christians and Muslims are precious tourist attractions, and as such important sources of revenue. But Jerusalem is not some kind of Disneyland of the spirit. Both Israel and the Palestinians have real roots in the Holy Land, and both want to claim Jerusalem as their

capital. The United Nations, supported by the Vatican, would have the city internationalized and under its jurisdiction. The issue, however, is not merely one of geopolitics. There will be no enduring solution to the question of Jerusalem that does not respect the attachments to the city formed by each faith. Whoever controls Jerusalem will always be constrained by the meaning the city has acquired over three millenniums of wars, conquest and prophetic utterance. Bless or cursed, Jerusalem is built with the bricks of the religious imagination. Were this not so, Jerusalem would be what it has never been: just another city on a hill.

Tribal Warfare

Before they can reach a settlement with the Palestinians, Israel's "five tribes" must navigate between Hebrew democracy and Zionist revolution.

BY BERNARD AVISHAI

On June 18, in broad daylight, Palestinian gunmen in a yellow taxi overtook Danny Yehuda—the father of three—as he drove on a highway near Homesh, a small Jewish settlement overlooking Nablus, the West Bank's largest city, and shot him to death at point-blank range. Taking responsibility for Yehuda's execution was a group calling itself Battalions of the victim Thabet Thabet." The organization claimed to be avenging the death of Dr. Thabet Ahmed Thabet of Tul Karm, who until last December, when he was gunned down by undercover Israeli forces, had been a dentist and director-general of the Palestinian Authority's health ministry.

In killing Thabet, the Israelis were apparently retaliating for a terrorist attack in the coastal town of Netanya just hours earlier, though nobody has established a connection between Thabet and the fatal explosion. A profile in the Israeli newspaper *Ha'aretz* later revealed that Thabet and his wife had been open advocates of peaceful negotiation with Israel; moreover, she credited their ability to have children to an Israeli friend who had pleaded with her to be treated by a Tel Aviv gynecologist. ("The Israelis gave me my life," Mrs. Thabet said, "and then the Israelis took it 19 years later.") In a state of depression following Thabet's assassination, one of his relatives shot and killed Israeli restaurateurs Motti Dayan and Etgar Zeituni, themselves peace advocates, as they shopped for supplies. At Danny Yehuda's funeral—scarcely a week into the cease-fire declared after 21 Israeli youths were blown up at the Dolphinarium dance club—grief-stricken settlers denounced Israeli Prime Minister Ariel Sharon for failing to declare war against the Palestinian Authority. "We need another Goldstein," shouted some of the mourners. They were referring to Dr. Baruch Goldstein, who killed 29 Arabs at prayer in the Tomb of the Patriarchs in 1994, before he himself was beaten to death.

SO CLOSE, AND YET SO FAR

The Oslo peace process—which dates back to secret negotiations in 1992 between Palestinians and Israelis in Norway, and which many hoped would move forward definitively in talks at Camp David a year ago—promised an era of confidence building, followed by a final agreement that would have resolved the status of Jerusalem and the territories. But what Secretary of State Colin Powell confronted when he arrived in the Middle East to begin a new round of diplomacy on June 26 was a grotesque reversal. Although the terms of what would have constituted a final deal between the Israelis and the Palestinians are clear, the violence that made reaching final terms impossible has now swept away the peace-seeking Labor Party coalition of Prime Minister Ehud Barak—who was unseated by Sharon in the February election—together with any accumulated good faith between Arab and Jew. Indeed, while the framework for a peaceful settlement is conceivable (in fact, such a framework exists), implementing it is not.

What would the deal have been? According to Yossi Beilin, the justice minister in Barak's government who served as a lead negotiator at the January talks in Taba, Egypt, Bill Clinton's "bridging proposals"—which were offered in the waning days of his administration, and went beyond Barak's offers to Palestinian Authority leader Yasir Arafat at Camp David in July 2000—put the parties just a few weeks from an accord. Here are the terms of the deal:

- A Palestinian state would be established on some 95 percent of the West Bank and Gaza.

- All Palestinian refugees would be compensated by Israeli and international aid; their "right of return" would be redeemed with cash, settlement in Palestine, or, on a case-by-case basis, settlement in Israel.
- The 1.4 million Palestinian refugees living in the West Bank and Gaza would be absorbed into the Palestinian state, while the 1.5 million Palestinians in Jordan, who were already Jordanian citizens, would be absorbed there.
- About 100,000 of the 300,000 Palestinian refugees now living in South Lebanon would be allowed back to Israel.
- Israeli settlements concentrated in about 5 percent of West Bank land around Jerusalem and Gush Etzion would be annexed by Israel. In return, Palestine would be compensated with Israeli land in the Negev to the south of the West Bank and a land corridor joining Gaza and the West Bank.
- About 40,000 Israeli settlers scattered on heights around Palestinian cities would return to Israel.
- The Arab neighborhoods of Jerusalem, including all but the Jewish Quarter of the Old City (about 320,000 people), would be absorbed into the Palestinian state, with the Haram al-Sharif (the Temple Mount) falling under Palestinian sovereignty, and the Jewish Quarter, the Wailing Wall, and the excavations adjacent to the Wall all falling under Israeli sovereignty.
- Israel would maintain a three-year security presence in the Jordan Valley, and security cooperation under U.S. mediation would continue beyond that date.

These terms represented the application of utilitarian principle to demographic facts; indeed, they are essentially what Beilin and a high PLO official agreed to in October 1995, days before Israeli Prime Minister Yitzhak Rabin was assassinated. But in the current atmosphere of terror, the practical details of such a compromise seem almost to mock Israel's condition. Arafat has never publicly accepted these terms, and his refusal to hunt down and jail Hamas radicals seems implicitly to condone terrorism. What, in the absence of a Palestinian peace partner, is Israel to do? Is its policy reduced to exacting vengeance?

The question cannot be divorced from how Israel conceives of itself, its purpose, and its relation to its neighbors. Consider Rehavam Ze'evi, the tourism minister, a leather-faced former Israeli general who has notoriously proposed mass transfers of Palestinians from "Judea and Samaria" to Jordan. His political party, Moledet, is marginal, but he's the voice of Israeli defiance when terror strikes. "Sharon knows the Arabs—they care most about their homes," Ze'evi told a TV interviewer. "One more shot from Ramallah and we'll take down the first row of houses." Israelis, Ze'evi insists, should not be *friarim*

("chumps"). The Intifada—the ongoing uprising against Israeli occupation of the territories—has become the most meaningful experience in the lives of destitute Palestinian youths; of 319 Palestinians killed by December 19 of last year, 121 were 18 years old or younger. In the absence of a signed agreement, the demand for the "right of return" could still mean three million Palestinians (refugees of the 1948 war, plus their children and grandchildren) exercising the right to inundate Israel with Arabs, a demand that gives pause even to peace advocates like Amos Oz. Would this not mean an end to Israel as a state with a Jewish majority?

Barak and others have advocated complete "separation" from the Palestinians, though how this would be possible around Jerusalem without the forced transfer of populations Ze'evi envisions, no one could say: The Wailing Wall abuts the Arab Quarter; the Hebrew University campus on Mount Scopus is on an exposed salient between two Arab towns. According to *Jane's Foreign Report*, Sharon has authorized the Israeli military to draw up a contingency plan for a month-long offensive to disarm the Palestinian Authority and expel (or kill) Arafat's circle of leaders—and is waiting for a terrorist bomb to supply the pretext. He argued through the 1980s that the Palestinians should topple the monarchy in neighboring Jordan and set up a Palestinian state there. His government, which includes Shimon Peres, would not dare pursue such a plan today. But if Sharon commands the Israeli Defense Force to start "taking down" rows of Arab houses in Ramallah, refugees will stream across the Jordan and the fat will be dangerously close to the fire.

Democracy requires a commitment to a more or less permanent Oslo process. What is democracy if not a peace process without end?

But there are other voices, too. On the day of Sharon's election in February, the novelist David Grossman wrote a column imagining what Israelis would say 50 years from now about a leadership that had believed it could impose by force what it could not expect to win by negotiation. What he was really doing, of course, was thinking back 30 years and envisioning how much better off Israel would be today if, in 1967, it had occupied the West Bank without settling it, held Arab Jerusalem and its mosques without annexing them, invited international investment and international forces into the West Bank and Gaza instead of turning these places into sites on an ancient map, and even conditionally recognized the PLO after the Rabat summit in 1974. Grossman was asking whether Israel, in laying the groundwork for the next generation, would conduct the occupation with liberal-democratic values or would revert to the previous state of affairs personified by Sharon. Democracy is not just majority rule, after all: It requires a commitment to the more or less permanent negotiation that aims to derive sovereignty from "the consent of the governed" (as former U.S. Secretary of State Cyrus Vance observed). A democratic Israel would promote peace, a framework for tolerance, not as a reward for Palestinian cooperation but as an acknowledgment of the inevitability of conflict, which must always be managed and subdued. What is a democracy if not a peace process without an end?

THE FIVE TRIBES

These voices underline that Israel, in spite of the terror, remains a site of contesting political cultures, habits of mind, and circles of loyalty in which different groups of citizens have experienced the peace process in quite different ways. Indeed, the people of Israel can be divided into five distinct "tribes" or demographic groups, each made up of about a million people, or 20 percent of the Israeli population. While each group has its contrarians—and while high rates of intermarriage among the tribes make bright lines difficult to draw—these blocs of Israelis nevertheless have distinct political profiles. And they have been talking past one another for at least a decade.

TRIBE 1: THE PRETTY SOULS This tribe consists of the more highly educated descendants of the old European Labor-Zionist establishment now living in northern Tel Aviv, Haifa, and Jerusalem's Baka'a. These *yefei nefesh*, or "pretty souls," held firm for the peace process. Seventy-five percent of the affluent northern suburb of Kfar Shmaryahu, for example, voted for Ehud Barak. Contrast this with the 88 percent who voted for Sharon in Beit Shemesh, whose residents are mainly descendants of the less well educated, more Orthodox, working-class and petit bourgeois *mizrahim*—Eastern Jews who arrived from North African Arab states during the 1950s and 1960s. The *yefei nefesh* see the state as a facilitator of their cultural life rather than as its embodiment. In this way, they are far closer to professional circles in the United States and Europe than to the Jewish settlers of the West Bank or residents of Jerusalem's pietistic quarters. Their children expect to be citizens of the world. They travel extensively—after serving in the army, during their university years, and throughout their careers. Today there are 200,000 highly skilled Israelis employed in Israel's 50 largest high-tech businesses. These firms contribute more than a quarter of Israel's total gross domestic product (GDP). This far outstrips the settlers in numbers and economic power. Over the past decade, Israelis have launched thousands of knowledge-based companies, which (until the recent downturn) have been thriving in Har Hahotzvim in Jerusalem, Herzliah, and the southern part of Haifa. Israeli entrepreneurs see tourism—which presupposes Palestinian cooperation—to be a necessary 15 percent of Israel's GDP and the sector most likely to provide good jobs for working *mizrahim* laid off from their jobs in Israel's rust belt.

Many Israelis who join the high-tech economy find themselves living in Amsterdam, Boston, or Santa Clara, whether they work for an Israeli company like Check Point or a global one like Intel. The real question is not whether the most talented young Israelis will leave; it is whether they will come back to raise their children and in the process become custodians of Israel's democratic culture. As the dean of a new business school told me, "The 20 percent of Israel that would be isolated by the collapse of the peace process cannot be expected to continue to provide the intellectual capital that translates into 80 percent of the country's wealth." The Israeli army's chief of staff, Lieutenant General Shaul Mofaz, recently warned that the brain drain from the research arms of the army and the defense ministry was Israel's greatest strategic vulnerability. Unlike the old Zionists who preached self-sufficiency, such people expect to be an integral part of a global culture.

TRIBE 2: THE SECOND ISRAEL The *mizrahim*, or "the second Israel," arrived in the country from hostile North African countries a generation after Israel was founded. These new immigrants discovered a strangely socialist society that was widely committed to the Zionist labor union Histadrut's owning the means of production, to sexual freedom, and to a Labor-Zionist aristocracy, which tried to steer the *mizrahim* into agricultural collectives. In reaction, the *mizrahim* embraced the populist Likud Party in the 1970s. In the 1990s, as integration and intermarriage accelerated, many migrated to the Shas Party, a hybrid movement of increasingly xenophobic Orthodoxy and proletarian resentment.

Tribe 2 does not oppose peace—only the social changes that would make it possible. Its members live on the edge of poverty, and their political tempers are easily triggered. They see themselves as having been no less dispossessed by the conflict than do the Palestinians. They envision an Israel as Jewish as the Arab states are Muslim—and as paternalistic. For as they once regarded themselves the chief victims of Labor-Zionist control over the economy, they now regard themselves as the chief victims of a post-Oslo global economy that favors the high-tech world of Labor-Zionism's children. They fear competition for jobs and housing from Israel's Arabs and want an Israel that resembles their large, warm families—observant, loyal, and gritty.

TRIBE 3: THE ORTHODOX Members of tribe 3, whose birth rates are twice the national average, fall along a spectrum ranging from Jerusalem's ultra-Orthodox *haredim* ("the awestruck") to followers of the messianic Zionism advocated by the ethnically European Mafdal—the National Religious Party—whose spiritual center is Bar Ilan University (where Yigal Amir, Rabin's assassin, was educated) and whose heroes are the West Bank settlers of Gush Emunim ("Bloc of the Faithful").

Both the *haredim* and the Mafdal have become champions—and wards—of the state. If a young man declares himself committed to a life of Torah study, he may be exempted from military service while his wife and children live on the dole. There are about 150,000 *haredi* men pursuing rabbinical studies in yeshivas. The state also supports Shas-sponsored schools attended by Israel's poorest children; Shas pleases their parents with rigid training in Orthodox observances, a hot lunch, and a longer school day. At the same time, defense and infrastructure investments subsidize as many as 100,000 people in the settlements. The *haredim* do not serve in the army (though the Gush Emunim serve with a vengeance).

On the whole, the institutional Orthodox see the state apparatus as a crucial force in protecting the Sabbath and other Jewish ritual law—and also the thousands of state jobs that go along with Rabbinic vigilance over marriage, burial, and kashruth. They want a Jewish state; equality for Israeli Arabs is anathema. Their leaders speak of liberal Jews as purveyors of an indecent materialism. They see the Jewish state as a chance to escape the theological challenges and physical threats of goyim. Though they joined Barak's government because it was victorious, they abandoned him, faction by faction, as soon as peace negotiations involved rethinking sovereignty in Jerusalem.

It IS IMPORTANT TO UNDERSTAND THAT THE ROUGHLY 40 percent of Israel's electorate who have persistently opposed territorial compromise are skeptical not only of Palestinian claims but of the cosmopolitan makeover any peace process would bring and the secular democratic coalition that it has engendered. Though Ehud Barak—a military man—got a marginally higher vote than previous peace candidates from tribes 2 and 3 in 1999, the peace camp has always assumed that these tribes are hard-liners. Indeed, after Barak failed at Camp David, losing the Shas Party's support in the process, he tried to rally peace forces with the promise of a "secular revolution" that would have banned the ministry of religion and mandated that all citizens, including yeshiva students and Arabs, serve in the army. These reforms were an attempt to fuse all the forces in the country who grasped, however dimly, that secular democracy and peace were two sides of the same coin and that Israel would emerge from the peace talks a different country from the one that entered them.

TRIBE 4: ISRAELI PALESTINIANS Israel's Arab citizens were intent on making a strong statement in the last election—and they did. In 1999, 75 percent voted, 95 percent of them for Barak; only 13 percent voted in 2001—and of those, 20 percent cast a blank ballot. It is cold comfort for the Labor Party that most of the small remainder voted for Barak. In Nazareth and Um el-Fahm, where 13

protesters were shot dead by Israeli police at the start of the new Intifada, the rate of voting was only 10 percent and 3 percent respectively.

The Palestinian Authority, in a last-ditch effort to get the peace process back on track, encouraged Israeli Arabs to vote for Barak, but the Arab members of Knesset who led the vote boycott told Palestinian Authority leaders to mind their own business. Aved Mar'am, an Arab Knesset member, said it was "the Israeli Arabs' declaration of electoral independence." Israeli Arabs have come to understand that they are not just 20 percent of the population but 40 percent of any conceivably triumphant peace coalition. Their electoral revolt was predictable, not least because the Barak government handled the tragic deaths with callousness.

Actually, the surprise is not the show of resistance but that it took so long. Per capita income of Israeli Arabs is roughly half that of Jews. Arabs are underrepresented in the civil service and in professional life and are still not permitted any effective program of national service that would enable them security clearances. Barak refused even to meet with Arab members of Knesset to discuss their possible participation in his coalition.

The growing political consciousness of Israeli Arabs portends the kind of political revolution that tribes 2 and 3 fear the most. If, as seems likely, the peace wing of the Labor Party (led by Beilin) joins informally with the left-wing Meretz Party to form a democratic peace coalition in the Knesset, the Arab parties will almost certainly cooperate with them. And this cooperation might well prepare the ground for social reform, including the retirement of anachronistic Israeli laws left over from the Zionist colonial period: the Law of Return (which bestows citizenship on all legally defined "Jews"); regulations regarding ownership of land that make it very hard to sell property to non-Jews; a prohibition of civil marriage, which makes intermarriage difficult; and others.

TRIBE 5: THE RUSSIANS Russian immigrants are the wild card of Israeli politics. Some 825,000 can now vote, and 70 percent did so in 2001 (90 percent cast ballots in 1999). Though 58 percent went for Barak in 1999, 63 percent went for Sharon this year. Its hybrid background makes the Russian voting bloc volatile. For one thing, Russians have come to Israel with higher levels of education than any other wave of immigrants. According to one estimate, a third of the software engineers and materials scientists who power Israeli start-ups are Russians; these professionals have raised standards in Israeli music, science, and the arts. For another, most Russians came to Israel not for Zionist reasons but to enjoy a style of life that they associate with the West. *Ha'aretz's* Lili Galili, who has covered the Russians extensively, says that a very small number practice Judaism and perhaps only half were (or considered themselves) Jews before they came. They dislike the Orthodox, whom they regard as a threat to the sophisticated and pluralist atmosphere of Tel Aviv, where the Russians are concentrated.

One would think that all this would make Russians staunch allies of the peace coalition, but that's not the case. Though most of them are cultural liberals, these veterans of the Soviet regime have generally retained both the refuseniks' suspicion of immanent world anti-Semitism and a Russian taste for the strongman. Barak was their ideal at first: Stanford-educated, sensitive to Israeli honor. His alleged capitulation to Palestinian demands over Jerusalem—at which point Russian leaders Natan Sharansky and Avigdor Lieberman left his government—and his decision to call off the secular revolution that the Russians supported left him looking like a paper tiger. "They are for the most part immigrants without a Jewish or deeply Zionist identity," writes Galili, "so national symbols, such as Jerusalem, have become an important component of their identity." But the émigrés from Russia are still getting used to their new country—the opportunities as well as the frustrations of freedom—and they may well change the political landscape again, especially when the economic impact of curtailing the peace process is fully felt.

GLOBAL SUPPORT FOR HEBREW DEMOCRACY

There is a pattern here. In a time of relative stability, tribe 1, the professional and economic elite, leads tribes 4 and 5, the Arabs and the Russians—and eventually also leads tribe 2, the *mizrahim*, while marginalizing 3, the Orthodox. This is the Israel Rabin was shaping until his murder. In a time of growing tension, however, tribes 2 and 3 will lead 5, alienate 4, and put 1 into a kind of internal exile—while presenting tribe 1's children with a choice between serving in the army to fight a war they believe could have been prevented or opting for exile in the global knowledge-economy. For the peace coalition to regain power and implement the deal, Israelis and Palestinians have to regain the stability that marked Oslo's early days. Can they?

Sharon says he will accept a demilitarized Palestine on 43 percent of the West Bank and sign a nonbelligerency agreement with its leaders—if the violence stops. His unity coalition promises to prohibit new settlements, limit existing ones to "natural" rates of growth, and negotiate partial agreements that defer decisions on refugees and Jerusalem. Saeb Erakat, one of the Palestinian Authority's most conciliatory negotiators, said that if these were the terms, he would meet his interlocutor in the "next life." So if Israel expects a cessation of violence, it will have to freeze all settlement activity—because to the Palestinians, settlements amount to aggression. Besides, why should Arafat's fragile Palestinian Authority risk a confrontation with radical Hamas activists if Israel's fragile coalition will not risk a confrontation with the settlers?

In retrospect, what was missing from Oslo all along was a stronger international presence to help contain outbreaks of violence and manage their aftermath in the context of continuing negotiations. If a cease-fire can be restored, Israel and the Palestinians need to achieve some kind of "separation of forces" like the agreement with Egypt that ended the post-1973 exchanges of fire. Each side desperately needs a strong third party to trust without having to trust each other. Sharon says he wants an "interim" arrangement. Secretary Powell could make the presence of international forces—billeted in a recognized, if temporarily small, Palestinian state—a condition of implementing the confidence-building measures outlined in the report of the Mitchell "fact-finding" commission, which was set up after October's Sharm el-Sheikh conference to ascertain the roots of the recent violence. As a quid pro quo to Israel, he could offer, say, to set up an American naval base in Haifa.

THIS IS NOT TO UNDERESTIMATE THE DIPLOMATIC AND logistical difficulties of deploying NATO forces, especially in and around Jerusalem, or the challenges to Israeli sovereignty such intervention might pose. Powell is famous for disliking American troops in a policing role and has endorsed only "outside observers" in the region. Israeli officials have a deeply ambiguous attitude toward the "blue helmets": They have bitter memories of UN forces evacuating the Sinai at Egyptian President Gamal Nasser's insistence in 1967—the umbrella that folded just when the rain began to fall, in Israeli diplomat Abba Eban's view. More recently, UN forces denied Israelis an unedited video they possessed of Hezbollah fighters kidnapping Israeli soldiers. One young officer told me he fears that UN forces, especially if they were European, would seriously undermine the Israeli Defense Force's freedom of action in the occupied territories and become a kind of shield behind which terrorists might operate, as in Lebanon. What's more, in the absence of a final-status agreement, would international forces have a clear mandate?

But on balance, these objections are unimpressive. NATO forces are going into Macedonia under equally chaotic conditions. And without international forces mediating cooperation between Israel and the Palestinian Authority, the two sides will always be hostages to terrorism. As for the young officer's wish to preserve Israel's freedom of action, well, the Israeli military has had freedom of action in the occupied territories since 1967. Besides, effective sovereignty does not mean military control, even if this were possible. What will happen to the stewardship of important utilities, public works, and transportation infrastructure without the cooperation of Palestine, other neighbors, and international partners? The water shortage has become a virtual emergency. If a Palestinian state is formed, neither side will be able to pump from the West Bank water table without affecting the other. Israel and a Palestinian state will have to work together on transportation links between the West Bank and Gaza, as well as on other matters of common jurisdiction, labor law, monetary policy (the Israeli shekel is still the major Palestinian currency), telecommunications policy, and more.

In this context, the fear of the Palestinians' "right of return" seems to be a failure of imagination. After all, the political and demographic forces unleashed by any negotiated settlement underwritten by the global powers will lead to pretty much the same result. Let's say 250,000 Palestinians are repatriated to Israel proper. What problems does a 25 percent Arab minority pose to Israel that a 20 percent minority does not? There would in any case be a dramatic expansion of Palestinian population in the triangle between Jerusalem, Ramallah, and Nablus—an increase of up to a million people that would eventually create a city the size of Amman. Israelis and Palestinians will consequently struggle with problems much like those of Singapore and Malaysia, or San Diego and northern Mexico. The Tel Aviv-Haifa corridor, and the roads to it, will swell with Palestinians working in industries like construction, light manufacturing, and tourism. At the same time, the promise of greater Israel will give way to that of greater Tel Aviv, a city that will remain materially and culturally hegemonic. The language of work for tens of thousands of Palestinians already is Hebrew. Tel Aviv will expand along the road and rail link that joins Herzliah, Netanya, and southern Haifa; it will become an international Hebrew-English megalopolis anchoring the technological development of the region up to Turkey.

True, this is not exactly the Israel envisioned by classical Zionist theorists. But if the fundamental purpose of their Zionist revolution was, as the movement's first great mentor Achad Ha'am argued, to have a place in the world where Jews could express the "Jewish spirit," compete in the world without self-effacement, and ask scientific and literary questions in Hebrew (free from the hold of Orthodoxy), then the prospect could be worse. Achad Ha'am had hoped that a Jewish national home would be heir to what he took to be Rabbinic Judaism's real achievement: a sense of divine intention that was endlessly debatable—an anticipation of the fractious, liberal values that he loved and believed had "overturned Judaism from within." If that hope is still worth cherishing, it will be realized, ironically, not by Israelis who consider their country a not-quite-finished Zionist revolution but by citizens of an internationally supported Hebrew democracy.

Writer and business consultant BERNARD AVISHAI *is the author of* The Tragedy of Zionism *and* A New Israel.

Will Arafat father a country?

By Samuel G. Freedman

Shortly after midnight on June 22, 1948, barely a month since Arab armies had attacked the newly founded state of Israel, a ship named the Altalena moored off the shoreline of Tel Aviv. It was carrying $5 million worth of arms to the Irgun, the radical underground of the Zionist movement, notorious for bombings and assassinations.

On the beach waited fellow Jews in the official national army, poised not for welcome but for assault. Because the Irgun had refused to disband, because its incoming weaponry bristled with the prospect of Jewish civil war, the Israeli leader, David Ben-Gurion, ordered his troops to sink the Altalena.

That episode carved a divide between the left and right wings in Israeli society that has lasted to this very day. And yet it made Israel, the nation, possible, for it demonstrated Ben-Gurion's commitment to preside over a single country with a single army, and his rejection of terrorism as a tactic.

Yasser Arafat faces the identical choice now. The man of a thousand and one opportunities, all of them squandered, has one more. With President Bush calling for Palestinian statehood and his administration pressing Israel to resume the peace process, with British Prime Minister Tony Blair hosting the Palestinian leader for talks—all this by way of helping to hold moderate Arab states in the American-led anti-terror coalition—Arafat has been presented another chance to be the peace partner of Oslo and the Nobel Prize, the father of a country instead of a fantasy.

What he must do, however, is act as decisively as Ben-Gurion did against renegades and rogues: the terrorists of Hamas and Islamic Jihad. When Arafat released them from the Palestinian Authority's prisons a year ago, in the early stages of the intifada, he may have calculated that just enough drive-by shootings and suicide bombings would

wring from Israel even more concessions than it had offered at Camp David. Now it must be apparent that the strategy has failed and the genie of terrorism refuses to slip back into the bottle.

All that the intifada has done is persuade Israelis to replace Ehud Barak, a prime minister prepared to divide Jerusalem and return more than 90% of the occupied territories, with Ariel Sharon, who would never make such offers, even in peacetime. All that the intifada has done is destroy a nascent Palestinian economy of industrial parks, tourism, agriculture, natural-gas deposits and construction labor, leaving Arafat's people to wring out subsistence under Israel's defensive throttle around Gaza and the West Bank.

Not so long ago, a majority of both American and Israeli Jewry was prepared to trade land for peace, to forever abandon the folly that an archipelago of Israeli settlements on Palestinian land could provide security, rather than a disconnected and vulnerable frontier. Now even many in the peace movement accept the targeted assassination of would-be terrorists as a necessity. After the events of Sept. 11, who can blame them?

Through it all, Arafat has juggled the roles of revolutionary and statesman, condemning the most abhorrent attacks on Israel, such as the suicide bombing of a Tel Aviv nightclub, without ever cracking down on the perpetrators. The Israeli settlers—most of whom would have been dislodged under the Camp David proposals—continue to be regarded by even mainstream Palestinian leaders as fair game for lethal attacks.

But the charade is over. The world has now seen Palestinians passing out candies to celebrate the Sept. 11 atrocities and marching behind posters of Osama bin Laden; the world has seen a university campus on the West Bank mark the first anniversary of the intifada with a scale model of the Jerusalem pizzeria where 15 Israelis perished in a suicide bombing, an exhibit replete with imitation body parts suspended from the ceiling.

Isolated voices within the Palestinian community have been warning all along of the futility, the self-destruction, of the intifada. The official Palestinian news agency, Wafa, in August urged Palestinians to resist "with stones and shoes instead of weapons," because only political means would enable them to achieve their goals. On the first anniversary of the latest uprising, the historian Samih Shabib wrote in the West Bank newspaper *Al-Ayyam*, "If only we had enough courage to criticize some of the means and methods that have weakened our situation, and damaged our past and future."

To undo that damage, Arafat must do more than donate blood for the Sept. 11 victims or renounce bin Laden's support for the Palestinian cause. He must do more than close the schools and universities in Gaza, as he did last week to quell demonstrations in support of bin Laden. He must do even more than turn Palestinian Authority police against pro-terror marchers. Welcome as those gestures are, they address only the immediate moment.

No matter how much pressure Bush and Western Europe apply, Israel will not consent to a Palestinian state that serves as a staging area for Hamas and Islamic Jihad. Only by subduing those murderous extremists can Arafat hope for an Israeli government to offer anything close to the Camp David compromises.

There will be apologists, of course, who will insist that Arafat risks being toppled by the Islamists in his midst. The risk of civil war is undeniably great. As it was, too, for Ben-Gurion in June 1948. But when he looked back later on the sinking of the Altalena, as the prime minister of a recognized state instead of the shaky potentate of feuding gangs, he said that the gun that struck the blow was "blessed."

Samuel G. Freedman, a professor of journalism at Columbia University, is the author most recently of Jew vs. Jew: The Struggle for the Soul of American Jewry. *He is a member of USA TODAY's board of contributors.*

Belonging in the West

Multiple challenges and concerns arise from the presence of ever-growing Muslim communities within Western society.

Yvonne Yazbeck Haddad

When Daniel Pipes sounded the alarm: "The Muslims Are Coming! The Muslims are Coming!" in the November 19, 1990, issue of *National Review*, it was clear that Muslims were already here. Indeed, they had become an integral part of the West. Since that time, Islam, particularly Islamic fundamentalism, has continually been depicted as the next enemy: as a force replacing communism as a challenge to the West.

Consequently, Muslims have often suffered from considerable prejudice. They have been accused of adhering to a religion that is devoid of integrity, that encourages violent passions in its adherents, that menaces civil society and is a threat to our way of life. Muslims are stereotyped as potentially bloodthirsty terrorists whose loyalty as citizens must be questioned. Not one promoter of political correctness has put them on a list of communities to be protected. But Muslims have been victims of hate crimes that include assault, murder, and the burning of mosques in both Europe and North America. As a result, their apprehension about their security and future in Western society has increased.

The Muslim encounter with the West dates back to the beginning of Islam. As Muslims spread into Byzantium and North Africa, they established their hegemony over large areas inhabited by Christian populations. While their expansion into western Europe was halted at Poitiers in 731, Muslims created a

thriving civilization in different parts of Spain, Portugal, Sicily, and southern France between the eighth and fifteenth centuries. In the East, Ottoman expansion into Europe was not halted until the failure of the siege of Vienna in 1683. While a significant number of Muslims

continued to live in eastern Europe, in Bulgaria, Romania, Albania, and Serbia, the fall of Grenada in 1492 and the Inquisition (which gave Muslims the options of conversion to Christianity, expulsion, or death) all but eliminated a Muslim presence in western Europe. Thus, the recent growth of the Muslim community in Europe and North America has been called the "new Islamic presence."

> *Some Muslim scholars have admonished Muslims to leave the West, lest they lose their souls.*

Indeed, since the sixteenth century, Muslims have encountered Western cultures as conquering and imperial powers, competing in their quest to subjugate Muslims and monopolize their economic resources. Consequently, some Muslims depict the West as bent on combating Islam not only through colonial conquest but through armies of missionaries. They perceive a West that is and ever has been eager to displace or eradicate Muslims. They find evidence in the Reconquista, the Crusades, and, more recently, in Palestine and Bosnia.

LIVING BEYOND THE ISLAMIC STATE

Muslim jurists have offered various opinions about whether it is permissible for Muslims to live outside the jurisdiction of an Islamic state. This issue has been raised during the last two decades, as some Muslim scholars have admonished Muslims to leave the West lest they lose their soul amid its wayward ways. Other jurists have insisted that as long as Muslims are free to practice their faith, they are allowed to live outside the house of Islam, while still others have said that it is Muslims' duty to propagate the faith in their new abode. Thus they not only have the opportunity to share the salvific teachings of Islam but must try to redeem Western society from its evil ways and restore it to the worship of God.

Muslims are repelled by what they see as a degenerate Western society with weak family values.

The question then is often asked: "Given their experience of the West, why do they come?" Surveys show that Muslims move to Europe and North America for the same reasons that other populations have chosen to come: for higher education, better economic opportunities, and political and religious freedom. Others are refugees, the by-product of Euro-American adventures in the world. Thus the first significant group of Muslims to come to France were North Africans and Senegalese who were recruited to fight in French colonial wars. Immigrants to Britain are from its former colonies and from the ranks of its Asian (Bangladeshi, Indian, and Pakistani) colonial civil servants expelled from Africa by the leaders of newly independent nations. In the Netherlands, the initial Muslim population came from the colonies of Indonesia and Suriname.

The majority of Muslims in Europe were recruited as temporary guest workers to relieve the shortage of labor in the post–World War II reconstruction. The host countries of Germany, the Netherlands, Austria, Britain, Switzerland, and France expected them to leave when their contracts expired. In the 1970s, a recession and growing unemployment prompted European governments to reduce imported labor. Some even provided

Here Yet Apart

Though an integral part of twentieth-century Western society, Muslims have lately been targets of considerable prejudice.

Many argue that it may not be possible to lead a Muslim lifestyle beyond the borders of an Islamic state.

Both Islamic and European governments have helped build mosques and Muslim centers in the West, in the hopes of blunting the rise of fundamentalism and aiding the assimilation of Muslim immigrants.

Muslims ask whether Western society, which prides itself on liberal democracy, pluralism, and multiculturalism, will be flexible enough to provide for Islamic input into the shaping of its future.

financial incentives for the laborers to return to their homelands. This policy led to an unintended growth of the Muslim community, as many opted to bring their families and settle for fear that they would not have another opportunity.

In European nations with an official state religion, such as Britain and the Netherlands, Muslims have sought parity with Jews and Catholics who have been given special privileges. But to no avail. Thus, during the Salman Rushdie affair, Muslims sought implementation of the blasphemy law, only to find out that it operates only to protect Anglicanism. In Britain, for example, the school day starts with a Christian prayer. In courts, the oath is taken on the Bible. Town council meetings start with a prayer. Anglican clergy celebrate marriage that is automatically legal without having to go to the registrar. While Catholic and Jewish marriages are recognized, those performed by imams are not. Catholics and Jews obtain state funding to support their parochial schools, but Muslim requests for parity have been denied.

Muslims have fared differently in nations that have historically welcomed immigrants—the United States, Canada, Latin America, and Australia. Muslim migrant laborers began coming to America in the nineteenth century. While many returned, a few settled permanently and formed the nucleus of what is now the fourth and fifth American-born generation of Muslims. The largest number of Muslims came in the 1970s on a preference visa and were accepted as citizens and given voting rights. Predominantly members of the educated elite, they are doctors, professors, and engineers.

Islam is the second- or third-largest religion in various European nations. It is estimated that there are five million Muslims in France, organized in over 1,000 mosques and prayer halls. They constitute about 10 percent of the population, making Islam the largest religion after Catholicism and with more active adherents than either Protestants or Jews. In Britain, the Muslim population is estimated at about two million, organized in over 600 mosques. The Muslim community of the United States is estimated at five million, about 10 percent of whom are involved in organized religion in over 1,250 mosques and Islamic centers. Canada has about half a million.

It is expected that Muslims will outnumber Jews in Canada and the United States by the first decade of the next century. The North American community is noted for its ethnic national, linguistic, and secretarian diversity. It includes over a million converts, mostly African Americans. While it is estimated that up to 18 percent of the slaves brought to America were Muslims, most had converted to Christianity by the beginning of this century. The conversion of African Americans to Islam is a twentieth-century phenomenon.

THE MUSLIM EXPERIENCE IN THE WEST

The Muslim experience in the West varies according to the immigrants' background, the nations they came from, their reasons for leaving, and their educational attainments. The host country's policies are also influential: whether it welcomes

Muslim Legal Expectations

Kathleen Moore

When a truck bomb shattered the Murrah Federal Building in downtown Oklahoma City on April 19, 1995—the worst terrorist act ever on American soil—many in the media and federal law enforcement jumped to the conclusion that an "Islamic fundamentalist" was responsible. Similarly, the downing of TWA Flight 800 and the Olympic Park explosion in Atlanta set off allegations that "Middle Eastern-looking" terrorists were to blame. Those hasty conclusions have proved groundless. However, Muslim defendants have been convicted for the 1993 bombing of the World Trade Center, and a Muslim suspect has been arrested in connection with the attack on traffic near the CIA headquarters in January of that year.

Instantly attributing blame to unknown Muslim terrorists was not just the result of the media and law enforcement officials letting their imaginations run amok. Such images were also conjured up—and in some instances acted upon—by the general public. Some 200 incidents of anti-Muslim harassment were reported in the days immediately following the tragedy in Oklahoma.

Consequently, American Muslim communities mobilized to an unprecedented degree. Existing organizations, such as the American Muslim Council and the Islamic Society of North America, were joined by newly formed groups such as the Council on American-Islamic Relations (CAIR) to defend Muslims' civil rights. Public relations and lobbying efforts and press conferences highlighted not merely the Muslim presence in the United States but also the American Muslims' experiences as targets of discrimination. Thus the rights consciousness of this growing segment of the American population is largely being shaped by Muslims' responses to media distortions and perceived demonization of Islam.

The fears that motivate anti-Islamic sentiment appear to derive from a sense of insecurity that has lurked just beneath the surface of our national life since the fall of the Berlin Wall in 1989. The prospects for world peace would seem to be greater than at any other time in this century, but our doubts about the future seem nevertheless to escalate. This post–Cold War malaise has its consequences for those who fear they may come to take the unenviable place of the "Red menace" in the public mind. Of great concern to many Muslims is the prospect that they will be increasingly subjected to various forms of discrimination in Western countries as negative portrayals of Islam and Muslims take their toll.

The visible effects of these concerns and experiences of mistreatment can be seen in the emergence of rights-advocacy groups that have used a variety of legal strategies to assert Muslim rights. For instance, in the United States, CAIR has conducted media campaigns over the last two years or so to bring to public attention instances where women have been prohibited from wearing the traditional Islamic hijab (head scarf) at work. Cases of harassment involving Muslims who have been taunted with epithets relating to prevalent prejudicial stereotypes have been documented and financially supported through the legal process by these advocacy groups. In Britain, a few Muslim activists have (so far, unsuccessfully) pressed the government for greater autonomy, particularly allowing Islamic courts to adjudicate issues of family law separate from the civil court system.

We are now witnessing the emergence of a distinctive Western Muslim identity, carved out of the secular social environment of the West. It would not be accurate, however, to assume that the Muslim identity being forged is uniform or monolithic. In fact, significant distinctions and disagreements exist within Muslim communities that are differentiated by sectarian, ethnic, regional, or generational traits. But it is meaningful to note that there are shared experiences and to recognize that the formulation of this identity is taking place under constraints imposed by the host societies. Muslim legal expectations and interpretations are thus voiced within particular contexts, in response to specific events, cultural characteristics, and historical pressures.

In an idealized sense, Muslims migrated to the United States and Britain with a centuries-old tradition in hand. In this legal framework are the classical traditions of Islamic jurisprudence that offer models for minority living. Historically, these models focus on three essential questions: First, under what conditions are Muslims allowed to live outside Muslim territory? In essence, the answer is only where religious freedom prevails. Second, what responsibilities do Muslim minorities have with respect to their host society? Here, answers are varied. Third, what is the relationship of Muslim minorities, living in places like the United States and Britain, to the global Muslim community as a whole? Again, answers are varied and problematic.

In general, the classical models suggest that if a Muslim minority does not encounter religious freedom and is unable to practice its faith, then it has the options of fighting back (jihad) or emigration (hirah).

Yet many see these traditions as out of touch with Muslim minorities' realities and in need of revision to fit today's circumstances. Recent calls have been made for the formulation of a "new" jurisprudence in light of changing conditions. A variety of issues have been singled out by the British and American Muslim communities as being crucial.

Some issues are the product of the secular environment in which Muslims

(continued)

(continued from previous page)

live. Do they have rights to religious freedom that require accommodation of their specific needs in the workplace, at school, or in the military? How will Muslims survive as a vibrant religious community in the West? Will they be able to freely and fully participate in its religious landscape and in defining the future as a pluralistic society? How can Muslim children be successfully integrated into the larger society, to function as hyphenated Americans or Britons without abandoning the faith? Can Muslims vote or run for political office in a secular society where the institutions of government are not based on Islamic values? What roles are women permitted to play in public life?

Attendance at mosques and Islamic centers (in the West) has gone up over the last decade or so. Mosques are now not only for prayer at the five prescribed times: They have become community centers and provide facilities for tutoring students in their school subjects, Qur'anic studies, marriage ceremonies, free counseling and mediation, and legal services.

In some of these places, Muslims are listening to those who warn from the pulpit that the encounter with the secular West is destructive and that the only option for Muslim survival is to remain marginal to public life. From this isolationist perspective, the Muslim minority should reaffirm a Muslim identity in isolation, untainted by the materialistic values of the West. This, it is thought, will have the effect of inviting others to Islam by providing an example of an incorruptible "city on a hill" in the midst of moral decay.

On the other side of the debate are the "accommodationists," who struggle to feel at home in the United States and Britain. Muhammad Abduh, an early twentieth-century reformer in Egypt, provides some insight into the accommodationists' position. Abduh gave a *fatwa* (religious legal opinion) permitting Muslims in South Africa to consume meat butchered for People of the Book (i.e., Christians and Jews) when no *halal* meat (i.e., food prepared or butchered in the Islamically prescribed way, similar to the Jewish tradition of kosher) was available.

Accommodationists advise cooperation with non-Muslims, provided that it benefits the Muslim community. As long as the Muslim who lives as minority is at liberty to maintain the "core" of the religion, he may adjust to the host society. Accommodationists argue that diet, as long as it is nourishing, need not comply with stringent Islamic strictures; attire, as long as it is clean and modest, need not be restricting (such as the so-called veil or head scarf is); and the architecture of mosques and Islamic centers need not slavishly imitate Middle Eastern styles as long as the buildings are accessible and functional.

In the last two decades the circumstances of Muslim minorities have come to the attention of various international Islamic organizations, such as the Muslim World League, which has established a Fiqh Council, a body that engages in the interpretation of Islamic law to address minority concerns. The council represents a wide variety of Islamic legal schools and advocates what is being called "jurisprudence of necessity" (*fiqh al-darurah*) and "jurisprudence of minority" (*fiqh al-aqalliyah*) to respond to issues of Muslim life in a non-Islamic environment.

Some critics within Islam, though, see this as an effort to impose a "top-down" understanding of Muslim contingencies and reject it in favor of a "bottom-up" approach. Efforts at using American legal rules and then sanctifying them as "Islamic" because they are fair and just can be seen at the local level. For instance, American laws governing marriage, divorce, and child custody, where the woman would, arguably, have greater rights than Islam affords, have been sanctified in places where the *imam* (leader of the mosque) has sanctioned a civil marriage license or divorce decree obtained by a member of his mosque.

The secular legal system has had its effect on Muslim legal consciousness. For example, one leader of a large mosque community in an urban area in the western United States asserts that the process of working out a set of rules to govern Muslim life must be thought of as a jurisprudence of "minority," not because of any specific Islamic tradition but because Muslims are living in the United States, where a significant body of case law on minority relations already exists. To be labeled a minority entitles one to rights. The word *minority* may connote weakness or vulnerability, but it is also a recognized basis for making claims to resources and privilege in America. Thus, it is imperative to accommodate Islamic practices to fit the opportunities provided by the local customs and laws of the community in which they are now a permanent part.

Kathleen Moore is assistant professor of political science at the University of Connecticut.

foreigners and/or grants them citizenship rights, its perceptions of Islam, and its laws governing the relationship between religion and state.

During the eighties, various Muslim countries began laying Islamic foundations in the West by providing funds for the construction of mosques and schools and the teaching of Arabic and Islam. For example, in a two-year period, Saudi Arabia spent $10 million to construct mosques in North America. In Germany, Sweden, and the Netherlands—where there are large Turkish and Moroccan communities—the fear of the potential for growth of Islamic fundamentalism among the *marginalized guest* workers led to arrangements with the Turkish and Moroccan governments to supervise the religious affairs of the community. Both governments welcomed the opportunity to blunt the growth of fundamentalism and curtail its dissemination in their countries. The European governments paid for construction of Islamic centers and mosques and imported the religious leaders to lead prayers and provide religious instruction.

Two issues are of paramount importance for both the immigrants and host countries: security and cultural coherence. All nation-states have developed a myth of national identity that has been inculcated in schoolchildren through literature, art, music, assumptions, legends, and a particular understanding of history. These myths have shaped several generations of Europeans and Americans through the cauldron of two wars and created distinctive identities marking the way the West sees itself and what it takes for granted, as well as what it identifies as alien, strange, and weird.

Educated Muslims who emigrated in the postwar period also have a preformed understanding of Western culture based on the experience of colonialism and neocolonialism. Their perceptions have been shaped by watching Western movies and television, which they perceive as imbued with drugs, violence, racism, and pornography. Muslims are repelled by what they see as a degenerate society with weak family values. They condemn premarital or extramarital sex and having children out of wedlock, both of which increase the fragility of marriage and hence the family bond. They believe that Western values concerning parent's and children's duties toward one another are lacking. There is too much emphasis on individual freedom and not enough on corporate responsibility.

A primary concern for Muslim immigrants is surviving in what they experience as a hostile environment and safeguarding the welfare of their children. They are fully aware that Europe and the Americas have been shaped by secular Christianity. They seek to maintain the right to practice their faith according to its tenets as revealed to them by God. They are concerned about perpetuation of the faith among their children and preservation of Islamic values. In this context they have sought to have employers provide them with time off to fulfill their religious duties during the

day, to attend the Friday prayer at the mosque, fast during the month of Ramadan, and celebrate the two major holidays (Eid al-Fitr and Eid al-Adha). Many are concerned about properly slaughtered meat (halal), while others seek the right to have their children excused from coed athletics and sex education (which they believe promotes promiscuity). They believe that religious freedom should provide the right to wear the head scarf (hijab) for women.

In France, the issue of wearing the hijab took on national significance when several female students were banned from wearing it on the grounds that such behavior is tantamount to proselytizing, a proscribed activity in the secular schools of France. For Muslims, the ban was seen as an anti-Muslim act, since Christians are allowed to wear a cross and Jews a yarmulke, both of which could then be interpreted as an act of propagating a faith.

The issue of the hijab has surfaced in other Western nations under different rubrics. For example, in Canada, feminists championed the banning of head scarfs, which they depicted as a symbol of oppression. Muslim girls who put them on insisted that it was an act of obedience to a divine injunction and therefore protected under the freedom of religion. More important, they viewed it as an instrument of liberation from being a sex object. In the United States, the Council on American-Islamic Relations reported that there was a 50 percent increase in 1996 in the number of incidents of discrimination against women who wear the hijab.

ISLAM IN A PLURAL SOCIETY

The Western experience is also shaping new forms of Islamic organization and administration. The imam not only leads prayer and worship but acts as an ambassador to the host culture, attempting to build bridges to other faith communities and representing Muslims in interfaith events. Moreover, the mosque, besides being a place of congregational prayer, has become a social center where the community meets for a variety of events that help cement relationships and pro-

vide for community celebrations. In this center for Islamic knowledge and education Islam is taught to the next generation, which reflects on its meaning in the new environment. The mosque has become an island of security and a venue for the sharing of one's experiences. It is not unusual to see people clothed in their ethnic dress for Sunday services, taking advantage of a chance to affirm primary identity in an environment where individuals can be themselves without being under constant scrutiny for conformity.

Some Muslims contemplate the option of returning to their homeland, should conditions of life in the West continue to be unacceptable. Their children, however, have been reared and educated in the West. The West is their homeland. They are bicultural and possess an intimate experience and knowledge of Western society, as well as a knowledge about the culture of the parents as remembered and reinvented in the West. While immigrants struggle to maintain their identity; they are increasingly being challenged and changed as their children become more indigenized into the surrounding culture.

Some Western authors have continued to question whether Muslims are worthy of citizenship in a democratic nation or whether their presence will alter the place where they settle. While some continue to debate whether they belong *in* the West, it is evident that Muslims are part and parcel *of* the West. An estimated ten thousand Muslims currently serve in the armed services of the United States, for example. There are two Muslim chaplains, one in the Navy and one in the Army and plans have been made to appoint one in the Air Force.

Muslims in the West generally favor keeping a low profile for security reasons. They are the latest victims of chauvinism and xenophobia. Events such as the oil embargo of 1973, the Iranian revolution, the holding of American hostages for 444 days, and the Pan Am bombing have created concern among many westerners. Irresponsible and irrational actions such as the bombing of the World Trade Center have heightened fears of Islamic fundamentalism. This has exacerbated the fear of Islam and tapped into a history of misunderstanding and vilification. Thus, Muslims fear they are becoming the new villains on the block, replacing Jews, Gypsies, Italians, and African Americans as objects of odium.

Muslims continue to ask whether Western democracies are liberal enough to include Islamic input into the national consensus, or if they will insist on an exclusively Judeo-Christian culture. Will Western pluralism or multiculturalism be flexible enough to provide for Islamic input into the shaping of the future of Western society? Or will Muslims continue to be marginaiized, ostracized, studied, and evaluated, always judged as lacking, always the "other"?

Yvonne Yazbeck Haddad is professor of the history of Islam and Christian-Muslim relations at Georgetown University.

This article first appeared in *The World & I,* September 1997, pp. 50–59. Reprinted by permission of *The World & I,* a publication of The Washington Times Corporation. © 1997.

In 'Little Kabul,' love of country, homeland

Afghans in California display allegiance to all things American

By MIKE ADAMS
SUN NATIONAL STAFF

FREMONT, Calif.—A poster of Osama bin Laden with an X across his face sits near the counter of the 98 Cent Plus store. The words under the photo say: "The Afghan community wants bin Laden out of their country and will not take the blame for terrorism."

The poster sums up the way many people feel here in "Little Kabul." About 40,000 Afghans live in the San Francisco Bay area, about a quarter of them in Fremont. Little Kabul, which takes its name from Afghanistan's capital, is a strip of small stores, restaurants and businesses on the city's main street, Fremont Boulevard.

The proprietor of the 98 Cent Plus store, Masood Haroon, 37, is an Afghan immigrant who has lived in the United States for 14 years. He resents the Taliban, the Islamic extremists who have taken over his homeland and are believed to be shielding bin Laden, the exiled Saudi terrorist accused of orchestrating the attacks Sept. 11 on New York and Washington that left nearly 7,000 dead or missing.

Haroon, like many others here, is quick to point out that bin Laden is an Arab—not an Afghan—and that much of the Taliban leadership received its religious and political training at Islamic schools in Pakistan. Neither the Taliban nor bin Laden has the support of most Afghans, he says.

Haroon wants the United States to take decisive action to neutralize bin Laden, but he's worried about the suffering that U.S. military action could bring to Afghanistan. He says that the United States could cut military casualties and civilian deaths by supporting the Northern Alliance, Afghan rebels already at war with the Taliban.

"We want to get rid of the Taliban any way possible, but we don't want innocent people to get killed by this war," he says.

While members of the Afghan community are paying rapt attention to events in their homeland, their allegiance to the United States and things American is much in evidence.

Shoppers who enter Haroon's variety store are greeted by two large American flags. Stacks of smaller flags are on display near the counter along with American flag key chains and ball point pens.

He also sells T-shirts that carry an American flag with the words "I love New York," a slogan with special significance after the attack that toppled the city's World Trade Center.

The best known local Afghan is an official All-American—quarterback Zamir Amin, star of nearby Menlo College, a Division III school, who set an overall NCAA record last year for passing 731 yards in a game.

Amin, who was born in Afghanistan but arrived in the United States as an infant in 1979 after the Soviet invasion, says he feels completely at home here. He says he has encountered none of the incidents of verbal abuse, vandalism and violence reported by Muslims, Sikhs and people of Middle Eastern origin since the terrorist attack.

"It's unfortunate for the people who are harassed," he says. "The people who do this are ignorant, and harassment doesn't accomplish anything."

He is much more concerned about the consequences of the attack for his homeland, which has been devastated by ethnic warfare, a war to drive out Soviet invaders a generation ago and years of misrule under the Taliban.

"I feel for the innocent citizens, the people that don't have anything to do with what's going on," he says.

During the Cold War, the United States helped Afghan freedom fighters in their campaign against the Soviet Union. But after the Soviets were expelled, the United States forgot about Afghanistan, Haroon says.

"The U.S. won the war, but unfortunately, they did not care after that," he says. "They left Afghanistan as a disaster, and they should have stayed with the Afghan people to help them build their country and bring a peaceful government there."

The United States is paying a price for its lack of concern about Afghanistan, Haroon maintains. Inaction by the United States made it possible for the Taliban to come to power, with assistance from elements in Pakistan, he says. Then bin Laden moved in and set up training camps for terrorists.

DENISE MURRAY : SUN STAFF

A devout Muslim, Haroon is appalled by the teachings of the Taliban and the violence of bin Laden. They have distorted his religion into something unrecognizable, he says.

"The Taliban is twisting Islam in a really harsh way, a bad way," he says. "The Taliban says women cannot go to school, that they cannot work. Nobody knows how many women have had their fingernails pulled out because they were caught wearing nail polish.... This is ridiculous because Islam does not say any of this."

A few stores away, talk of the Taliban draws angry words from Homayoun Khamosh, 38, the owner of the Pamir Food Mart. "Everyone calls them government; they are not our government, the Taliban is against our government," he says. "We have a legitimate government, the Northern Alliance." The Taliban have never been recognized as Afghanistan's legitimate government by more than a handful of countries, and two of them, Saudi Arabia and the United Arab Emirates, withdrew recognition in the past week. Pakistan is the only country that maintains diplomatic relations with them. The

Northern Alliance, which contains elements of the government ousted by the Taliban in 1996, controls less than 10 percent of the country.

The alliance's efforts to reclaim more territory suffered a major blow days before the terrorist attacks on the United States when its leader, Ahmad Shah Masood, was killed by a suicide bomber posing as a journalist. Khamosh is not alone in believing that the assassination was bin Laden's work and that there was a link between Masood's killing and the terrorism that followed in the United States.

Khamosh has lived in the United States for 11 years. During the war with the Soviets, he served as a medic. He views the Taliban as an alien element.

"I don't like the Taliban at all because they are not our people," he says. "The Taliban is made up of Arabs and Pakistanis, and people who are paid by the Taliban to fight with them against our people, the Northern Alliance."

He also wonders why they seem to be shielding bin Laden and accuses them of violating Muslim precepts.

"They are not Muslims, they are not Islam, they just use the name of Islam," he says "Nowhere does the holy Quran say you should kill innocent people or attack them."

Farid Noori, 38, walked into the food mart as Khamosh spoke. He immediately joined the conversation by saying, "I support George W. Bush 100 percent."

"Muslims are peaceful people. The Quran says that if you kill innocent people, God will punish you. You will go to hell," he says. "The Taliban just made up a lot of stuff to take advantage of people with low education by telling them that they will go to paradise with 72 women around them if they kill people in acts of terror. I read the Quran many, many times. There is no such thing in the Quran."

Noori concedes that the Taliban have some support in the Afghan community in the United States. He says that the number of supporters is small but that they are fanatically loyal. He maintains that some people, particularly those who are less educated, are more likely to believe the Taliban's teachings.

"Even when they see what bin Laden has done, they still support it," he says. "They believe what they believe. You can't teach them.

"The United States has to take serious action, find these people and send them back home. They don't belong in this country. They live here, and they eat here and make their lives here, but they support terrorists. I cannot believe it, but unfortunately, it's true."

Arab Americans

Protecting Rights at Home and Promoting a Just Peace Abroad...

Until recently, the establishment of Arab Americans as an organized political constituency had been, for the most part, in a formative process. This year, however, Arab Americans have arrived as an independent-minded and highly motivated political force with a common agenda.

A Zogby International (ZI) study recently completed for the Arab American Institute (AM) sought to explore the attitudes of Arab Americans on a range of domestic and foreign policy issues.[1] Before examining its findings about those issues that are of special concern to Arab Americans, it is interesting to sketch the portrait of the community's characteristics that emerge from the study's results.

I. DEMOGRAPHICS AND CHARACTERISTICS

Arab Americans are part of the American success story.

From the earliest settlements in the industrialized Northeast and Midwest to those in the Southwest and West, Americans of Arab descent have played an important part in building communities and institutions in most major cities in the United States.

Today, the more than three million Arab Americans are, according to U.S. Census figures, quite an impressive group and those surveyed in the study were representative of such success.[2] Thirty percent earn more than $75,000 a year (second only to the Jewish community). The small percentage (22%) that report earning under $25,000 is also one of the lowest of all the ethnic groups surveyed. Arab Americans also claim the highest per capita ownership of business of any ethnic group in America and have a higher ratio of advanced degrees and membership in the professions.

Two-thirds of those Arab Americans who were polled reported being born in the United States (this is a lower number than the actual 80% of Arab Americans who were born in the United States). And one-third of all the Arab

Americans in the survey reported that they were second, third or fourth generation Arab Americans.

Other indications in the study show that Arab Americans, while maintaining a strong sense of community and ethnic ties, are also a much-assimilated group. Over 60% of those who are married chose someone from their ethnic background, and 85% prefer that when grown, their children remain living in their community. This is the highest of any group in the study. At the same time, Arab Americans and Italian Americans reported living in the most ethnically diverse neighborhoods and having the most friendships outside of their own ethnic communities.

The Arab American community is also quite accomplished and upwardly mobile. Almost one-half of the Arab Americans in the study (48.5%) have at least a college education. Fifty-six percent report that their financial situation is better than it was four years ago and 87% (the highest of all the groups in the study) report that they have an optimistic view of the future.

As for ideological preferences, Arab Americans are difficult to pigeonhole. They are not single-issue voters, and they do not back one party exclusively, often switching from one candidate to another depending on the election. Arab Americans, whether Democrats or Republicans, make important contributions to the national election debate over a wide range of domestic and foreign policy issues.

Indeed, because of the culture and values that have shaped the Arab American experience, the community has a great deal to offer in policy discussions regarding education, support for small business development, and issues that involve strengthening and protecting families and communities. There is also considerable consensus among Arab Americans on critical issues of U.S. policy in the Middle East and the world as a whole.

In 2000, the Arab American political and electoral agenda is aimed at protecting civil and constitutional rights and ensuring that the promise of freedom and equality applies to all Americans. At the same time, the community is dedicated to promoting strong ties and a

Other demographic information from the study

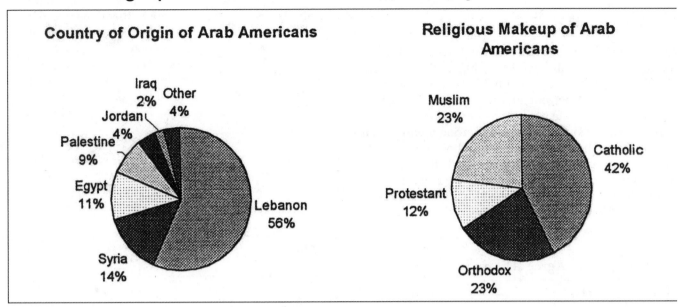

Country of Origin of Arab Americans

Iraq 2%
Other 4%
Jordan 4%
Palestine 9%
Egypt 11%
Syria 14%
Lebanon 56%

Religious Makeup of Arab Americans

Muslim 23%
Catholic 42%
Protestant 12%
Orthodox 23%

just peace in the Middle East as the best way to promote U.S. interests in the entire region.

II. POLITICAL ACTIVITY

The recent Zogby/AAI "Culture Poll" reveals that Arab Americans show some of the highest levels of political participation. According to the results, Arab Americans led many other ethnic groups in being registered to vote (88.7%). Only African Americans (90.1%) and Jewish Americans (92.3%) were registered to vote in higher numbers.

Furthermore, Arab Americans vote in greater percentages (62% in 1996) and are more politically active than average Americans. In the "Culture Poll," over ninety percent of Arab Americans indicated that they were very likely to vote in the upcoming national elections.

While Arab American voting behavior has shifted between various parties for the past couple election cycles, Arab Americans retain higher levels of political participation in relation to other ethnic groups in the following campaign activities:

1. Visiting a presidential candidate's web site?

Arab American	Asian American
13.1%	12.6%
Hispanic	Jewish American
12.5%	8.1%
African American	Italian American
7.7%	7.2%

2. Donated money to a presidential candidate?

Arab American	Jewish American
16.0%	15.6%
Hispanic	African American
12.8%	14.1%
Italian American	Asian American
11.9%	10.2%

3. Watched a presidential debate?

Arab American	African American
81.6%	78.6%
Italian American	Asian American
76.5%	77.2%
Hispanic	Jewish American
73.2%	70.0%

III. DOMESTIC ISSUES

Abortion

Abortion has been one of the most hotly debated issues in recent decades. Arab Americans, like other Americans are divided on this issue and hold rather strong views. For example, 52 percent of Arab Americans describe themselves as pro-life (that is, they are opposed to abortion in most cases). Conversely, 45 percent identify themselves as pro-choice (that is, those who approve of the right to an abortion in most cases). While these numbers reflect a more conservative view than the population as a whole, Arab American attitudes on abortion are similar to other ethnic immigrant communities.

Statement	Agree	Disagree	Not Sure
Banning partial birth abortion	52.1	41.4	6.6
Banning all abortions	53.5	42.8	3.7
Parental notification for abortions for female under 18	78.5	20.1	1.4

Education

Arab Americans tend to favor conservative proposals on education. 69 percent support the use of federally funded vouchers to allow parents the choice of schools to which they will send their children.

Statement	Agree	Disagree	Not Sure
Provide parents with school vouchers	68.9	27.1	3.7
Restriction on teaching of evolution	35.9	58.5	5.6
Racial preferences in hiring or school admissions	21.2	75.2	3.6

Health Care

Arab Americans have a more liberal perspective on health care. 86 percent support using the federal budget surplus to support a federally sponsored health insurance program. 92 percent support strengthening the Medicare program. 89 percent support allowing patients to sue health insurance companies (HMOs).

Statement	Strongly Agree	Disagree	Not Sure
Strengthen Social Security and Medicaid	91.8	6.3	2.0
Allow patients to sue their HMO	88.8	7.9	3.3
Use government surplus to provide health care for working poor and children	86.4	11.4	2.2

Social Security

Plans for addressing Social Security concerns have received significant news coverage. As a group, Arab Americans hold strong views about Social Security as over eighty percent support allowing individuals to invest a portion of their Social Security pension in personal retirement accounts, suggesting that they agree with Governor Bush's recent proposal.

Statement	Agree	Disagree	Not Sure
Strengthen Social Security and Medicaid	91.8	6.3	2.0
Allow investment of Social Security pensions in personal retirement accounts	80.9	15.2	3.9

Crime

Arab Americans have relatively conservative views on crime. At the same time, 72 percent of Arab Americans support the use of the death penalty in cases of capital crimes. And 83 percent support treating 14 to 16 year olds as adults if they commit crimes using guns.

Statement	Agree	Disagree	Not Sure
Prosecute as adults youth 14-16 who have committed a violent crime	82.8	14.0	3.2
New gun control laws	76.0	20.2	3.9
Death penalty for heinous crimes	71.7	24.1	4.2

Table 1: Statements on Arab-Israeli conflict

Statement	Agree	Disagree	Not Sure
Independent Palestinian state	87.2	6.6	6.4
Clinton's handling of peace process	68.7	24.1	7.2
U.S. policy biased towards Israel	74.4	16.6	8.9
U.S. policy is even-handed	46.9	36.6	6.5
U.S. policy shows respect to Islam	63.1	26.0	10.8

V. MIDDLE EAST ISSUES

Overall, Arab Americans hold that the Middle East, and especially the Arab-Israeli conflict, is an issue of utmost importance. Over two-thirds place it among their top five issues of concern, while 79 percent say that a candidate's position on this conflict is important for their vote. This attitude is shared by both those born in the United States (77 percent) and those who are immigrants (83 percent)—although it is more strongly felt by recent Arab American immigrants, 61 percent of whom say that the Arab-Israeli conflict is the "single most important" issue in determining their vote.

The results from the study show that despite the community's tremendous diversity in country of origin, religion and generation, Arab Americans come together on critical Middle East issues. In regards to specific issues, the table below indicates the community's agreement or disagreement with the following statements:

Areas of consensus:

- 87 percent of all Arab Americans agree that there should be a Palestinian state—with a strong consensus existing among all subgroups on this issue.

- Despite misgivings about U.S. policy not being evenhanded and biased in favor of Israel, Arab Americans generally agree with President Clinton's handling of the peace process by nearly 70 percent.

In regards to other issues also related to the Middle East, Arab Americans also hold strong opinions, with an impressive level of consensus. Table 2 shows their relative degree of importance of the following Middle East issues:

Areas of strong consensus:

- 81 percent support the sovereignty of Lebanon—with immigrants feeling somewhat stronger about this issue than those born in the United States.

- 77 percent support securing Palestinian rights in Jerusalem—with 86 percent of immigrants and 72 percent of those born in the United States holding this view.

- 87 percent of Arab Americans support promoting human rights in Arab countries—with a strong consensus on this matter shared by all sub groups.

- 83 percent support the U.S. normalizing relations with the Arab world—with a strong consensus on this matter shared by all sub groups, especially Palestinian-Americans.

Economic sanctions on Iraq:

Only on the question of lifting economic sanctions on Iraq is there a division among various groups of Arab Americans. Overall, 54 percent support lifting these sanctions while 40 percent do not.

VI. OUTLOOK

The political progress of the Arab American community over the past several elections has been remarkable. Voter

Table 2: Middle East issue importance				
Issue	Important	Neither	Not Important	Not Sure
Securing the rights of Palestinians	74.1	14.3	8.6	3.0
Sovereignty of Lebanon	80.4	9.7	7.0	2.8
Normalized U.S. relations with Arab countries	83.2	8.0	7.7	1.1
Status of Jerusalem	74.0	13.9	9.3	2.7
Promote human rights in Arab world	87.3	6.4	5.3	1.0

registration is up, as is voter turnout. Arab Americans now participate in major fundraising for candidates and parties, further enhancing the role of the community. Furthermore, it is expected that this year, as in the past three presidential elections, over 80 Arab Americans will be elected as delegates and party leaders to both the Democratic and Republican national conventions.

Of equal importance for Arab Americans is the fact that the community is now better recognized as a political constituency. The efforts of Arab Americans over the past few elections have created an awareness of the "Arab American vote." As a result, outreach to the community is on the agenda of both major political parties. Nearly all of this year's major presidential candidates have spoken before Arab American audiences and addressed the concerns of the community.

Perhaps the factor that attests to the greatest potential of the Arab American vote however, is the strategic location of the community across the country. Indeed, the so-called "battleground states" for the 2000 presidential and congressional elections are home to the largest numbers and concentrations of Arab Americans as almost one-third of the community (more than one million) is located in this critical belt of states stretching from Illinois to New Jersey. With current polls showing a close race between Vice President Al Gore and Texas Governor George W. Bush, Arab Americans could represent a pivotal voting bloc in several key states of the presidential election.

"If Arab Americans go to the polls in this election in Michigan, Illinois or New Jersey, which are tightly contested battles, they may provide the swing vote in these states," says John Zogby, an independent pollster, himself an Arab American.

Not to be forgotten are this year's congressional elections in which a handful of truly competitive races will likely determine what party controls the U.S. House of Representatives and Senate after November. With concentrations of Arab Americans in a number of these districts, the community is uniquely positioned to play a decisive role in the key races. Indeed, the national Arab American registered voter database shows that Arab American voters are well represented in 55 congressional districts across the United States, making up between 1.5% and 4.5% of the total voting population.

VII. ENDNOTES

45. The ZI/AAI study interviewed 501 Arab Americans during January and February of 2000. The poll's margin of error is +4.5%.
46. The ZI/AAI study was part of a much larger examination of the opinions of six major U.S. ethnic groups (African American, Asian American, Hispanic, American Jews, Italian Americans and Arab Americans). Useful comparisons can be made between the attitudes and characteristics of Arab Americans and those of the other groups.

BEHIND MUBARAK

Egyptian clerics and intellectuals respond to terrorism.

BY JEFFREY GOLDBERG

The Mohandessin section of Cairo is a fashionable district on the west bank of the Nile that contains a number of embassies, boutiques, and American fast-food restaurants. It also houses the Mustafa Mahmoud Mosque, which is named after a physician and Islamic television personality who founded it, twenty years ago. On Friday, September 21st, I arrived at the mosque just as the first worshippers were making their way there, and the egalitarianism that is one of the great virtues of the Muslim prayer service was evident: they were dark-skinned and light, rich and poor; one man drove up in a blue Jaguar; others, wearing grease-stained galabiyas and crude sandals, came on foot, or by donkey cart. (Women, as is customary, prayed apart, in another, smaller hall.) I had arranged to meet the mosque's imam, Sheikh Nasser Abdelrazi. A slight, anxious man, he preëmptively offered up the observation that "Muslims are gentle and Islam is peace."

Many in Cairo are on the defensive in the wake of the terror attacks on New York and the Pentagon. Greater Cairo, a city of sixteen million people, is the intellectual capital of the Arab world—home to its moviemakers, many of its great writers, and some of its most respected interpreters of Islam. Muslim leaders here are sensitive to the image of their faith—especially now, because Egyptians are among those allegedly involved in the attacks. Muhammad Atta, who is believed to have flown one of the hijacked planes into the World Trade Center, is the son of a middle-class Cairo lawyer. Ayman al-Zawahiri, a former leader of the Egyptian Islamic Jihad, a fundamentalist group that sought to turn Egypt into an Islamic state, is said to

be second-in-command to Osama bin Laden, the Saudi exile who is suspected of directing the attacks.

I did not dispute the Imam's assertion, but the speaker at the service that Friday, Ahmed Youssef—an elderly, bespectacled professor at Cairo University, who joined us before the service got under way—did. "Look, what happened in New York is the work of a gangster mentality, but America must learn not to take the side of the aggressor," he said. "I hope America learns from the mistake before it makes another mistake."

In his view, the aggressor is Israel, which signed a peace agreement with Egypt almost twenty-three years ago. This historical fact is not immediately noticeable in Cairo, where the public obsession with Israel is overwhelming. Youssef said that the nineteen terrorists who on September 11th committed mass suicide in the course of committing mass murder engaged in an un-Islamic act. They killed civilians, which is *haram.* or forbidden, and they killed themselves, which is also *haram.* Only against Israel is it permissible to engage in a "martyrdom attack," he said, and this is because it is "only the Jews who kill innocent people." He added, "There are no Israeli civilians, only soldiers, so this is a legitimate tactic."

At this, Sheikh Abdelrazi blanched. "He is not speaking for the mosque," he whispered. The mosque, like all mosques in Egypt, ostensibly comes under the supervision of the government, whose position on suicide attacks against Israeli civilians is ambiguous. When I asked President Hosni Mubarak's chief spokesman, Nabil Osman, if his government condemns such attacks, he would say only, "One can-

not condemn these acts without condemning the acts of the occupier."

I asked Sheikh Abdelrazi and Youssef if they believed that the Palestinian cause was the motivating factor in Muhammed Atta's alleged act.

"I don't know what happened in New York," Youssef said. "I don't have the answer."

The mosque's muezzin began calling the faithful to prayer. "God is Greater," he chanted, his voice carried by speakers across Arab League Street, beside the mosque. "I bear witness that there is no God but God. I bear witness that Muhammad is the messenger of God."

Some of the men who went to pray asked if I was a man of the Book; Christians and Jews, as monotheists, however flawed, still hold a certain status in Islam, and I was invited to perform the ablutions that would purify me for the prayer service. As we stepped outside to the fountain, where a great number of Muslims were already washing, an old man, sallow-skinned and stooped, moved our way, surrounded by courtiers.

"*He* has the answer," Sheikh Abdelrazi said, pointing to the mosque's founder, Mustafa Mahmoud himself. But Mahmoud hobbled into the mosque; the answer would wait until after prayers.

By now, two thousand or so worshippers had assembled. The Friday service was short, and the sermon lasted only a few minutes. In it, Youssef acknowledged that an injustice had been done in the United States but cautioned America to stay its hand. "Don't say that one should not kill civilians and then kill civilians yourself."

After prayer, Youssef found me and gave his interpretation of the differing outlooks of Christianity and Islam.

"In Islam, if I slap your cheek"—he slapped my cheek—"you should slap my other cheek. But in Christianity, Jesus says turn the other cheek. The U.S. is Christian, so why doesn't it turn the other cheek?"

The discussion was curtailed by the announcement that Mustafa Mahmoud was ready to meet with me. I made my way to an austere office where Mahmoud, who is eighty, was already sitting. "I understand you want the answer," Mahmoud said.

I said yes.

"Waco," he said. At my silent surprise, he went on, "The Branch Davidians attacked the World Trade Center, the McVeigh people. The Mossad gave them help. Did you know that the Israelis who work at the World Trade Center were told to stay home that day?"

He had learned this, he said, from research on the Internet.

"It is impossible for Osama bin Laden to do this," Mahmoud continued. "No Arab could have done this."

For moral reasons? I asked.

"No!" he said. "For technical reasons. Arabs are always late! They aren't coördinated enough to do this, all at once on four airplanes. What does Osama bin Laden know about American air travel, anyway? He lives in Afghanistan."

Mustafa Mahmoud is not a marginal figure in Egyptian society. He is an eminent surgeon and onetime Marxist who found religion; his popular television show, "Science and Faith," explores the connections between religion and reason; a charitable organization that bears his name runs several clinics and hospitals in Cairo, including an eye institute that is reputed to be one of the most advanced in the Middle East.

Mahmoud told me that he is not sorry about the destruction of the World Trade Center. "Even Rome was a great empire once," he said. "This was an attack on American arrogance."

He said I could read more about his beliefs in a newspaper column that would appear the next day. In addition to his other achievements, Mahmoud regularly contributes articles to *Al-Ahram,* which is the largest and most respected daily newspaper in Egypt.

I later found, on the Internet, a translation of one of Mahmoud's columns, from late June. Its headline was "ISRAEL—THE PLAGUE OF OUR TIME AND A TERRORIST STATE." Much of the column is taken up with a recounting of the main points of the notorious turn-of-the-century tsarist forgery "Protocols of the Elders of Zion." "What exactly do the Jews want?" he wrote on June 23rd. "Read what the Ninth Protocol of 'The Protocols of the Elders of Zion' says: 'We have limitless ambitions, inexhaustible greed, merciless vengeance and hatred beyond imagination. We are a secret army whose plans are impossible to understand by using honest methods.'"

The image of Anwar Sadat and Menachem Begin joyously clasping hands with Jimmy Carter at the signing of the Egyptian-Israeli peace accord is indelible but misleading because it did not herald a true peace between two peoples. It has been a cold peace, particularly on the Egyptian side. Israelis have visited Egypt by the thousands, but the Egyptian government has long discouraged its citizens from visiting Israel or doing business with Israelis. And since the latest outbreak of the Palestinian uprising, a year ago, and the attendant photographs of Israeli soldiers firing on Palestinian rock throwers, the relationship has turned frigid. Mubarak supports the peace treaty signed by his predecessor, Sadat—an American-aid package of two billion dollars a year fairly demands this of him—but he has discouraged the normalization of relations between the two states.

It is in the domain of the press that Mubarak's position is most evident. *Al-Ahram* is often described in the American press as a "semi-official" daily newspaper, but this may be an understatement. Its editor, two government officials told me, is chosen by President Mubarak, who also chooses the editors of other government newspapers and magazines. Even supposedly independent or opposition newspapers are said never to criticize the President. The one area in which they are given especially wide latitude is in criticizing Israel and, to a lesser extent, America.

One day last week, I visited the offices of the newspaper *Al-Usbu,* an independent weekly that is distinctly anti-Israel and critical of ministers in the Mubarak government—though not, of course, of Mubarak himself. Its editor, Mustafa Bakri, who is in his forties, was in his office, watching Al-Jazeera, the Pan-Arabic cable channel. He was impeccably dressed, polite and deferential. I had wanted to meet him for some time, ever since I read a translation of a column in which he described a dream. The dream began with his appointment as one of Ariel Sharon's bodyguards, assigned to protect the Israeli Prime Minister at Cairo's airport, and in the column, which appeared in February, he wrote:

The pig landed; his face was diabolical, a murderer; his hands soiled with the blood of women and children. A criminal who should be executed in the town square. Should I remain silent as many others did? Should I guard this butcher on my homeland's soil? All of a sudden, I forgot everything; the past and the future, my wife and my children and I decided to do it. I pulled my gun and aimed it at the cowardly pig's head. I emptied all the bullets and screamed.... The murderer collapsed under my feet. I breathed a sigh of relief. I realized the meaning if virility, and of self-sacrifice. The criminal died. I stepped on the pig's head with my shoes and screamed from the bottom of my heart; Long live Egypt, long live Palestine, Jerusalem will never die and never will the honor of the nation be lost.

Bakri offered me an orange soda, and talked of the attack on the World Trade Center. He spoke in terms that, in the current shorthand, are considered Nasserist, after Gamal Abdel Nasser, the revolutionary leader and Egypt's first President. Nasserism today combines populism, Pan-Arab socialism, and opposition to all relations with Israel. Nasserists also resent American economic influence.

"The new globalists want to impose American thinking on the Arabs," Bakri said. "This is a reaction to their thinking." Bakri blamed the September 11th attacks on the American right wing, with help from the Mossad. "Five Israelis were arrested the day before the attack outside the World Trade Center for taking pictures," he said, and added that he knew this from reading American newspapers. If America responds militarily to the attacks, he continued, "American targets will be legitimate targets of Arab anger."

I also went to the offices of *Al-Ahram* to talk about this phenomenon. I met with Abdel Monem Said Aly, the director of the Al-Ahram Center for Political and Strategic Studies, a respected moderate think tank attached to the newspaper. I asked him about the many anti-Israel and anti-American articles published in the official Egyptian press in the year leading up to the terror attacks. He himself has not disseminated anti-American ideas, and has fought the spread of conspiracy theories in Egyptian life.

"We have anti-Semitic papers and fanatics, yes, but these are garbage magazines," he said. "*Al-Ahram, Al-Akhbar,* these are very moderate newspapers. Sometimes they are highly critical of the U.S., but that does not mean that they're anti-American."

Nevertheless, *Al-Akhbar* this year has run opinion pieces defending Hitler. I found one of them translated on the Web site of the Middle East Media Research Institute, a watchdog organization based in Washington. "Thanks to Hitler, of blessed memory, who on behalf of the Palestinians took revenge in advance, against the most vile criminals on the face of the Earth," the *Al-Akhbar* columnist Ahmad Ragab wrote in April. "Although we do have a complaint against him, for his revenge was not enough."

Holocaust denial is a regular feature of *Al-Gomhuriya,* another government daily. Its deputy chief editor, Lotfi Nasif, sat with me in his windowless office in downtown Cairo last week and explained that the Holocaust is "an exaggeration" and that gas chambers are a product of the "Jewish imagination." He told me, "The crimes of the Zionists against the Palestinians far outweigh any of the crimes committed by the Nazis."

Colin Powell has frequently been denounced in the government press, sometimes in racial terms, and, shortly before the attacks in New York and in Washington, the *Al-Akhbar* columnist Mahmoud Abd Al-Munim Murad wrote, "The Statue of Liberty in New York Harbor must be destroyed because of… the idiotic American policy that goes from disgrace to disgrace in the swamp of bias and blind fanaticism." He also declared that "the age of the American collapse has begun." This is a not uncommon theme among members of the Egyptian intellectual class.

On one subject of international controversy—the use of suicide bombers against Israel—there is near unanimity: despite slight shades of difference, as seen at the Mustafa Mahmoud Mosque, most people agree that it is sometimes allowable. Some Islamic moderates believe that suicide attacks are doctrinally permissible only against Israeli soldiers; a more extremist position holds that all Israelis are legitimate targets.

Before September 11th, American officials who worked closely with Egypt tried to downplay the role of anti-Israel and anti-American incitement in the local press. One of the few incidents that provoked a public American response came in 1998, when the newly appointed American Ambassador in Cairo, an Orthodox Jew named Daniel Kurtzer (who is now the Ambassador to Israel), was attacked in anti-Semitic terms in the Egyptian press.

Dennis Ross, who guided Middle East policy under the first Bush Administration and was the chief Middle East negotiator for Bill Clinton, told me last week that he and others had underestimated the influence that the press and the imams had in creating a climate hostile to Israel and America.

"The media have been a kind of safety valve to release tensions, and you could even say that a safety valve is a legitimate way to approach such problems," Ross, who is now a distinguished fellow at the Washington Institute for Near East Policy, said. "But in doing so they appeased extremist sentiments rather than countering them. A climate has been created in which the practice of suicide attacks has come to be seen as legitimate. I'm concerned that there are those who say that if it's O.K. against Israelis, then it's O.K. against Americans."

When I summarized Ross's view to Muhammad El-Sayed Said, the deputy director of the Al-Ahram Center, he blamed Ross for the failure of the peace process. "Dennis Ross is behind it all," Said said. "The Americans should be blamed for the disaster we are in," he continued, referring to the collapsed peace process, and, indirectly, to the terror attacks on the United States. "There's an ambivalence about the World Trade Center. I saw so many people crying when they heard the news, but the other side of it is that many Egyptians saw this as a useful blow against American arrogance. The sense is that it will help the Americans learn that they, too, are vulnerable. That they are paying a price for their total support for Israel."

Egyptian political élites, unlike the makers of street opinion, do not suggest that Israel, either alone or in concert with American extremists, carried out the attacks, but they blame Israel for creating an atmosphere of despair which leads to terrorism.

Last Tuesday, I met with Amr Moussa, the secretary-general of the Arab League, which is housed in a palatial building on Tahrir Square, in the center of Cairo. Before being appointed secretary-general, Moussa served as President Mubarak's foreign Minister. He is known as an outspoken critic of Israel. Moussa is a dapper man who, like many veteran diplomats, can speak at great length without giving much away. He said first that he hoped the World Trade Center would be rebuilt; then he outlined the current thinking of the Mubarak regime.

"There is a wide menu of coöperation," he said. "Countries will choose the areas where they can do best. All of us will fight terrorism, confront terrorism, but not necessarily by conducting a military campaign."

Moussa said that the World Trade Center attack should provide the impetus for America to "reassess" its Middle East alliances. "When it comes to the crunch, such as the Persian Gulf War, ten years ago, or the situation today, America has to sideline Israel," he said. "If Israel intervened on the side of America, it would be destructive to any coalition against terrorism." Many Arab governments have stated that they will not participate in a coalition in which Israel plays a part, and the Bush Administration has agreed. Moussa said that Israeli behavior in the occupied territories is contributing to instability and unease throughout the Muslim world.

Last October, during a visit here to attend an Arab summit on the Palestinian uprising, I spent a morning with a Muslim cleric named Muhammad Sayed Tantawi. Tantawi is the highest-ranking cleric in Egypt, and an influential figure across the Sunni Islamic world. I met him in his office near Al-Azhar University, the venerable Muslim theological center, which he oversees. Tantawi is known as the Sheikh of Al-Azhar.

Tantawi was appointed by Mubarak, whose official photograph hangs in Tantawi's office. Sheikh Tantawi usually has taken the side of Islamic moderation and believes in interfaith dialogue, but he also supports the development of an Arab nuclear weapon. Last October, the Palestinian uprising was in its infancy; there had not been a waive of suicide bombings since 1997. But in the interview Tantawi forcefully addressed the issue of jihad. "If someone takes something from you by force, it is your right to take it back by force," he said. "This is a requirement of Islam. If the Israelis would stop transgressing Muslim land, then there no longer would be a requirement to rise up and fight them."

I asked if Muslims were forbidden by Islamic law to engage in specific acts of retribution. "The killing of civilians is always wrong," he said. "Women, children. This is abhorrent to Islam."

Tantawi has since endorsed some suicide attacks against soldiers. In an interview earlier this year, he said, "The Palestinian youth who bomb themselves among people who fight against them are considered martyrs." Last week, though, he would not talk about suicide attacks. When I spoke to him briefly outside his office, he said only that he was sorry for the attacks on America, and he approved the notion of an international conference on terrorism. I noticed that he moved with a serious-looking security detail; men with submachine guns hanging under their jackets shadowed him through the building.

I asked one of Sheikh Tantawi's aides if there had been a specific threat against the Sheikh's life. No, he said, but added, "Egyptians are the victims of terrorism as well." He was referring to the anti-government campaigns of the nineteen-nineties, in which terrorists operated on behalf of two fundamentalist Muslim groups: the Egyptian Islamic Jihad and the Gama'a al-Islamiya. In this wave of terror, Egyptians and foreign tourists alike were murdered in a brutal campaign to convert Egypt into an Islamic state. Fundamentalists killed President Sadat in October of 1981, and they have tried to kill Mubarak as well. But the security around Tantawi suggests that they might want to kill him, too—and they could find, in a liberal interpretation of Tantawi's ruling favoring suicide attacks against "oppressors," a new and devastating way to carry out their vision.

From an Islamic theological perspective, perhaps the most significant suicide attack to have taken place in the last two weeks occurred on September 9th, in northern Afghanistan. Two men suspected to be operating under the command of Osama bin Laden blew themselves up along with the leader of the Afghan opposition, Ahmed Shah Massoud. It is one thing for Muslim extremists to martyr themselves while attacking infidels; it is quite another for them to begin defining religious Muslims such as Massoud as infidels. Even among the Islamic Jihad and Hamas clerics of the Gaza Strip, I never heard anyone justify the use of suicide bombers against Muslim targets.

For some fundamentalists, the Massoud murder seemed to have significantly

shifted the boundaries of what is considered permissible. Some Islamic scholars, including those under Sheikh Tantawi's supervision at Al-Azhar, have argued that, if one could attack Israelis, one could also attack anyone who stands in the way of their vision of what the world should look like.

To better understand the thinking of Muslims who have killed fellow-Muslims in holy war, I went to see Montasser al-Zayyat, the spokesman of the Gama'a al-Islamiya, which is the larger of Egypt's two fundamentalist terrorist groups. He is a lawyer and has represented, among others, his organization's spiritual leader, Sheikh Omar Abdel Rahman, who is in prison in America for plotting to blow up a number of New York landmarks, including the Holland and Lincoln Tunnels, the Empire State Building, and the United Nations.

When I arrived at a decrepit building in downtown Cairo, where al-Zayyat has his office, it was 9 P.M., and in his waiting room were several bearded men who were seeking an audience with him. They were noticeably hostile toward me, but I could not tell if they were upset by the presence of an American or by the fact that the American was jumping the line.

Al-Zayyat himself, a heavy featured, bearded man, was friendly, but, in the wake of the World Trade Center attacks, he was evasive. At a press conference in Cairo earlier this year, he had warned, "The U.S. will reap a bitter harvest if it continues humiliating Dr. Omar"—Sheikh Rahman. "The continuation of the Sheikh's abuse may result in an explosion of events targeted against U.S. interests. Sheikh Omar has many followers." That night, he said that his threats were not to be taken literally. "I'm very sorry for what happened in New York," he said.

Although Muslim fundamentalists in Egypt have been less visible since President Mubarak ordered a crackdown in the mid-nineties, they have been especially discreet over the last two weeks. The Gama'a al-Islamiya declared a ceasefire in 1999, but thousands of its members remain in jail. Like its rival, the ideologically similar Islamic Jihad, the Gama'a grew out of the Muslim Brotherhood movement, which for decades has been advocating the Islamization of Egyptian society. Unlike the Gama'a, which is illegal, the Muslim brothers exist in an ambiguous political state described to me by one government official as "illegal but tolerated."

The Egyptian Islamic Jihad is also illegal, and in any case seems to have trans-

ferred its operations to Afghanistan and merged with Osama bin Laden's Al Qaeda network, with the help of Jihad's Ayman al-Zawahiri. Though they represent rival organizations, al-Zayyat considers al-Zawahiri a friend.

"He's a very sensible man, a very quiet man," al-Zayyat said, when I asked him to describe al-Zawahiri. "When he speaks, you listen to him carefully."

I asked al-Zayyat what might have driven al-Zawahiri to help organize the American attacks. He replied that he had no knowledge of the attacks, and also said, "I'm not going to be a witness against my friend."

I had a final question: What is it about America that incites the fury of so many Islamists? I suggested that it is American values, especially as they relate to sex and the role of women in society, which Islamic conservatives abhor. "We have sex in Egypt," al-Zayyat said, laughing. Then he went on, "We don't have feelings of hatred toward the people of the U.S., but feelings of hatred toward the government of the U.S. have developed because you support Israel so blindly." At that moment, Montasser al-Zayyat's views seemed inseparable from those of Mubarak's spokesmen.

One evening, I met a friend, a member of the small Egyptian upper class, for drinks in a hotel by the Nile. Cairo isn't Islamabad: Muslims are free to drink alcohol, and there are movie theatres and belly dancing, although the percentage of women wearing traditional headscarves seems to have increased dramatically since I first visited, ten years ago. What people aren't encouraged to do is express interest in democratic reform. My friend asked that I not name him in anything I might write; he believes that the soft despotism of the Mubarak government is hardening, and he wants to stay out of jail. Earlier this year, a prominent sociologist and democracy advocate, Saad Eddin Ibrahim, was sentenced to seven years' hard labor on trumped-up charges, and, like the Egyptian peace camp, the number of those who support true democracy is purposefully shrinking from view.

We spoke about the Egyptian preoccupation with Israel. He is no friend of Israel—"I'm an Arab, how can I have warm feelings for such a place?" he said—but he believes that hatred of Israel, and, to a lesser extent, hatred of America, is fomented by the Mubarak regime as a diversion; as long as Egyptians think about Palestinians, they aren't thinking about themselves. "Egyptians live in just appalling conditions today," he said.

Per-capita income in Egypt is less than the per-capita income on the West Bank. Cairo is a tumultuous, decaying city with a wealthy élite and great masses of the destitute and the near-destitute. The universities are turning out thousands of graduates each year for whom there are no jobs. "The gap between rich and poor is widening, and what does the government give us? Hatred of the peace process." He ascribes to Mubarak's circle the ability to turn on and off anti-Western rhetoric.

All of this, he went on, is indirectly the fault of America, which gives Egypt two billion dollars a year in aid but demands little in return. "You allow them to manipulate you. Every time anti-American feelings appear here, Mubarak says, 'Support me or else you see what you'll get.' But the suppression and the corruption and the anti-democratic behavior will create much worse fundamentalism over time. Washington never stands up to them." He cited the imprisonment of the democracy advocate Saad Ibrahim, and said, "Look what they just did on the Queen Boat."

The boat in question, a well-known disco that allegedly attracted a gay clientele, was anchored a short distance from where we sat. ("Queen" is thought to refer to the wife of the deposed King Farouk.) Following a police raid of the vessel in May, fifty-three men were arrested for presumed homosexuality; these men are now on trial in Cairo. Two weeks ago, the first

sentence was handed down: a seventeen-year-old received three years' hard labor.

"What does the U.S. do about this? Nothing," my friend said. The only prescription is the robust export of democratic values. "There's no Cold War anymore. You can't drive him into an alliance with the Soviets."

There are few Egyptian intellectuals who still argue publicly in favor of normalization with Jerusalem. They are despised, and for the most part quiet. One of them is Ali Salem, a playwright recently expelled from the Egyptian Writers' Union for making frequent visits to Israel and for assuming a pro-normalization stance.

I wanted to ask Salem, who is sixty-five years old and looks like the literary critic Harold Bloom, what had happened, but he said that he was interested in talking about "something deeper than that." We sat in a cafeteria not far from the Mahmoud mosque. Salem drank coffee and chain-smoked Marlboros. "History is cruel," he said. "It is trying to drag America backward. But I think in this case history is right."

He explained, "We here need to be more progressive, but you need to take a step back. If the bureaucrats in your airports were just a little more paranoid, like us, it would be a different world. Really, America is a beautiful place: no one even asked why all these guys wanted flying lessons. You should learn to be suspicious. A little backwardness would be healthy."

I asked him to identify the cause of the attacks on America.

"People say that Americans are arrogant, but it's not true," he said. "Americans enjoy life and they are proud of their lives, and they are boastful of their wonderful inventions that have made life so much easier and more convenient. It's very difficult to understand the machinery of hatred, because you wind up resorting to logic, but trying to understand this with logic is like measuring distance in kilograms. These are people who are afraid of America, afraid of life itself.… These are people who are envious. To them, life is an unbearable burden. Modernism is the only way out. But modernism is frightening. It means we have to compete. It means we can't explain everything away with conspiracy theories."

Ali Salem paused to order another cup of coffee.

"Bernard Shaw said it best, you know. In the preface to 'St. Joan,' he said Joan of Arc was burned not for any reason except that she was talented. Talent gives rise to jealousy in the hearts of the untalented."

Soon after seeing Ali Salem, I ran into Muhammad Atta's father, Muhammad al-Amir Atta, outside a downtown Cairo hotel. He was agitated, alternately aggressive and disconsolate. He had spent much of the week defending himself to reporters and defending his son. I asked him the same question: What, in his mind, lay behind the attack on the World Trade Center?

"The Mossad kidnapped my son and stole his papers," he told me. "Then they spread those papers out at the World Trade Center in order to make it seem like he did it."

From *The New Yorker*, October 8, 2001, pp. 48-55. © 2001 by The New Yorker.

UNIT 10

Understanding Cultural Pluralism

Unit Selections

Key Points to Consider

- What signs have you seen of an increase in racist, anti-Semitic, anti-immigrant, and anti-minority group acts that recent studies apparently confirm?

- What explains the fact that large population studies confirm that Americans are more tolerant than ever in the areas of ethnic, racial, and religious differences?

- Why do teenagers commit 80 percent of all biasrelated acts?

- What problems does conflict in ethnic and race relations pose for corporate and governmental institutions?

- What media images of race and ethnicity are dominant?

- What avenues are available for the authentic cultural resources of ethnic communities and traditions?

- How can multiethnic expressions of traditions intersect with the breakdown of community and the isolationist tendencies related to individual and personal achievement?

- How can dialogue among conflicting parties about dilemmas that are essential to technological and economic change enable us to share and shape the burden of social change?

- Contrast local knowledge with national and local media as sources of information on race and ethnicity.

- Why should advocates of multicultural development and diversity argue for the following: (1) fair and equal protection under the law; (2) the compilation of full and accurate data on the ethnic composition of the American population; (3) corporate and governmental leaders who are focused on issues that do not exacerbate relations among persons because of ethnicity and race

- What are the benefits of ethnic groups meeting regularly with other ethnic groups and engaging in friendly "What's your agenda" meetings?

- Who, if anyone, benefits from the persistence of ethnic tension and conflict?

Links: www.dushkin.com/online/
These sites are annotated in the World Wide Web pages.

Anthropology Resources Page, University of South Dakota
http://www.usd.edu/anth/

National Center for Policy Analysis
http://www.ncpa.org

Patterns of Variability: The Concept of Race
http://www.as.ua.edu/ant/bindon/ant101/lectures/race/race1.htm

STANDARDS: An International Journal of Multicultural Studies
http://www.colorado.edu/journals/standards/

The September 11, 2001, attacks on New York and on the Pentagon have thrust the significance and magnitude of racial conflict and ethnic hatred into the public eye. The burdens of pluralism and diversity are manifested on campuses, in neighborhoods, in the workplace, and in relationships to public services and the marketplaces through general prejudice and specific exclusionary acts and omissions ranging from hateful speech to physical violence; and from profiling to being ignored. Strategies for dealing with this problem include increased awareness through mandatory ethnic studies, empowering the targets of violence, and fostering social and cultural interaction through festivals, folk-arts fairs, and literary and political forums. Systematic knowledge about ethnic groups has not been a central scholarly concern. In fact, main-

stream literary, humanistic, and historical disciplines have only recently begun to displace sociological attention to the pathologies of urban ethnicity as the primary contact and source of information and interpretation of ethnic traditions. Thus, the benefits and burdens of pluralistic traditions and heritages have begun to shift our approaches to understanding ethnic/racial heritage and culture.

The debate regarding the relationship of Islam to terrorism invites us to search for an understanding that creates particular skills and rules for dialogue among religious, ethnic, and political traditions in support of civilization and a peaceful means of resolving differences. The historic role that voluntary groups have played in the reduction of bias and bigotry also needs to be acknowledged and revitalized. Voluntary associations can take part in a host of state and local initiatives to improve intergroup relations. Schools and parents can help children understand commonalities and differences among ethnic traditions and groups. The incorporation of the experiences of families and a formal pedagogy rooted in accurate and locally relevant resources are essential building blocks for understanding diversity.

The reemergence of the discussion of race, religion, and ethnicity that is included in the selections found in this unit reveals the embeddedness of interpretive categories that frame the analysis of group relations.

The enormity of the educational effort that is required as we attempt to move beyond the ethnocentrism and racism that bred hatred and destructive relationships between persons and communities is revealed in a number of ways. Philosophic and theological reflection on the foundations of anthropological and epistemological issues associated with explaining human variety and the characteristics of human consciousness are important in this time of national and world crisis. It is precisely at this intersection of social philosophy and science and its grappling with evil that the crucial breakthroughs in understanding are likely to appear. The continual mismeasures of intelligence and misreading of meaning indicate the long-term need for critical reformulation of the very ideas of race. Concrete strategies for improving this situation call upon both the public and the private sectors in areas of relief, instituional building, education, employment, and training. Suggestions for meeting future needs of this population and pragmatic policy responses also will help.

At this time a variety of ways of measuring the development of race and ethnic relations and results are being proposed, and all evidence points to the expectation of a spirited debate. This unit challenges us to rethink the assumptions, contradictions, and aspirations of social-development models.

the Geometer of Race

In the eighteenth century a disastrous shift occurred in the way
Westerners perceived races. The man responsible was Johann Friedrich
Blumenbach, one of the least racist thinkers of his day.

STEPHEN JAY GOULD

INTERESTING STORIES often lie encoded in names that
seem either capricious or misconstrued. Why, for example, are
political radicals called "left" and their conservative counterparts "right"? In many European legislatures, the most distinguished members sat at the chairman's right, following a
custom of courtesy as old as our prejudices for favoring the
dominant hand of most people. (These biases run deep, extending well beyond can openers and scissors to language itself,
where *dexterous* stems from the Latin for "right," and *sinister*
from the word for "left.") Since these distinguished nobles and
moguls tended to espouse conservative views, the right and left
wings of the legislature came to define a geometry of political
views.

Among such apparently capricious names in my own field of
biology and evolution, none seems more curious, and none
elicits more questions after lectures, than the official designation of light-skinned people in Europe, western Asia, and North
Africa as Caucasian. Why should the most common racial
group of the Western world be named for a mountain range that
straddles Russia and Georgia? Johann Friedrich Blumenbach
(1752–1840), the German anatomist and naturalist who established the most influential of all racial classifications, invented
this name in 1795, in the third edition of his seminal work, *De
Generis Humani Varietate Nativa* (On the Natural Variety of
Mankind). Blumenbach's definition cites two reasons for his
choice—the maximal beauty of people from this small region,
and the probability that humans were first created in this area.

Caucasian variety. I have taken the name of this variety from Mount Caucasus, both because its neighborhood, and especially its southern slope, produces the
most beautiful race of men, I mean the Georgian; and

because... in that region, if anywhere, it seems we
ought with the greatest probability to place the autoch-
thones [original forms] of mankind.

Blumenbach, one of the greatest and most honored scientists
of the Enlightenment, spent his entire career as a professor at the
University of Göttingen in Germany. He first presented *De Generis Humani Varietate Nativa* as a doctoral dissertation to the
medical faculty of Göttingen in 1775, as the minutemen of Lexington and Concord began the American Revolution. He then re-
published the text for general distribution in 1776, as a fateful
meeting in Philadelphia proclaimed our independence. The coincidence of three great documents in 1776—Jefferson's Declaration of Independence (on the politics of liberty), Adam Smith's
Wealth of Nations (on the economics of individualism), and Blumenbach's treatise on racial classification (on the science of
human diversity)—records the social ferment of these decades
and sets the wider context that makes Blumenbach's taxonomy,
and his subsequent decision to call the European race Caucasian,
so important for our history and current concerns.

The solution to big puzzles often hinges upon tiny curiosi-
ties, easy to miss or to pass over. I suggest that the key to understanding Blumenbach's classification, the foundation of much
that continues to influence and disturb us today, lies in the peculiar criterion he used to name the European race Caucasian—
the supposed superior beauty of people from this region. Why,
first of all, should a scientist attach such importance to an evidently subjective assessment; and why, secondly, should an
aesthetic criterion become the basis of a scientific judgment
about place of origin? To answer these questions, we must compare Blumenbach's original 1775 text with the later edition of
1795, when Caucasians received their name.

Blumenbach's final taxonomy of 1795 divided all humans into five groups, defined both by geography and appearance—in his order, the Caucasian variety, for the light-skinned people of Europe and adjacent parts of Asia and Africa; the Mongolian variety, for most other inhabitants of Asia, including China and Japan; the Ethiopian variety, for the dark-skinned people of Africa; the American variety, for most native populations of the New World; and the Malay variety, for the Polynesians and Melanesians of the Pacific and for the aborigines of Australia. But Blumenbach's original classification of 1775 recognized only the first four of these five, and united members of the Malay variety with the other people of Asia whom Blumenbach came to name Mongolian.

We now encounter the paradox of Blumenbach's reputation as the inventor of modern racial classification. The original four-race system, as I shall illustrate in a moment, did not arise from Blumenbach's observations but only represents, as Blumenbach readily admits, the classification promoted by his guru Carolus Linnaeus in the founding document of taxonomy, the *Systema Naturae* of 1758. Therefore, Blumenbach's only original contribution to racial classification lies in the later addition of a Malay variety for some Pacific peoples first included in a broader Asian group.

This change seems so minor. Why, then, do we credit Blumenbach, rather than Linnaeus, as the founder of racial classification? (One might prefer to say "discredit," as the enterprise does not, for good reason, enjoy high repute these days.) But Blumenbach's apparently small change actually records a theoretical shift that could not have been broader, or more portentous, in scope. This change has been missed or misconstrued because later scientists have not grasped the vital historical and philosophical principle that theories are models subject to visual representation, usually in clearly definable geometric terms.

By moving from the Linnaean four-race system to his own five-race scheme, Blumenbach radically changed the geometry of human order from a geographically based model without explicit ranking to a hierarchy of worth, oddly based upon perceived beauty, and fanning out in two directions from a Caucasian ideal. The addition of a Malay category was crucial to this geometric reformulation—and therefore becomes the key to the conceptual transformation rather than a simple refinement of factual information within an old scheme. (For the insight that scientific revolutions embody such geometric shifts, I am grateful to my friend Rhonda Roland Shearer, who portrays these themes in [her] book, *The Flatland Hypothesis*.)

BLUMENBACH IDOLIZED his teacher Linnaeus and acknowledged him as the source of his original fourfold racial classification: "I have followed Linnaeus in the number, but have defined my varieties by other boundaries" (1775 edition). Later, in adding his Malay variety, Blumenbach identified his change as a departure from his old mentor in the most respectful terms: "It became very clear that the Linnaean division of mankind could no longer be adhered to; for which reason I, in this little work, ceased like others to follow that illustrious man."

Linnaeus divided the species *Homo sapiens* into four basic varieties, defined primarily by geography and, interestingly, not in the ranked order favored by most Europeans in the racist tradition—*Americanus, Europaeus, Asiaticus*, and *Afer*, or African. (He also alluded to two other fanciful categories: *ferus* for "wild boys," occasionally discovered in the woods and possibly raised by animals—most turned out to be retarded or mentally ill youngsters abandoned by their parents—and *monstrosus* for hairy men with tails, and other travelers' confabulations.) In so doing, Linnaeus presented nothing original; he merely mapped humans onto the four geographic regions of conventional cartography.

Linnaeus then characterized each of these groups by noting color, humor, and posture, in that order. Again, none of these categories explicitly implies ranking by worth. Once again, Linnaeus was simply bowing to classical taxonomic theories in making these decisions. For example, his use of the four humors reflects the ancient and medieval theory that a person's temperament arises from a balance of four fluids (*humor* is Latin for "moisture")—blood, phlegm, choler (yellow bile), and melancholy (black bile). Depending on which of the four substances dominated, a person would be sanguine (the cheerful realm of blood), phlegmatic (sluggish), choleric (prone to anger), or melancholic (sad). Four geographic regions, four humors, four races.

For the American variety, Linnaeus wrote "*rufus, cholericus, rectus*" (red, choleric, upright); for the European, "*albus, sanguineus, torosus*" (white, sanguine, muscular); for the Asian, "*luridus, melancholicus, rigidus*" (pale yellow, melancholy, stiff); and for the African, "*niger, phlegmaticus, laxus*" (black, phlegmatic, relaxed).

I don't mean to deny that Linnaeus held conventional beliefs about the superiority of his own European variety over others. Being a sanguine, muscular European surely sounds better than being a melancholy, stiff Asian. Indeed, Linnaeus ended each group's description with a more overtly racist label, an attempt to epitomize behavior in just two words. Thus the American was *regitur consuetudine* (ruled by habit); the European, *regitur ritibus* (ruled by custom); the Asian, *regitur opinionibus* (ruled by belief); and the African, *regitur arbitrio* (ruled by caprice). Surely regulation by established and considered custom beats the unthinking rule of habit or belief, and all of these are superior to caprice—thus leading to the implied and conventional racist ranking of Europeans first, Asians and Americans in the middle, and Africans at the bottom.

Nonetheless, and despite these implications, the overt geometry of Linnaeus's model is not linear or hierarchical. When we visualize his scheme as an essential picture in our mind, we see a map of the world divided into four regions, with the people in each region characterized by a list of different traits. In short, Linnaeus's primary ordering principle is cartographic; if he had wished to push hierarchy as the essential picture of human variety, he would surely have listed Europeans first and Africans last, but he started with native Americans instead.

The shift from a geographic to a hierarchical ordering of human diversity must stand as one of the most fateful transitions in the history of Western science—for what, short of railroads and nuclear bombs, has had more practical impact, in this case almost entirely negative, upon our collective lives? Ironically, Blumenbach is the focus of this shift, for his five-race scheme became canonical and changed the geometry of human order from Linnaean cartography to linear ranking—in short, to a system based on putative worth.

I say ironic because Blumenbach was the least racist and most genial of all Enlightenment thinkers. How peculiar that the man most committed to human unity, and to inconsequential moral and intellectual differences among groups, should have changed the mental geometry of human order to a scheme that has served racism ever since. Yet on second thought, this situation is really not so odd—for most scientists have been quite unaware of the mental machinery, and particularly of the visual or geometric implications, lying behind all their theorizing.

Scientists assume that their own shifts in interpretation record only their better understanding of newly discovered facts. They tend to be unaware of their own mental impositions upon the world's messy and ambiguous factuality.

An old tradition in science proclaims that changes in the theory must be driven by observation. Since most scientists believe this simplistic formula, they assume that their own shifts in interpretation record only their better understanding of newly discovered facts. Scientists therefore tend to be unaware of their own mental impositions upon the world's messy and ambiguous factuality. Such mental impositions arise from a variety of sources, including psychological predisposition and social context. Blumenbach lived in an age when ideas of progress, and the cultural superiority of European ways, dominated political and social life. Implicit, loosely formulated, or even unconscious notions of racial ranking fit well with such a worldview—indeed, almost any other organizational scheme would have seemed anomalous. I doubt that Blumenbach was actively encouraging racism by redrawing the mental diagram of human groups. He was only, and largely passively, recording the social view of his time. But ideas have consequences, whatever the motives or intentions of their promoters.

Blumenbach certainly thought that his switch from the Linnaean four-race system to his own five-race scheme arose only from his improved understanding of nature's factuality. He said as much when he announced his change in the second (1781) edition of his treatise: "Formerly in the first edition of this work, I divided all mankind into four varieties; but after I had more actively investigated the different nations of Eastern Asia and America, and, so to speak, looked at them more closely, I was compelled to give up that division, and to place in its stead the following five varieties, as more consonant to nature." And in the preface to the third edition, of 1795, Blumenbach states that he gave up the Linnaean scheme in order to arrange "the varieties of man according to the truth of nature." When scientists adopt the myth that theories arise solely from observation, and do not grasp the personal and social influences acting on their thinking, they not only miss the causes of their changed opinions; they may even fail to comprehend the deep mental shift encoded by the new theory.

Blumenbach upheld the unity of the human species against an alternative view, then growing in popularity (and surely more conducive to conventional racism), that each race had been separately created.

Blumenbach strongly upheld the unity of the human species against an alternative view, then growing in popularity (and surely more conducive to conventional forms of racism), that each major race had been separately created. He ended his third edition by writing: "No doubt can any longer remain but that we are with great probability right in referring all... varieties of man... to one and the same species."

AS HIS MAJOR ARGUMENT for unity, Blumenbach noted that all supposed racial characteristics grade continuously from one people to another and cannot define any separate and bounded group. "For although there seems to be so great a difference between widely separate nations, that you might easily take the inhabitants of the Cape of Good Hope, the Greenlanders, and the Circassians for so many different species of man, yet when the matter is thoroughly considered, you see that all do so run into one another, and that one variety of mankind does so sensibly pass into the other, that you cannot mark out the limits between them." He particularly refuted the common racist claim that black Africans bore unique features of their inferiority: "There is no single character so peculiar and so universal among the Ethiopians, but what it may be observed on the one hand everywhere in other varieties of men."

Blumenbach, writing 80 years before Darwin, believed that *Homo sapiens* had been created in a single region and had then spread over the globe. Our racial diversity, he then argued, arose as a result of this spread to other climates and topographies, and to our adoption of different modes of life in these various regions. Following the terminology of his time, Blumenbach referred to these changes as "degenerations"—not intending the modern sense of deterioration, but the literal meaning of departure from an initial form of humanity at the creation (*de* means "from," and *genus* refers to our original stock).

Most of these degenerations, Blumenbach argued, arose directly from differences in climate and habitat—ranging from such broad patterns as the correlation of dark skin with tropical environments, to more particular (and fanciful) attributions, including a speculation that the narrow eye slits of some Australian aborigines may have arisen in response to "constant clouds of gnats… contracting the natural face of the inhabitants." Other changes, he maintained, arose as a consequence of customs adopted in different regions. For example, nations that compressed the heads of babies by swaddling boards or papoose carriers ended up with relatively long skulls. Blumenbach held that "almost all the diversity of the form of the head in different nations is to be attributed to the mode of life and to art."

Blumenbach believed that such changes, promoted over many generations, could eventually become hereditary. "With the progress of time," Blumenbach wrote, "art may degenerate into a second nature." But he also argued that most racial variations, as superficial impositions of climate and custom, could be easily altered or reversed by moving to a new region or by adopting new behavior. White Europeans living for generations in the tropics could become dark-skinned, while Africans transported as slaves to high latitudes could eventually become white: "Color, whatever be its cause, be it bile, or the influence of the sun, the air, or the climate, is, at all events, an adventitious and easily changeable thing, and can never constitute a diversity of species," he wrote.

Convinced of the superficiality of racial variation, Blumenbach defended the mental and moral unity of all peoples. He held particularly strong opinions on the equal status of black Africans and white Europeans. He may have been patronizing in praising "the good disposition and faculties of these our black brethren," but better paternalism than malign contempt. He campaigned for the abolition of slavery and asserted the moral superiority of slaves to their captors, speaking of a "natural tenderness of heart, which has never been benumbed or extirpated on board the transport vessels or on the West India sugar plantations by the brutality of their white executioners."

Blumenbach established a special library in his house devoted exclusively to black authors, singling out for special praise the poetry of Phillis Wheatley, a Boston slave whose writings have only recently been rediscovered: "I possess English, Dutch, and Latin poems by several [black authors], amongst which however above all, those of Phillis Wheatley of Boston, who is justly famous for them, deserves mention here." Finally, Blumenbach noted that many Caucasian nations could not boast so fine a set of authors and scholars as black Africa has produced under the most depressing circumstances of prejudice and slavery: "It would not be difficult to mention entire well-known provinces of Europe, from out of which you would not easily expect to obtain off-hand such good authors, poets, philosophers, and correspondents of the Paris Academy."

Nonetheless, when Blumenbach presented his mental picture of human diversity in his fateful shift away from Linnaean geography, he singled out a particular group as closest to the created ideal and then characterized all other groups by relative degrees of departure from this archetypal standard. He ended up with a system that placed a single race at the pinnacle, and then envisioned two symmetrical lines of departure away from this ideal toward greater and greater degeneration.

WE MAY NOW RETURN to the riddle of the name Caucasian, and to the significance of Blumenbach's addition of a fifth race, the Malay variety. Blumenbach chose to regard his own European variety as closest to the created ideal and then searched for the subset of Europeans with greatest perfection—the highest of the high, so to speak. As we have seen, he identified the people around Mount Caucasus as the closest embodiments of the original ideal and proceeded to name the entire European race for its finest representatives.

But Blumenbach now faced a dilemma. He had already affirmed the mental and moral equality of all peoples. He therefore could not use these conventional criteria of racist ranking to establish degrees of relative departure from the Caucasian ideal. Instead, and however subjective (and even risible) we view the criterion today, Blumenbach chose physical beauty as his guide to ranking. He simply affirmed that Europeans were most beautiful, with Caucasians as the most comely of all. This explains why Blumenbach, in the fist quote cited in this article, linked the maximal beauty of the Caucasians to the place of human origin. Blumenbach viewed all subsequent variation as departures from the originally created ideal—therefore, the most beautiful people must live closest to our primal home.

Blumenbach's descriptions are pervaded by his subjective sense of relative beauty, presented as though he were discussing an objective and quantifiable property, not subject to doubt or disagreement. He describes a Georgian female skull (found close to Mount Caucasus) as "really the most beautiful form of skull which… always of itself attracts every eye, however little observant." He then defends his European standard on aesthetic grounds: "In the first place, that stock displays… the most beautiful form of the skull, from which, as from a mean and primeval type, the others diverge by most easy gradations…. Besides, it is white in color, which we may fairly assume to have been the primitive color of mankind, since… it is very easy for that to degenerate into brown, but very much more difficult for dark to become white."

Blumenbach then presented all human variety on two lines of successive departure from this Caucasian ideal, ending in the two most degenerate (least attractive, not least morally unworthy or mentally obtuse) forms of humanity—Asians on one side, and Africans on the other. But Blumenbach also wanted to designate intermediary forms between ideal and most degenerate, especially since even gradation formed his primary argument for human unity. In his original four-race system, he could identify native Americans as intermediary between Europeans and Asians, but who would serve as the transitional form between Europeans and Africans?

The four-race system contained no appropriate group. But inventing a fifth racial category as an intermediary between Europeans and Africans would complete the new symmetrical geometry. Blumenbach therefore added the Malay race, not as a minor, factual refinement but as a device for reformulating an entire theory of human diversity. With this one stroke, he produced the geometric transformation from Linnaeus's unranked geographic model to the conventional hierarchy of implied worth that has fostered so much social grief ever since.

I have allotted the first place to the Caucasian... which makes me esteem it the primeval one. This diverges in both directions into two, most remote and very different from each other; on the one side, namely, into the Ethiopian, and on the other into the Mongolian. The remaining two occupy the intermediate positions between that primeval one and these two extreme varieties; that is, the American between the Caucasian and Mongolian; the Malay between the same Caucasian and Ethiopian. [From Blumenbach's third edition.]

Scholars often think that academic ideas must remain at worst, harmless, and at best, mildly amusing or even instructive. But ideas do not reside in the ivory tower of our usual metaphor about academic irrelevance. We are, as Pascal said, a thinking reed, and ideas motivate human history. Where would Hitler have been without racism, Jefferson without liberty? Blumenbach lived as a cloistered professor all his life, but his ideas have reverberated in ways that he never could have anticipated, through our wars, our social upheavals, our sufferings, and our hopes.

I therefore end by returning once more to the extraordinary coincidences of 1776—as Jefferson wrote the Declaration of Independence while Blumenbach was publishing the first edition of his treatise in Latin. We should remember the words of the nineteenth-century British historian and moralist Lord Acton, on the power of ideas to propel history:

> It was from America that... ideas long locked in the breast of solitary thinkers, and hidden among Latin folios, burst forth like a conqueror upon the world they were destined to transform, under the title of the Rights of Man.

FOR FURTHER READING

Daughters of Africa. Margaret Busby, editor. Pantheon, 1992. A comprehensive anthology of prose and poetry written by women of African descent, from ancient Egyptian love songs to the work of contemporary Americans. The collection features the work of Phillis Wheatley, the first black to publish a book of poetry in the United States.

Stephen Jay Gould, a contributing editor of Discover, *is a professor of zoology at Harvard who also teaches geology, biology, and the history of science. His writing on evolution has won many prizes, including a National Book Award, a National Magazine Award, and the Phi Beta Kappa Science Award. For* Discover's *November 1993 special section on ten great science museums, Gould wrote about the glass flowers at Harvard's Botanical Museum.*

Notes on Prejudice

Isaiah Berlin

Isaiah Berlin liked to allude to a passage in Bertrand Russell's History of Western Philosophy *where Russell says that, if we are to understand a philosopher's views, we must "apprehend their imaginative background,"[1] or the philosopher's "inner citadel," as Berlin calls it.[2] The character of one of the main rooms in Berlin's own citadel is vividly expressed in some hurried notes Berlin wrote for a friend (who does not wish to be identified) in 1981. His friend was due to give a lecture, and wrote to Berlin to ask for suggestions about how he might treat his theme. Berlin had to go abroad early on the day after he received the request, and wrote the notes quickly, in his own hand, without time for revision or expansion. The result is somewhat breathless and telegraphic, no doubt, but it conveys with great immediacy Berlin's opposition to intolerance and prejudice, especially fanatical monism, stereotypes, and aggressive nationalism. Its relevance to the events of September 11, 2001, hardly needs stressing.*

Berlin's manuscript is reproduced here in a direct transcript, with only a few adjustments to make it easier to read. I have omitted material relevant only to the specific occasion.

—Henry Hardy

1.

Few things have done more harm than the belief on the part of individuals or groups (or tribes or states or nations or churches) that he or she or they are in *sole* possession of the truth: especially about how to live, what to be & do—& that those who differ from them are not merely mistaken, but wicked or mad: & need restraining or suppressing. It is a terrible and dangerous arrogance to believe that you alone are right: have a magical eye which sees *the* truth: & that others cannot be right if they disagree.

This makes one certain that there is one goal & one only for one's nation or church or the whole of humanity, & that it is worth any amount of suffering (particularly on the part of other people) if only the goal is attained—"through an ocean of blood to the Kingdom of Love" (or something like this) said Robespierre[3]: & Hitler, Lenin, Stalin, & I daresay leaders in the religious wars of Christian v. Moslem or Catholics v. Protestants sincerely believed this: the belief that there is one & only one true answer to the central questions which have agonized mankind & that one has it oneself—or one's leader has it—was responsible for the oceans of blood: but no Kingdom of Love sprang from it—or could: there are many ways of living, believing, behaving: mere *knowledge* provided by history, anthropology, literature, art, law makes clear that the differences of cultures & characters are as deep as the similarities (which make men human) & that we are none the poorer for this rich variety: knowledge of it opens the windows of the mind (and soul) and makes people wiser, nicer, & more civilized: absence of it breeds irrational prejudice, hatreds, ghastly extermination of heretics and those who are different: if the two great wars plus Hitler's genocides haven't taught us that, we are incurable.

The most valuable—or one of the most valuable—elements in the British tradition is precisely the relative freedom from political, racial, religious fanaticism & monomania. Compromising with people with whom you don't sympathize or altogether understand is indispensable to any decent society: nothing is more destructive than a happy sense of one's own—or one's nation's—infallibility, which lets you destroy others with a quiet conscience because you are doing God's (e.g. the Spanish Inquisition or the Ayatollas) or the superior race's (e.g. Hitler) or History's (e.g. Lenin–Stalin) work.

The only cure is understanding how other societies—in space or time— live: and that it is possible to lead lives different from one's own, & yet to be fully human, worthy of love, respect or at least curiosity. Jesus, Socrates, John Hus of Bohemia, the great chemist Lavoisier, socialists and liberals (as well as conservatives) in Russia, Jews in Germany, all perished at the hands of "infallible" ideologues: intuitive certainty is no substitute for carefully tested empirical knowledge based on observation and experiment and free discussion between men: the first people totalitarians destroy or silence are men of ideas & free minds.

2.

Another source of avoidable conflict is stereotypes. Tribes hate neighbouring tribes by whom they feel threatened, & then rationalize their fears by representing them as wicked or inferior, or absurd or despicable in some way. Yet these stereotypes alter sometimes quite rapidly. Take the nineteenth century alone: in, say, 1840 the French are thought of as swashbuckling, gallant, immoral, militarized, men with curly moustachios, dangerous to women, likely to invade England in revenge for Waterloo; & the Germans are beer drinking, rather ludicrous provincials, musical, full of misty metaphysics, harmless but somewhat absurd. By 1871 the Germans are Uhlans storming through France, invited by the terrible Bismarck—terrifying Prussian militarists filled with national pride etc. France is a poor, crushed, civilized land, in need of protection from all good men, lest its art & literature are crushed underheel by the terrible invaders.

The Russians in the nineteenth century are crushed serfs, darkly brooding semi-religious Slav mystics who write deep novels, a huge horde of cossacks loyal to the Tsar, who sing beautifully. In our times all this has dramatically altered: crushed population, yes, but technology, tanks, godless materialism, crusade against capitalism, etc. The English are ruthless imperialists lording it over fuzzy wuzzies, looking down their long noses at the rest of the world—& then impoverished, liberal, decent welfare state beneficiaries in need of allies. And so on. All these stereotypes are substitutes for real knowledge—which is never of anything so simple or permanent as a particular generalized image of foreigners—and are stimuli to national self satisfaction & disdain of other nations. It is a prop to nationalism.

3.

Nationalism—which everybody in the nineteenth century thought was ebbing—is the strongest & most dangerous force at large to-day. It is usually the product of a wound inflicted by one nation on the pride or territory of another: if Louis XIV had not attacked & devastated the Germans, & humiliated them for years—the Sun King whose state gave laws to everybody, in politics, warfare, art, philosophy, science—then the Germans would not, perhaps, have become quite so aggressive by, say, the early nineteenth century when they became fiercely nationalistic against Napoleon. If the Russians, similarly, had not been treated as a barbarous mass by the West in the nineteenth century, or the Chinese had not been humiliated by opium wars or general exploitation, neither would have fallen so easily to a doctrine which promised they would inherit the earth after they had, with the help of historic forces which none may stop, crushed all the capitalist unbelievers. If the Indians had not been patronized, etc., etc.

Conquest, enslavement of peoples, imperialism etc are not fed just by greed or desire for glory, but have to justify themselves to themselves by some central idea: French as the only true culture; the white man's burden; communism: & the stereotypes of others as inferior or wicked. Only knowledge, carefully acquired & not by short cuts, can dispel this: even that won't dispel human aggressiveness or dislike for the dissimilar (in skin, culture, religion) by itself: still, education in history, anthropology, law (especially if they are "comparative" & not just of one's own country as they usually are) helps.

Notes

1. *History of Western Philosophy* (Simon and Schuster, 1945), p. 226.

2. For example, in *Four Essays on Liberty* (Oxford University Press, 1969), p. 135.

3. Berlin may be referring to the passage where Robespierre writes that *"en scellant notre ouvrage de notre sang, nous puissons voir au moins briller l'aurore de la félicité universelle"* ("by sealing our work with our blood, we may see at least the bright dawn of universal happiness"). *Rapport sur les principes de morale politique qui doivent guider la Convention nationale dans l'administration intérieure de la République* [Paris, 1794], p. 4.

Mideast clerics, speak out

By DAVID MAKOVSKY

WASHINGTON—America has come full circle.

In 1983, the idea of jihad, or Muslim holy war, was introduced in the contemporary Middle East as 241 American servicemen were killed in Beirut.

The United States beat a hasty exit, and Islamic militants saw this as a vindication that suicide bombing was religiously sanctioned as well as being deadly effective. It took the terror strikes of Sept. 11, almost exactly 18 years later, to galvanize America to action, resolving it to the idea that such terrorism must be eradicated.

President Bush made clear that this campaign is not just about Osama bin Laden but confronting an ideology that justifies killing in the name of religion. While correctly praising Islam as a religion, Mr. Bush declared, "Those who commit evil in the name of Allah blaspheme the name of Allah. The terrorists are traitors to their own faith, trying in effect to hijack Islam itself."

This is a battle that the United States cannot wage alone, nor should it. The Islamic militant challenge is not directed just at the United States. When confronted with such radicalism, Egypt stemmed the challenge and ultimately defeated these religious opponents in the 1990s.

Yet while Egypt, Jordan, Saudi Arabia and Syria have sharply (and often ruthlessly) put down challenges from Islamicists, they have never laid a glove on Islamicism as an ideology so long as it was directed at others such as the United States. Thus the regimes deflected attention from their own failing economies.

It is wholly insufficient for Middle Eastern leaders and their clerics to denounce the perpetrators of the Sept. 11 attack. This is too easy. It's now time for them to do the hard part and discredit this revived ideology. If not, it only will be a matter of time before they once again face these militants. They need to make clear to their faithful that Islam does not sanction the wanton killing of innocents. Period. Terror attacks are utterly antithetical to Islam.

Dealing with the religious underpinning is at the core, and this must be addressed by Islamic clerics in the Middle East.

For the last decade, bin Laden has issued a number of religious rulings (*fatwas*) declaring that his goal was to uproot the United States from Saudi Arabia, Yemen and the Horn of Africa.

ELEANOR MILL

His group, Al Qaeda, says its goal is to "unite all Muslims and to establish a government which follows the rule of the caliphs." He has consistently invoked religion to justify his cause. In a 1998 *fatwa,* bin Laden appealed for attacks on Americans in order to drive the United States out of "the lands of Islam in the holiest of places," alluding to Saudi Arabia's holiest city of Mecca.

There is a fiery resentment among Islamic radicals of all that America represents as a military, cultural and economic power and its focus on the individual at the center of society. America is viewed by these radicals as a revolutionary power that is disruptive of traditional Islamic society.

Indeed, the state-appointed Sheik Mohammed Sayed Tantawi of Cairo's Al-Azhar, Islam's oldest and most prominent religious institution, and the mufti of Saudi Arabia recently have been the exception among clerics in condemning terrorism.

Yet even in the aftermath of Sept. 11, the mufti of Jerusalem, Ikrima al-Sabri, opposed the killings in New York and Washington but reaffirmed that suicide bombings against innocents are allowed so long as they are carried out to liberate Palestine. It must be made clear that terrorism in any form is unacceptable, whether it is perpetrated against children at a Jerusalem pizzeria or a bond trader in lower Manhattan.

Dealing with Islamic clerics in halting violence is as important as dealing with them in attaining peace. Americans don't fully grasp the political sway religious leaders often hold in the Middle East, possibly because the United States separates church and state. An international political coalition against terrorism must be matched by a religious coalition inside the Middle East of mainstream Islamic clerics who disavow a twisted ideology that claims to speak in the name of Islam.

David Makovsky is a senior fellow at the Washington Institute for Near East Policy and is a contributing editor to U.S. News & World Report.

From the *Baltimore Sun,* September 30, 2001, p. 3F. © 2001 by the Baltimore Sun. Reprinted by permission of David Makovsky.

Arabs Have Nobody to Blame But Themselves

BY FOUAD AJAMI

We should be under no illusions about our struggle against Osama bin Laden and the cultists and terrorists arrayed around him. Although we control the sea lanes and skies of that Arab-Muslim world, he appears to hold sway over the streets of a thwarted civilization, one that sees him as an avenger for the sad, cruel lot that has been its fate in recent years.

A terrible war was fought between rulers and Islamists; the regimes in Algeria, Tunisia, and Egypt won, but the insurgents took to the road, and vowed to return as triumphant conquerors after the dynasties and the despots were sacked. Rich, famous, free and young, bin Laden taunts the rulers of a silent, frightened Arab world seething with resentments of every kind. He and his lieutenants cannot overthrow the Arab ruling order, so they have turned their resentments on us.

Consider the three men who taunted us in the video that came our way on Oct. 7, courtesy of the Qatari satellite channel, Al-Jazeera. In it, bin Laden is flanked by two lieutenants. The older one, a man of 50 years, is an Egyptian physician, Dr. Ayman al-Zawahiri, a sworn enemy of the regime of Hosni Mubarak. Twenty years ago, he had been picked up in the dragnet that followed the assassination of Anwar Sadat. He was tortured, and imprisoned for three years. He drifted to Pakistan, then made his way to the Sudan and Afghanistan, and took to the life of terror.

The younger man, spokesman for bin Laden, is a Kuwaiti theocratic activist by the name of Sleiman Abu Gheith, who hails from a quaint, stable principality, with generous welfare subsidies and an American trip-wire to protect it against a predatory Saddam. Abu Gheith had been an employee of the Kuwaiti state, an imam of a government-sponsored mosque, and a teacher of Islamic studies. Those who know him tell of a man who had become fanatical in his view of Islam's role in political and social life.

A foul wind had been blowing in Arab lands. The rulers had snuffed out endless rebellions and the populace had succumbed to a malignant, sullen silence. It prayed and waited for the rulers' demise. It dreamt of an avenger and a band of merciless followers who would do for it what it could not do for itself.

It is no mystery that reporters from Arab shores tell us of affluent men and women, some with years of education in American universities behind them, celebrating the cruel deed of Mohamed Atta and his hijackers. The cult of the bandit taunting the powerful has always been seductive in broken societies. Bin Laden and Zawahiri and Abu Gheith and Atta did not descend from the sky: They are the angry sons of a failed Arab generation. They are direct heirs of two generations of Arabs that have seen all the high dreams of *Asr al Nahda* (the era of enlightenment and secular nationalism) issue in sterility, dictatorship and misery. The secular fathers begot this strange breed of holy warriors.

A suffocating hate separates the ruler from the ruled in Arab lands. The former own those lands, they have closed up the universe, and their dominion stretches as far as the eye can see. Their scions stand at the ready to claim the good things of the earth. Imagine the way Arabs read the ascendancy of the sons of the dictators of Syria, Egypt and Iraq in public life; a trick has been played on them. Under their eyes, the republics have metamorphosed into monarchies in all but name. Alone, in God's broad lands, it seems to them, they are to be excluded from a share of today's democratic inheritance. The rulers can't deliver to us these sullen, resentful populations and—shrewd men—the rulers know it. They have ducked for cover as America blew in asking them to choose between the terrorists' world and ours.

We were "walk-ons" in this political and generational struggle playing out in Araby. America and Americans have a hard time coming to terms with those unfathomable furies of a distant, impenetrable world. In truth, Atta struck at us because he could not take down Mr. Mubarak's world, because in the burdened, crowded land of the Egyptian dictator there is very little offered younger Egyptians save for the steady narcotic of anti-Americanism and anti-Zionism. The attack on the North Tower of the World Trade Center was Atta's "rite of passage."

In the same vein, bin Laden and Abu Gheith can't sack the dynastic order of the Gulf. (Were they to do so, they would replace it with a cruel reign of terror that would make the yuppies of Jeddah who have been whispering sweet things in the ears of foreign reporters about bin Laden yearn for the days of Al Saud). So the avengers come our way. Our shadow, faint and mediated through hated rulers and middlemen, has fallen across their world. They struck at the shadow, but it is the order that reigns in their lands that fuels their righteousness. And it is the sense of approval they see in the eyes of ordinary men and women in their societies that tells them to press on.

The military campaign against bin Laden is prosecuted, and will surely be won, by the U.S. But the redemption of the Arab political condition, and the weaning of that world away from its ruinous habits and temptations, are matters for the Arabs themselves.

A darkness, a long winter, has descended on the Arabs. Nothing grows in the middle between an authoritarian political order and populations given to perennial flings with dictators, abandoned to their most malignant hatreds. Something is amiss in an Arab world that besieges American embassies for visas and at the same time celebrates America's calamities. Something has gone terribly wrong in a world where young men strap themselves with explosives, only to be hailed as "martyrs" and avengers. No military campaign by a foreign power can give modern-day Arabs a way out of the cruel, blind alley of their own history.

Mr. Ajami, author of "The Dream Palace of the Arabs" (Vintage, 1999), teaches at the Johns Hopkins School of Advanced International Studies.

History Is Still Going Our Way

By Francis Fukuyama

A stream of commentators has been asserting that the tragedy of Sept. 11 proves that I was utterly wrong to have said more than a decade ago that we had reached the end of history. The chorus began almost immediately, with George Will asserting that history had returned from vacation, and Fareed Zakaria declaring the end of the end of history.

It is on the face of it nonsensical and insulting to the memory of those who died on Sept. 11 to declare that this unprecedented attack did not rise to the level of a historical event. But the way in which I used the word *history*, or rather, History, was different: It referred to the progress of mankind over the centuries toward modernity, characterized by institutions like liberal democracy and capitalism.

March of History

My observation, made back in 1989 on the eve of the collapse of communism, was that this evolutionary process did seem to be bringing ever larger parts of the world toward modernity. And if we looked beyond liberal democracy and markets, there was nothing else towards which we could expect to evolve; hence the end of history. While there were retrograde areas that resisted that process, it was hard to find a viable alternative type of civilization that people actually wanted to live in after the discrediting of socialism, monarchy, fascism, and other types of authoritarian rule.

This view has been challenged by many people, and perhaps most articulately by Samuel Huntington. He argued that rather than progressing toward a single global system, the world remained mired in a "clash of civilizations" where six or seven major cultural groups would coexist without converging and constitute the new fracture lines of global conflict. Since the successful attack on the center of global capitalism was evidently perpetrated by Islamic extremists unhappy with the very existence of Western civilization, observers have been handicapping the Huntington "clash" view over my own "end of history" hypothesis rather heavily.

I believe that in the end I remain right: Modernity is a very powerful freight train that will not be derailed by recent events, however painful and unprecedented. Democracy and free markets will continue to expand over time as the dominant organizing principles for much of the world. But it is worthwhile thinking about what the true scope of the present challenge is.

> ### *Political Islam doesn't provide a viable long-term alternative to principles championed by America.*

It has always been my belief that modernity has a cultural basis. Liberal democracy and free markets do not work at all times and everywhere. They work best in societies with certain values whose origins may not be entirely rational. It is not an accident that modern liberal democracy emerged first in the Christian West, since the universalism of democratic rights can be seen in many ways as a secular form of Christian universalism.

The central question raised by Samuel Huntington is whether institutions of modernity such as liberal democracy and free markets will work only in the West, or whether there is something broader in their appeal that will allow them to make headway in non-Western societies. I believe there is. The proof lies in the progress that democracy and free markets have made in regions like East Asia, Latin America, Orthodox Europe, South Asia, and even Africa. Proof lies also in the millions of Third World immigrants who vote with their feet every year to live in Western societies and eventually assimilate to Western values. The flow of people moving in the opposite direction, and the number who want to blow up what they can of the West, is by contrast negligible.

But there does seem to be something about Islam, or at least the fundamentalist versions of Islam that have been dominant in recent years, that makes Muslim societies particularly resistant to modernity. Of all contemporary cultural systems, the Islamic world has the fewest democracies (Turkey alone qualifies), and contains no countries that have made the transition from Third to First World status in the manner of South Korea or Singapore.

There are plenty of non-Western people who prefer the economic and technological part of modernity and hope to have it without having to accept democratic politics or Western cultural values as well (e.g., China or Singapore). There are others who like both the economic and political versions of modernity, but just can't figure out how to make it happen (Russia is an example). For them, transition to Western-style modernity may be long and painful. But there are no insuperable cultural barriers likely to prevent them from eventually getting there, and they constitute about four-fifths of the world's people.

Islam, by contrast, is the only cultural system that seems to regularly produce people, like Osama bin Laden or the Taliban, who reject modernity lock, stock and barrel. This raises the question of how representative such people are of the larger Muslim community, and whether this rejection is somehow inherent in Islam. For if the rejectionists are more than a lunatic fringe, then Mr. Huntington is right that we are in for a protracted conflict made dangerous by virtue of their technological empowerment.

The answer that politicians East and West have been putting out since Sept. 11 is that those sympathetic with the terrorists are a "tiny minority" of Muslims, and that the vast majority are appalled by what happened. It is important for them to say this to prevent Muslims as a group from becoming targets of hatred. The problem is that dislike and hatred of America and what it stands for are clearly much more widespread than that.

Certainly the group of people willing to go on suicide missions and actively conspire against the U.S. is tiny. But sympathy may be manifest in nothing more than initial feelings of *Schadenfreude* at the sight of the collapsing towers, an immediate sense of satisfaction that the U.S. was getting what it deserved, to be followed only later by pro forma expressions of disapproval. By this standard, sympathy for the terrorists is characteristic of much more than a "tiny minority" of Muslims, extending from the middle classes in countries like Egypt to immigrants in the West.

This broader dislike and hatred would seem to represent something much deeper than mere opposition to American policies like support for Israel or the Iraq embargo, encompassing a hatred of the underlying society. After all, many people around the world, including many Americans, disagree with U.S. policies, but this does not send them into paroxysms of anger and violence. Nor is it necessarily a matter of ignorance about the quality of life in the West. The suicide hijacker Mohamed Atta was a well-educated man from a well-to-do Egyptian family who lived and studied in Germany and the U.S. for several years. Perhaps, as many commentators have speculated, the hatred is born out of a resentment of Western success and Muslim failure.

But rather than psychologize the Muslim world, it makes more sense to ask whether radical Islam constitutes a serious alternative to Western liberal democracy for Muslims themselves. (It goes without saying that, unlike communism, radical Islam has virtually no appeal in the contemporary world apart from those who are culturally Islamic to begin with.)

For Muslims themselves, political Islam has proven much more appealing in the abstract than in reality. After 23 years of rule by fundamentalist clerics, most Iranians, and in particular nearly everyone under 30, would like to live in a far more liberal society. Afghans who have experienced Taliban rule have much the same feelings. All of the anti-American hatred that has been drummed up does not translate into a viable political program for Muslim societies to follow in the years ahead.

The West Dominates

We remain at the end of history because there is only one system that will continue to dominate world politics, that of the liberal-democratic West. This does not imply a world free from conflict, nor the disappearance of culture as a distinguishing characteristic of societies. (In my original article, I noted that the posthistorical world would continue to see terrorism and wars of national liberation.)

But the struggle we face is not the clash of several distinct and equal cultures struggling amongst one another like the great powers of 19th century Europe. The clash consists of a series of rearguard actions from societies whose traditional existence is indeed threatened by modernization. The strength of the backlash reflects the severity of this threat. But time and resources are on the side of modernity, and I see no lack of a will to prevail in the United States today.

Mr. Fukuyama, a professor of international political economy at the Johns Hopkins School of Advanced International Studies, is author of "The End of History and the Last Man."

Appendix A

2000 Census Ethnicity Data
Aggregated from Ancestry, Race, Hispanic Questions

Total population	273,643,269					
	Raw data			Percentage of Total		
	Estimate	Lower Bound	Upper Bound	% Est.	% Upper Bound	% Lower Bound
German	46,452,074	45,973,229	46,930,919	17.0%	16.8%	17.2%
Hispanic/Latino	34,341,066	34,112,977	34,569,155	12.5%	12.5%	12.6%
Black/African American	34,034,908	33,693,068	34,376,748	12.4%	12.3%	12.6%
Irish	33,026,795	32,761,244	33,292,346	12.1%	12.0%	12.2%
English	28,255,308	27,962,176	28,548,440	10.3%	10.2%	10.4%
Mexican	21,500,506	21,280,744	21,720,268	7.9%	7.8%	7.9%
American	19,643,045	19,193,912	20,092,178	7.2%	7.0%	7.3%
Italian	15,903,962	15,656,376	16,151,548	5.8%	5.7%	5.9%
Asian	11,768,717	11,586,795	11,950,639	4.3%	4.2%	4.4%
French (except Basque)	9,768,319	9,529,623	10,007,015	3.6%	3.5%	3.7%
Polish	9,050,122	8,852,693	9,247,551	3.3%	3.2%	3.4%
Scottish	5,418,746	5,337,540	5,499,952	2.0%	2.0%	2.0%
Scotch-Irish	5,223,468	5,128,205	5,318,731	1.9%	1.9%	1.9%
Dutch	5,219,074	5,038,432	5,399,716	1.9%	1.8%	2.0%
Norwegian	4,547,291	4,312,938	4,781,644	1.7%	1.6%	1.7%
Swedish	4,332,226	4,190,984	4,473,468	1.6%	1.5%	1.6%
American Indian/Alaska Native	4,184,387	3,983,343	4,385,431	1.5%	1.5%	1.6%
Puerto Rican	3,455,802	3,363,856	3,547,748	1.3%	1.2%	1.3%
Russian	2,987,143	2,911,641	3,062,645	1.1%	1.1%	1.1%
French Canadian	2,201,977	2,125,858	2,278,096	0.8%	0.8%	0.8%
West Indian (excl. Hispanic origin groups)	1,928,658	1,860,498	1,996,818	0.7%	0.7%	0.7%
Welsh	1,899,196	1,850,712	1,947,680	0.7%	0.7%	0.7%
Hungarian	1,516,645	1,462,106	1,571,184	0.6%	0.5%	0.6%
Subsaharan African	1,504,985	1,421,726	1,588,244	0.5%	0.5%	0.6%
Danish	1,499,804	1,447,474	1,552,134	0.5%	0.5%	0.6%
Czech	1,395,867	1,324,881	1,466,853	0.5%	0.5%	0.5%
Portuguese	1,311,008	1,259,546	1,362,470	0.5%	0.5%	0.5%
Arab	1,249,160	1,178,487	1,319,833	0.5%	0.4%	0.5%
Cuban	1,232,736	1,178,451	1,287,021	0.5%	0.4%	0.5%
Greek	1,179,737	1,131,989	1,227,485	0.4%	0.4%	0.4%
Swiss	996,671	937,043	1,056,299	0.4%	0.3%	0.4%
Ukrainian	862,416	822,260	902,572	0.3%	0.3%	0.3%
Slovak	820,711	773,848	867,574	0.3%	0.3%	0.3%

2000 Census Ethnicity Data
Aggregated from Ancestry, Race, Hispanic Questions

	Raw data			Percentage of Total		
	Estimate	Lower Bound	Upper Bound	% Est.	% Upper Bound	% Lower Bound
Native Hawaiian/Other Pacific Islander	796,736	743,987	849,485	0.3%	0.3%	0.3%
Lithuanian	714,729	685,239	744,219	0.3%	0.3%	0.3%
Foreign Born Population						
Total Foreign-born population	30,520,323	30,247,060	30,793,586	11.2%	11.1%	11.3%
By Region						
Europe	4,768,602	4,680,814	4,856,390	1.7%	1.7%	1.8%
Asia	8,397,093	8,276,674	8,517,512	3.1%	3.0%	3.1%
Africa	836,248	785,578	886,918	0.3%	0.3%	0.0%
Oceania	181,799	161,044	202,554	0.1%	0.1%	0.0%
Latin America	15,501,472	15,295,664	15,707,280	5.7%	5.6%	0.0%
Northern America	835,109	801,517	868,701	0.3%	0.3%	0.3%
NCUEA Data File derived from 2000 United States Census						

Index

Index

Test Your Knowledge Form

We encourage you to photocopy and use this page as a tool to assess how the articles in *Annual Editions* expand on the information in your textbook. By reflecting on the articles you will gain enhanced text information. You can also access this useful form on a product's book support Web site at *http://www.dushkin.com/online/*.

NAME:

DATE:

TITLE AND NUMBER OF ARTICLE:

BRIEFLY STATE THE MAIN IDEA OF THIS ARTICLE:

LIST THREE IMPORTANT FACTS THAT THE AUTHOR USES TO SUPPORT THE MAIN IDEA:

WHAT INFORMATION OR IDEAS DISCUSSED IN THIS ARTICLE ARE ALSO DISCUSSED IN YOUR TEXTBOOK OR OTHER READINGS THAT YOU HAVE DONE? LIST THE TEXTBOOK CHAPTERS AND PAGE NUMBERS:

LIST ANY EXAMPLES OF BIAS OR FAULTY REASONING THAT YOU FOUND IN THE ARTICLE:

LIST ANY NEW TERMS/CONCEPTS THAT WERE DISCUSSED IN THE ARTICLE, AND WRITE A SHORT DEFINITION:

We Want Your Advice

ANNUAL EDITIONS revisions depend on two major opinion sources: one is our Advisory Board, listed in the front of this volume, which works with us in scanning the thousands of articles published in the public press each year; the other is you—the person actually using the book. Please help us and the users of the next edition by completing the prepaid article rating form on this page and returning it to us. Thank you for your help!

ANNUAL EDITIONS: Race and Ethnic Relations 02/03

ARTICLE RATING FORM

Here is an opportunity for you to have direct input into the next revision of this volume.
We would like you to rate each of the articles listed below, using the following scale:

1. **Excellent: should definitely be retained**
2. **Above average: should probably be retained**
3. **Below average: should probably be deleted**
4. **Poor: should definitely be deleted**

Your ratings will play a vital part in the next revision.
Please mail this prepaid form to us as soon as possible.
Thanks for your help!

RATING	ARTICLE	RATING	ARTICLE
	1. *Dred Scott v. Sandford*		30. Academic Haven for Blacks Becomes Bias Battleground
	2. Racial Restrictions in the Law of Citizenship		31. Laying Down the Burden of Race
	3. In a Judicial 'What If,' Indians Revisit a Case		32. Reparations for American Slavery
	4. *Brown et al. v. Board of Education of Topeka et al.*		33. Racism Isn't What It Used to Be
	5. *University of California Regents v. Bakke*		34. Misperceived Minorities: 'Good' and 'Bad' Stereotypes Saddle Hispanics and Asian Americans
	6. Freedom of Religious Expression: *Shaare Tefila Congregation v. Cobb and Saint Francis College v. Al-Khazraji*		35. Arranged Marriages, Minus the Parents
	7. New Answers to an Old Question: Who Got Here First?		36. Wartime Hysteria
	8. American Indians in the 1990s		37. Please Ask Me Who, Not 'What,' I Am
	9. Migrations to the Thirteen British North American Colonies, 1770–1775: New Estimates		38. Who Are We?
	10. The Enduring Legacy of the South's Civil War Victory		39. Where We Stand on Issues
	11. Racial Viewing Habits Move Closer, but Big Gaps Remain		40. A City That Echoes Eternity
	12. Black America		41. Tribal Warfare
	13. White Girl?		42. Will Arafat Father a Country?
	14. America 2000: A Map of the Mix		43. Belonging in the West
	15. What's White, Anyway?		44. In 'Little Kabul,' Love of Country, Homeland
	16. All White, All Christian and Divided by Diversity		45. Arab Americans: Protecting Rights at Home and Promoting a Just Peace Abroad
	17. Should Immigrants Assimilate?		46. Behind Mubarak
	18. New Immigrants and Refugees in American Schools: Multiple Voices		47. The Geometer of Race
	19. Surveying the Backgrounds of Immigration Scholars: A Report		48. Notes on Prejudice
	20. Following the Chain: New Insights Into Migration		49. Mideast Clerics, Speak Out
	21. Ellis Island Finds an Immigrant Wave Online		50. Arabs Have Nobody to Blame but Themselves
	22. As Others Abandon Plains, Indians and Bison Come Back		51. History Is Still Going Our Way
	23. Culture Corrosion in Canada's North		
	24. Inside the Arctic Circle, an Ancient People Emerge		
	25. Hispanic Diaspora		
	26. Specific Hispanics		
	27. The Blond, Blue-Eyed Face of Spanish TV		
	28. Latino, White Students Cling to Own Social Circles		
	29. 10 Most Dramatic Events in African-American History		

(Continued on next page)

BUSINESS REPLY MAIL
FIRST-CLASS MAIL   PERMIT NO. 84   GUILFORD CT
POSTAGE WILL BE PAID BY ADDRESSEE

McGraw-Hill/Dushkin
530 Old Whitfield Street
Guilford, Ct 06437-9989

ABOUT YOU

Name   Date

Are you a teacher? ☐   A student? ☐
Your school's name

Department

Address   City   State   Zip

School telephone #

YOUR COMMENTS ARE IMPORTANT TO US!

Please fill in the following information:
For which course did you use this book?

Did you use a text with this ANNUAL EDITION? ☐ yes ☐ no
What was the title of the text?

What are your general reactions to the *Annual Editions* concept?

Have you read any pertinent articles recently that you think should be included in the next edition? Explain.

Are there any articles that you feel should be replaced in the next edition? Why?

Are there any World Wide Web sites that you feel should be included in the next edition? Please annotate.

May we contact you for editorial input? ☐ yes ☐ no
May we quote your comments? ☐ yes ☐ no